Sync

Stylistics of Hieroglyphic Time

JAMES TOBIAS

TEMPLE UNIVERSITY PRESS
Philadelphia

TEMPLE UNIVERSITY PRESS
Philadelphia, Pennsylvania 19122
www.temple.edu/tempress

Published 2010

Library of Congress Cataloging-in-Publication Data

Tobias, James S.
Sync : stylistics of hieroglyphic time / James Tobias.
p. cm.
Includes bibliographical references and index.
ISBN 978-1-4399-0201-1 (cloth : alk. paper)
1. Motion pictures. 2. Motion pictures and music. I. Title.

PN1994.T63 2010
791.43—dc22 2009048502

⊗ The paper used in this publication meets the requirements of the American National Standard for Information Sciences—Permanence of Paper for Printed Library Materials, ANSI Z39.48-1992

Printed in the United States of America

2 4 6 8 9 7 5 3 1

Contents

List of Illustrations

Acknowledgments

Very early seeds for the research that would become a doctoral dissertation and now this complete, extended study were planted in 1994, when I joined Joy Mountford's "Expressions" design group at the Interval Research Corporation in Palo Alto, California. A number of recent studies emphasizing computational media as "expressive media" do not fully acknowledge that in the early 1990s, for such designers as Mountford, Bill Verplank, Rachel Strickland, David Levitt, and others, understanding computation as expression was a clearly articulated project, to the extent of providing the title and research focus of Mountford's work at Interval. Senior Interval staff, including Mountford and Bob Adams of the Expressions group, understood that the mainstreaming of the Internet in the form of the World Wide Web meant that networked computation had become a matter of everyday experience, yet one that nevertheless lacked the dynamic cognitive affordances, communicative aesthetics, critical capacities, and affective power we associate with expressive media instruments.

With Mountford's team—and while enjoying her expansive vision of the importance of communicability, aesthetics, critical usability, and emotional power for computing, along with her ability to offer often startlingly incisive analyses of complex design questions—we explored musicality at the digital interface as a key problem area for expressive media generally. We also designed alternative displays and controllers for composing, displaying, sharing, and revising data in prototypes prioritizing affect over computation:

computers as musical instruments. It was with Mountford's encouragement that I began serious research on historical and contemporary visual music animation; and it was with her urging that I corresponded with or informally interviewed visual music artists, including David McCutcheon, David Brody, Sara Petty, Stephen Beck, Stephen Malinowski, Vibeke Sorenson, and Michael Scroggins, as well as other figures, including Elfriede Fischinger, the wife of visual music pioneer Oskar Fischinger, whom I interviewed at her Long Beach, California, home in 1995.

In the context of interface and interaction design, visual music animation provided an alternative to the classical understandings of audiovisual synchronization that Sergei Eisenstein or Hanns Eisler and Theodor Adorno offer, but it also provided an exemplar of variable, expressive audiovisuality that the computational display had not reached and that interaction design theorists had only vaguely conceived (often on the basis of such historical sources as Eisenstein, Eisler, and Adorno). In this context, I realized that, more than visualization, sonification, or other forms of transcoding data from one realm into another, expressive computation depended on synchronization and style in broadly historical ways that were crucial for, but were in important ways neglected by, studies of computing and of media alike. I was fortunate to have Sandy Cohen of San Francisco State University twice provide me with the opportunity to present guest lectures on "Styles of Synchronization," which allowed me to share my research with his eager, engaged students. The insights I developed during that early period of research at Interval would ultimately lead me to the materials I present in Chapter 3 of this study. But more generally, my experience with Mountford's Expressions team and with the many brilliant artists, technologists, designers, and engineers who populated Interval during my time there informs many aspects of this project in more ways than I can describe. While I ultimately developed the work I initiated at Interval in terms of media historiography, critical theory, and cultural studies of music rather than in terms of those theories and practices of interaction design with which I began, nonetheless, Mountford's early and generous support of my research framing visual music animation as a rich historical archive for the design of expressive computation had profound impact on this project.

Subsequently, at the University of Southern California's (USC) School of Cinematic Arts (then the School of Cinema-Television), the extraordinary luxuries of a three-year fellowship and the opportunity to carry out doctoral research with Marsha Kinder, David James, Vibeke Sorenson, Daniel Tiffany, and Dana Polan provided me with the critical rigor, creative insights, intellectual frameworks, academic community, time, and material support I needed to place the early ideas forged in Silicon Valley into more nuanced critical, historical, and theoretical frameworks. In particular, Kinder's dual expertise in world cinemas and digital media, her dazzling critical and creative use of digital media as a combine of theory and praxis, James's brilliant modeling of historical and historiographical media critique, and both colleagues' deeply passionate intellectual commitments to analytics of labor, sexuality, gender, race, and power relations provided me with treasured intellectual and affective resources that I have internalized in my way and that I invoke constantly in my own thoughts and work. To attain their degree of analytical precision, historical vision, and passionate commitment remains a cherished goal. Also at USC, the critical rigor, intellectual generosity, and inspired insights that Michael Renov, Todd Boyd, and Tara McPherson brought to media scholarship provided me with models of rigorous, ethical, and caring scholarship at its finest. No less crucial to this project were the love, support, and admiration shared among my graduate student peers, included among them Nithila Peter, Deborah Levitt, and Alison Defren.

USC/Annenberg Center's fertile hybridization of critical and cultural theory with experimental new media practices—an approach whose long-term productivity has been evident in ventures ranging from Kinder's Labyrinth Project to USC's Institute for Multimedia Literacy and the *Vectors* journal—was a crucial and formative site especially important for the development of Chapter 2; I thank Kristy Kang, art director of several Labyrinth Project productions and an emerging new media theorist in her own right, for the countless hours of inspiration that helped make our work together on *Mysteries and Desire* a revelation in collaborative digital praxis. USC's Cinema Library and the USC Doheny Library's Feuchtwanger Archive provided me with irreplaceable archival assistance and access to historical documents as a graduate student and in years since.

More recently, George Haggerty, my colleague in the English Department at the University of California at Riverside (UCR), read drafts of Chapter 2 on Eisenstein and provided the rigorously insightful suggestions that are, for Haggerty, de rigueur and that greatly improved the chapter's focus and readability. I presented a portion of Chapter 3 at the 2009 Conference of the College Art Association on a panel organized and chaired by Janeann Dill, to whom I express my gratitude for including me on an inspiring panel of media art scholars and practitioners. Over the past few years, Cindy Keefer of the Center for Visual Music has provided countless hours of her time in illuminating conversations about Fischinger scholarship; the joys and challenges of archiving precious, yet often neglected, works of visual music animation; and the state of the art of visual music animation today. In addition to talking me through insights from her own publications, Keefer very generously read a prepublication draft of Chapter 3 and provided a number of helpful suggestions, corrections, and insights for which I am deeply grateful. Keefer also arranged with the Fischinger Estate the reproduction of a film still from *Motion Painting No. 1* that appears in Chapter 3.

The Rockefeller Archive Foundation in New York State provided a deeply appreciated grant-in-aid that allowed me to spend precious days in their archives; without the assistance of the Rockefeller Foundation's extremely helpful staff of archivists, the discussion of Eisler in Chapter 4 would not exist in its current form. The City Library of Berlin, along with various and sundry new and used bookstores of the German capital, provided research assistance and access to materials that helped me complete Chapter 4. The Rivera Library of UCR provided a number of key research sources for Chapter 5, which also benefited from my reading published work by and having conversations with colleagues at UCR, including Lindon Barrett—to whose memory I dedicate Chapter 5—as well as Vorris Nunley. The origins of Chapter 6 were an invited talk hosted by David James at USC, at which I was delighted to see graduate students singing along, on cue, with a clip from *Hedwig and the Angry Inch.* Chapter 6 revises and extends a previously published version of that talk, which was anthologized in Blackwell's seminal 2007 collection of contemporary research on LGBT/Q studies, edited by my colleagues Haggerty and Molly McGarry, whom I thank for including me in their extraordinary project.

At an early stage of this project, Roseanna Albertini happily insisted that I take account of Steina Vasulka's work, a suggestion that I gladly took up and that informs my concluding Chapter 7. NTT InterCommunication Center of Tokyo generously provided archival videotape of the Vasulkas' performance and workshop in Tokyo in 1998. Steina Vasulka kindly provided the still image from *Voice Windows* appearing in Chapter 7. The Zentrum für Kunst und Medientechnologie (ZKM; Center for Art and Media) in Karlsruhe, Germany, maintains a standing exhibition of some of the finest interactive artworks of the past few decades in its MedienMuseum, without which resource I would not have been able to complete Chapter 7. I thank ZKM, too, for providing the installation image of Stephan von Huene's *Tischtänzer* appearing in this concluding chapter. The Los Angeles County Museum of Art very generously provided me with access to its collections to view von Huene's *Kaleidophonic Dog,* which was not on public view at the time of this writing. Patrick Crogan of the University of West England provided extremely helpful feedback on the discussion of cognition and technical synchronization appearing in Chapter 7. Finally, I am grateful to Stanford University Press for providing me with advance copies of English translations of Bernard Stiegler's work, which allowed me to compose the concluding chapter in a timely way.

UCR provided several grants supporting research as well as acquisition of research materials that were instrumental in the completion of this project. UCR's libraries have patiently provided their consistently high level of expertise and invaluable collections resources at every turn. Editor Micah Kleit, production editor Joan Vidal, copy editor Heather Wilcox, and the editorial board and production staff of the Temple University Press have provided the finest manuscript review and publishing support possible, and in the most timely of ways, for which I express my profound appreciation. The anonymous peer reviewers for the manuscript made critical, constructive suggestions that greatly strengthened the final draft. Elizabeth Hamilton made thoughtful proposals that significantly improved clarity. However, although this project bears debts historically deep and geographically broad for the extensive assistance that has made it possible, I alone am responsible for any error that may appear in these pages.

An earlier introduction to this book appeared in *Film Quarterly* in 2003–2004, but when it came time to finalize this book's contents in the spring and summer of 2009, I had learned so much, and the disciplines and transdisciplines intersecting the interests of the project had changed so much, that I jettisoned the earlier introduction, rather than update it, and wrote an entirely new introduction. Writing a new introduction while finishing a new concluding chapter and continuing with revisions to other chapters resulted in the elevated levels of stress and exhaustion familiar to many an author facing a looming, fixed deadline. Still, however common deadline anxiety and the overwork accompanying it may be, these feel nothing like shared experience, despite the constant need for shared everyday time that this kind of work in particular demands. Here at the peak, and much as he did once before in a very low valley, Lutz stepped in, into the midst of my extended hyperfocus on sync and style and my chronic distraction from everyday things, and, cooking and cleaning and seeing me through each day, carried me through it all and, when it was done, drove me away to the sea. Love: the first cipher to be styled, and the last—for Lutz.

1
Ciphers of Hieroglyphic Time

Here again music gives the most extreme expression to certain characteristics of the artistic, though this too by no means bestows any primacy on music. Music says "We" directly, regardless of its intentions.
—Theodor Adorno, *Aesthetic Theory*

Clocks That Don't Tell Time: Temporal Diagrams of Personhood and Publicity in Time-Based Media

Cinema or the digital interface: We consider these time-based expressions to be, variously, "technologies," "media," or perhaps, when thinking of these technical industrial expressions in specific historical contexts, "institutions," "discourses," "practices," or "forces." *Sync* begins from the observation that such complex exhibition installations are, very generally, something more like queer clocks: devices that diagram, express, and interpret unfamiliar temporal relations. This observation that time-registering devices, such as cinema—or telephony, phonography, radio, television, or the World Wide Web—equip us with situations for expressing and interpreting time is a weak one. It may mean that temporal, temporalizing media devices may have no more value than as devices—perhaps heterogeneous, arcane, opaque, or as yet imperfect in terms of their temporal presentation—for registering, storing, exhibiting, expressing, and exploring the passage of historical or lived contemporary time. Alternatively, such a claim may mean that queer clocks may be so powerful as to determine entirely their receivers' capacity to know and to move in time.

Think of Freder in Fritz Lang's *Metropolis* (1927). He goes in search of the elusive and entrancing Maria, but, leaving the Elysian heights of the city-state's leisure gardens, he receives a visual shock from which he physically recoils. In a much sampled and appropriated scene, troops of laborers wrestle in a choreography of human and machine, struggling to hold on to gears resembling the hands of clocks to maintain their balance on the precarious tiers of the great "Moloch machine" and the energetic balance of the city. He sees that their efforts utterly exhaust them, but the callow son of *Metropolis*'s director has to know this corporeal exhaustion to experience it.

Young Freder relieves one of the exhausted workers and takes hold of the clock-hands-as-gears, struggling to hold the truth of the energies animating modern industrial time in his own hands. His grappling with this haptic knowledge of the force of modern temporalities is not enough: Freder spends much of the subsequent duration of the film in a fever dream, visualizing an alchemical-industrial enactment of the ultimate transgression. His patient, caring social worker, Maria, is transformed in a magical, technological experiment into a machine-woman whose choreography of erotic surface and machine movement reduces the individual perspectives of *Metropolis*'s leisured male elites to a collective mass of protoplasmic, ocular lust. Then, the erotic, robotic dancer shifts her energies to revolutionary agitation, inciting *Metropolis*'s exhausted workers to leave their posts at the gears of industrial time and to run amok, ruining the tentative historical order of the vertical city and causing catastrophe for all.

Reading *Metropolis* as a narrative entry in the modernist project of a rhythmic cinema, Michael Cowan[1] points out that the film focuses "on the central question at stake in the [period's] broader rhythm debates: namely that of the limits between technology and organic life" (236). As rhythmic cinema, Cowan explains, it dramatizes then-current debates about tensions between corporeal rhythm and machine rhythm (*takt*) but, further, clarifies tensions between Marxian and Bergsonian understandings of history and temporality. *Metropolis* prompts reception, then, of a double, temporal aspect. Its clock-machines do not "tell" time; it diagrams a relation between contemporary debates about historical transformations in labor and in contemporary cinema.

First, it mobilizes complex affective tensions that it puts to work in presenting untenable and more manageable organizations of personhood and public being. And it dramatizes personhood and publicity in relation to autonomy and governmentality. It characterizes these tensions in temporalized, energetic terms: The masculine pleasures of leisure time are suspended over the masculine toil of work time. Director Freder's televisual surveillance is ultimately powerless to constrain the energies that accumulate, and the escalating state of oppression, in which male workers are feminized as exhausted machines maintaining *Metropolis*'s heights, reaches an inflection point of technological transgression when the machines become superlibidinally human. Innocent Maria, the feminized embodiment of care, and robotic Maria, the feminized embodiment of machine time (and of cinematic spectacle as alchemical double of industrial labor), first channelize attention to, and then disastrously incite and release the explosive forces of, industrial clock time. The disorganized energies of the revolting workers throw the vertical balance of power in the city into disarray. The film's escalation of time as chaos—revealed by wild sequences in which montages of hallucinatory labyrinthine detours to secret depths lead to frenzied pursuits back to spectacular heights—is followed by the thermodynamic exorcism of techno-magic, as robot Maria is burned at the stake, and her alchemist-inventor Rotwang falls to his death. The film closes with a horizontal chain in which Freder and his father clasp hands on the broad steps of the city cathedral. The unsustainable vertical heights of the city are leveled to more horizontal relations between worker, mediator, and owner.

Surveillance in the form of televisual information pales in comparison to the energetic forces of technologized divisions of labor and leisure, but, finally, gendered, classed divisions of labor remain intact. What *Metropolis* proposes is only a tempering and rebalancing of the rhythmic expression of energetic industrial time. *Metropolis* is a temporal diagram of complex temporal relations; it presents wildly fluctuating temporal transformations in the streams of time-based image and nonsynchronized musical accompaniment. Cinema's doubled temporality, presenting temporalized expression in time-based sequences, proposes an expression and an interpretation of the historical, material, and affective relations determining personhood and publicity, autonomy and governmentality.[2]

Lang's film exemplifies the two observations from which this study departs. *Metropolis* as cinematic exhibition may have no more value than as an arcane exhibition device presenting a heterogeneous, opaque, and imperfect temporal diagramming of history, modernity, labor, personhood, publicity, and power. It also claims, in its spectacular aspects and its narrative form, that distributed industrial ensembles, such as power networks or cinema, may be so powerful as to determine entirely their receivers' capacity to make sense of or to move in time. The informatic, networked, televisual processes of surveillance become powerless to control the larger exhaustions and eruptions of energetic relations primed in that energetic inflection point where technology becomes magic, whereby Maria becomes a spectacular, dancing agitating machine. In *Metropolis*'s temporal diagramming of material, technical, and affective labor, information power pales in comparison to energetic power. *Metropolis*'s diagramming of audience reception and historical temporality presents the biopolitical governing of personhood and publicity as still more a bioenergetic than a bioinformatic dynamic.

Metropolis is a temporal diagram of historical transformations that emerges from a particular, transforming historical moment. It tells us only something about its own period and production from the vantage point of our own. It does not represent its time but diagrams complex relations between its own moment and the larger historical period in which it was made. The film is a clock that does not tell time but diagrams temporality, and we diagram some relation between its complex temporalities and our own in receiving it. Between the two limit points of presenting an entirely indeterminate and an entirely determining temporalized expression of time entangled within the time-determined series of cinematic images, along with the great ambivalence with regard to historical and contemporary meanings this entanglement entails, to say that technical, such presentational ensembles as cinema or the computational display are complex, queer "timepieces" more than presentations of representational or denotational images or enframed world pictures means, simply, acknowledging that such complex ensembles as cinema *may* express temporality in terms of the clock time in relation to which their disparate technical mechanisms function and to which they were viewed. Such works as *Metropolis* do not exhibit the contents of their displays as historical or as contemporary clock time in any reliable way—despite our possible identifications with young Freder's shocked gazing on the choreography of exhausted workers.

Cinema or computational interface channel and express streaming, temporalized expressive material like series of recorded images or sounds; in this sense, they are "media." Cinema or computational interface derive their capacities for time-based expression from techno-scientific processes deriving from nineteenth-century thermodynamic sciences and are motivated in materialist geopolitics. They rely on inventions produced in large-scale transformations of industrial production systems whose increasing automation over historical time is achieved in compressing and channelizing the serial production processes that they draw on and redistribute; in this sense, cinema or interface are "technologies."

But however closely we may attend to the clock faces that cinema or computational display may present, these temporalized, technical exhibitions of mediated sound and image do not represent clock time. Clock time is some temporal standardization for measuring elapsed duration on local, geopolitical, planetary, or cosmic scales. Time-based presentational ensembles, such as cinema or digital interface, cannot fully, actually, or factually represent clock time, nor can they actually represent historical or contemporary time. The materiality of the display ensures that the representation of time and our apperception of it are, however apparently precise, to some degree contingent on some larger series of time. As the saying goes (familiar, perhaps, in Orbital's sampling, looping, and remixing of it), "even a stopped clock tells the right time twice a day." Any temporalized audiovisual display presents some measured ratio of—a temporal diagramming of—complex relations between the order of historical time and contemporaneity, expressed as complex relations of personhood and publicity, autonomy and governmentality.

And the deployment of these time-based displays of temporalized expression is itself part of the large-scale reordering of geopolitical world space. Synchronized devices, whether the synchronized gear mechanisms of the synchronome, the cinema, or the synchronized semiconductor mechanisms of computing displays, relate historiality and contemporaneity, personhood and publicity in displacements of historical time and space. As complex as the queer clock faces of cinema or digital interface seem, we can carefully match critical description to particular instances, historical contexts, and interpretations to determine how technologies, media, a particular work, and their complex historical social situation and resituation of time and space become expressive in reception.

Consider, in this light, Charlie Chaplin's *Modern Times* (1936). Like *Metropolis, Modern Times* also presents a time-disciplined factory setting surveilled and controlled by television. As in *Metropolis, Modern Times*'s factory disciplines workers whose movements are stressed by their synchronization with the speed of industrial production and within a larger temporal stream whereby production is synchronized in divisions of property and labor. In both films, televisual communication surveys the "liveness" of the workers' movements and dramatizes the displaced nature of the labor animating the production of everyday life from the surface of everyday life. Famously, Chaplin's Tramp persona, appearing as "A Factory Worker," naively accepts the factory ownership's increasing demands to synchronize his every living movement with serialized machine production, helping prototype a new "feeding machine," which shovels food at him faster than he can consume it. Subsequently, a frenetic musical accompaniment punctuates the Tramp's strained efforts to keep up with the increasing speed of the assembly line. In the converse of his test run of the feeding machine, though, now he is run through, consumed by, the assembly line. As Christian Hite[3] observes, the Tramp's frenzied automatisms result in his disgorgement from the factory in a case of "indigestible" labor.

But before his choreographed path out the factory door, and as he is fed through the machine, we see a cross-section view revealing the innards of the assembly line through which he "unreels" (Figure 1.1). The Tramp is flattened like a filmstrip as he streams through the gears of the machine, reflexively diagramming the film projector apparatus that we, as audience, are watching. *Modern Times* reminds its audience of the technical labor whose intensified automation continues to displace material labor; and, more incisively than *Metropolis*'s ostensive analogy of "feminized machine" with cinema reception, it reminds audiences that cinema itself is a site where these historical displacements occur. Chaplin's familiar Tramp persona plays a large part in this revelation. Then, too, there is the loose yet incisive synchronization of rhythmic pulse and melodic tone with the Tramp's hysterical movements in the factory sequence, contrasting with the general quietude of the anxious director's office; the intertitles used

FIGURE 1.1 *Modern Times* (1936): The Tramp as factory worker consumed by the factory (frame capture). (*Modern Times,* dir. Charles Chaplin [Charles Chaplin Productions, 1936].)

throughout the film; and Chaplin's performance near the end of the film, when, before a working-class diner crowd, he sings a nonsense song whose polyglot lyrics telegraph an echo of cinema as "universal language"—all these audiovisual stagings recall formal and technical aspects of, as well as the affective aspirations of, cinema before the coming of synchronized sound.

Modern Times uses synchronized sound, then, as needed, and while deploying the higher fidelity and mixing techniques characterizing new studio sound-production methods and technologies of the mid-1930s. But it does so in the interest of articulating its own capacity to prompt our recall of nonsynchronized (silent) cinema. By charting relative changes in volume balancing music, dialog, and sound effects during the formative years of synchronized cinema sound tracks, Rick Altman, McGraw Jones, and Sonia Tatroe argue that the Hollywood sound track resulted from specific negotiations of "social and cultural work as well as technical labor, and thus from conflicting contemporary commitments to differing sound types and uses."[4] Studio sound methods, too, exist within the changing soundscape, and, as Altman and many others have emphasized, understanding cinema sound also means understanding the everyday soundscapes exterior to cinema.[5] In fact, *Modern Times* presents similar observations and critique, although in diagrammatic rather than scholarly form. Its narrative form models tensions in the advance of sound-film technologies, which Altman and his team track from the late 1920s to the mid-1930s.

It uses musical sound in the manner of silent cinema but also scores such scenes as the one depicting the factory director in his office without music or dialog—that is, "real" feeling or actual communication. Too, synchronization of sound and image in the factory sequence as frenetic labor evokes the noisy factory floors that such theatrical sound designers as Harold Burris-Meyer helped the Muzak corporation balance with efficiency-prompting musical sound tracks during the 1930s and 1940s and that he hoped might be deployed for cinema. And it also provides a shrill rendition of the bustling soundscapes of urban metropoles, which, as Emily Thompson[6] notes, prompted soundproofing as an architectural technique while contributing to the iconic musical motifs decorating such buildings as New York's Rockefeller Center. By emphasizing the director's suite as anxious, soundproofed quietude, *Modern Times* depicts anxious internalized stress as the counterpoint to energetic laboring excess.

The film's rendition of the affects of modern industrial labor is double. First, it synchronizes musical imagery as contemporaneity: A working frenzy becoming hysterical in the effort to keep up with the speed of industrial machines or musical quietude as Tums-popping stress, *Modern Times* evoke the soundscapes of metropole and factory using the new sound technologies of the mid-1930s to telegraph the affective tensions of contemporary life.[7] But *Modern Times* does not only propose a critique of contemporary work, consumption, and leisure with cinema projected, as the Tramp and the Gamin (Paulette Goddard) hit the road, as a momentary critical escape from more unobserved forms of these activities. The film also provides a history lesson on cinema sound by way of musical synchronization. It diagrams an *earlier* period of nonsynchronized cinema sound and image as historically immanent to the contemporary synchronized cinema. *Modern Times* does not depict contemporaneity; it does not tell time. It diagrams time, in time.

Using contemporary sound-image synchronization techniques to recapitulate expressive aspects of the earlier, nonsynchronized cinema as well as the earlier cinema's often-progressive aspirations for mass cultural expression, *Modern Times* musically prompts, while reflexively diagramming, its audience's recall of the industrial history through which, sitting in the site of reception, it is again passing and displacing. The historical energies of nonsynchronized cinema are projected as dated but enduring: not up-to-the-moment like the feeding machine, yet still to be fully exhausted, still historically resonant. The set piece of the factory scene, with its closely choreographed synchronization of shrieking music with Chaplin's herky-jerky performance and its reflexive cross-sectioning of industrial cinema as a displacement of historical labor, is also a "timepiece." This sequence prompts apperception of the passage of cinematic time as a strange and complicated historical time: a queer clock ticking away public moments of Chaplin's familiar aging persona. *Metropolis* and *Modern Times* make clear that synchronization, in networks of ensembles that cannot tell time, is first a matter of coordinating the *contemporaneity* enframing audience reception with the *historiality* of the streaming composition. Whether the ensemble we receive refuses our interpretations and gestures or incites them, it precedes the contemporaneity in which we receive it and from which we are excluded. Complex temporal diagrams, such as cinema or the computational interface, whatever their capacity to hold or to program cultural or technical memory, begin for receivers as materialized, antimemorial ensembles of the streaming temporalities in which they are diagrammed—and that, in turn, they, too, partially diagram.

Chaplin's historical persona in *Modern Times* is prepared by Chaplin and the studio ensemble; but the synchronization of his frenetic gesture with the frenzy of factory "music" is rendered not simply by the "filmmaker," as Michel Chion[8] generally insists, but also by the audience for whom it is projected in reception. As we "hear" *Modern Times*'s "silent cinema musical sound" carrying the Tramp's commoditized serial image object through that cross-section of the assembly line/film projector, as we see and hear the results of up-to-date 1930s Hollywood sound technologies interpreting the film's time-out-of-joint expressive tactics, we travel backward down that path to an earlier period of cinema whose forward transitions Altman and his team have excavated. Though it cannot accurately represent time and space because it helps displace them, cinema begins with a synchronization of reception and production as exhibition, where historiality and contemporaneity are diagrammed via affective means that audiences feel: differentiations of personhood or publicity, autonomy or governmentality. Cinema reception—whether within the production process or in exhibition—*also* distributes the process of any cinema's own historical displacement. The disappearance of the Tramp and the Gamin is the trail of the leading edge of a never fully elaborated allegory of reception—that is, when it is not just a tentatively happy ending.

Exhibition Diagrams, Reception Diagrams

The reasons for starting from the very weak claim that "technological media," such as cinema, are more like clocks that cannot accurately tell time or register space in the site of reception and that become expressive in spite of themselves become apparent, I hope, when we consider the highly musicalized synchronization strategies of such canonical works as *Metropolis* or *Modern Times.* Classic apparatus studies, such as those of Jean-Louis Comolli,[9] demonstrated that any complex exhibition installation, such as cinema, is always a sum of more than simply the material parts constituting its earliest concrete instantiation. As Martin Jay[10] notes, the apparatus theories of Paul Narboni, Comolli, Jean-Louis Baudry, or Christian Metz may well have been a "culminating moment in the

French critique of ocularcentrism." But the aspects of Comolli's argument that stress cinema's needs to meet specific material historical conditions of perspectival imaging to become viable for viewing remain worth noting. Further, as genealogical and discursive analyses, such as those of Friedrich Kittler,[11] suggest, describing large-scale shifts in the means of knowledge production (in Kittler's *Discourse Networks,* a shift from literary, philosophical, and pedagogical networks of distributing literary epistemologies to technical, mechanical, and probabilistic networks) may be more revealing than presuming static ontologies, epistemologies, and ethics for highly socially freighted, technically sophisticated, and historically fraught conduct, such as "writing." It can never be entirely clear at any particular moment of historical time the precision with which any particular media apparatus may render its meanings, ideologies, or effects, as cultural studies of time-based media from Walter Benjamin onward have long observed.

But, as Benjamin's writing on language and on cinema also make clear, that aspect of the contemporary we may experience as glassine sphere of everyday life rolling forward from a continuous, retrospectively accessible historical past that we need only turn around and view before equipping ourselves to wheel on forward may, with closer consideration, appear as cracked surface. Perhaps it is patched together as much by the effect of historical eventuality or of some form of spoken or unspoken consensus—or by some ensemble of scientist, artist, historian, or critic. Perhaps it is simply some willful desiring cognitive agent who, diagramming time in time, conveys discovery, insight, recollection, elaboration, even tentative conclusions as to the meanings of profound displacement, disruption, or destruction. A willful, desiring cognitive agent does not need to mean "an individual person."

Metropolis and *Modern Times* today demonstrate that whatever the shortcomings of the works or the ensembles of people who made, exhibited, and received them, cinematic works also diagram cracks and patches, relate historical time to contemporary time, in being projected. When the interpretation of recorded, distributed, and exhibited data depends on synchronizing the operations of an intervening technical device with those of the archival medium in which the message is encoded, any "social" meaning may, in fact, be written as "noise," as Kittler argues, rather than as historical "signal." Yet history finds ways of biding its time while the gears or discs of our technological sense and sensation synchronize in action or strain and fall apart. Even in spite of the material conditions they may impose or withdraw, and as Theodor Adorno argues for music, cinema or computing displays say "we." But contrary to Adorno's insistence, they say "we" indirectly: They ultimately diagram historiality and contemporaneity in only expressive terms, however abstract, of personhood and publicity. If *Metropolis* hedges its social observations about material labor and creative labor by diagramming their spectacular inflection as choreographed, gendered, gestural movement, *Modern Times* diagrams its own filmic history as the value retained by musical synchronization of sound and image in a transformed regime of studio production practices.

As clocks that don't tell time but diagram temporality, these films raise the key questions that *Sync* attempts to answer: why and how musicality and gesture have been so frequently, consistently, and broadly deployed for emphasizing the synchronization not simply of sound and image streams but of historical and contemporized time, in streaming media undergoing radical transformations in their technological materialities, in their medium specificities, in their formal variations, and in their reuse. My own textual diagrams describing highly compressed interpretations of *Metropolis* or *Modern Times*, above, begin to offer evidence of this problem and an initial attempt at the answers. Films such as these do not propose their visual imagery only as concepts or necessarily as logical propositional images presenting literal space, movement, or motion in historical or in contemporary terms. Rather, such works propose complex temporal relations as complex temporal diagrams. Still, as we can already see, weak claims grant great plasticity. We need to attach a bit more ballast to the ballooning elasticity becoming apparent in my temporal diagrams if they are to be at all critically descriptive.

Recent scholarship provides wide precedents for reading streaming media as diagrammatic or emblematic presentation. As Charles Altieri[12] notes, although Gilles Deleuze is appreciated as one of the twentieth century's most sophisticated thinkers on affect, his long initial engagement with Bergsonism from the late 1940s into the mid-1960s increasingly engaged with diagrammatic semiotics after that point. Felix Guattari's notes on their work together during the 1970s make clear the debt the two collaborators owed to Charles Sanders Pierce's mid-nineteenth-century understanding of diagram as "icon of relation."[13] Pierce's notion of diagram as icon of relation allowed Deleuze and Guattari to advance a still significant if expansive solution of the tensions between the historical tendencies of organicism and mechanism that had taken on urgent, critical import with the elaboration of cybernetic semiotics for network computing between 1950 and 1970. In the context of the growing sophistication and wide proliferation of global computing networks and media networks, and with no indication of an abatement in the pace at which the automation of symbolic processes proceeded yet no clear evidence of the ability of cybernetics to fully account for thought, memory, or feeling, Deleuze and Guattari pronounce the machine a "subject" and derive from Pierce's semiotics of the diagram a generative theory of nature, history, and capital that they articulate in terms of serial, symbolic-material "machines."[14]

More recently, in ways closer to more conventional phenomenologies of vision and language and more willing to engage rhetorical interpretations of cinema as well as audience commentary on computer-generated imagery (CGI) reception, Vivian Sobchack[15] considers CGI in narrative industrial cinema as diagrammatic. Sobchack follows Peter Wollen's 1972 derivation of Pierce's theory of the sign for cinema semiotics. Wollen points out that in Pierce's semiotics, a diagram is not precisely an image but a sign presenting relations between parts of two referents; the diagram tends toward "emblematics" in a larger historical tension between the emblem and the photograph. Describing the computer-graphics animation in *Final Fantasy: The Spirits Within* (2001), Sobchack suggests that this fully CGI-animated film's promise of convincing photorealism invites audiences to read the computer-generated images as photorealistic images and as diagrammatic emblems as they compare CGI animation to the historical dominant of photorealism. Sobchack argues that the result of audiences reading CGI as a diagram of its own similitude to the photorealistic image toward which it strives is that they find *Final Fantasy*'s attempt at CGI photorealism too detailed but also lacking in its "illusion of life."[16]

Sobchack's cinema-receiver scans for tensions between image and diagram in reception but also for contemporary rhetorics and ideologies around recent computer-generated animation and performs a historical comparison of contemporary CGI realism to historical photorealism. While Sobchack argues that CGI presents a diagrammatic emblem of the photorealistic image it strives to present, her discussion also suggests that receivers also project temporal diagrams. As the cinema-CGI audience reads the time of exhibition and relates exhibitionary time to the historical dominance of photographic realism and the advent of CGI realism, more than assigning a (negative or positive) value to the realism of industrial feature-length CGI cinema, the audience is *also* relating two complex material and temporal durations. It is diagramming its reception of cinematic time to the historical transition between the introduction of computer-graphics animation and its uses. *Final Fantasy* prompts this diagramming on the part of its audience in its production, in its advance advertising, or in the ideological rhetorics circulating around both.

Despite the fact that the great majority of audience members are not likely to assign precise historical calendar dates delimiting either of these durations as specific periods in calendar and clock time, still, if audiences are weighing CGI animation with regard to the antinomies of image and emblem, as photorealistic image and as emblematic diagram, then audiences are also diagramming two portions of streaming time to one another. We create a ratio of lived contemporary time to the historical emergence of computer graphics, and we thus grant a particular type of *historicity* to *Final Fantasy*'s exhibition: its "historic" nature. The film is trivially historic, Sobchack finds, a matter of actual exhibition not living up to ideological promise or rhetorical premise. Perhaps, for others, it is significantly historic, diagrammed, say, as an entry in a series of photorealistic CGI feature films integrating the epistemologies of navigable CGI computer gaming of the 1990s with feature-length cinema animation and Web-based social marketing and fan production whose material, technical, and affective values are yet to solidify completely. More than simply evaluating CGI's photorealism or its perceptual realism,[17] then, audiences also diagram contemporary and historical time. Temporal diagramming proposed in the streaming work and differently conducted by audiences is not exclusive to works expressing recent media transitions or technical deployments. *Modern Times* mobilized this capacity on the part of audiences by designing the reception of its narrative form as a temporal diagramming of synchronized sound cinema's historical derivation from nonsynchronous cinema.

In just this way, though, we should consider temporal diagrams more as doubled proposals, as doubled projection, rather than as logical propositions or concepts. They orient us toward streaming media in the streaming history that they in part displace. And because the considered duration of the contemporary or the historical temporality such diagramming relates may be adequate, confused, wrong, or entirely false, temporal diagrams evaluate commensurate or incommensurate expressions of time. We may believe we experienced an event at a moment impossible for us to have done so, or we may assign the historiality of computer graphics to, say, that of computer games—so the ratio we diagram for contemporaneity and historiality may be partial, negative, or even a compounding of the negative. Temporal diagrams may be a kind of shorthand held for time we have never experienced or grasped or for time that has never passed.

Such diagramming may help us adjust habits or adapt new ones. But temporal diagramming always risks *some* commensuration of lived historical experience with a diagrammatic measure of times never personally lived and or not yet having had historical passage other than in some medial reception (fantasy, fiction, dream, speculation, and so forth). Remote, irrelevant, forgotten, lost, fictive, fantastic time, nonevents, or nondurations belonging either to a sense of historical order *or* to our reception of some sensation of it may be recollected as emblems of contemporaneity that has passed, is being lived, or is impending. The historicity we grant within partial or negative temporal diagramming may describe, replace, or destroy the historicity of the lived moment. A replacement or destruction of lived time by what we may call "mediatic" time, of course, is the threat that apparatus theories attempted to frame as a matter of political, ideological determination. They are also the tendency Kittler less dramatically describes as the discursive noise of technical networks historically replacing prior networks of written literacy. In their negative forms, temporal diagramming may amount to absolute, passive human dependency and subjection (the human as machine) on one hand or the dissolution of history as entropic fragmentation recouped in the automatisms of new technologies (the machine as history) on the other. Addiction and noise, in their negative cases, are the two limit points of incommensurate or noncommensurate synchronization. Time becomes hieroglyphic.

Echoes of Eisenstein

Barbara Stafford's[18] reading of a range of art-historical works as "echoic objects" goes some way toward helping explicate the difficulties involved with the understanding of temporal diagrams as complex synchronization I offer here. Stafford's goal is to guide the arts and humanities and the cognitive neurosciences into more productive interactions with one another. Stafford observes that, first, in borrowing historically from the arts and humanities, cognitive neurosciences may be overestimating many of their discursive claims and, second, that neuroscience cannot fully account for the cultural and historical dimensions of that cognitive work that artistic images do or the problems such images continue to raise in the present. "As both filtering and immersive new media are demonstrating, we are far from reaching the end point of the long tradition in Western philosophy of identity as *autarkeia*—that is, the withdrawal or maximal independence of the subject from all external factors as the highest goal" (211), despite many neural researchers' claims to this effect. She acknowledges the "neural Darwinism" of such cognitive researchers as Gerald Edelman, who suggests selective pressures cause changes in "populations of synapses" throughout the brain, resulting in transformed mental capacities over time. Contemporary cognitive neuroscience, Stafford thinks, suggests that the "invasive and metamorphosing 'phatic' products of visual culture might, in turn, reenter our brain strengthened":

> Such augmented images would then reconfigure the neural-synaptic organization of the brain before getting distributed in the outside world again. Explicit advertisements, shock waves of video, salient film clips, "mashed" digital media, the polymorphous World Wide Web, all design the neurons and the neural networks re-design popular culture. . . . Apparently vast populations of neurons must become synchronized at around a 40 hertz frequency of electrical pulses for conscious activity to occur. Similarly, at the macro level, for unrelated people to form coherent social groups, their divergent behavior must somehow also become synchronized. (211–212)

Synchronization at the social level depends on acquiring "social skills." Cooperation between people and environment happens, then, in macro- and microscale networked synchronization, but between neural or social synchronization, historical cultures fill the material, symbolic gaps, building complex ensembles and associations in mimetic, "compound images" affording empathy between self and other. The "work of the senses" goes beyond vision; it is affective, configurative, and performative. "Compound images" are not simply visual but "are the medium or interface where world and subject get co-constructed, that is, echoically presented to one another's view" (211–212).

If mechanistic synchronization determines neural patterning, Stafford observes, understanding patterns of attention to the images we create is all the more crucial (216). The "compound images," "inlay art," or "emblazoned interfaces" that Stafford explores encompass, then, the antinomies of realist image and emblem interpreted by Sobchack's viewer. If cognitive scientists must embrace the cognitive work such compound "inlay images" or "echo objects" do, then humanists too will have to accept a cognitive grammar of perception, those "pathos-laden *schema*" that over the course of human history have "unified self-consciousness, consciousness of one's body, and environmental consciousness into a formal logic. Visual 'universals' or visual formulas capture how we synoptically structure neural content" (209).

Heraldic devices, blazons, mosaics: These and more work as "inlay, mesh, net, lattice, or grid" (136), devices of fitness assisting in the narrative construction of the self, and demonstrate the ways thought interpenetrates the "components" of sensation and how the elements of sensation enter into thought. Familiarity with the world will not suffice: "The problem inlaying art formats specifically illuminate is interaction or the cognitive work of conscious crafting" (215). Echoic objects afford interaction between universal biological grammar and living thinking bodies making sense out of the sensations of a changing, historical world. Echoic objects are diagrams in the sense that Pierce, Wollen, or Sobchack describe: They relate portions of larger referents. But their "echoic" nature indicates that they are also reflexive, temporal diagrams.

Such echoic objects relate some portion of the synchronizing sequences of temporal patterning in mechanistic neural activity with partial sequences of social networks. *What* they relate by compounding affective empathy and mimetic construction is "pathos." Echoic objects are temporal diagrams that hold, distribute, and differentiate pathos otherwise out of reach of the synchronized processes of biological neural networks or social networks. Yet Stafford's description flattens specific historical geopolities or historical epochs, while making technological deployments or media transitions appear as aftereffects of neuro-cognitive aesthetic interaction recoverable as echo objects mediating the overlapping projects of neurological and aesthetic research.

Demonstrating the value of historical art for contemporary neuro-cognitivism, echoic objects are Stafford's resolution to the great historical tensions of organicism and mechanicism that Deleuze and Guattari resolve by pushing the meaning of "machine" away from that of functional, nonliving energetic systems of instruments. Instrument, technology, or medium ceases to retain specificity in Deleuze and Guattari's treatment of "social machines," dynamic and complex ensembles animated in historical immanence and manifesting in and across historical time as enfleshed material-symbolic sense and sensation. In Stafford's work, where synchronized informatic mechanisms now clearly determine the development and processes of organic neural material, sense and sensation are mediated in echo objects: "The dialogical motion of mimesis enabling shared affective, experience suggests that learning, affective control, and the capacity to distinguish self from others is echoic. As social beings, we seem to bounce off one another" (76).

Chaplin's film comedy and Sergei M. Eisenstein's *Battleship Potemkin* (1925) help Stafford illustrate how echoic objects mediate sense and sensation in cinematic mimesis, where pathos is effected as a synchrony of cognition resulting as a network effect coordinating viewers' responses. *Potemkin*'s Odessa Steps sequence, Stafford suggests, succeeds in presenting a unified and realistic orienting view for the mass audience by animating facets within the streaming spatiotemporal flow of the sequence. Editing modulates continuity and rupture by ordering in-frame composition against cross-frame cuts, emphasizing salient "facets" within Eisenstein's "conspicuous modernist geometry" (84). Stafford does not describe the larger network effects initializing, activating, distributing, culminating, and subsiding as historical pathos in this sequence, as if the crowd were a flock of gentle doves hunted by a ruthless military machine: sudden alarm; initial shock; mass flight; a cascade of brutality; enervation of the tragic process; and after all of these events are presented by virtue of complex rhythmic modulations, the final exhortation to remember Tsarist violence in the name of the revolution—*and* this last, not only in a final title but also in the often-noted hand-tinted red flag borne by the battleship at the film's finale. Stafford speaks of montage as echoic schemata apparent in one rhythmic swing of pathos within the larger seriation of historical pathos that Eisenstein designed the Steps sequence to telegraph. Stafford notes the cut: from a longer view of soldiers marching diagonally down the stairs cutting down the madly fleeing mass to a close-up of a defenseless sick boy fallen among the chaos. This cut, Stafford notes, produces a "nonnarrative diagrammatic starkness" (84) communicating pathos beyond metaphor by animating salient detail amid general flow.[19] In contrast, Chaplin, she observes, achieved comedic diagrammatic mimesis by making his own actions salient within more continuous cinematic duration (84). Narrative is cognitive work rather than a matter of aesthetic or cinematic form.

Eisenstein's own argument about *Potemkin* is not entirely dissimilar to Stafford's account of echoic objects but diverges in important ways. Eisenstein, too, appropriates all manner of art-historical resources in his arguments for that "organic unity" achieved by Soviet montage cinema in such films as *Potemkin*. But he contrasts U.S. or German cinemas with Soviet montage as a matter of their historical development of aesthetic resources and of the temporal diagramming of pathos. Soviet montage improved on the tempo characterizing D. W. Griffith's films by mobilizing metaphor beyond visual or narrative representation in a "*relentlessly* affective rhythm."[20] Rhythmic series trace the line of a successful film's "organic" pulse through a play of the "inner contradictions" the work exhibits. This streaming pulse is never reducible to object or objectivity.

Where Stafford's echoic object engages a dialogical crafting of interaction between neural microsynchronization and social macrosynchronization allowing the narrative constitution of self and other, in Eisenstein's work, montage projects a "microcosm" (235) bearing inner contradictions rather than an object.

For Eisenstein, rhythmically diagramming historical pathos in montage art results not simply from technological advance, as Stafford seems to agree, but also in terms of historical, social, political, and art-historical differentiation that Eisenstein believes montage expressed but that Stafford sees as independent of the dialogical echoic object. Eisenstein's essay on "Synchronization of Senses"[21] helps make the point. Here, typically, Eisenstein cites sources as disparate as Karl von Eckartshausen's account of inventing a color organ influenced by Père Castel,[22] recent writing on jazz as "disunion," or German romantic author and philosopher Novalis, Hermann von Helmholtz, and Arthur Rimbaud (and again, in the essay "Color and Meaning," Walt Whitman or Havelock Ellis in the development of what we may call a bioenergetic notion of color sensation and sense). For Eisenstein, synchronization of the senses in cinema means creating terms of correspondence using such materials as temporal rhythm or color, so as to afford a rhythmical "fusion" between the streams of phenomena projected. A successful qualitative "fusion" has nothing to do with fusing, say, "yellow" and a particular sound but is a dynamic effect discovered in the *compositional* process. The work cannot be taken apart from the compositional labor that produces it; but at its best, "fusion" arising in the composition of rhythmic streams results in a diagram that literally "reproduces" historical sense and association: "the very *image of an epoch and the image of the reasoning process* of those who are linked to the epoch" (100). This linkage becomes concrete in reception but arises from the various phases of compositional labor.

Such a projection of an epochal image via a link to those who lived its history relates to the contemporary audience *some* measure of historical time in that qualitative fusion. This diagram of a link to remote historical contradictions (rather than conditions or objects) also models the expressive internal contradictions of the present in the dynamic microcosm of montage, as well. Montage expands in reception into a microcosm relating two historical, sociopolitical streams in some measure of their contradictions. For Eisenstein, of course, this measure itself is temporal, and it must move forward as a historical development. The temporal diagram must be a positive commensuration not simply of the mass reception of mass art but the collectivized, socialist production and reception of mass art. Temporal diagramming as rhythmic stylization takes the measure, finally, of an ethical streaming of cinema exhibition.

The montage stream is not simply a dialectical object as opposed to a dialogical one. The specific art-historical dynamism of montage's double modeling of dynamic internal contradictions results from Eisenstein's own production context: his "worldview both monistic and dialectic."[23] The streaming nature of the montage sequence projects the phases of the cinematic work's production; it expands the flat notational series of planning documents, serial images, musical accompaniment or optical sound, and technical exhibition in reception. Streaming forth, it bears with it complex potentialities: It is plastic and affective, a living cell but also historical rupture. The "harmonic recurrence" Eisenstein describes (241) as defining montage, and lacking in Griffith's work, stylizes cinema in resounding "harmonic series": that is, temporalized streams, not objects.[24] The macrocosm would be the historical stream, the microcosm of montage linking to history by virtue of accomplishing a leap in the present. For monistic immanence to prepare and to animate dialectical contradiction and synthesis, pathos must be composed in production, projected in exhibition, and then made concrete, by audiences, in reception. Cinema composition and reception are the sites where that monad as cell breaks open and expands in series. It changes history—if not socialist history, at least art history.

This rhythmic and haptic expansion that montage effects in reception *is*, further, a matter of historical specificity and of metaphor and narrative passing beyond representational limits. To extend cinema's plastic capacities for meaning beyond representation, through metaphor, as affective rhythm expressing historical pathos took time; cinema had to develop from modeling eye and vision to becoming capable of presenting "the image of an embodied viewpoint" (233). The haptic embodiment of perspective is double: "Organic unity" of montage unifies production workers and audience in complex synchronization—of reason, affect, and history—arising in diagrammatic, rhythmic gesture.

Montage as streaming, temporal diagram, then, performs the configurative and cognitive work Stafford ascribes to echoic objects in the present but further makes complex historical claims. This work is achieved in a rhythmic, pathic act rather than through nonnarrative presentation of cognitive objects. In other words, Eisenstein conceived of the historical contingency also unfurling through the montage stream (allowing such critics as Stafford or myself to isolate a cut or a montage sequence) as having been historically necessary. Eisenstein's description of *Potemkin* makes greater claims for cinema as monistic, dialectic diagramming than those Stafford makes for dialogical echoic objects. Such films as *Potemkin* achieve a (socialist) synchrony of production, exhibition, and reception streams, differentiating the expressive power of montage from the metaphoric poverty and less-developed temporal relations Eisenstein observed in Griffith—and from Griffith's casual racism (234).

Stafford resolves the historical tensions between mechanicism and organicism by observing autonomic neuronal and social synchronization mechanisms mediated in an echoic organic crafting of aesthetic experience. Thus, Stafford isolates a single cut from Eisenstein's Odessa Steps sequence from its narrative. But montage becomes nonnarrative, because narrative now exists in cognition, not in the material object of the film or the material stream of temporalities the film conducts. For Eisenstein, historical tensions between mechanicism and organicism, cognition and aesthetic form are less important than an elaboration of monistic and dialectical materialisms. His shift away from more conventional concerns of human-as-machine is not surprising, since, as I discuss in Chapter 2, in postrevolutionary Soviet Russia it was the capitalist state "machine" that had been seen as synchronizing sovereign power and social, technological, and political underdevelopment. Machine extension was not a symptom of social decay but a problem to be overcome through industrial, political, and cultural labor. Narrative was a quality of the *work* of art, its history, and its reception: Narrative or metaphor could be transmuted into rhythm or gesture in exhibition only with a doubling of the meanings of pathos—pathos in art's composition and in its material, historical, and political reception.

What is important, though, is Eisenstein's doubling of pathos as rhythmic energetic potentials: pathos immanent to privileged instances of art appropriated from the historical past (Charles Dickens, Whitman, Griffith, and so many more) *and* to the immanent historiality of the postrevolutionary present. Pathos connotes the material, aesthetic historicity of Soviet montage—its artistic achievement—but also a historicity that we associate with "liveness" in contemporary critical terms. In philosophical terms, what expands the flattened cinematic series into the organic unity of its embodied viewpoint is the streaming of rhythmic gesture informed by Marxian understandings of historical, dialectical potential and Bergsonian understandings of potential as virtuality.[25] The montage of historical and contemporary pathos takes the ratio of a complex temporal diagramming of sociopolitical and aesthetic experience. More than echoic object, its rhythmic pulse elaborates a line, the musicality of lyricism or phrasing, to trace doubled potential. Montage *scores* the moving image as complex musical diagram deciphering the hieroglyphic of modern contemporaneity as the becoming historical of Soviet art. Relating compositional labor and creative, interpretive labor to historical temporality, pathos expressing "affective logic" (250) or "sensual thought" (251) in Eisenstein is an expression of what has been recently described as "affective labor."[26]

An important point of Stafford's argument is that if the synchronization of contemporary sociality may be determined in a blast of "polymorphous" digital media forms evolving our neuronal connections collectively and autonomously while feeding through social forms and practices, then how and what we attend to as we craft our interactions with one another and the world around us are crucial. Yet even while neural cognition defines the limits of human cognition and affect, neither neuroscience nor echoic objects respond to any need for a critical history of neuroscience, as Stafford allows when deferring from pursuing biopolitical considerations. Nor do we learn of the pathos of intimate or grand historical failures of artistic, neural, or social synchronization not evident or recoverable in the cognitive-affective emblematics of echoic objects. We are left wondering how "salience" and "attention" might be expanded to Eisenstein's "devastating rhythm."

In Eisenstein, stylizing cinema as devastating rhythm claims the most advanced capacities of cinema to conduct historical pathos in the memorialization of traumatic violence. Too, if temporal diagrams may reproduce affect as commensurate, incommensurate, or noncommensurate relation between contemporaneity and historiality, Eisenstein's consideration of montage as having a doubled potential for such ends suggests pathos as commensurate and noncommensurate relation. It can only be affective labor as an expression of synchronizing composition and reception that reproduces historical pathos as pathic act. In Eisenstein, affective labor expresses the fluctuating capacities of the temporal diagram in a medial ethics, as if to say, "This is what aesthetics can do; this is what we can do; this is what history can do." Temporal diagramming does not tell time; it risks wild, even destructive relations. But it expresses the ethical capacities of the medium in affective labor. Yet why echoic objects or rhythmic pathos? Why should a medial ethics arise in rhythmic, musicalized temporality rather than a literal description or representation of world space?

Echoes, of course, present displacements of space and spatial objects: Think of sonar. Stafford's echoic objects present an ethical hinge between aesthetics and science trading echoes in a shared world or interdisciplinary space. Rhythmic line, though, has to do with continuous, streaming displacement of temporal streams. Indeed, whether in early nonsynchronized or synchronized cinemas, exhibition prompted observations of the cinematic exhibition's unreeling of the serial image in terms of time as musical diagram—as various of Eisenstein's writings attest. I have noted[27] the broader significance of French critic Emile Vuillermoz's comments that the nonsynchronized cinema might "orchestrate our images, *score* our visions and memories according to a strictly musical process."[28] Musicality seemed to *score* the cinematic image and diagram it in time, a more dynamic version of the way that Sobchack describes computer graphics as diagramming their own photorealistic image. Thinking about cinema as musical scoring of the serial image allowed such critics as Vuillermoz to attribute specific historical capacities to the emergent mass art: what it could do—that is, its ethical capacities.

Musicality, as the term is used in this study, comprises those effects of music as they may be performed or represented in other than auditory media: performances that may only mime or otherwise do not produce audible music, or qualities specific to music presented in visual terms. Musicality may inform visual lyricism in the mediated work even as it invites performative actions by audiences in response: foot tapping, head nodding, hand clapping, or even simply breathing. Musicality is what Eisenstein attempts to exploit in his plans for isomorphic movements between visual and sonic domains. It is what Eisler aims to enrich by means of a film music counterpointing the filmic image. It is this same musicality in which Berkeley immerses the audience of the classical Hollywood musical with kaleidoscopic visual patterns set to music; that music video uses to advertise the body of the pop star; that television jingles implement to enhance the appeal of cars, cigarettes, or hygiene products; and from which film and television narratives draw to clarify for viewers what are often ambiguously sequenced image fragments.

Musicality synchronizes medial or narrative form with audience knowledges and practices to create emergent meaning out of the conflict between what is given to us, what we demand, and how we respond. In this conflict of narrativity and enunciation, music begs the investigation of materials synchronized as instrumental mediation: the ways in which the noise of a representational apparatus is transformed into an instrument. Attending to musicality in these terms requires a radical decoupling of musical meaning so that aesthetic effect is no longer strictly tied to material form, visual or auditory perception, or mode of reception. *Sync* aims to address this need for a transmedia, transcritical, *and* affective description of musicality emergent within synchronized streams of time-based media. At the same time, *Sync* responds to the historiographical concerns raised by new media claims of digital transcodability of all prior forms.[29] As the following chapters show, musical meaning in time-based media today extends explicitly to the indexical gesturality of interactive digital media, so it should not be surprising that, historically speaking, musicality and gesturality provided key registers for prototyping the heterogeneous futures of media out of which digital cultural forms have arisen.

Transposing Diagrams for Affective Labor

During the 1940s, preparations for the industrial deployment of television also prompted musical proposals for television broadcast. Much early U.S. commercial television, indeed, was first programmed by such industrial behemoths as CBS, according to models informed by studies of programmed radio listening, such as those Paul Lazarsfeld carried out at Princeton and Columbia. But more speculative proposals suggested that the television image might be broadcast most effectively as a musical synchronization of studio production ensemble with domestic viewing audience—whether the televisual broadcast communicated news or music and whether it featured live action drama, more abstract imagery, or musical performance.

In a 1946 *Hollywood Quarterly* essay, Carl Beier[30] brainstorms television broadcast as something like a streaming version of Stafford's echoic object, a musical synchronization of the gamut of film-studio techniques—including mise-en-scène, *mise-en-cadre,* visual montage, sound performance, mixing and dubbing—and even suggests hypothetical, live electronic compositing. The references in Beier's article are so lively as to make television an unintentional musical pastiche of the "seven arts":[31] cinema; the framed sprawl of action in a Breughel painting; the Living Newspaper theater experiments (where Joseph Losey gained initial fame); Orson Welles's production of *Julius Caesar*; sound cartoons; techniques proper to the vast archive of cultural expression, properly prepared, may be presented unrehearsed along the lines of improvised jazz, "less of an orchestral performance than of a jam session" (5). This mélange of studio production, broadcast network, and domestic reception might become an ensemble of dynamic, musical process:

> Since this televisual "orchestra" is not sufficient unto itself, the director's position during a performance is comparable to that of the conductor in the pit at a musical play. . . . The pace and flow laboriously achieved in the shooting of a motion picture, and in the cutting rooms and special-effects laboratories, must be given to a television production *as it goes.* The texture and tempo of the sound that is achieved in recording, cutting, scoring, and dubbing must all be "played" in television, instead of being finally assembled as in films. All the processing of film (both sound-track and picture)—exposure, development, cutting, the addition of special photographic effects, dubbing, and projection—is compressed, in television, into the instant of electronic pickup and transmission. . . . It is not enough for the director to conceive and rehearse the actions of his performers: he must "conduct" them in performance as well.[32]

Beier's interest in what Eisenstein described as ideological-intellectual and professional-technical matters,[33] however extravagantly presented, is still crucial to the historical experience of diagramming contemporary time and historical time in terms of material, technical, and affective labor. Conceiving the TV director as an improvisational, multimedia conductor invokes jazz epistemologies while associating quality television with contemporary musical art rather than with the production of information: "Spontaneity is no substitute for skill, but art need not always be deliberate" (5). For the young Eisenstein working in theater, jazz rhythms were coordinated with other modernist influences to enliven a theatrical montage of attractions in which a "potentate-automaton" is overthrown.[34] Here, jazz epistemologies, transposed from a minor jazz cinema, allowed a speculative temporal diagramming of live television broadcast in a streaming ratio of revered historical aesthetic expressions to contemporary networked mass culture on the cusp of another industrial transition.[35]

Perhaps Beier was aware of Oskar Fischinger's visual music animation in *Allegretto* (1936), which floats the receiver through a closely synchronized but expressive creative visualization of Hollywood jazz as illuminated radio broadcast. The work of the John and James Whitney in synchronized synthetic sound and image, like the work of Fischinger, was also discussed in *Hollywood Quarterly* during this period, along with proposals of "audivisual music" and "cineplastics" in numerous articles proposing speculative research or technical procedures for more expressive or more efficient synchronization of sound and image.[36] In any case, for his part, Beier imagines the new television studio as an improvisational, industrial combine of cinema production, radio networking, and jazz performance. Beier overestimates the technical capabilities he thought would afford synchronizing the studio ensemble with broadcast networking and with domestic reception in his vision of musical televisual conducting of improvisational performance. But, in doing so, he also raises estimations of the skills this live musical television would require of the director-conductor: the aesthetic and technical expertise of the film director, the conducting skills of an orchestra leader, and the turn-on-a-dime facility of the jam-session improviser—with access to an internal technical network worthy of *Metropolis*'s Freder. The television director would be the lead player shaping all elements of the orchestration of a massive, musically synchronized social and technical apparatus. As for program material for this apparatus, an "*Information Please* movie short is no trick to shoot, but Gjon Mili's *Jammin' the Blues* [1944] should, I think, be ranked as superior because it is brilliantly produced" (9). Beier is thinking, then, of the range from information to contemporary musical cinema. But aiming for a live conducting of television as networked cinematic improvisation allows him to sketch a speculative medial ethics: what television should be made capable of doing. This proposal invests a premium on the new director's labor. As a speculative temporal diagram, Beier outlines an ethics of material, technical, and affective labor worthy of television as history-making new medium.

Beier's reference model for the content of televisual expression as improvisational multimedia conducting is Mili's critically acclaimed jazz "soundie" (1944). The *Life* magazine photographer, known for his work with jazz musicians and time-lapse photography using electronic flash, shot the short for Warner Brothers; it features Lester Young in a synthetic cinematic jam session. Marie Bryant scats to "Sunny Side of the Street" between the slow blues that kicks off the short and the jitterbug choreographed to the ensemble jam of the title track that concludes the film. *Jammin' the Blues* dramatizes apparently spontaneous and continuous musical temporality using carefully choreographed camera work, editing, and sound mixing. It also uses optical printing to reproduce multiple exposures, duplicating saxophonist Young in a cascade of echoing repetitions across the breadth of the frame. Further, it carefully combines special-effects superimposition with precision editing so that singer Bryant first appears as a reflection in the surface of the piano, following a series in which the pianist is reflected above its keyboard and on its lid. Then, Bryant materializes out of the rippling mesh of her own reflection.[37]

Jammin' the Blues is a complex temporal diagram in its own right. Its careful compositing of jazz sound and image as personified gesture reflecting, rippling, disjoining, or even bouncing off one another in dance stresses synchronization as musical continuity rather than as Eisenstein's "devastating rhythm." Although we routinely refer to the expert synchronization of sound and image in such a composition as this as "montage," it is important to differentiate the emphasis on improvisational continuity that *Jammin'* creates synthetically. Jazz instrumental, vocal, dance, and cinematic composition are all made to flow rhythmically together, whether as a cascade of serial disruptions within the frame as Young's image doubles and quadruples across it or as the rippling mesh from which Bryant's image emerges across the cut.

Differently from Eisenstein's early use of jazz in the theater, here, jazz stages the improvisational continuity of Young's saxophone breaking the coherent spatial geometry of the framed image or, alternatively, Bryant's song staged as emerging across the breaks of serial composition. Jitterbugging, along with the camera choreographed to follow dance movements or to contrast dance against instrumental gestures, then intrudes on the space of musical performance, redefining its framed, geometric coherence so that musical swing tests and expands the camera's perspectival foci and its energetic limits. Disjuncture and conjuncture are synchronized within the sound mix to project the effect, then, of improvisation continuing in the audiovisual stream even as musical performance or visual emphasis passes between performers. *Jammin' the Blues* indicates the important role that musical innovation played in expressing and recasting historical and emergent stresses in the temporal fabric of midcentury modern life in Los Angeles. It diagrams the "meshes of the evening," relieving the "meshes of the afternoon" that Maya Deren notably diagrams as oceanic wave energies crashing on the psychic littoral of a subject whose selfhood refracted, attenuated, and tracked to the point of self-obliteration in the harsh everyday sunlight of the studio capital.

As Arthur Knight[38] points out regarding Warner's cinematic capitalization of midcentury bebop's creative innovations, "The setting never intrudes because there is none—only apparently limitless blackness or whiteness surrounding the players" (33). In fact, an *audio* setting exists, and although it frames the entire piece along with the title credits it follows, it withdraws its authority early on: An announcer's voice frames the film by explaining that it demonstrates the stylistics of a jam session often taking place "at midnight." Otherwise, the customary framing of cinematic orchestras often balanced against and anchoring song-and-dance fantasies in period musicals, such as Busby Berkeley's *The Gang's All Here* (1943), is adjusted to better characterize the musical personalities, the creative productivity and expressive power of their performances, and the similarly virtuoso dancing they excite. The spectacular staging and editing of production numbers in such film-musical fantasies as Berkeley's *Gang* are also deferred here in favor of shifts between shots of varying range that call, carry, shift, elaborate, and punctuate the receiver's improvisation of memory, attention, and anticipation, as audiovisual stream moves from soloist to ensemble or between instrumentalists and dancers. *Jammin'* conducts audience reception as "hot," improvisational performance.

Jammin's temporalized forms and rhetorics emphasize synchronization not simply in terms of auditory or visual continuity, then, but in terms of jazz epistemologies; indeed, as Knight observes, they emphasize the distinct performers' musical mastery and the currency of their recognizable personas, also identifiable in their title credits (30). Knight concludes that although the film attempts to present a filmic jam session as a fusion of the jazz players' productivity with a fraught, less-expressive national, racial, and ethnic imaginary, "the categories that *Jammin' the Blues* partakes of and tries to fuse mark the complexity of the film's project, the complexity of music as a social-cultural, visual, and aural representation, and the contradictions of the United States as a 'community' in the mid-1940s" (47). The film "simultaneously" emphasizes the creativity and humanity of black musicians, desiring to achieve "colorblindness" but also to be racially mixed, all at a moment "when the impulse behind such simultaneity was not yet widely acceptable" (47).

However, the synthesis of hot performance distinguishing this film from that of the film musical, and the aspect that Beier seems to have in mind, is less that of a national communitarian simultaneity and more a through-composed audiovisual continuity inflecting a distributed, networked musical temporality fusing innovative, local media production with circulating musical knowledges. This complex continuity *is* achieved in the choreography of sound and image streams in the cinematic rendering of musical performance, not as failing national imaginary but of radio broadcasts and local dance spots. *Jammin'* does not, in fact, attempt to present a jam session as if it were a live session. For example, we never see any technical equipment, such as that typically apparent in live performance, and the sound mix is typical of 1940s radio: Even when Bryant sings from the background, we neither see a microphone nor hear a shift in volume. As the announcer's voice-over makes clear, the film presents a jam session that usually would take place at midnight—a cinematic *demonstration* of the affective labor associated with radio broadcast or with jazz dance spots, not simply an imaginary presentation of a live jam session.[39]

As the camera tracks dancers whose movements nudge the frame along to make room for their movements, the image emphasizes cinema's accommodation of radio broadcasting while making adjustments for localized performance and production. Audiovisual synchronization as "jammin'" musical continuity animates jazz photography to visualize music heard somewhere between radio-network sound and such jazz spots as those of south Los Angeles on Central Avenue. Bryant appears as a credited singer in *Jammin'*, but Central Avenue musicians such as Clora Bryant (no relation) remember Bryant from the Central Avenue scene as a talented choreographer who produced routines for Betty Grable and Marilyn Monroe.[40]

Knight's conclusion that the film presents a model for a U.S. jazz cinema that would go unfulfilled during its own period indicates that *Jammin' the Blues* could hardly model the audiovisual representation of race, race mixing, and colorblindness as a mediation of a sovereign national imaginary. Viewing the film as a complex series whose parts incorporate musicalized disjuncture and conjuncture to communicate improvisation as continuity distinct from other modes of cinematic continuity, we can see that it synchronizes sound and image in a meshing of affective knowledges associated with radio broadcast and contemporary popular dance. The Central Avenue music and dance scene supported undervalued, behind-the-scenes studio contractors, such as singer-dancer Bryant, and prompted Hollywood residents to travel south of Pico Boulevard to segregated South Central, contributing to official concern about race mixing that was expressed through increased policing of Central Avenue's "sidewalk university." That increased policing helped cement Central Avenue jazz's demise in the 1950s, as musicians' unions integrated and segregationist housing policies were struck down.[41] In this context, *Jammin'* attempts less to imagine a national imaginary than to animate cinema as a "radiophonic" locale where national jazz stars play with local stars to demonstrate a jam session as if in a Hollywood studio appearance. It dramatizes, in other words, a boundary breaking *localization* of network dissemination. This network dissemination of musical meaning in the continuous productivity of *Jammin*'s gestural scenics, then, is transposed in Beier's proposal for conducting improvisational television.

The stylization of a cinematic jam session in *Jammin'* derives from its entangling of two historical sources. First, as Paul Gilroy[42] observes, "Dislocated from their original conditions of existence, the sound tracks of the African American cultural broadcast fed a new metaphysics of blackness elaborated and enacted in Europe and elsewhere within the underground, alternative, public spaces constituted around an expressive culture that was dominated by music" (83). Twentieth-century black music distributed in rhizomic form (including tours, local musical productions, print, and media recordings) cultivated four antifoundational antiessentializing epistemologies communicated in musical kinesics: the political language of citizenship, justice, and equality; commentary on work's relation to leisure and the respective freedoms associated with these opposing worlds; a folk historicism reclaiming historical experience through music; and the representation of sexuality and gender identity, particularly in antagonistic relationships between black women and men, inviting identification across color lines. The tensions between instrumental performance and dance movements in the film amply translate tensions between working and leisure freedoms; between the management of race mixing in the film and the political languages of citizenship; between masculine instrumental mastery and Bryant's vocal mastery as gendered antagonisms; and between the construction of the film itself as a historic surfacing of talent, innovation, technical mastery, and contemporaneity modeled on jazz itself as a changing folk historiality.

The second historical resource I have already mentioned: that of the visual-music cinema, which, in contrast to montage cutting, emphasized the through continuity of the audiovisual work, whether consisting of profilmic materials or graphical materials. Just as Fischinger's *Allegretto* illuminates network radio in closely synchronized musical visualization, *Jammin'* presents the abbreviated radiophonic version of a midnight jam session whose broadcast is localized as dance. Beier's proposal, then, reverses this localization.

The year his *Hollywood Quarterly* article appeared, Beier, a New Yorker who had made training films for U.S. Air Force pilots during World War II, directed a CBS radio documentary on the positive uses of radioactivity in cancer treatments called *The Sunny Side of the Atom*; the next year, he directed the late-November broadcast of *Joy to the World* for the Ford Theater series for CBS television. The Princeton alumni Web site indicates the pride Beier took in having assisting blacklisted artists—the blacklisting of artists began in 1947, the year after Beier prioritized the jazz soundie *Jammin'* over the radio quiz show *Information Please* as a model for TV production in his *Hollywood Quarterly* essay.

In the transition from the war economy to the peacetime economy, amid the rising tension of what would soon become the Cold War and the revival of commercial television's long-delayed deployment, the pedagogical effects of national media production became complicit with sovereign disinformation produced to exclude skilled creative laborers whose output was considered dangerously and spontaneously expressive.[43] At this complex juncture, black affective labor modeled creative labor for a new media director who proposed conducting the televisual broadcast as quality, improvisational music: spontaneous art that does not always need to be deliberate, controlled as information. The continuity conducted in audiovisual synchronization as a skilled modulation of ecstatic form bounding beyond but then returning within energetic limits is irreducible either to the conceptual or logical information producing it. The ecstatic, skilled indeliberation of *Jammin'* also typifies the synchronized continuity of that form commonly known as visual music. As Fischinger once said of his *Motion Painting No. 1* (1947), which I discuss in more detail in Chapter 3, "The film isn't 'cut,' it is a continuity, the absolute truth, the creative truth. Any observer can verify that, and I consider myself an observer."[44]

Visual music continuity is the classical antinomy of montage cutting. Fischinger inscribed an even-tempered, affective labor of self-observation into *Motion Painting*'s spiraling textured displacements. Meanwhile, Deren and Alexander Hammid's *Meshes of the Afternoon* (1943) cuts and structures durations of sound and image patterns to capture the creative and destructive waves of psychic energy from everyday light and shadow and to render cinematic reception as the subjective refraction of more distant waves of oceanic, quantum energies. *Meshes* appears something like an intimate optical telegraph, tipping askew the cinema's meshing of thermodynamic power and informatic inscription for its audience, casting the cinematic image as a shadow projected by the vital energies of space-time. For its part, *Jammin'* demonstrates historical black epistemologies animated by an ensemble of skilled jazz masters whose energies bound through and across or push aside the frame.

Each of these strategies pursues continuity between the site of reception and some larger temporality in an ecstatic disciplining of the doubled entangled potentialities of the technicized media stream exhibits as materialized time: immanence and information. Whether mythifying jazz performance, reusing Bach, or introducing drastic disruptions into cinematic subjectivity, these strategies deciphered the hieroglyphic of midcentury modern time to exhibit an ecstatic continuity rather than the historical pathos animated in Eisenstein's montage. Taken together, Fischinger's *Motion Painting,* Mili's *Jammin',* and Deren and Hammid's *Meshes* serve to expand the notion of visual music from a cinematic genre dedicated to illustrating musical sound toward a particular ethics of affective labor. Chapter 2 presents Fischinger's visual music animation as ecstatic stylization of cinematic temporalities and posits a historical reading of cinema and painting within Fischinger's work of this period.

Diagramming Critical Distance

Cinematic continuity is never airtight in any of these ecstatic cinematic diagrams of modern, hieroglyphic time—it is, rather, the opposite: necessitated in historical contingency. Each of these works constitutes a locally situated but widely resounding exemplar produced in 1940s Los Angeles, understood as a media capital through which a range of epistemologies circulated, especially in relationship to New York and San Francisco, as David James[45] has extensively documented. Each of these cinematic diagrams provides a distinct expressive and technical resolution to the problem Hanns Eisler and Theodor Adorno diagnose in their critique of Hollywood and Soviet cinemas: the hopeless mythification of cinematic time *as* representation of historical reality with the use of advancing technologies of synchronization whose unconsidered power of amalgamation worked to the detriment of cinematic art, musical art, and creative labor. Fischinger's, Mili's, or Deren and Hammid's films are temporal diagrams of affective labor and of ethical media composition and reception.

But Eisler develops a more specifically dialectical expression in response to concerns about the increasingly automated means of synchronization used in commercial and noncommercial cinemas (see my discussions of Eisler and Adorno's critique in *Composing for the Films* [1947] in Chapters 2 and 4).

A two-year grant from the Rockefeller Foundation running from 1940 to 1942 allowed Eisler to investigate the uses of serialist music composition in cinema's serial production processes and imagery; this funding gave Eisler *his* chance in the role of director-conductor.[46] Having worked in cinema composing from the nonsynchronized cinema of the late 1920s and through the maturing sound era of the early and mid-1930s, Eisler nonetheless had never produced a thorough conception and execution of cinema music as the final determinant of meaning in the site of reception. Instead, he had reused musical material composed for different films, illustrating a dialectical conflict, progression, and synthesis recoverable across different films.

For example, musical material Eisler composed for Joris Ivens's *New Earth* (1933) leads to the film's concluding sequence, in which its quasi-triumphal images of ocean reclamation in the Netherlands are punctuated with musical commentary—and hesitation. We hear Eisler's "Ballad of the Sackslingers," a sarcastic ode whose caustic lyrics, sung by Ernst Busch, note the glut of worldwide production being thrown away to shore up consumer prices; the song closes with a rousing demand to throw the capitalists into the sea, instead. The jaunty march tempo of "Sackslingers" is inflected throughout with slight jazz syncopation that develops into the more resounding musical agitprop lyrics of its conclusion. The song's aural and textual materials first parody economic doublespeak and then counter it with the defiant finale.

However, the same harmonic and developmental materials of the musical cues anticipating "Ballad of the Sackslingers" in *New Earth* also appear in Eisler's score for Ivens's *Komsomolsk* (*Song of Heroes*; 1932). Here, underscoring the Magnitostroy Workers Recruitment sequence, where jobless laborers are interviewed and given positions building the giant Magnitostroy plant, Eisler's cue segues into a workers' chorus incorporating folk music and then factory sirens. Musical material Eisler scored for *Komsomolsk* as the synthesis of dialectical conflict appears as prefatory to a coming conflict in *New Earth.* Musical synchronization performed distinct stages of a dialectical progression. Still, by the time of his residence in the United States, Eisler had little faith left in any further potential for the Soviet model he had celebrated in *Komsomolsk.*

Eisler's Film Music Project gave him the time, the New School for Social Research's institutional support, and the financial and technical assistance to reconsider cinema production from the point of view where musical production would determine final production stages and exhibition. He and Adorno wrote in *Composing for the Films* that film music, deploying advanced techniques of musical composition *and* advanced technical means of production and synchronization, must become visible in its own right in the site of cinema reception: It must "sparkle and glisten" apart from the streaming image. It may join with but develops essentially apart from the contents of the image. Here, the dialectical conflict, opposition, and synthesis are prompted by sound and image streams, but while reflecting the film composer's touch, they are resolved by the cognition and feeling on the part of the audience. In Eisler's dialectical stream of sound and image, the audience maintains, or perhaps gains, critical distance from the cinematic exhibition by virtue of music's autonomous development sharing in the autonomous development of the serial image.

Rather than organic unity and historical pathos, or continuous ecstatic musicality in reception, in Eisler, musical exposition splits the totalized social and technical architecture of cinematic reception into two parts by virtue of active musical listening. Eisler and Adorno's description of this process encompasses the technical-professional and the ideological-intellectual positions, of which Eisenstein claimed the latter. For Eisenstein, the technical-professional axis was less important because of the character of Soviet labor, which tended to deploy professional specialization in relation to ideological and structural needs. But for Eisler and Adorno, both of whom were cultural workers in the United States when they wrote *Composing for the Films,* a critique encompassing both these axes worked toward emancipating film music composition not, say, *for* California farm workers, but *from* prejudices and bad habits. The often-observed counterpoint of sound and image for which Eisler is known does not specify a total formal separation or immediately political contestation of sound against image. Rather, it proposes that the cinema audience ultimately resolves any dialectical synthesis of art and labor beyond the site of exhibition. This reorganization of dialectical aesthetics aims at deflating, even musically diagnosing, the hysteria that Eisler and Adorno associate with the subjection of human feeling to mass-produced, standardized cultural-industrial prescriptions. It also insists on access to greater technical advances: adapting post-Schoenberg techniques for music on the one hand, but also the further automation of sound-image sync on the other.

So far, we have observed a central problem, that of the production of modern temporality as hieroglyphic: cut off from historical time or the sensible tip of radically expanded, relativistic space-time; and time contested in terms of labor and in terms of advancing technologies. And we have seen the ways in which a wide range of cinema diagrams this hieroglyph by mobilizing sound-image synchronization. Exhausting individual workers in the massive instrumentalities of networked technical systems seemed to produce not simply exhaustion or apathy but also hysteria. The films and the creative processes that produced them or that they inspired that I have introduced here thus aim at synchronizing the newly observed materiality of the streaming temporalized image *as* musical affect: the pathos of Eisenstein's devastating rhythm, the ecstatic continuity of Fischinger's visual music or *Jammin*'s cinematic jazz ensemble, Eisler's dialectical stream as diagnostics of hysteria. These musical diagrams stylize the hieroglyphic of a contemporaneity entangled in, but also separated from, the understandings of historical change their creators held. Too, all these projects anticipated further mediations of time in terms of production labor, technology, and critical interpretation. In diagramming audiovisual synchronization as musical rhythm, each project diagrammed affective labor on the part of the audience in terms of musical gesture. The "synchronization of sense" in Eisenstein allows the contemporary audience to "link" to remote historical times, to receive their immanent historical meanings, and to reframe the contemporary contradictions that they lived in everyday life. The choreography of cinema as a musical apparatus in Fischinger allows observation of an otherwise invisible but creative energetic temporal continuity. Eisler's musical essayism prompts critical apperception of the exhibition itself as a site of streaming but conflicted material temporality. In each case, the site of exhibition is not so much a historical repetition of a Platonic cave of flickering images as that of a Pythagorean cavern.

For Alfred North Whitehead, writing in 1925, the Pythagorean roots of "logical harmony" had served to renew and to redeem an exhausted "scientific materialism"; music rivaled philosophy as a way of thinking the limits of modern techno-science, although Whitehead himself carefully keeps to philosophy.[47] Eisenstein, Fischinger, and Eisler, whose work I explore in more detail in Chapters 2 to 4, are less reticent. After nineteenth-century thermodynamic physics had produced the technical epistemologies necessary for automating the calculation of harmonic series whose technics and expressive power had once belonged primarily to music, animating the technological ensembles of streaming media as musical cavern allowed the measure of contemporaneity to be taken in relation to the history from which it seemed split. The measure taken in streaming media, then, is not that of form to appearance but of a relation of contemporary time to historical time.

In each of the cases I have introduced here, the musical animation of an unstable ratio of historical stream and materialized temporality prioritizes energetic temporality over informatic inscription. In each case, musical reception is understood in one or another sense as active mobilization calling, carrying, shifting, and elaborating audience gesture or kinesics beyond any specific informatic inscription of sound or image. Yet, in each case, historical time takes over. A final example from the history of cinema helps illustrate how. In Ib Melchior's minor science-fiction film *The Time Travelers* (1964), a small group of men and one woman working in a science lab rush to finish a project to open a cybernetic, televisual window to the future before they lose institutional support. As they make final adjustments, technician Carol White (Merry Anders) notices a shadow flitting across the lab; shortly afterward, in a fluke of technical function, time pressure, and group effort, they notice that the window to the future has opened—and that it is a door, not a window.

One after another, the scientists walk through the door, first to explore the future's desert landscape, then to run after colleagues fleeing the future's hostile denizens. The door closes behind them, but they are rescued from aggressive mutants by the beautiful if severe Gadra (Joan Woodbury), who leads them to a secret laboratory where a small band of humans unaffected by the radiation of a nuclear holocaust make plans to leave Earth for good. Earth after nuclear holocaust is depicted at its most advanced in a sequence in which electrician Danny McKee (Steve Franken) is seduced by Reena (Delores Wells), who plays a futuristic color organ for him. As she moves her hands lightly over an organ keyboard, the display reacts: A series of multicolored waves ripple over its surface. The futuristic color organ's sensual special effects, in fact, were those of an actual instrument: Fischinger's Lumigraph, the gestural color instrument he patented in 1950 and presented in performance at the Coronet Theater and the Frank Perls Gallery in Los Angeles in 1951 and again at an Art in Cinema screening in San Francisco in 1953. The version seen in *The Time Travelers,* like the later brighter one seen on *The Andy Williams Show,* had been rebuilt for bright studio lighting by Fischinger's son Conrad.[48]

The narrative of *The Time Travelers,* however, does not present color-music seduction as a replacement for sex in the way William Moritz argues: In fact, one reclining couple listening to Reena's performance leaves to consummate sensuous musical pleasures in private. Rather, Reena's sensuous musical cavern counterpoints the final denouement of the film. After mutants wreck the rocket built to escape Earth, scientists and future humans must reopen the door of time and step back into the past. But when they do, they find *themselves* in a mutation of time: They learn that they were the shadows that had flickered momentarily through the lab as they tested their equipment. Now, they have closed a temporal circuit: from the branching of time diagramming actual technical development, to the future attempt to displace Earth once and for all, and back to the retrospective voyaging into a technical, instrumental time they can no longer embody.

If caring Maria could not coexist with lascivious robotic Maria, Reena's futuristic color organ alternates with but is finally dominated by Carol's computer window (Figure 1.2). Carol and her colleagues observe their own bodies as if they are a wax museum exhibit and then step through the door of time again. From this point, they unleash an algorithmically escalating loop that accelerates to the point of absolute temporal incoherence. This loop is presented as an ever-faster montage sequence, with ever-greater portions of duration deleted from it and proceeding in ever-shorter durations. At first, then, the voyagers find a musical cavern of sensuous, continuous pleasures; then, they grasp the pathos of their situation by virtue of repiecing it together; finally, they are frozen in a technical overview that obliterates any critical, situated relation to self-imaging, world imaging, or time imaging.

Their displacement in time cannot itself be displaced and so annulled, but only further compounded. Finally, then, montage cutting and visual music continuity are eclipsed in a computational feedback loop whose violent acceleration results in extreme hermeneutic violence: historical pathos, instrumental ecstatic

FIGURE 1.2 *The Time Travelers* (1964): Carole's "time window" and Reena's "musical cavern" (frame captures). (*The Time Travelers,* dir. Ib Melchior [American International Pictures, 1964].)

play, critical distance—all become illegible. In its informatic version, cinematic audiovisuality is at once frozen and exploded. The new instrument folds into its power the pathos of montage, the ecstasy of visual music, and the critical distance provided in a dialectical streaming of cinematic time. The scientists meet a fate that is opposite that of the dodo: They go extinct precisely by flying through time. The audience gains no critical grasp of a historical transformation from which it might critically extricate itself; rather, caught in the escalating loop, the audience is confused, unable to process either the media stream or its historical relations.

Of course, the film's play of, as Mary Anne Doane puts it, narrative and probabilistic tendencies was and remains legible. *The Time Travelers* diagrams the emergence of a new configuration of *bioinformatic* temporalities that disturb the old, *bioenergetic* ones, even as they incorporate them. The long metamorphosis of hieroglyphic time, whose tensions had developed in the nineteenth century and reached a peak in the mid-twentieth century, appears in its new aspect. Hieroglyphic time is doubled, its energetic aspect now subsumed to the informatic.

Moritz notes that Fischinger's influence would continue in traditional hand-drawn, computer-generated, and videographic forms. Yet Fischinger's work would also be studied as a model for expressive computer-interaction design at think tanks, such as Silicon Valley's Interval Research Corporation, along with a wide range of visual-music animation, by the effort called "Expressions" led by Joy Mountford—who supported my own research into the historical and contemporary values of visual music animation for more expressive human-computer interfaces and interaction devices.[49] This was the same context in which Marc Davis's "Media Streams" video remixing project—an important phase of whose justification reconsidered Eisenstein's theory of montage as collision of dynamic ideograms—was developed for possible commercial deployment. Other projects, meanwhile, continued the automation of synchronized media streams that Eisler and Adorno saw would reach new, as yet undetermined forms. For example, Malcolm Slaney's development of "Video Rewrite" automated the laborious processes of synchronizing synthetic lip sync so that it appears natural regardless of whoever originally spoke what is heard.[50] Inspired by such films as Robert Zemeckis's *Forrest Gump* (1994), Video Rewrite prototyped the automation of laborious processes required to produce spectacular synchronization effects, whereby historical figures might speak words they never uttered to fictive characters. Video Rewrite structured video databases for computational access to prerecorded gestures of body and voice actors, whether fictional or historical. The semantic content of the sound did not matter, only sound as recorded vocal gesture. Demonstrations of the prototype used ideal conditions: talking-head shots of staff members presenting in direct address without moving their heads, or three-quarter profile shots of JFK from digitized video.

Such projects, then, made immanent to the new histories they were attempting to create those older inventions, relations of everyday life, or media productions originating in locations as far flung in time and space as Palo Alto, Moscow, Berlin, Los Angeles, or New York in the nineteenth and twentieth centuries. To the extent that informatic epistemologies, ontologies, and ethics were, by the 1990s, considered adequate to describing not only everyday life but also transcoding historical experience, such projects attempted to configure the mediation of experience in informatic terms, displacing the very energetic formats and methods upon which they drew. Their efforts, nonetheless, require the reconfiguration of experience and expression in terms of affective labor: the creative and interpretive task of reshaping historical time, as in user-generated content. Neither a Marxian analysis of labor value fetishized as money[51] nor Michel Foucault's discursive analysis of the statement *(enoncé)*[52] can sufficiently describe the transpositions of affective labor differentiated over time in streaming media.

Sync begins with the observation that streaming media devices are timepieces that don't tell time, then, but diagram it in affective labor. Chapters 2 to 4 explore in more detail the ways that Eisenstein, Fischinger, or Eisler *stylized* the hieroglyphic time of streaming media reception in and as temporal diagrams. In Chapters 5 to 7, *Sync* explores streaming media as complex temporal diagrams revising the classical stylistics of synchronization seen in Eisenstein, Fischinger, and Eisler after the rise of what Langston Hughes calls "an IBM land." In the final case study, I extend the implications of stylizing cinema or the digital interface as temporal diagrams of historical affective labor. We see again a familiar patterning: Where contemporaneity seems exhausted, dying out, or dangerously complex, temporal diagramming turns to music and gesture to stylize time become hieroglyphic. In every case, as temporal diagramming attempts to resolve the entanglement of material, technical, and affective labor, not only do the capacities or "medial ethics" of streaming media become clear but we also begin to discern the ways that displacements of material labor and the affects of creative labor determine publicity and personhood in relation to changing historical relations. This changing relation is not simply determined by new technologies, by new media industries, or by new formations of capital. Personhood or publicity, autonomy or governmentality, diagrammed in affective labor suggests that affective labor is biopolitical: *Biolabor* is the resource via which one historical apparatus transposes its concerns to another.

The goals of this study, then, are to explore the ways in which temporal diagrams relate determinations, displacements, and differentiations of material, technical, and affective labor according to five distinct capabilities. First, temporal diagrams presume, whether they depict them or not, the initial material, developmental conditions in which they arise. Second, they specify relations with prior work or treatments in or of the varying ontological, epistemological, and ethical aspects of those material conditions. Third, temporal diagrams propose some disjuncture and conjuncture with those conditions and the materialities, epistemologies, and pragmatics according to which conditions become actionable. Fourth, they propose, rightly or wrongly, some measure of the relations they propose and the conditions and treatments to which they relate. Fifth, temporal diagrams propose further, not yet undertaken elaboration in other conditions and according to other treatments for other problems and resolutions.

As a result, the historical, exhibitionary, and ongoing and incomplete aspects of those situations in which temporal diagrams arise and are received may be deeply entangled in the diagrams themselves—like Chaplin's resorting to early-cinema sound conventions while using synchronized cinema sound technologies. More demonstrative or pedagogical temporal diagrams, like those of the conventional scholarly abstract of an essay or talk, may proceed with these five capabilities in sequence and as statements. But the most interesting temporal diagrams rarely do, and these are the most interesting, informing the choice of works presented here. Further, while any of these five conditions, treatments, problems, resolutions, or incomplete elaborations may be representational or propositional, they can never be exclusively so; temporal diagrams, then, may be, alternately, techno-scientific, aesthetic or expressive, or critical and reductive. Unlike James Elkins's's[53] recent work on diagrammatic images from art to quantum mechanics, and unlike Stafford's echoic objects resounding between their uses in the arts and the cognitive neurosciences, *Sync* concentrates only on diagrams of affect whose presentation is primarily aesthetic and critical: those elaborated in streaming media ensembles and works.

But this focus also allows us to propose a nonteleological determination of the ways in which technology and media are deployed where personhood and publicity are related to each other in complex ensembles also relating contemporaneity and historicity. In other words, we are able to see the ethical capacities of technology and media respectively and differently. As biopolitical deployments, technology builds capacities for temporal diagramming of material, technical, and affective labor outward, through bodies, built modernity, geopolitical world space, and historical time in biopolitical tensions between sovereignty and autonomy. Conversely, media relay capacities for temporal diagramming inward through historical time, geopolitical world space, built modernities, and bodies, expressing the biopolitical tensions between personhood and publicity. Thus, more than the material labor displaced in technical operations or media exhibition, temporal diagrams exhibit affective labor. To clarify affective labor as the exhibition and reception of pathos, I turn to the first of three canonical stylistics of streaming media synchronization: Eisenstein's montage cinema. I begin with a review of the ways in which Eisenstein has functioned as an avatar of new media since Benjamin's embrace of *Potemkin* in 1927.

2

Eisenstein's Gesture

Breaking Down Alexander Nevsky

Aren't the eyes capable of seeing in the dark with the aid of infra-red glasses; aren't the hands capable of guiding missiles and aircraft from a very great distance by means of radio; isn't the brain capable, with the help of electronic computers, of calculating within a few seconds something that used to require months of work on the part of a whole army of accountants; isn't the consciousness, waging an incessant struggle since the end of the war, shaping a concrete image of a truly democratic International ideal; doesn't all this demand absolutely new arts of unheard-of forms and dimensions, arts that should leave far behind all such palliatives as the traditional theatre, traditional sculpture and traditional . . . cinema?

—Sergei M. Eisenstein, "Stereoscopic Films"

My observations lead me to the conclusion that homosexuality is in all ways a retrogression—a going back to the state where procreation came with the dividing of the cells. It's a dead-end. A lot of people say I'm a homosexual.

—Sergei M. Eisenstein, quoted in Marie Seaton, *Sergei Eisenstein*

"Eisenstein and Dziga Vertov were both liars. . . . Their films can be regarded as fantasies completely divorced from historical reality. These directors had great technical skill, but their work can only be taken seriously as formal exercises in editing and cinematography. . . . Man is always free to go to prison. . . . Eisenstein simply should not have made the films he did, or at least"—and here I thought I detected some Slavic humor—"he should not have made them so well."

—Néstor Almendros (reporting the response of a member of the delegation of new Soviet filmmakers at the Los Angeles Academy of Motion Picture Arts and Sciences, 1989), quoted in Annette Michelson, "Eisenstein at 100"

Sergei M. Eisenstein: Avatar of New Media . . . or Director of History Films?

For Soviet director Sergei M. Eisenstein, changing technologies were secondary to the social meanings of a historical totality that had been politically transformed by war. That Eisenstein's cinema became, even in his own time, an emblem of transformed technological media standing in for historical transformations occurring in political terms is surprising in many ways.

From Walter Benjamin's 1927 defense of *Battleship Potemkin* (1925) to designers of novel interfaces for streaming media in our own time, Eisenstein's montage cinema has been repeatedly configured as a signal instance of art-technological innovation representing historical continuity in terms of technological change instead of political conflict or historical rupture—emphasizing technical innovations in combinatorial media *in spite of* the director's oft-stated interests in the pathos of historical expression and in aesthetic expression itself as a site of historical rupture. Eisenstein's treatment of pathos, indeed, seems willing to sacrifice the representation of history. As he puts it in *Nonindifferent Nature: Film and the Structure of Things,* the "construction of pathos" requires a "passage of representation into music" (216).[1]

The citations above schematize my concerns in this chapter. Taken in order, they indicate the political fallacy—and ethical failure—we mobilize when we read technologies as media, read media as the affects experienced in reception, and then understand affect in terms of either partial or excessive reception or, as a result of inadequate or misdirected technology, failed political engagement, and so, subjection, passive subservience, or an entropy of affect: the exhaustion of human creativity, finally, "a lie." This chain of proposals almost always terminates in requiring some intensified technologization of media to repair the damage it incurs, so that the history of conditions is canceled out, prompting, conversely, the positive reading of such figures as Eisenstein as technological innovator rather than the negative one as homosexual liar. Either interpretation results in a biographical misreading or a misdirection of historical meaning, however productive.

Of course, Eisenstein himself seemed to commend precisely this logic when he stated his conviction in socialist technology rather than, say, in socialist sexual variegation. But, if his reasoning was that new media would continue to express a concrete image of an expanded, dynamic international socialism—rather than allow new forms of socialization under capital—he also reasoned that self-expression through the montage principle would relieve him of suspicions of the failed corporeal affect, affective death, or entropic degeneration associated with homosexuality. Neither technology nor sexuality, then, is adequate, though both are required, to understand the ways Eisenstein's montage relates temporality and historicity in the cinematic work.

I begin by reviewing the ways Eisenstein's montage has been diagrammed for new media approaches in a politics of technology tending to make affective labor secondary to technological change. Then, conversely, I explore the ways in which Eisenstein's montage diagrammed an affective politics of historical labor by stylizing cinema montage in terms of musicality and gesture. Here, I explicate the problem of affective labor in Eisenstein with reference to what Gilles Deleuze emphasizes as the organic, pathetic, and pragmatic dimensions of Eisenstein's "movement-image" as it strained toward becoming a "time-image."[2] I suggest instead that montage diagrammed synchronization in a doubled ratio—musical, gestural—of aesthetic labor expressing personhood and publicity. In this non-indifferent ratio of music and gesture, pathos as diagrammatic *ratio* expresses the complex historical relation between composer of montage and receiving audience and a historial relation, where montage construction emerges as a modality of cinematic time to impinge upon the larger biopolitical relation of laboring autonomy and state governmentality. Eisenstein's stylization of montage developed over the course of the historical period in which he lived, but while both the technical means available to cinematic expression and the political context in which he worked changed, the expression of the relation between composition and reception as historical and affective—that is, as pathos—did not.[3] Certainly, he modulated his stylization of montage: I argue that Eisenstein's was a *modal cinema* critiquing not only the expressive contradictions of other national cinemas but also the role and function of the party-as-historical-image in postrevolutionary Soviet Russia.

Eisenstein's modal cinema raises the question, then, as to what resource, if not cinema technologies or the Soviet State, provided the creative capacities of Eisenstein's montage. In the fourth section, I clarify the key transmedia negotiation through which Eisenstein derived his early style of montage as rupture and the more plastic theatrical style of his final films: Eisenstein deployed the rhythmic elaboration of streaming, energetic materiality typifying Vsevolod Meyerhold's theatrical workshops in biomechanics, along with Vladimir Mayakovsky's poetry, to express precarious affective labor as pathos—in this instance, creative affective labor rupturing and realigning aesthetico-political experience. The result is that Eisenstein's temporal diagramming of precarious homoaffectivity as pathos made the director's labor inseparable from, rather than a waste product of, a natural and technical history of expression, allowing his audiences to know and to remember the turbulent history they lived.

One lesson in particular to be taken from Eisenstein's modal cinema is that cinema is not simply a medium obsolescing as novel techniques, such as digital computation or network computing, arise. Rather, cinema or the computational interface is an exhibitionary idiom deploying technological means for channelizing compositional sense and receiver sensation in time-based networks. Further, the montage cinema was Eisenstein's *idiom*; and he *styled* montage to express historical transformations—including the exhibitionary capacities of the time-based work itself—as expressions of historical, affective labor: Experience, suffering, and pathos are divisions of precarious affective labor shared between creative producers and creative audiences. Explicating Eisenstein's montage as a modal stylization of the idiom of montage cinema allows me to introduce several concerns important for the chapters on Oskar Fischinger and Hanns Eisler that follow: (1) the temporal and, therefore, historical specificity of informal affective labor in media composition and reception; (2) the primary need to synchronize composition, exhibition, and reception in complex temporal schema for audiovisual media to become expressive; (3) the roles musicality and gesture have played in diagramming expressions of complex, lived, historical time; and (4) the diagrammatic expressivity that cinema or the digital interface attains as each becomes capable of expressing historical relationships between receivers and the complex temporality that we live.

Eisenstein's cinema remains one of the clearest instances of a stylization of complex, conflicted temporality; his work is oriented emphatically toward history. On the surface, of course, all his films, even given the contemporary subject of agricultural collectivization taken up in *Old and New* (also known as *The General Line*; 1929), are always, in the end, history films: Even contemporary subjects are treated as expressing complex historical processes. But more importantly, Eisenstein's historicizing montage exemplifies pathos as pathic act elaborated through the doubled potentiality of the streaming media work; in his case, pathos is the work doubling potentiality, the affective labor making material history palpable. Of the three classical stylistics of synchronizing cinema to express authorial sense and audience sensation, Eisenstein's cinema montage tends to express the historicity of pathos in streaming media.

Immanence and Information

Boris Barnet's *The Girl with the Hatbox* (1927), a feature-length film advertisement for Soviet state lottery tickets, provides a succinct image marking the tensions mediating personhood as a networked mass during the years of the Soviet Union's New Economic Plan (NEP, 1921–1929). In *Girl,* hatmaker Natasha's laboring potential is frustrated by her customers, the dissolute tax-dodging milliner Madame Irène and her husband, a querulous and abusive couple who have secured the large spare room in their apartment for their own use by registering it in Natasha's name. Natasha's hats, too, pile up in excess in the room she is supposed to occupy, where Madame Irène's husband relaxes as if in a private office or hosts lavish dinner parties. Instead of paying Natasha for her output, Madame Irène's husband gives Natasha a lottery ticket he believes worthless. Of course, the slip of paper turns out to hold the winning number, dramatizing the artificiality of currency and wealth. The ensuing madcap pursuit of Natasha and her winning ticket dramatizes inequalities accruing not simply in classed divisions of labor (those who block the girl from her rightful rewards resist any productive activity) but in technological divisions of privilege and privation. Natasha's employers lounge about in house robes, putting on airs while using up resources and money rightfully belonging to workers like Natasha by virtue of her and her grandfather's precarious labor designing, fabricating, and distributing hats. Meanwhile, Natasha goes the extra mile, not only supporting herself and her grandfather but also resettling the hapless, homeless Ilya Snegiryov,

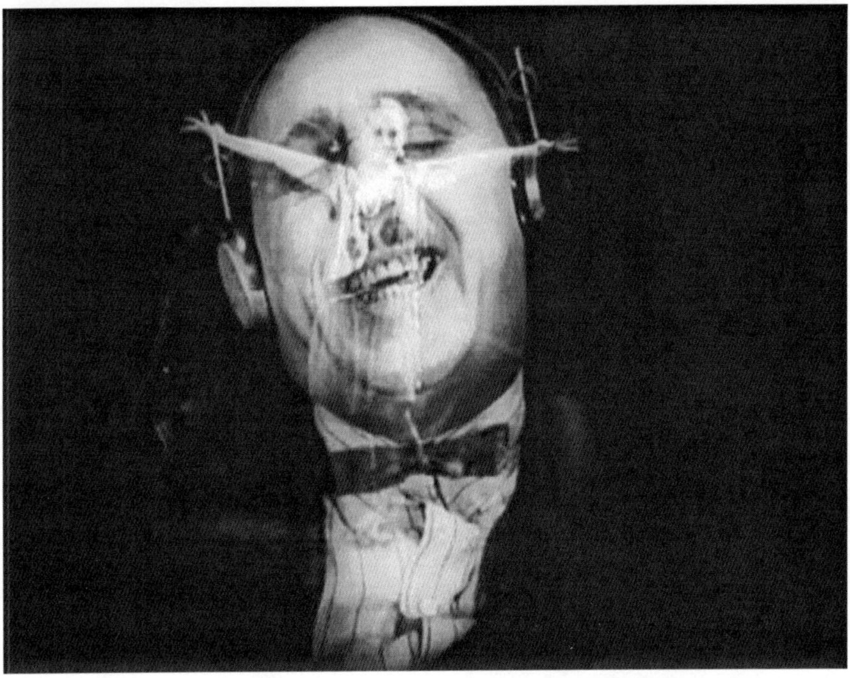

FIGURE 2.1 Barnet's *The Girl with the Hatbox* (1927): Networked listening (frame capture). (*The Girl with the Hatbox,* dir. Boris Barnet [Mezhrabpom-Rus, 1927].)

who, in spite of his initial disorientation in the new society, becomes Natasha's love interest and ultimately helps her claim her prize.

The turning point in Natasha's destiny comes in an image of Madame Irène's husband learning of the wealth he has thoughtlessly gifted to the working girl he intended to exploit. He sits relaxed, listening through a headset to a radio broadcast while a series of superimposed images reveal the content of the radiophonic sound he hears (Figure 2.1). We see a luxuriously dressed female vocalist accompanied by violins superimposed over the reclining radio receiver, suggesting a feminized, unearned leisure in listening. Then, a state official wearing proletarian clothes and cap interrupts his musical reverie with the announcement of the winning ticket, drawn by a similarly roughly dressed boy. The voice of the workers' state replaces the sound of musical leisure. In this nonsynchronized film, sonic and network epistemologies indicating clashing rhythms, habits, and affective positions are amply communicated by the superimposition of the radio singer's image, then that of the worker announcing the lottery winner, and that of the boy drawing the winning ticket, over the image of Natasha's nemesis. First sinking into a state of listening plenitude accompanied by the singing voice, Madame Irène's husband sits up in alarm as he checks a notation of the ticket he has given to Natasha.

Labor's power to create and to distribute wealth in the production of the networked mass is visualized here as an unerring wheel of Soviet fortune interrupting unearned leisure with a rude awakening to the new reality. The sequence of superimpositions shows the voice of the state directing the workers' collective fortune away from the radio listener hoarding goods, living space, access to communication technologies, and leisure time, while directing it toward the working girl whose place as rightful receiver of state benefits has been usurped. The rest of the film's plot disentangles Natasha from a complex narrative network of technical, class, and gendered disadvantages, finally recognizing her and Ilya as history's protagonists. Privation and privilege are resolved in favor of Natasha, not the idle radio listener using new media to accumulate the benefits of labor's new, productive power.

The worker inherits the return of the party's representation of networked mass labor; advantage taken in privileged access to the network of masses counts negatively in comparison to being, probabilistically, one of the hundreds of millions producing the wealth of those networks.[4] Creative, or, in thermodynamic terms, negentropic, labor trumps decaying, or entropic, waste. These polarities are designated from the outset in terms of personhood: The bourgeois Francophilic Madame Irène and her boorish husband receive derision; characters with the familiar names "Natasha" and "Ilya" experience setbacks on their way toward material and affective rewards. Together, their earnestness—and their productive potential for romance—overtakes the wasteful greed of the postrevolutionary bourgeoisie holding on to status and property that are no longer theirs to claim. Natasha and Ilya reap the benefits of combining material labor (hat making) and affective labor (care) as ethical labor. They warrant recognition in a cinematic diagram of networked mass culture asserting negentropic labor as the mediator of personhood and publicity.

For Benjamin, Eisenstein's *Potemkin,* seen in 1927 during his visit to Moscow toward the end of the NEP, provides the dialectical image of personhood in this networked mass. In Moscow, Benjamin describes the new men and women of the USSR, as in *Girl,* living the precarious tensions of poverty and reconstruction, but in areas where powerful images of party activism dramatized everyday close contact and attestations of conviction, where, for instance, legal proceedings provided "pedagogical theater": "For mobilizing the public on questions of Bolshevik morality in accordance with party wishes, there can be no more effective means. . . . The austere forms of such educational work are entirely appropriate to Soviet life, being precipitates of an existence which requires that a stand be taken a hundred times each day."[5] Ethical labor as negentropic excess organized image networks to overcome the legacies of capitalist underdevelopment in the *byt* ("everyday life") of the Soviet body politic. The proletarian "physiognomy" was permeated by a "new rhythm,"[6] in a "mandate, however virtual," to integrate "personal thoughts with a preexisting force field" incessantly producing "organized, guaranteed contact with comrades" (30) on the basis of party membership as "caste." *Potemkin*'s technologization of narrative, then, is another way of imaging this force field, otherwise seen only from an airplane "of the industrial elite of [Moscow], the film and automobile industries" (39).

Benjamin's ambivalence about state production of industrial images of ethical labor within a virtual public sphere explains his treatment of technology in his 1927 response to a German critic who dismissed *Potemkin*'s politicization of cinema as lacking in realism. Benjamin responds that *Potemkin* is ideologically, not realistically, descriptive—not simply of everyday life in Soviet socialism but of revolutions in technology and media and their broader meaning for art and culture: "The technical revolutions are the fracture points of artistic development; it is there that the different political tendencies may be said to come to the surface. In every new technical revolution the political tendency is transformed, as if by its own volition, from a concealed element of art into a manifest one";[7] cinema having "exploded [the] prison-world" of modern industrial life, "the technological revolution takes precedence over both [new content and new forms]" (17). Soviet montage shared with American slapstick a pragmatic case-by-case resolution of deeply motivated historical tensions in cinema's social form and content not directly observable but legible in cinema's technical imaging of social and political transformations. But, anticipating Deleuze's evaluation of Eisenstein's montage as demonstrating materialist reason where U.S. film narrative provided spectacular equivalencies, Benjamin argues that "the obverse of a ludicrously liberated technology [in U.S. slapstick] is the lethal power of naval squadrons on maneuver, as we see it openly displayed in *Potemkin*" (17). The montage method's technical mediation of industrial and state power gives *Potemkin* its special value: Its production "in a collectivist spirit" (18) emphasized the vital role of collectivist organization that was a primary concern in the Soviet Union.

Since postrevolutionary Soviet life allowed private thought, Benjamin thinks, only as a form of "solitary confinement,"[8] the collectivized montage cinema—in its complicity with the modern "milieu that rebukes it," in the bloody violence of its imagery, and in its foregoing of coherent narratological form—succeeded in annihilating the bourgeois subject's self-reflection in art.[9] What Barnet's hat girl did for the NEP bourgeois radio listener, *Potemkin*'s mutinous sailors did for the bourgeois spectatorship that Benjamin thinks decayed along with the remnants of romantic systems of the arts. Barnet's networked, musical listener is shocked into reactive self-consciousness of his historical loss of personhood by the radiophonic voice of the state. For Benjamin, Eisenstein advanced cinema's expressive capacity by deploying rhythm on the level of montage construction rather than by narrativizing rhythmic pulse or melodic line as diegetic events or characterizations.

But to make *Potemkin* render a dialectical image of Soviet life, Benjamin flattens the complex relationships between party and masses into a single force field: The "virtual mandate" to which Benjamin refers is epiphenomenal to the already realized force field making subjection to state power possible in every act and belief. Distinctions between Soviet policy and actual economic or technical development or between material and affective labor were not crucial for Benjamin's purposes. Transposing the montage cinema to his own critical context was a matter of establishing its value not simply as art but as critical, collective, technical mass art: historically necessary for conceiving the expression of an ethical relation between culture and politics. Benjamin's flattening of detail in *Potemkin,* then, made power relationships patent despite the opaque postrevolutionary context or Eisenstein's supposed attenuation of narrative content.

But Benjamin is selective in his emphasis of the film's narrative details. Less important than the collusive relation between church and state the film depicts (the ship's priest and captain are the two authorities whom the rebelling sailors most spectacularly attack) is the ship's doctor who prompts the mutiny. The "sadistic acts of the ship's doctor . . . become interesting only if we establish a relationship between the medical profession and the state"; while "no other medium could reproduce this collective in motion" (18–19). *Potemkin* provides, then, a dialectical image of *biopolitical resistance* in postrevolutionary Soviet life, where the probabilistic field of statistics demonstrated an epistemological relationship between newly transformed material ontologies of everyday life, the transformed governmental epistemologies of the body politic, and an ethical, collectivist mode of production. To a degree, this reading mitigates fears about *Potemkin*'s promulgation of revolution abroad.

At this historical remove, Benjamin's reading makes general questions around cinema's conditions of production, its medium specificity, or its aesthetic criteriology less important than observations as to the montage cinema's historical, material, expressive necessity. Configuring the film's energies as resistant rather than as memorializing recent memory, Benjamin reads *Potemkin* as *informatic* in rendering the technical force field modulating Soviet health and governmentality, mass contact and mass conviction. Meanwhile, montage is *immanent* to a critical, historical mediation of everyday biopolitical life in aesthetico-political terms. As for an immanence of affect, more than the energies of historical, memorial pathos, an enervated, pervasive melancholia glows dully through Benjamin's account of *Potemkin*'s technical achievement,[10] while Benjamin's logic of "new media"—more precisely, of medial succession—configures collectivist organization as the salient content of a biopolitical diagram relating historicity to technicity in the Soviet context, and beyond it.

Diagramming historicity and contemporaneity in terms of immanence and information continues to condition the theoretical reception of montage cinema. What has changed, though, is the degree to which a bioenergetic conception of immanence and information gives way to a bioinformatic one. Historically, the overriding tendency in contexts where advances in technology rather than in politics mediate discourses of social transformation is to valorize the montage cinema in some logic of medial succession—cinema conceived as new technology or digital computation as new media—rather than explicating political revolution as a historical event. In such accounts, however, whether bioenergetic or bioinformatic, "technology" either animates or exhausts "affect"; here, montage becomes a key instance of a technological advance and a technical expression that share priority. For example, in Bernard Stiegler's recent account of consciousness as "montage flux," the exhaustion of affect resulting from the informaticization of everyday life is more pronounced even than in Benjamin's melancholic account of technological modernity. From Hollywood cinema to global digital networks, Stiegler argues, we suffer a planetary "exhaustion of the desire for histories."[11] In such accounts, Eisenstein's montage becomes a signal historical exception, where the time-based medium's capacity for historical expression does not suffer a predictable discursive transfiguration into affirmations of the priority, desirability, and thus inevitability of technological change over social or political change.

But these accounts may relinquish historical, political specificity for Eisenstein's cinema. Logics of medial succession proceed by taking the medium in which the work is made for a larger given: The production of contemporaneity appears in terms of technology, technology appears as medium, medium as idiom, and the stylization of an idiom (here, Eisenstein's cinema montage) as an instance of a revelatory use, perhaps a historic, even political use, of the new technology. Historical contemporaneity is thus determined in relation to the technical instance of expression.[12] All such accounts configure some complex relation of historicity to contemporaneity in terms of material, technical, and affective labor *but* prioritize the relation of historicity to technical transformations.

Neither Benjamin's melancholia nor Stiegler's melancholic "symbolic misery," then, describes pathos in Eisenstein's cinema montage. And while for these critics technological change becomes the key transformation observed, still, cinema technologies, production methods, and output were not as advanced in the Soviet Union as they were in other industrial economies. Generally, the claim of the *montageurs* was not that Soviet cinema was more technologically advanced or new but that the Soviet montage cinema was more expressive of the historical material dynamics producing social, technological, and political transformations in modes of belonging best characterizing advanced industrial culture (such as collectivist socialism). Benjamin's appreciation of the technical and expressive achievements of Eisenstein's montage cinema and the uses of appropriating Eisenstein for critical melancholia concretize a long-enduring tendency in Eisenstein's reception, one that becomes clear when we reconsider cinema as biopolitical expression. Where information exhausts (bioenergetic) immanence in a technological conditioning wherein collectivist cinema best expresses the conflicts of everyday life, or where information entirely renovates (bioinformatic) immanence in the wealth of new possibilities engendered by the dissemination of new digital media, Eisenstein's montage methods—considered in part or entirely a matter of transformed technological expression—are transposed away from their historical conditions to different contexts.

For Soviet critics, Eisenstein's montage principle became a matter of debate around formalist aesthetics and socialist epistemologies symptomatic of more complex movements and events in Soviet politics and culture.[13] A Soviet documentary titled *Sergei Eisenstein* made in 1958, the year of *Ivan the Terrible, Part Two*'s belated and posthumous release, indicates a hesitant remembrance of the director: Characterized as a cultural worker of genius and generosity, with the capacity to "work, and work, and work," he was, the voice-over explains, subject to occasional delusion and ideological error. At this point in the film, the camera pans over Eisenstein's diagrammatic score of *Alexander Nevsky*, which thus becomes an index of nervous exhaustion. By the collapse of Soviet socialism during the late 1980s, such characterizations had been distilled to simple condemnations of the director as a canny liar, as in the epigraph cited at the beginning of this chapter.

In Western criticism, Benjamin's review of *Potemkin* concretizes a series of debates wherein Eisenstein's montage method becomes a matter of advancing technics and modernist (or postmodernist) epistemologies and where the expressive capacities of audiovisual media become a matter of informatic new media or of opportunities to recuperate epistemologies associated with older media for a transformed technological context. The concerns Victor Hugo expressed during the mid-nineteenth century—that the culture of the book would kill that of the cathedral—are transposed to streaming media.

In their 1947 critique of Eisenstein's claims of isomorphic synchronization of sound and image in *Alexander Nevsky* (1938), Eisler and Theodor Adorno produce the negative version of Benjamin's affirmation of *Potemkin*. Their well-known critique takes on claims that Eisenstein makes in his essay "Vertical Montage" (1939)[14] and that he illustrates with a graphical score diagramming simultaneously rising and falling movements in sound and image in a key sequence of his cinematic collaboration with Sergei Prokofiev on *Nevsky* (Figure 2.2). In "Vertical Montage," Eisenstein claims that any correspondence between sound and image of the sort associated with modernist painters, such as Wassily Kandinsky, must be an artifact of historical material circumstances rather than an expression of some ambiguous spiritual dimension of aesthetic experience. He asserts that the *Nevsky* diagram's rising and falling rhythm shows how the sequence's

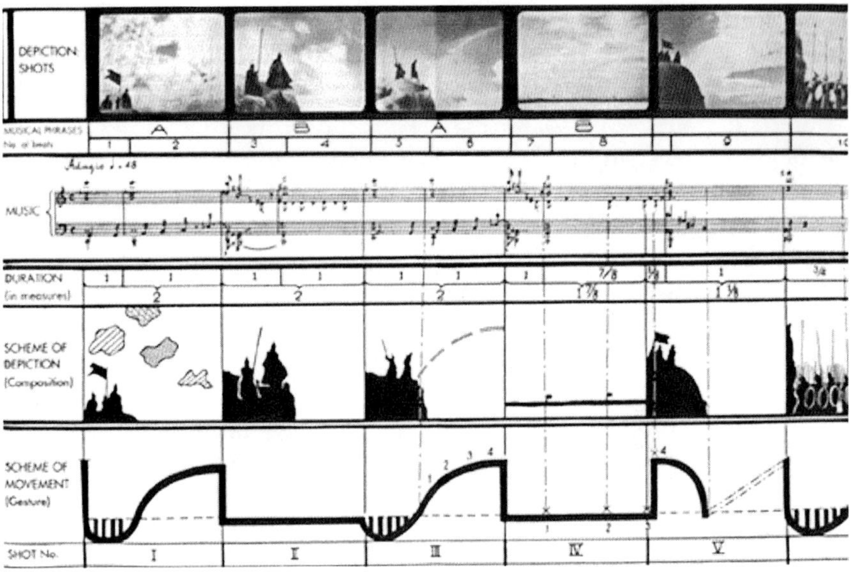

FIGURE 2.2 Eisenstein's controversial *Nevsky* diagram (detail). (S. M. Eisenstein, "Vertical Montage," *Selected Works Volume 2: Towards a Theory of Montage* [London: BFI, 1991], 327–399, insert.)

isomorphic sound and image reproduce a gesture of "breath."[15] This portion of the film depicts the Russian Prince Nevsky's late medieval army anxiously awaiting, on the shores of a frozen lake, an impending attack by invading Teutons.

Eisler and Adorno acknowledge that Eisenstein's interest in gesture in music and in plastic, serial imagery agrees with their contention that gesture has primacy in the audiovisual work as in ballet or pantomime (77). Eisenstein is also right, they think, in considering "rhythm" as an important consideration for auditory and visual registers of the audiovisual work. Rhythm is evident in the musical illustration especially common in synchronized cartoons ("Mickey Mousing") but more significantly describes the "higher aesthetic quality" of the work (68). As Benjamin does, they acknowledge the importance of collective or collaborative production. But rather than construe montage rhythm as a cinematic engagement with the superstructure promulgating technical advancement while denying the specific meanings of collective production, as Benjamin does, Eisler and Adorno argue that any rhythmic correspondence arising in sound and image would have to be metaphorical, refuse any phenomenological status for any qualitative fusion of sound and image, and dismiss any other source of metaphor apart from audience interpretation as a claim of *musica ficta*: the musical score forced to "represent something to which it refers instead of merely being itself" (85). This tendency to deploy music in service of the image originated, they argue, in the ghostly quality of the moving image, its living and nonliving quality, where musical accompaniment became useful "to exorcise fear or help the spectator absorb the shock" (75) of this entangled exhibition of living and dead labor. It is motivated in a cultural symptom, in other words, that should not be indulged.

Eisler and Adorno instead present a plan for film scoring informed by Eisler's experiences in a recent Rockefeller Foundation–funded Film Music Project and in Hollywood and by Adorno's experience as consultant on the Princeton Radio Project, another Rockefeller Foundation–funded project that helped facilitate Eisler's grant. The means for emancipating cinema music will be "objective planning, montage [methods for sound and music], and breaking through the universal neutralization" (88) of musical value and audience affect resulting from then-inferior sound-production practices as well as standardized composition practices. Acknowledging further technical advances in synchronization while insisting on access to those uses for advanced aesthetic uses, they read the *Nevsky* diagram as an informatic fallacy. All Eisenstein's graphical score of isomorphic breath gesture in *Nevsky* proves, Eisler and Adorno argue, "is that there is similarity between the *notation* of the music and the sequence. But the notation is already the fixation of the actual musical movement, the static image of a dynamic phenomenon. The similarity between the music and the picture is indirect, suggested by the graphic fixation of the music; it cannot be perceived directly, and for that reason cannot fulfill a dramatic function" (153).

Eisler and Adorno attribute to Eisenstein's chart a parametrical, informatic character that Eisenstein does not, in fact, explicitly claim for it. This reading of the *Nevsky* diagram and of "Vertical Montage," like Benjamin's appropriation of *Potemkin,* serves numerous purposes: Eisenstein becomes a useful straw man for Eisler and Adorno's argument.[16] But it indicates Eisler and Adorno's larger interests: making advances in compositional technique parallel advances in recording technique so that musical scoring would have greater autonomy in the production process and in cinema reception. Synchronization techniques shortly would be "automated," they argue (109), and given the reduction in value for musical labor such advances implied, film music must become visible in its own right rather than disappear in subservience to the filmic image. It should "sparkle and glisten" without illustrating what is already on screen (133). Eisler and Adorno advocate a kind of doubled screen for the streaming audiovisual work. Disney's higher-definition stereo sound for *Fantasia* (1940) provided the problematic reality their program might improve. The composer of a "visible" film music would no longer be taught that "he is only a cipher" (115)—that is, a creative worker become hieroglyph.

The difference, then, has to do with the ways distinct critical methods considered labor and cultural reproduction. For Eisenstein, sound and image might reproduce a gesture, such as breath; this was not a technological advance but an aesthetic and political one. For Eisler and Adorno in Hollywood, film music workers had to plan montage using the most advanced technologies possible as a way of being gainfully employed, but, further, epistemology and cognition for Eisler and Adorno must pass through the concept rather than through musical affect, precisely because Hollywood's incipient automation of synchronization techniques threatened to automate cognition as false feeling. The sound-image *combinatoire* had to be pulled apart and submitted, in separate streams, to audience reflection.

During the 1960s, Christian Metz and Peter Wollen produced new versions of Benjamin's and Eisler and Adorno's pro-and-con valorizations of Eisenstein's montage. In both accounts, the newly perceived dominance of cybernetic processes is clear. For Metz, Eisenstein's montage fetishizes an informatic approach. Just as Eisler and Adorno claim in regards to the *Nevsky* diagram, Metz asserts, in essence, that Eisenstein had confused immanence with informatics, helping prepare the way for a general triumph for the cybernetic apparatus:

> The machine has ground up human language and dispenses it in clean slices, to which no flesh clings. Those "binary digits," perfect segments, have only to be assembled (programmed) in the requisite order. The code triumphs. . . . It is a great feast for the syntagmatic mentality . . . [as the natural object is] analyzed, literally and figuratively, and its constituent parts are isolated; this is the moment of *breakdown analysis*, as in the cinema. Then the parts are distributed into isofunctional categories: straight tracks to one side, curved to another. This is the paradigmatic aspect—and it is only preparatory, as was the filming of individual scenes for Eisenstein. The grand moment, which one has been waiting for and thinking about since the beginning, is the syntagmatic moment [in which a duplicate of some original object is fabricated so that it will be] "perfectly grasped by the mind, since it is a pure object of the mind."[17]

Metz argues for an urgent distinction between cybernetic technics and the cinema's exhibition value as utterance within a negative logic of medial succession wherein cybernetics had parceled out idealized reality as binary code and where cinema might resist that totalization as actualized speech, not idealized mental copy. In response, Wollen[18] perfects the opposite response to the "old-new" axis where new technologies replace the old. Much as Eisler and Adorno think that rising technical standards for sound reproduction necessitate "the free and conscious utilization of all musical resources," Wollen describes cinema generally as requiring an eclectic, political aesthetics. For Wollen, cinema as new medium draws on extensive, motley media archaeologies and thus requires historicization in relation to older modes of expression (just as, in a less pointed way, Eisler and Adorno compare cinema to ballet or mime). Rejecting the cybernetic implosion of Saussurean semiotics Metz theorizes, Wollen draws on Charles Sanders Pierce's semiotics of icon, index, and symbol to argue that distinct referential qualities mingle in the same cinematic sign. Cinematic meaning can never be reduced to a single syntagmatic encoding. Wollen thus understands multifarious historical artifacts belonging as much to the history of cybernetics and robotics as providing cinema's impure origins, like automata. Cinema becomes not a final holdout against cybernetic idealization but wildly combinatorial and incorporative:

> The cinema is not simply a new art; it is also an art which combines and incorporates others, which operates on different sensory bands, different channels, using different codes and modes of expression. It poses in the most acute form the problem of the relationship between the different arts, their similarities and differences, the possibilities of translation and transcription: all the questions asked of aesthetics by the Wagnerian notion of the *gesamtkunstwerk* and the Brechtian critique of [Richard] Wagner, questions which send us back to the theory of synaesthesia, to [Gotthold] Lessing's *Laocoön* and [Charles] Baudelaire's *Correspondences.* (8)

Wollen's account recalls Benjamin's sense of immanent historical fracture lines brought to the surface in the expressive power of a new technological medium, although here, the fracture lines seem to be radio "bands" or television "channels," while Eisenstein becomes the exemplar for a second, combative avant-garde rather than for collective production of mass art. Whether in Metz's totalized account of Saussurean logic giving way to cybernetic idealism or in Wollen's heterogeneous semiotics, the laboring indexes of the director and his collaborators on the work and those of the audience interpreting the work tend to be erased.

Later, Eisenstein's "montage of attractions" serves as a generative, supple logic for locating historical points of media origin or transition and for new historicizations of transnational modernisms, and not only in scholarly works. As such accounts as Tom Gunning's influential elevation of cinematic attractions to the status of neglected modern vernacular[19] tended to generalize the excavation of cinema memory in order to reveal the displacement of alternative modernities, citations of Eisenstein become a mark of directorial mastery in Hollywood industry. Roughly concurrently, Brian De Palma's *The Untouchables* (1987) is one of numerous cinematic works to knowingly reference *Potemkin*'s Odessa Steps sequence or to otherwise pay homage to Eisenstein to emphasize their mastery of cinema's historical, spectacular display: Roller coaster–like attraction is integrated with historicist fiction. In *The Untouchables,* at a moment of imminent suspense, a runaway baby carriage recalls the carriage released from the hands of a murdered woman to bounce down the Odessa staircase in *Potemkin.* Here, it rolls down the marble staircase of 1930s Chicago's Union

Station, caught in the crossfire of Al Capone's gangsters. The reference challenges the audience with a formal riddle about film-studies academicism and pop-culture interpretation but for meanings that are the very opposite of those Eisenstein intended: Baby and mother survive in *The Untouchables,* of course.

Zbigniew Rybczynski's video *Steps* (1987) parodies the appropriation of Eisenstein's montage into Hollywood cinema and Western film studies according to logics of new media succession and cinema historicism. The video mobilizes tensions between immanence and information to question whether montage-as-technological-attraction is not actually a sophisticated form of historical kitsch. In *Steps,* a visiting Eastern Bloc director restages the Odessa Steps sequence on a U.S. blue-screen stage as an experiment in media immersion. Dramatizing the power of electronic compositing technologies, whereby the blue-screen studio-as-computer expands the spectacular qualities of cinema into participatory immersion, *Steps* presents a group of Eisenstein fans and tourists of cinema history who enter the Steps sequence and climb a "virtual" form of the steps presented somewhere between the blue-screen stage, a supervisory control booth, an unseen digital computer performing a live composite, cinema history, and commercial appeal. The tourists climb the Steps to "touch" film history come alive, to explore the power of electronic "reality," or, simply, to become "stars." One couple's attempt to secretly film erotica and others' attempts to touch the blood of a dying woman make a point shortly made even more glaringly obvious, as the Steps tourists mime gestures suggestive of hungry vampires or slowly rioting zombies in a Romero film. The user of participatory, immersive digital media risks becoming more a vampire-zombie of late capital than a participatory media revolutionary who will know what to do with the future of image production soon to be available at his or her fingertips. Immersion in electronically composited environments holds the promise to renew the political aspirations of montage or the political meanings held in cinema memory but instead only fetishizes cinema history and memory, appropriating these in illusionistic participation whereby the interactive media attraction mines historical pathos less for historical lessons than for greed, lust, and ignorance—at least, in this director's vision.

But by the mid-1990s, with the novelty of digital compositing increasingly a thing of the past and interactive forms widely available in computer games or CD-ROMs, its very lack of novelty allowed digital compositing to serve as memory theater. Oleg Kovalov's compilation film of 1996, *Sergei Eisenstein: Autobiography,* loosely excerpts Eisenstein's memoirs while using digital composition to reassemble fragments from a broad range of European modernist cinema experiments from the 1920s into the 1930s. Fernand Léger and Dudley Murphy's *Ballet mécanique* (1924) or Fischinger's early musical motion studies circulate through the film as reflections in Eisenstein's mind's eye: evocative but vague art-historical references seen from a pseudoautobiographical point of view guiding the receiver through the narrated excerpts of Eisenstein's diary. Although the narrative of the film is drawn from Eisenstein's memoirs, a montage of modernist cinema stands in as his cinematic autobiography and as testament to an almost plastic everydayness seemingly transforming as he moves through it. Here, Eisenstein's own contributions are subsumed to a European field of practice whose retrospective geopolitical generality defies the historical fault lines that fractured it.

With the dissemination of digital-media technologies underwriting Kovalov's fictive Eisenstein autobiography, interdisciplinary approaches ranging from information design,[20] film music and musicology,[21] or narratology and digital media theory[22] explored Eisenstein's theories with renewed insight, emphasizing Eisenstein's sense of the active engagement of the cinema viewer, his recognition of the capacity for musical meaning to arise in visual as well as auditory registers, or montage's emphasis on affect, breakage, and association. Marc Davis's 1995 doctoral dissertation explicates the design of his Media Streams authoring system for video remixing by acknowledging the social nature of fan remixing that Henry Jenkins[23] observes and by working through Eisenstein's theories of montage as prior work in recombinant cinema semiotics. Media Streams was not an early version of YouTube.com but a proposal for more advanced versions of the video-authoring interfaces typified by such programs as Adobe Premiere or Adobe After Effects. Davis expands on a central insight of Eisenstein's *Nevsky* diagram: Specific elements of an audiovisual work might be isolated as gestures, such as Eisenstein's breath gesture. In Media Streams, icons allowing elements to be parametrically controlled appear in a stacked column on the left-hand side of the interface window, while their tracks to the right show changes over time. Authoring video elements by icon rather than simply adjusting timing information of audio and visual tracks allows any semantically meaningful component of an audiovisual work to have its own stream.

Davis, like Metz, situates Eisenstein's work in relation to Saussurean semiotics but, like Eisler and Adorno, reads the *Nevsky* diagram as an incomplete proposal of informatic synchronization. Davis writes, "Eisenstein was on the right track though [he was theorizing] at the wrong level of representation. Shots are not letters or even words, but utterances whose semantics does radically depend on their position in a syntagmatic structure" (98). Davis's graphical language for video remixing describes an "invariant" semantics independent of the sequence in which it occurs and a "variable" semantics dependent upon the sequence in which it occurs; interactions between the two account for the play of meaning arising in video remixing. Davis separates, in the manner characteristic of bioinformatic epistemologies, the medium substrate (the hardware) from the medium of expression (the software interface). Davis proposes two semantics, then, but by removing the substrate of computation, implicitly includes three. Any original context, content, or exhibition becomes subject to an independent semantics allowing the work to be input, analyzed, and reordered; the Media Streams interface allows the determination of new dependent semantics rendered in output; but beyond these, the manipulability of the temporal sign at the graphical interface itself evinces a further semantics. At this third level, the gestural of Eisenstein's breath gesture is transposed to the interface icon and the hands of the computer user (rather than being transposed between composer and audience in exhibition). This third semantics is that of the interface design itself; that the software design might be broken apart and redistributed is not part of Davis's design (at least in this documented version).

Because the nature and number of semantics proposed remain unclear, Davis is able to collapse software design of video production, exhibition, and reception into a double articulation whereby semantic variability wins out over syntactic determination, meaning over context; video remixing wins out over the givenness of content or historical authorship. Media Streams reconfigures the material, technical, and affective gesture of Eisenstein's montage for video remixing and social networking; its ostensible value would be its capacity to facilitate novel exhibitions of personhood and publicity.[24] Davis's video remixing software is not so much medium as instrument. It models the variegation of authorship as a straightforward activity for which exemplars and concepts circulate widely in professional and informal domains. Why would participatory media practices grown up around existing, often low-quality tools require such a fine-grained tool? A theory of user-generated content in search of a participatory user base that is also a software consumer base, Media Streams remains interesting in the ways it works through a series of important questions around instrumentality and participation in the form of software design: what counts as historical and what counts as social, what counts as medium and what counts as tool, and how digital tools mediate participation differently from the exemplars they call on.

For Eisenstein, active interpretation of historical pathos in reception was crucial to expressing and revising the memory of political transformations in streaming image and sound. For Davis, active reauthoring and circulation of any content in any sense would have been crucial for Media Streams in the event of commercialization. The meanings of history become an effect of what can be made to circulate rather than what can be marked as a memorial, affective event. As we have seen in the works of Benjamin, Eisler, and Adorno, as well as in those of Metz, Wollen, De Palma, and Rybczynski, Media Streams did not originate this problematic. Davis's software, steeped in but resisting Eisenstein's theory of pathos as creative, ethical labor, presents a clear articulation of a long-emerging problematic wherein immanence is displaced by information. Meanwhile, informal users of video seem less interested in fine-grained composition of digital video content but doubly interested in digital video as a medium for variegated self-exhibition and in the networked site of video exhibition as a medium of commentary—that is, in scoring the mediated historicity of personhood and publicity.

In the obverse of Davis's interpretation of Eisenstein, such critical media comparatists as Marsha Kinder draw insights from Eisenstein's cinema that help explain this interest in exhibitionary scoring of comparative personhood and publicity. Kinder argues that Eisenstein's specific characterizations of the cinema sign, which varied widely, are less important than his self-conscious appropriation of prior works of art and his insistence on reframing art-historical material for streaming exhibition and reception: "It was not just the conflict between the object and its framing that provided a new resource for dialectic montage but also the way he framed this conflict through a *comparison* across contextualizing media, cultures, and periods, a process that generated a productive analogy between framing and adaptation" (160–161).[25] Framing and appropriation emphasize the expressive power of open-ended association mobilizing desire, not computation, yet also exhibit immanent historical conflict on the media screen rather than the subjection of historical meaning to informatic structuring. This conflict of framing and adaptation arises as an expression of highly mediated but historically expressive desire playing out in transmedia appropriations ranging from Peter Greenaway's *A TV Dante* (1989) to children's gaming software. Kinder's reformulation of psychoanalytic theories of desire requires a rethinking of theories of digital media reception as self-exhibition: Any engagement of Eisenstein's montage means writing oneself into the processes of "promiscuous" association according to which contemporary transmedia production proceeds.[26]

"Promiscuous association" rather than technical instrumentality enchains desire and cognition in Kinder's account of adaptation and reframing, working across historical and contemporary fields of expression. Similarly, more than any single dominant technical instrumentality, Eisenstein himself invokes the ways in which technical ensembles were adapted to and expressed reframed association. In "P-R-K-F-V," he writes admiringly of Prokofiev's cognitive capacity to submit telephonic communication, alphanumeric mnemonics, and compositional expertise in the composer's signature emblem made up of the consonants in his surname.[27] Eisenstein's own fascination with configurable medial forms, such as the "spherical book,"[28] the adjustable quadratic screen, or the ancient scroll as a protocinematic panorama, similarly, is a claim about his own facility to compress historical *or* technological ensembles into new expressions that might then be given an explosive new power.

For Kinder, similarly, biographical memory may be narrativized in computational forms—for example, as "database narrative"—but association is motivated and elaborated in terms of affect. In her interactive CD-ROM *Mysteries and Desire: Searching the Worlds of John Rechy* (2000), Kinder and art director Kristy H. A. Kang implement a contemporary version of Eisenstein's spherical book: The notion of a vast spherical projection of montage materials becomes a cylindrical scrapbook of photos and text from the archives of gay Chicano writer John Rechy.[29] The project speaks to Stiegler's fears of a general exhaustion of desire for history as a result of the symbolic work demanded by programmed media; it insists on a desire for biographical, historical narration. In *Mysteries and Desire,* the mysteries are the personal history, motivations, or historical significance of Rechy's exploits in U.S. literature. The CD-ROM draws on cinematic as well as literary and life-writing epistemologies to frame desire as motivating Rechy, the readers of his works, and the user of the interactive biography's interface.

Using the navigable panorama technology of QuickTime VR—more often employed to present perspectival, quasi-immersive touristic scenes—Kinder and Kang design the introductory "Memories Zone" of *Mysteries and Desire* as an intimate but navigable collage of Rechy's personal archive, a collection of associations programmed as embedded hotlinks leading the reader to additional pathways and into other "zones" of Rechy's biography. Where a navigable panorama presenting a cylindrical scrapbook motivates user navigation in this first primary encounter with Rechy's life and work, cinematic and literary epistemologies are invoked in the pathways to which associations programmed into the scrapbook lead. Linearly sequenced, often containing animated imagery, and sometimes including digital video or sound, these pathways fill in historical details not apparent on the psychic surface of writerly memory. The reader travels through primary and secondary mediations of intimate and public memory, then, breaking elements blurred together in the first level of the collage out into secondary series where historical associations or cultural meanings are filled out.

The archive of personal history turns out to be the precipitate of accumulated but partial, not entirely recoverable intersubjective experiences or events, which are further elaborated and complicated in other zones of the CD-ROM. The other zones are devoted to creative depictions of affective labor imbricated in the complex collage of personal and public self and that are paradoxically more descriptively presented as fictive rather than documentary or historical interpretation. These consist of illustrated, annotated, or reinterpreted versions of Rechy's writing, presented via a fictive navigation of factual obsessions: fiction, life writing, sexuality, bodybuilding. The aesthetico-political shaping of concrete reality undertaken by Rechy is delivered over a navigable media stream but with no promise of radical extension or of infinite navigation or variation.

In *Mysteries and Desire,* conflict is presented, on the surface, as beautifully informatic: a polished, if also blurred and worn, resolution of personhood and publicity in a sphere of memory. But the meaningful associations making this exhibition of selfhood cohere, the user learns, lie in additional conflicts immanent to that surface, requiring energetic actions on the part of the user to crack and to unfurl. At key moments between select sections, Kinder directs that a random number generator determine which section will be the next destination. Rather than promise infinite interactivity, at moments when energetic movement exhausts a sequence, the ensemble of technically prepared associations, animated by desire, introduces entropic calculation into the navigable path, scrambling and renewing the sequencing of associations. Kinder and Kang's design of digital biography treats history and the desire for history as factic and fictive by turns: made, but generative, given to be remade in repeated revision of pathways, even if users are no more allowed to remix the CD-ROM's contents than Davis's users are allowed to remix his authoring program. The drawback of this design is that the play of fact and fiction is most illuminating to readers of Rechy's work, whose reading habits may or may not adapt easily to this gestural-technical versioning of literary repetition. If Media Streams's potential digital authors remixed without needing such sophisticated software, *Mysteries and Desire*'s readers' habits may not have found immediate points of literary entry with the CD-ROM's navigable associations.

Barbara Stafford[30] argues that *Potemkin*'s montage creates "animated, salient images . . . generating interbrain correspondences" that unify its audience.[31] Stafford argues that such a generation of correspondences across thinking bodies exemplifies the "cognitive work" that artistic images do as "echoic objects," vibrant diagrammatic emblems binding the thinking body and its surrounding environment in a mimetic "interface" (233). Davis's Media Streams prototype and Kinder and Kang's *Mysteries and Desire*'s experimental biography each suggest, though, that revisions of cinema montage animate desire for mediological expression—that includes the cognitive work Stafford describes but is not limited to it—to introduce or to rediscover historical meanings not apparent in the "compound image." In other words, the echoic object arises in and is subject to, historical change beyond any specific work that it does. This lesson about historical relation is proffered in Eisenstein's work, in his reception, and in these prototypes: The historical play of personhood and publicity engages affective labor informally where technical development differentiates and displaces material work. Potential historical, social, or cognitive-corporeal correspondences diagrammed through media streams (whether in the energetic sense of bodies resonating together in the modulation of personhood and publicity in a single site and moment or in the more general modulatory dissemination of programmed media networks) are transduced as *certain* possible gestures to be taken or deferred—and not as other gestures that thereby become impossible or go unrealized. This larger, complex historical relation is not directly subject to cognition in the sense of a cognitive, thinking self.

Affective labor determines an informal difference between potential and possible gesture-technical act. But *Mysteries and Desire* prompts us to ask: What kind of act is the affective labor of pathos for Eisenstein? For Nicholas Cook, the *Nevsky* diagram is an exemplar of the plasticity of affective meaning that becomes available in the dynamic, cognitive combination of image and sound. Cook notes Eisler and Adorno's concern that rhythmic gesture in audiovisual synchronization is metaphorical and glosses Eisenstein's *Nevsky* diagram with reference to cognitive theories of metaphor. Cook argues that when two expressions, in whatever medium, are made coextensible in some aspect, metaphor results in the transfer of meaning proper to one expression to the other, so long as the two different expressions share some attribute. Sound and image may transfer meaning to one another, then, if they share, or are interpreted as sharing, attributes. Eisenstein's *Nevsky* score thus diagrams a complementary synchronization of sound and image: The metaphors presented in sound or image roughly agree. More precisely, shared meaning results in conformant synchronization; negative transfer results in expressions that contest one another. The cognitive theory Cook calls on to make sense of the *Nevsky* diagram reads it in terms of metaphor and reference, but here, metaphor becomes something more like metonym. It references attributes of formal expressions by indexing sets of attributes to the nominal identity of the expression. This cognitive model of metaphor parallels the nominal referencing structures of object-oriented computing, where attributes of objects may be called to pass parametrical expressions from one object to another, creating computable chains of transfer and inheritance between software objects using dynamic referencing. Beyond the close readings Cook provides of media works ranging from Eisenstein's cinema, record-album covers, Disney's *Fantasia,* or film works by contemporary European auteurs, Cook's reading suggests how the *Nevsky* diagram might partially anticipate certain aspects of object-oriented media expression, at the cost of turning metaphor into metonym. Cook's explanation also does not explain how a gesture of breath structured as an emergent quality of an event arising in the shared duration of a musical phrase and an image sequence communicates *historical* pathos as an artifact of its being composed and received.

The argument made in "Vertical Montage" and by the *Nevsky* diagram is that the complex contrapuntal meanings of the synchronized image as gesture are not simply produced in collision, as in Eisenstein's 1923 montage of attractions, nor are they simply "stratigraphic," as in the four layers of montage he hypothesized in 1929. Rather, building on these earlier approaches, the *Nevsky* diagram presents four isomorphic layers of composition—visual composition, shot, musical score, and final synthetic gesture—in a larger contrapuntal flow. Each contrapuntal voice helps shape a larger combined expression whose gestural concreteness is also partly determined by its audience reception; interpretation may also, as in counterpoint, pull out voices on the basis of combined relation. But these streams correspond to the material and collaborative process of making meaning, not simply to cognitive meaning inhering in the film (or the diagram of it). Vertical montage, then, emphasizes a specific collaboration and a specific production history in Soviet sound film (rather than a general collectivization of labor), does not map music and image as informatic and parametrical, and does not insist that music follow image. The enfolding of polyphonic and contrapuntal rhythm and lyricism results from the collaborative labor of production and reception. The *Nevsky* diagram, in other words, is a compressed production and exhibition history of compositional sense and audience sensation, charting a quasi-autonomous breath projected and received within a "cinema Soviet." This breath draws immanent history as pathos into everyday time and releases possibility into everyday life through the complex temporal expression of precarious affective labor. Its production history and exhibition occupy a key phase in Eisenstein's work, during which he moved further away from historicizing the violent memory of the revolution in forms relying on profilmic materials and toward historicizing the revolution's sustained meanings in the face of futural violence, where the correspondence of pathos between the historical and the contemporary is effected with intensified attention to plastic symbolic forms rather than materials familiar from everyday Soviet life or recent history. (The comparison of his later works to Disney animation is, in this latter respect, justified.)[32]

As Davis's and Cook's discussions make clear, some aspects of Eisenstein's graphical score do anticipate formally and conceptually the graphical authoring interfaces for contemporary software products ranging from digital video authoring to special effects authoring to consumer entertainment software. The interface displays of authoring tools, such as the various versions of Adobe Premiere or Adobe After Effects, allow audio and visual media to be graphically co-positioned and processed according to a common, mathematically determined time base specific neither to auditory nor to visual material and not intrinsically subject to the limits or constraints thereof. This time base, though, is subject to the limits of the clock ticks of the digital computer; the algorithmic modulation is subject to the hardware and software limitations of the computer. Here, rather than creative labor and audience gesture, binary sound and image material become inputs, and the compressed final segment of digital video becomes the output. Placing media of historically distinct materialities as logical materiality within a generic time base subject to hardware clock, programmed algorithm, and software memory is a basic desideratum informed by the temporal contingencies of production labor or of audience reception. This same temporal modularity also informs the play or authoring modes presented in the diagrammatic interfaces of such musical computer games as *Frequency* (Harmonix, 2002), *Amplitude* (Harmonix, 2003), or *Guitar Hero* (Harmonix, 2005). These programs produce value to the degree that they can reduce disparate media materials to the logical convertibility of the binary digit. This reducibility indicates not a ready extension of Eisenstein's affective labor as pathos but rather a massive intensification of the fragmenting of labor power in abstract general labor distributed according to exchange value, as argued by Karl Marx in his analysis of the alienated commodity object.[33] The historical pathos Eisenstein aimed to express to his audiences as gesture is intensified and fragmented as part and parcel of the gestural-technical modulation of tensions between personhood and publicity animating contemporary bioinformatic belonging. In this sense, Davis's or Kinder's prototypes are useful: They stress the extreme and often fragile modulation, not the historical inevitability, of technical function and possibilities for exhibition in the contemporary production of personhood and publicity. But the only parametricization here is what Eisenstein describes in his memoirs as a "charmed parameter":

> There is deep within me a long-standing conflict between the free course of the *all'improviso,* flowing line of drawing or the free run of dance, subject only to the laws of the inner pulse of the organic rhythm of purpose (on one hand); and the restrictions and blind spots of the canon and rigid formula (on the other).
>
> Actually, it is not entirely appropriate or fair to mention formulae here.
>
> The charm of a formula is that, while laying down a general rule, it allows, within the free current which filters through it, "special" interpretations, special cases and coefficients.[34]

The rhythmic diagramming of breath in the *Nevsky* diagram illustrates the pulse of serialized expressive materials articulating not an advance for automation but a claim of deep historical belonging, enabling cinema to reproduce powerful plastic gestures in the collaborative hands of two cultural workers who shared tendencies and in those workers' audiences.[35]

In comparison, gesture remains radically underrepresented, undertheorized, and underdeveloped in terms of material and affective labor at the digital interface—it is pointedly and strategically reduced. The working body at the software interface belongs to a bioinformatic capitalization of attention, gestural action, and programmed process. Gesture at the interface is implemented within a distinct regime of affective and technical labor as a negative form of laboring exchange: Programmed gesture works as a productivity gain for the producer of the intellectual property output in the computational process before it works for an audience or the state. The exhibition and commentary of user-generated or remixed video express tensions of personhood and publicity in this bioinformatic regime.

The *Nevsky* diagram read in this light allows us to confront a certain fissure and fusion of two regimes of modern historical corporeal production that are not limited to the uneven economies of either capitalism or socialism during the 1920s and 1930s or to contemporary digital media but that have to do with energetic and symbolic processes. The first regime is that of the bioenergetic, in which the body is understood as having a complex ontology, epistemology, and ethics for producing meaning between the energetics of the living body and the energetics of industrial machines: Ergonomics, for example, arose to study the fatigue this interaction produced.[36] The second regime is that of bioinformatics, also a complex ontology, epistemology, and ethics, but one for the production of engagements between the symbolic materiality of the corporeal body and the symbols of information streams.[37]

The difference between the two regimes has to do with the relationship between energetic and symbolic streams powering the production of corporeal experience and sense. As N. Katherine Hayles[38] has shown, cybernetics did not arise in a vacuum; its historical context was marked precisely by a formulation of informatic messaging requiring that context as such be discarded from the cybernetic message, as well as by subsequent reformulations arising in part because of the deferral of historical or social context from the cybernetic sign. The result was that information streams, while requiring energetic resources, made energetic interactions *either* internal *or* external to the content of the symbolic stream of information. But the future of our own bioinformatic regime lies in the fact that it cannot separate itself fully from the thermodynamic, energetic regimes from which it derives historically.

In Eisenstein's time, the transformed political context meant that bioenergetic epistemologies were reconsidered by such theatrical artists as Meyerhold in theatrical biomechanics; these epistemologies were stops on the way toward bioinformatic corporeality but neither aimed at nor achieved its conception. Meyerhold's biomechanics or other modern vernaculars of bioenergetic production required further symbolic elaboration; Eisenstein's cinema montage was one response. Cybernetics in its modern form as the automation of symbolic processes was also a distinct aspect of vernacular responses to the demands of bioenergetic technocultures. To the degree that bioinformatic regimes require the bioenergetic regimes to which they seem to defer in their emphasis on symbolic processing as nature, bioinformatic corporeality continues to require the production of bioenergetic corporealities. The robotic as a diagrammatic flag for bioenergetic history continues to mark our time along with a menagerie of other corporeal ontologies, epistemologies, and ethics: Donna Haraway's ironic cyborg or Deleuze's "spiritual automaton," rubrics for the manufacture of the automatic out of the involuntary.[39]

Eisenstein's theory of vertical montage, then, takes on what appears to be a more total and completely formalized appearance in terms of musicality and gesture at precisely the moment at which the cybernetic automation of work becomes feasible (instead of the nineteenth century's "social cybernetics"—that is, harmonic civil governance).[40] On the cusp of a historical transposition from bioenergetic industrialism to bioinformatic industrialism, Eisenstein's composition methods for *Nevsky* travel to the point of the bioinformatic regime's concrete appearance in world historical materiality and turn back toward the symbolic and even the constructivist tendencies of Meyerhold's biomechanical theater. The moment at which Eisenstein returns to symbolic theories by then immanent to Soviet history rather than those of an emergent bioinformatic regime constitutes a bifurcation point in the alignment of montage practices within Soviet politics: By the time Eisenstein composed "Vertical Montage," Meyerhold had been assassinated, a "catastrophe" to which Prokofiev, Eisenstein's musical collaborator on *Alexander Nevsky* and *Ivan the Terrible, Part One* (1944), refers in a letter to the director in July 1939.[41] Organizing montage as symbolic, musical affective labor had value: This stylistics of media composition provided Eisenstein an ethical mode of conducting public personhood while generating an aesthetico-political sequence of work diverging from conventional spectacles dramatizing state power.

Modal Cinema

We now need to come to terms with the imbrications of pathos and instrumentality and, more broadly, the entanglement of organicism and mechanism Deleuze resolves with his account of cinema's "spiritual automaton" in *Cinema 2: The Time-Image.* How does cinema unreel the serialized indexical traces it captures photographically in an automated exhibition of memory and thought? Cinema's stream of serial images is not simply projected on the screen but cleaves to our innermost consciousness, Deleuze observes. The organization of temporalized narrative in D. W. Griffith or Eisenstein emerges from cinema's capacity to shape spectatorship not for an individual viewer but for a "spiritual automaton." Deleuze argues that the "pathetic" dimension of Eisenstein's montage—for my purposes, the affective labor of pathos, what I have called a "pathic act"—constitutes a dialectical materialist aesthetics insofar as it could be expressed in terms of the energetic visuality of early and classical cinema.

Deleuze gives Eisenstein's achievements a privileged status within the cinema of the movement image, the first of two successive historical epochs of a "universal cinema."[42] Eisenstein's "dialectical assemblage" of pathos adds a "developmental" reason to montage, differentiating Soviet montage from U.S. film style. Privileged moments are not composed as contingent, equivalent individual persons, places, or events, as in Griffith's editing. Rather, dialectical, affective reason motivates pulsating transitions where Deleuze notes a "leap into the opposite," where transitions develop from one point of intensity to another—from sadness to anger, from doubt to certainty—resulting in an upsurge of the new quality born in the transition (35). These pathetic "movement images" include the sudden appearance of color in the hand-tinted red flag at the end of the otherwise monochrome *Potemkin.* Such moments "compress" then "explode" the film's development, so that such transitions express "the dawn of consciousness and consciousness attained, revolutionary consciousness attained" (36).

The painterly images of Leonardo da Vinci or El Greco that Eisenstein analyzed require their perceivers to fabricate any possibility of movement with regards to them; choreographic or dramatic movement, too, remain attached to a moving body. Eisenstein's movement images begin to build on cinema's historical expression of a shock to thought: "It is only when movement becomes automatic that the artistic essence of the image is realized: *producing a shock to thought, communicating vibrations to the cortex, touching the nervous and cerebral systems directly*" (156). Cinema finally makes potential—that is, "virtual"—what had been only a possibility for the other arts. Cinema's "spiritual automaton" no longer refers to the logical, abstract deduction of thoughts from one another. Now, "spiritual automaton" refers to "the circuit into which [thoughts] enter with the movement-image, the shared power of what forces thinking and what thinks under the shock; a *nooshock*" (151–152). As D. N. Rodowick[43] explains, this understanding of cinema as effecting a long destined shock to the receiver of the streaming image means that "what cinema contributes to the history of thought is a powerlessness—in fact, a dispossession of thought in relation to the image—that is equivalent to the division of the subject by the pure form of time" (190). Thus, the earlier cinema semiotics of Griffith or Eisenstein would break apart into the virtual "time image" of postwar cinemas, characterized by narrative disjunctions, hallucinatory sequencing, or wandering dream states rather than coherent spatiality and sensorimotor movement.[44] The time image relates the identity of the temporal image itself: It shows time. The time image haunted the classical cinema's movement image, but, Deleuze argues, it requires a fragmenting of spatiality in the interest of the temporality of the image itself, toward which Eisenstein strained but never reached, according to Deleuze.

For Deleuze, potentiality as virtuality is real, immanent, and unrepresented, not a possibility to be realized. Deleuze believes that understanding the manifestation of material reality as possibilities realized results in a severe problem: It means that differentiating material existence from the concept of material existence is unnecessary. The result is that we get lost in representation. The movement image, then, strains toward the virtuality of the time image, but to the degree that it remains a representation of time in space rather than a communication of temporality as such, it is still bound up in a false problem. If the modern subject is split from the historical world, the time image communicates, without representing the spatial world, the flux of time splitting the subject in modernity. The time image relates the spiritual automaton to its historicity through an affective ratio of cinematic duration.

In spite of Deleuze's recognition of pathos at the heart of Eisenstein's rhythmic developments and transitions, his reading of Eisenstein's montage as projecting coherent space and sensorimotor movement is strange—too close, in fact, to the claims that Eisenstein's cinema lacks adequate narrative structure, distorts history, or indulges in scientistic, quasi-parametrical formalisms. The historical, representational, spatial, or descriptive aspects of Eisenstein's films are fraught precisely *because* he engaged in *possible* reproductions of the revolution while projecting these reproductions as *virtual* image. This paradox of virtually streaming image projecting a possible gesture is not the movement image straining toward a time image. It is rather an action feeling, a pathic act, engendered by musicalizing the media stream. It has, too, a historicizing, memorial aim *as well as* the futural calling Deleuze theorizes as an essential aspect of modern art's function: to invoke a not-yet-formed community, a coming community, a "missing people."[45] For Eisenstein, a socialist people *had been* achieved *in part,* but the socialist body politic itself was historically traumatized, excessively stressed in the present, and futurally unfinished. In this situation, any "world historical consciousness" of an unfinished socialist people, because their governmentality had been settled for the moment by the party as state, could be furthered, at least for such film artists as Eisenstein, only by articulating its immanent historical potential via cinematic possibility. Still, today, the ethical force of pathos as affective labor in Eisenstein's cinema remains to be brought alongside the ontological and epistemological dimensions of montage as "epistemophilia" or "figural philosophy."[46]

The concern with projecting a virtual streaming image in exhibition to be received as possible gesture is consistent across Eisenstein's theories of montage. Eisenstein's (now much-studied) rejoinder to Dziga Vertov's proposal of the Kino-Eye, for example, was what he called *The Strike*'s (1924) "cine-fist." The stylistics Eisenstein's cinema instantiates in each case from his earlier theater works through his late films demonstrate the variegation of his responses to historical tensions between aesthetic and political epistemologies. *The Strike* depicts a parable, set in 1912, of a wrongly accused worker who hangs himself, prompting workers' agitation and an ensuing strike. The eventual mass liquidation of the strikers depicted in the film conveys historical agitation for worker autonomy under the tsar in images of revolt against capitalists of the sort Vladimir Lenin invoked: The key sequences follow a boiling over of movement into organized, directed action. But the film also diagrams struggles taking place in the Soviet cultural sphere in 1924, the year of Lenin's death. Eisenstein's conflicts with the postrevolutionary Soviet institution for proletarian arts and culture, Proletkult, center on the rationale according to which the audience as mass receiver was conceived. Rather than a more geneticist account using adaptive means to educate through cultural production, *The Strike*'s montage insists on a teleological, instrumental, and interventionist account of reception. Eisenstein's notably intensified editing techniques—using an average of 379 edits per reel instead of the conventional 40 to 60 cuts and including corresponding shifting—dissociate perspectives.[47] *Strike*'s finale of dying workers intercut against shots of an abattoir is, then, the synthesis of a teleological aesthetics attempting to force the conveyance of a historical motive for the coherence of mass, laboring corporeality and agitating against developmental or otherwise adaptive deployments of mass culture. Contrarily, the breath gesture of *Nevsky* elicits a correspondence between contemporary Soviet audiences anxious about hostilities with Germany and the medieval Russian army awaiting the approaching Teutons on the frozen lake. Instead of the earlier, more instrumentalist gesture, this gesture is adaptive.

And as Joan Neuberger notes, Eisenstein's *Ivan the Terrible* is a "richly political" work; the montage of the film, including its development of the narrative thematics with the use of color as well as music, is worked out on the basis of inspiration from Russian icon paintings.[48] Central to the film is a dualism reflected in the highly visual narrative that Neuberger suggests Eisenstein developed from historical icons to illustrate the dialectical tensions inherent in *Ivan* as a "soul torn by contradictory impulses, a 'unity of opposites'" (385). Neuberger allows that these "dualisms" include dualisms of gender, such as androgyny or bisexuality, but cautions that in *Ivan,* these have more to do with a philosophical problem than with sexual affect as such. Yet the transcoding of philosophical problems into the affects of the ecstatic or the pathetic via a dynamically projected montage image with "richly political" meanings could hardly be restricted to philosophical implications. And thus here, too, the means of this transcoding immediately raise temporal concerns whereby musicality and gesturality become primary. Further, here, the tension between monadological temporalities and dialectical materialisms—that is, between Bergsonisms and Marxisms—is turned specifically toward the problem of the projection, exhibition, and reception of affect in musical and gestural terms. The archaic site where state identity is reproduced is rendered not in terms of essentialized, biological destiny but rather in terms of a tense relation between social exhibition and self-projection: circus and masquerade. This is a materialist, affective, sexed theory of differential technocultural reproduction.

Eisenstein designed the sequence of *Ivan the Terrible, Part Two* (1958) in which Ivan murders Vladimir Staritsky such that the lighting of the rotund set invokes a sense of the embryonic, with Prokofiev's music proceeding in a dramatic pulsing. Ivan was, as Joseph Stalin believed, the first to unify Russia and thus lent a historical rationale for the violence of his own regime.[49] And as Oksana Bulgakowa points out, *Ivan the Terrible, Part One* and *Part Two* were, Eisenstein knew,[50] a state assignment from Stalin to mythify his image, even while historical research had speculated about Ivan's homosexuality. In *Ivan,* then, the (historically) homosexual despot Ivan kills the feeble-minded effeminate usurper Vladimir as a gesture of traumatic, violent birth, not justifying state violence under Stalin, and not simply drawing a tragic figure according to the dialectical synthesis of opposites, but affirming a brutal profiling of homoaffectivity—that is, the range of affect according to which same-sex feelings relate personhood and publicity: homophobia, homosociality, homoeroticism, homosexuality, and homophilia. The black-and-white sequence in which Vladimir is fatally stabbed as he takes Ivan's place in a procession punctuated by rhythmic groans follows the previous scene, whose palette is designed in shades of red and is punctuated by a recurring bacchanale of dancing and drinking in which Ivan seduces Vladimir into believing in his own future destiny as tsar. Alternating circus with masquerade, *Ivan* depicts the complex homoerotic, homophobic violence at work in the historical installation of a legendary state image, which repeats in the modern biopolitical drama of the party as state.[51]

The montage transposition of circus into masquerade, of spectacular streaming image into a haptics of pathic gestural act, attributes Russian/Soviet identity to a perverse, traumatic, and repetitive political labor through which some dangerously undifferentiated homoaffective violence circulates. *Ivan* makes the action of Soviet-imperial unification *felt* in the audiovisual sequencing of slaughter birth, but in ambiguous conceptual terms. Bulgakowa notes that Stalin interpreted it as his recent murder of Nikolai Yezhov, the brutal chief of police. Eisenstein's stylization, then, unfolds homoerotic violence by virtue of the pathic cinematic act as a diagrammatic, dead-end gesture of uninterrogated homophobic violence grounding state power. As Eisenstein explains in *Nonindifferent Nature*, rather than a subject, a contrapuntal theme "uncoils" (340) in *Ivan*. His description of counterpoint here is not simply of musical form but of historical and cultural force fields The funeral scene in which Ivan grieves his wife's murder has a specific contrapuntal theme—"the theme of power" (324). If blood and sacrifice is immanent to the historicity pouring forth on Eisenstein's screens, looking for either a technological or a modernist vernacular leaves us blind to the pathic impulses and acts animating the works, differentiating the works from the dependencies that threatened them or, in other cases, that mutilated or destroyed them. The cultural labor producing transpositions of spectacular, haptic image into felt, concrete gesture, was, if perverse, perversely different from Stalin's politics: This stylistic of action feeling was achieved in an aesthetico-political mode rather than in the political one.

Eisenstein's revision of his thoughts in "Montage in 1938"[52] makes his tactics more clear than elsewhere in his writings. Composing sequenced or sequenced and layered materials in time, montage assembles "partial representations" not as "readymade," but so that a projected image "*comes into virtual being*" (77). Spectators, "included in the creative process," "concretize" this virtual image—that is, they may receive it in as a possible, pathic act.[53] The profilmic image serially recorded in the shot and cut into the sequence is *not* the image montage projects in exhibition. The image in exhibition is virtual and is made concrete in reception; its indexing of historical temporality is not the profilmic indexing of material reality in the photogram. Instead, montage's virtual image is an image "of the dynamic process" that does not project representation as seen by the director and captured by machine, but historical materiality as it "was experienced by the author [or director]" (77).

Montage projects immanent historicity before representing possibility for the audience. What transforms the virtual stream of projected imagery into possible concrete representation, affect into pathic gesture, is pathos, upon which Eisenstein insists throughout his writings. Eisenstein's montage thus produces reception as a site where two series, virtual and possible, are mutually disjoined and fused. The precipitation of a pathic act from the virtual streaming image maintains the director's experience in projection but fissures the director's experience from possible audience reception, inasmuch as it becomes generalized affective labor. Invariably, the director describes this fissuring and fusing of history in musical terms, such as rhythmic, lyrical, contrapuntal, and so forth.

Such directors as Eisenstein and Vertov, in spite of their polemics against one another during the mid-1920s, shared a need to justify to their state sponsors the value of their creative methods *and* of the questionable possibilities around the reception of their works. For both, montage expression provides claims about the generative merits of their creative labor. Vertov, like Eisenstein in "Vertical Montage" and *Nonindifferent Nature,* responds to the acclaim he garnered for *Three Songs about Lenin* (1934) by asserting the value of his general methods: "In [requiring exceptionally complex editing] the experience of *The Man with a Movie Camera, One-Sixth of the World,* of *Enthusiasm* and *The Eleventh Year* were of great help to our production group. These were, so to speak, 'films that beget films.'"[54] This socialist, socializing montage carries forward the revolutionary subject of history not fully within political or social orders, but in an aesthetico-political *mode* of Soviet production. At the same time, this modulation of adaptation and instrumentality suggests that the exhibition or audience of cinema is never fully and finally social. Montage cinema required an audience capable of quasi conduct: a virtual public sphere mandated by the force field organizing the possibilities of everyday life. Reconsidering Eisenstein in relation to political, social, cultural, and technological change means rethinking the relation of style and idiom to historical experience. Eisenstein reconsiders this relation by turning to musicality to mediate virtuality and possibility and to gesture to mediate creative and interpretive labor as pathos: The ecstatic aspect of Eisenstein's cinema is the successful case of *pathos* attaining an ethical force in reception.[55]

Eisenstein's depiction of the Odessa uprising is hardly literal in terms of historical record, geopolitical space, or identifications of energetic movement. Hearing the news of the 1905 mutiny, Lenin dispatched party agents to Odessa, but they arrived *after* the *Potemkin*'s mutineers had already left port after the massacre near the famed stairs dramatized in *Potemkin.* State telecommunications trumped Lenin's agents, and Lenin's subsequent understanding of the value for coalitions of workers and peasants during the period of world war, revolution, and civil war between 1914 and 1918 responded to his observation that "spontaneous" uprisings by nonpartisan worker Soviets could not finally effect a decisive seizure of power from even a weakened state. If "spontaneous" revolutionary struggle could not compete with capital's organizational command, the party form *itself* must find a more immediate logic by which to bring the lacking motive force of workers and peasants to a breaking point.[56]

Capitalist temporality as much as its abstraction of general labor had become central. Lenin's subsequent theories turned what had been treatments of immanent contradictions (tensions of capital and labor) into contradictory possibilities to be directed within and as party organization.[57] Sylvain Lazarus summarizes the shifts in Lenin's thought vis-à-vis the larger sequence of events: "History and politics are thus out of phase" for Lenin in 1917; shortly, the role of the revolutionary party would shift:

> Politics is charged with assuming its own thought, internal to itself. This is the condition for its existence, and it is also this point that requires the disjunctions. As we know, the Stalinist mechanism was quite different: circulation of notions between politics, philosophy, and history, the party no longer being the system of condition for politics but the real subject of all knowledge and decision. . . . [W]e enter a historicist problematic of politics in which the key word becomes *revolution*.[58]

In this transposition between governing toward the revolutionary event and governing the maintenance of the meaning of that event as the historical datum originating and validating the party's coherence, generalized socialist labor was split between adapting to actual needs and instrumentalizing futural outcomes.[59] The party became a national-imperial simulacrum of revolutionary workers' action, a simulacrum of which the labor of conducting the party itself stands as first exponent, the vanguard. The party displaced the interests of varied parties and classes or factions of workers, peasants, minorities, women,[60] and sexual minorities[61] with its own interests, while directing and shaping these corporealities' energies within a labor now generalized to produce excess. The revolution as event warranted the gap between actual adaptation and futural teleology, but by the end of the NEP years, it would be filled with programmatic industrialization according to technical means[62] along with a massive variety of programs designed to produce laboring excess: "reforging" criminals as laborers in the system of prison camps[63] shock labor; Stakhanovism, from the mid-1930s (159); or, starting at the end of the 1930s, the massive expenditure of generalized human labor in the industrialization and militarization required for war.[64] Overall, structuring general labor as excess allowed the maintenance of party metastability by enacting a division between the larger populace and the "pyramid of bureaucrats" who constituted party membership (numbering, by the 1930s, into the millions).[65] As the metastable party form increasingly mediated its own image of governmentality, the result was collectivization without individuation rather than the pursuit of industrialization through some never-identified collectivist individuation.[66] Dan Healey documents the ways in which these concerns and measures coincided with the recriminalization of homosexuality in 1934.

The process beginning with Lenin's dissolution of the constituent assembly in 1918 proceeded henceforth with centralization of political and media functions in or around the Bolshevik party apparatus. In the course of this large-scale transposition, Eisenstein trained in state workshops, including Meyerhold's workshop. That Eisenstein never held party membership while receiving (or being denied) state support points to the deeply entangled conditions for cultural and political labor that characterized his entire career.[67] In Eisenstein's or Vertov's cinemas, the material and affective labor of the directors and their collaborators tend to provide the energetic value, the "conviction" behind the "formalist delusions" such directors were sometimes believed to harbor.[68] Eisenstein's return to a style reminiscent of Meyerhold's theater, then, had illuminating implications.[69]

Circus and Masquerade

In his memoirs, Eisenstein recalls the bravado of the young artists' collective who joined him to mount *Enough Simplicity for Every Wise Man* at Proletkult in 1923, with Grisha Alexandrov starring in an acrobatized reconfiguration of the original play. He writes of revisiting the theater, but, instead of listening to the banter of a British official he accompanied, he reminisced about "a whole horde of young enthusiasts, on the very spot where we sit now, climbing no mountain with puritanical slogans, but up the slope of a cable to the balcony, turning somersaults on mats, making love to each other at night on roll-up carpets, under stage flats plastered with dried-up placards, and bringing into this very hall . . . a live camel to participate in one of my productions." Their labors unexpectedly birth "a camel!" in Eisenstein's retelling: the wild "reproduction" achieved by musicalizing precarious affective labor. An important point, however, is the implied subject of "making love." In this translation, Eisenstein is included within the horde of love-making artists; the Richard Taylor translation of this chapter in *Eisenstein at Ninety: A Celebration of the Life and Work of Sergei Eisenstein* allows a similarly ambiguous reading: "making love to one another under the drying posters for the sets."[70] A more recent English translation of this chapter excludes Eisenstein from the crowd by specifying a subject for this clause in the third-person plural: "They made love here at night, under the drying posters for the sets."[71]

An effect of our reception of Eisenstein as master of advanced technical art is that we are left to wade through a vast, partial archive of films, theories, and still emerging accounts to wonder about the reproductive power of Eisenstein's affective labor. Marie Seton early on raises this question in terms of sexuality and state power. More recently, Bulgakowa follows the conventional reasoning in attributing Eisenstein's often seemingly tortured logic or images to the creative sublimation of his homosexuality. This convention contains Eisenstein's deployment of the range of homoaffective exhibition with a psychosexual interpretation of a sad masquerade. Eisenstein thus functions as an avatar of new media even as he provides a virtual object of mourning in historical cinema and cultural studies marking a dead wish for political revolution entangled with a refusal to acknowledge queer affect as precarity. This tendency is most highly pronounced in readings of sublimation in the films.[72]

Susan Buck-Morss efficiently sums up the approach, finding that a sadomasochistic aesthetic pervades the imagery of a director "remarkably capable of sublimating desire into artistic creativity"; "but his own homoeroticism, for which Soviet society had no place, took the form of sadomasochism, thus paralleling the erotics of domination and submission generated by the power of Stalin's regime."[73] For Buck-Morss, Eisenstein's films sublimate sex but mirror the corporeal anguish of workers under Stalin's competition with capitalist industrialization where laboring excess formed the "underside of the monumentality of Stalinist style," "their ecstatic smiles expressing pleasure at physical pain."[74] Elsewhere, Buck-Morss describes "technology" as concretization of material, social relation. The result is that Eisenstein appears not to know the pathos he suffers, even as he forces it into spectacularly technical images of masochistic subjection. Buck-Morss reads against the very trope of the open secret Eisenstein proposes as a reading strategy for his autobiography, a trope he designed partly to not shame "the Americans."[75]

The need to not waste labor power in bourgeois or tribal excess *and* to deploy labor *to* excess to overcome underdevelopment in the historical articulation of party identity as class identity isomorphic to state identity meant particular investments with regards to affect and to homoaffectivity: the range of affects mediating same-sex personhood or publicity, from homophobia to homosociality to homoeroticism to homosexuality or homophilia. Individual corporealities, too, like social, cultural, or political programs, were reconsidered in terms of postrevolutionary energetics. Where all image or belief is granted a contingent power to reproduce, in fact, nonbiological corporeal reproduction becomes tactical and strategic, poetic and pragmatic. Viktor Shklovsky, returning to Moscow in 1924 after exile in Berlin, invokes public sex between men as the bioenergetic image of German decadence. Here, the concerns around masculinity and purity that Healey describes as instrumental in 1930s trials of men arrested after the recriminalization of homosexuality are projected as foreign impotence. Defeated German soldiers "fragment" into haunted homosexual *flanerie*; music overflows Berlin's cafés. Western capitalist powers divert Germany's resources as if picking the pockets of the desperate cocksuckers:

> *The old Germany has disintegrated.*
> *The fragments of the old army haunt cafes and indulge in pederasty.*
> *The streets are filled with terribly subdued cripples.*
> *Three hundred thousand Russians of various nationalities wander aimlessly in the cracks of a perishing city.*
> *The cafes are filled with music.*
> *An enclave of waiters and singers within a conquered nation.*
> *Meanwhile, in the dark public toilets of Berlin, men indulge in mutual onanism. They are suffering from a devalued currency and hunger; the country is perishing.*
> *And slowly, gobbling up the spoils, foreigners pass among them.*
> *The whole thing is simple—straightforward and elementary.*
> *Down with imperialism.*
> *Long live the brotherhood of peoples.*
> *If one must perish, let it be for that.*
> *Was it conceivably for this piece of knowledge that I journeyed so far?*[76]

Shklovsky's narrator barely avoids perishing.

By the time Eisenstein wrote his memoirs, homoaffect had become even more instrumental, in part through the recriminalization of homosexuality. Maxim Gorky would demonstrate the renewed values succinctly: "Destroy the homosexuals—Fascism will disappear."[77] Eisenstein, of course, celebrates Gorky in his essay "Montage in 1938" while working with Prokofiev on *Nevsky*. Eisenstein's writerly relations with Shklovsky or Gorky were a means of styling his modal practice of cinema in print, integral for sustaining crucial friendships, for winning back official support, or for successfully hiding Meyerhold's personal archive after his murder.[78]

That all artistic production was subject to state organization by 1921 and to central review and censorship by 1934[79] indicates that the party as state and cinema directors alike understood the liabilities and benefits of crafting a singular style in Soviet arts as well as the forms and limits of official style in the 1930s.[80] Eisenstein's exercise of power in his cinema productions resembles Stalin's political exercise of power, in one way—characteristically for Eisenstein, not by channeling Stalin's particular brand of governmentality but in the circulation of homoaffective labor. Stalin's subordinates resented him for making members of his inner circle engage in homoerotic slow dancing, a humiliating ritual about which one participant noted that these humiliations at least gave the dancers a chance to whisper comments in each other's ears that otherwise could not be spoken aloud at Stalin's drunken parties.[81] Eisenstein, too, was faulted for abuses of authority. Mikhail Nazvanov, who played Andrei Kurbsky in *Ivan,* commented, "Ever since his rough cut [of *Ivan the Terrible, Part One*] was enthusiastically received in Moscow, Eisenstein has become a complete boor. He yells at everybody. In the studio he is so inaccessible and so prickly that it has become unpleasant to talk to him. But that doesn't stop him from fawning over young men."[82]

A key difference between Eisenstein's montage and that of other Soviet montage directors is his structuring of the laboring excess demanded by postrevolutionary Soviet policy in the temporalized sign itself rather than in images of the power of the state. He mediated affective precarity to excess in the temporal diagram: in preproduction and production, in technical exhibition, in reception. In this excess, two topoi are doubled in fissioned, fused montage: Circus and masquerade emblematize the pathic gesture of Eisenstein's cinema in a Dionysian machine.[83] But I should stress that affective precarity takes precedence over any notion of machinic, desiring generativity. The excess of "circus": a rhythmic revelation of publicity whose energies overflow in a larger transposition. The excess of masquerade: a rhythmic revelation of personhood as affective precarity in some larger transposition. Eisenstein's doubled, Dionysian ensemble, rather than psychic sublimation, exhibits homoaffectivity not solely in terms of waste but rather as having profound historical meaning despite its improbable representation.[84]

Whether collaborating with such figures as Shklovsky or complimenting such figures as Gorky, Eisenstein develops methods for synthesizing rhythmic pathos drawing on exemplars provided by Mayakovsky, Lev Kuleshov, or Meyerhold. Eisenstein elaborates the rhythmic exemplars of Mayakovsky's constructivist poetry or Meyerhold's biomechanics in an expressive musical gesture for the at once living and nonliving, material and streaming imagery of the montage cinema. In Meyerhold's experiments with precision synchronized ensemble movement, Eisenstein encounters a rigorous theorization of corporeal, verbal, and dramaturgic pulse and line within dramatic theatrical narrative aimed at an active audience. Eisenstein viewed Meyerhold's *Masquerade* in 1917.[85] Demobilized from the Red Army and having worked a short stint as scenic director for Proletkult, Eisenstein joined Meyerhold's workshop in 1921. In Meyerhold's conception, biomechanical dramatic method enables the conceptual parameterization of stage movement according to a supratemporal compositional scheme. Biomechanical diagramming enables, then, rhythmic modulation of dramatic movement and audience states, such as calm or excitement, as if by "pressing a button," as Eisenstein's early collaborator in Meyerhold's workshop, Sergei

Yutkevich, later recalled:[86] "It was interesting to observe how this born improviser would teach us a system in which for every execution no coincidence might arise."[87]

Meyerhold insisted on knowing "how to act 'with the music,' and not 'to the music.' There is a colossal and not yet completely understood difference."[88] In this context, Yutkevich and Eisenstein set Pierrot's bohemian revolt against the capitalist taskmaster-as-automaton to jazz rhythms, with costumes inspired by those Pablo Picasso designed for Jean Cocteau's *Parade* (1916–1917): Such were the elements assembled in the pair's theatrical production of *Columbine's Garter* (1922).[89] Although Wollen[90] cites Yutkevich as evidence of a problematic Americanism placing the younger Eisenstein at odds with the postrevolutionary context, Yutkevich remembers that while riding the American-style roller coaster Wollen mentions, he and Eisenstein would scream out verses by Mayakovksy.[91] While the influences explored by the two collaborators (and many other of their contemporaries) included a wide array of postromantic staging theories[92] or musical correspondence theories such as those of Alexander Scriabin, Meyerhold's emphasis on biomechanical rhythm, Vertov's or Kuleshov's montage experiments, and Mayakovsky's rhythmic appropriation of "unliterary" advertising, musical hall, or satirical news[93] for poetry provided the immediate contacts in the postrevolutionary context.[94] Rhythmic and lyrical diagramming pushed Eisenstein's cinema aesthetics forward: "Thus [in *Battleship Potemkin*] as the sail of the passing ships slowly closes in the aperture, so the wound-up sails on the yawls announce the beginning of a new, so-to-say musical phrase. The pilgrimage of the people on the jetty to the dead body of Vakulinchuk begins"; or again, in the celebrated sequence of the stone lions in *October*, "rage and vengeance" arise in the most dramatic rhythmic intersection of the film's action.[95]

These contacts are important to reestablish, because, as Yutkevich points out, in the Soviet context, Eisenstein's *Potemkin* would be confused with "factographic" or "historical films," of a piece with Vertov's Kino-Eye—or, as I have shown, seen as the revelatory sheen on the technological surface serving state power from abroad. Whether as historical document or as technological surface or notation, immanence is confused with information. Yutkevich argues, though, that shaping the "immanence of montage art" (380) in terms of the "informing rhythm" of "revolutionary pathos" (382) results in effective, agitational art: "What is distinguished in the staging of these films lies directly in that from all fundamental situations much humanism shines out, and man is seen to be found not in a 'mechanical world,' but in one of men" (374).

Eisenstein could not easily adduce in any predictable or repeatable way the operative principles for recreating earlier achievements.[96] On one hand, vast art historical impulses may come to inform the construction of cinematic event streams in this musicalized principle of montage—a powerful capacity in a time out of joint. On the other, new efforts at continuing this modal cinema's mediation of international cinema and the state image also upended Eisenstein's own practices, requiring him to transform them. The rhythmic parameters of montage are charmed: musical mediation of an unstable aesthetico-political relation; affective precarity excessive to general informatic law; circus and masquerade, personhood and publicity.[97]

The range of homoaffective positions that Eisenstein compounds as pathos marking the powerful production of affective precarity in his gesture of resistance to the image of party as state was lived in the *byt* as a marked form of resistant and public sexual relation punished in irregular ways by the party as state, as Healey documents.[98] Eisenstein's montage diagrams a modal cinema in which the stylization of an aesthetico-politics of pathic gesture counterpoints sovereign governmentality. His cinema projects its displaced working publics in the expression of negentropic labor as historical and transformative rather than simply presenting what appear to be cinematic representations of important historical dates, figures, or events. In *October* (1928), as Anne Nesbet describes, an actor's portrayal of Lenin risks demythifying Lenin's historical personage.[99] In *The Strike,* NEP values are battled; in *Potemkin,* heroism is overlaid on images of sailors conforming to homoerotic ideals; or instrumentality of collectivization programs is upended as villages are modernized but also retraditionalized, as in *Old and New,* where Marfa, the progressive village maid, is masculinized, inseminating and fertilizing the sleepy superstitious backwardness of her village via the new technology of the cream separator and dreams of a traditionally festooned bull.

In Eisenstein's failures to complete film projects—*¡Que Viva Mexico!* (1932) or *Bezhin Meadow* (1937)—we also discern violent conjunctures and disjuncture around the politicization of affective labor and aesthetico-political form after the more genetic policies of the NEP period gave way to the more instrumental policies of the 1930s. *¡Que Viva Mexico!* is a case in point. Its sweeping panoramic portrait of autochthonous Mexican history could hardly have been amenable to more intensively instrumentalized central planning. Further, complicating matters were Upton Sinclair's naiveté regarding funding a feature film and, as Nesbet and Bulgakowa document, controversies around Eisenstein's sexual conduct in Mexico during its making. Sinclair viciously uses news of Eisenstein's homosexual activities in Mexico against the director in his correspondence with Stalin in disputes over the footage after the production had been dissolved.[100] In this case, Eisenstein's modal cinema works at counterpurposes to U.S. regimes of bioenergetic knowledge as well.

Affective precarity as gendered, sexed pathos refracts in the archived remains of *¡Que Viva Mexico!* The film's epilogue, edited differently in distinct versions of the film compiled, when viewed along with Eisenstein's plans for the film, speaks to the reservoir of value produced in Eisenstein's modal cinema methods and utilized by others who have edited the footage. This conclusion was to be a "Soldaderas" segment dramatizing the women who had trailed Mexico's revolutionary armies in 1910. What remains of the footage suggests that this finale depicts the unresolved and immanent contradictions of contemporary Mexico in terms of women's histories and realities but also in relation to the film's initial invocations of matriarchal traditions and local historical variations in sexual customs.

The footage of this final sequence[101] features vibrant images of Day of the Dead festivities. After an extraordinary series of masked dancers shimmy in skeleton costumes before a Ferris wheel, a young girl takes a healthy bite out of a candied skull—the Mexican equivalent, perhaps, of shouting out Mayakovsky verses while riding a roller coaster. Circus, masquerade, the young girl's sugary snack: a future yet to be metabolized concretely but virtually presented as immanent, historical rhythm.[102] Eisenstein's version of Mexico's history begins with matriarchy and fond glances between young peasant men but ends with a young girl snacking on death, invoking the given, historical possibility of revolution and the pathos actualized in the becoming historical of its virtual duration—that is, its future lies in transforming the past dancing in the present.

In Eisenstein's films, corporeal characteristics denote affective correspondences developing over time, subject to modulation in network effects: inhibition, excitation, distribution, catastrophe, reformation—a circus and masquerade of pathic expression. Individual bodies diagram enfleshed affective labor where aesthetico-political exhibition mixes virtual temporality through representational possibility. What is communicated is affective precarity in transformation: Bodies proliferate in masses or die in succinct configurations, but not strictly according to their sexed, gendered capacities to reproduce. Bodies break apart or come together in rhythmic, pathic effects; complex temporality becomes sensible; the conditions of political being are transformed into aesthetico-political being. Rhythm or lyrical line as musical energy makes the generation of affiliation in affect primary rather than the reproduction of cognition of kinship.

Musicalizing pathos means that the sacrificial valiance of *Potemkin*'s heroic mutineer, Vakulinchuk, is redeemed in mass mourning, but, then again, it is also compounded in the bloody massacre of the mourning masses on the steps. The homoaffectivity of the sailor as type is not recouped as individual sacrifice but is rather redeemed in a temporal sequencing of yet greater excess demonstrating undeniable historical motive—that is, the ostensive, affective cause for and conditions of the revolution and civil war. Or, again, in *Nevsky*, the woman warrior Vasilisa, named the most valiant fighter of Russia's battle with the Teutons, is for a split second awarded the virgin bride whose pure body is the sacrifice promised to the soldier drawing the most blood. Only as a slight necessary adjustment does the bride get reoriented toward one of the male clowns who also fought bravely. Marriage is an aftereffect, adjusted for appropriate ends within networked mass personhood. *Nevsky* concludes according to the socialist-realist telos of conventional Stalinist family values, but in the modal cinema diverging from official values, the woman warrior is named, for a pregnant, confused instant, as the winner of the bride's blush.[103] For a moment, the circus mask of homoaffectivity is brandished in relief from socialist-realist instrumentalities.

Even when struggling to maintain his capacities and status as state artist, Eisenstein commingles circus and masquerade in the pathos of hiding in plain sight: "I do not look for help. But what I find I do not hide; I bring it out into the open—in lectures, books, magazines, newspapers. And . . . did you know, the most effective way of hiding something is to put it on display?"[104] Circus and masquerade provide rhythmic, energetic modes of presenting precarious affect as deeply productive, deeply memorial pathos: a temporal resource for stylizing a diagrammatic production of everyday life as cinematic time.

Critical Tools for Modal Media

Eisenstein's cinema gives us a key, critical stylistics of synchronization where immanence and information animate aesthetico-political transformations, and key critical tools as well. First, Eisenstein's cinema was more significant for demonstrating the differential reproduction of precarious, affective labor—pathos—rather than technical reproducibility. Second, Eisenstein's stylization of a modal cinema diverging from other national cinemas and from official Soviet aesthetics indicates the theory and practice of a modal cinema, an ethical practice relating historicity and contemporaneity, personhood and publicity. Third, each work in this modal series is instantiated according to a developing stylistics for synchronizing compositional and receptive labor, requiring some suprarepresentational or complex temporality opened up in the instance of reception, provided by rhythm or music. The orchestration of monistic and dialectical potentiality elucidates an energetic thematics of biopower in musicalized pathos rather than projecting a unified historical subject. Fourth, such modal media evinces the ethical force of a time-based work as we identify its theoretical and pragmatic stylistic divergence.

These conceptual tools will help clarify the ways that other stylistics of synchronization developed in other musical cinemas, which also may be obscured within logics of medial succession. In Chapters 3 and 4, I extend this analysis of the stylistics of synchronized streaming media to two additional cases. In Chapter 3, I show how Fischinger's stylization of visual music deploys musicality to express the sense of an ecstatic futurity for time-based media. In Chapter 4, I show the ways in which Eisler's stylization of film music deploys film scoring to defer any historical pathos or futural ecstasy attributable to the media apparatus back toward the present site of reception—that is, to the listening audience.

Stylizing audiovisual synchronization to express affective labor as history, as future, as present: These are the three classical stylistics of audiovisual synchronization. Each case study isolates what are more commonly the mixed temporal inflections of streaming media, whereby mass personhood and mass publicity are expressed.

If Eisenstein's musical montage stylized cinema as a bioenergetic idiom, how have montage style or other classical stylistics of audiovisuality been reworked in bioinformatic cinemas? The chapters on Larry Clark's *Passing Through* (1977), John Cameron Mitchell's *Hedwig and the Angry Inch* (2001), and Steina Vasulka's video work each provide answers. However, Eisenstein's approach also prompts another question I can only raise: If new means often justify critical ends, whereby changes in technological medium become representative of radical transformations in labor, affect, politics, history, and personhood, then what practices might relate personhood and publicity in properly political—that is, democratic—terms? Beginning to answer this question does not require that we transpose Eisenstein's montage to our own time, but rather that we relate our own conflicted moment to his.

3

For Love of Music

Oskar Fischinger's Modal, Musical Diagram

"My Statements Are in My Work"
—Title of short essay by Oskar Fischinger in 1947 Art in Cinema catalog

Visual Music as Style and Idiom

Throughout Oleg Kovalov's *Sergei Eisenstein: Autobiography* (1998), a veritable catalog of modernist experimental cinemas is edited into a quasi-historical semifictional account of Sergei M. Eisenstein's travels through industrial modernity. Fragments from Dudley Murphy and Fernand Léger's *Ballet mécanique* (1924) or Oskar Fischinger's *Liebesspiel* (*Love Games*; 1931) are cut into the work, suggesting that Eisenstein's montage is a way of seeing modernisms as much as or more than the creative response to postrevolutionary Soviet modernity the director himself describes in his own writings. Here, long marginalized by art histories of the modernist avant-garde, visual music becomes a kind of flowering patch on the modernist aesthetic horizon, but only from within that perspective where montage produces cinema as the pathos of personal and cultural memory.

In a diametrically opposed rendering, excerpts from such works as Fischinger's *Radio Dynamics* (1942), along with an entire archive of other visual music animators, appear sampled, processed, and repurposed in the digital video of a mash-up artist whose work is presented in a U.S. university course on "open source" aesthetics. The course blog describes the artist's methods in the following way: "Fake data or real data, surveillance cameras or internet spy software, in the end, [this artist] is tracking the vibe of the interface itself."[1] The visual music canon this artist mashes up in his often-collaborative work might amount to, in that description, "fake data," appropriated historical resources going unattributed in the videos' credits. Here, media of the past become a kind of historical noise open for reinterpretation and resale by "new media artists" stylizing the "vibe" of the interface to demonstrate digital media's apparently unfettered historical and creative power.

These contrary and contemporary uses of visual music animation summarize the degree to which montage permeates modernist aesthetic production (in Kovalov, even visual music becomes montage) on the one hand, or the ways in which "new media" art often grounds its own medium specificities by appropriating, while denying, those of "old" media art (classical visual music sampled to represent "the vibe" of the interface) on the other. But they also present two crucial historical problems. First, however much they mischaracterize the historical sources they appropriate, still, neither characterizes visual music cinema in the conventional terms by virtue of which visual music has been marginalized in histories of the avant-garde: as an attempt to render the forms and meanings of the animated screen musical in some way; as a modern and industrial recapitulation of neo-Pythagorean philosophies or color organs; as an attempt at modeling synesthetic experience in technical forms; and as speculative, pure, or visionary cinema. Rather, visual music animation appears as a kind of historical evidence somehow exceptional and mundane, a given of mediatic invention and reinvention that requires no account.

Additionally, these examples prompt our notice of the protean capacities the visual music cinemas offer for appropriation, receiving continuous acclaim *and* formal neglect in a wide range of academic histories and theories of cinema and the historical avant-gardes.[2] Appropriations of visual music animation for the purpose of historicizing or characterizing a new medium are hardly original. As I note in my introduction, in the 1940s, work by Fischinger or John and James Whitney was cited as evidence for far more than technicized synesthesia or some postindexical moment when the expressive capacities of time-based media were liberated, a moment from which everything can be transcoded. Before being intensively studied in Silicon Valley for lessons in interaction design during the 1990s, Fischinger's work served as a model for resolving the chicken-and-egg problems of new medium specificities and the complex historical relation of emergent technologies to dominant and residual ones during the 1940s and 1970s. The 1940s was a period when audiovisual production was broadening to include preparations for early television as well as increasing fidelity in sound production, including stereo exhibition. Fischinger's and the Whitneys' work, as well as Walt Disney's *Fantasia* (1940), are either cited or ostensively referenced in articles grappling with these expansions in such journals as *Hollywood Quarterly* as well as in the archival documents of Hanns Eisler's Film Music Project (see Chapter 4). In my introduction, I point out the ways in which Gjon Mili's *Jammin' the Blues* (1944) provided Carl Beier[3] with a model for "conducting" the new medium of television as improvisational multimedia performance. Ralph Potter[4] reasons that since the work of contemporary "animationists" (Fischinger, Mary Ellen Bute, Len Lye, the Whitney brothers, Disney, and Norman McLaren) developed from earlier efforts by Walter Ruttmann, Viking Eggeling, or Eggeling and Hans Richter to achieve the fusion of sound and image in a synthetic "music," applying aesthetic insights to that development might be more effective for deploying "audivisual music" for the mass audiences of film and television "at once" and as "rule," rather than as exception (69). Technological development programs, Potter thinks, would be too long and drawn out. His reasoning is partly based on what he sees as common principles whereby musicality had been graphed in a wide range of image types: filmstrips by the Whitneys; an image automatically derived from musical sound in Cecil Stokes's Auroratone process; samples of "bird song motion" from a spectrum analyzer; and spectrograms of cymbal clashes and violin tones. Potter, like many before and after, thinks Fischinger's musical synchronization of audience with the exhibition of sound with image expressed new capacities to visualize sound. The term "audivisual music" confuses Fischinger's visual music animation with scientific visualization of sound rather than seeing it as achieving a higher-order continuity for the temporalities of reception.

If visual music cinema during this period was often seen as successful artistic expression of processes enabled by sound visualization rather than as musical expression in its own right, this confusion arose because of a presumption of convergent media practices enabled by deploying new technologies as new media: Potter is proposing visual music cinema for television as well as cinema. At the same time, Potter's proposal also foresees programming capacities for television to "visualize" those typical of more established, commercial-radio practices and the more marginal but nonetheless historically important practices associated with the modernist avant-gardes of the 1920s. Fischinger's preeminence in that context, though, goes unacknowledged: Potter describes him as a contemporary, even though artists Potter mentions (Lye, McLaren) describe him as an inspiration.

As Beier's or Potter's articles suggest, the production processes of visual music animation and jazz improvisation provided ways of thinking through new processes of creative labor amid technological and media transition: ways of retaining innovative aesthetic expression while engaging new "improvisational" modes of creative labor composing streaming media in technology intensive workflows. Beier's notion of the television director as improvisational conductor or Potter's analysis of workable approaches to synchronizing sound and image to create a fused "audivisual music" indicate then-emergent problems for television as programmed *and* live production. New production processes needed to arrange and to modulate a broad number of workers and processes in time, and television's material conditions and aesthetic limits for future audiences were unclear; visual music or jazz shorts described temporal processes and, further, emphasized the affective and improvisatory effects at which Beier and Potter think television should aim.

Similarly, the increasing availability of microelectronics during the late 1960s and early 1970s allowed such artists as Stephen Beck to engineer "color sound" processing equipment, allowing "real-time" manipulation of a synthetic audiovisual stream. Here, too, historical documents indicate, was the familiar goal of a musical animation of a new apparatus. An unpublished 1969 proposal by Beck to the Zenith Corporation[5] identifies "new uses for color television"; a 1976 San Francisco *Examiner* article gives an overview of Beck's subsequent work. Having received a grant to collaborate with Jordan Belson on the film *Cycles* in 1974, at the time the article appeared, Beck was working on "a dozen TV games [that is, video games] for National Semi-Conductor Corporation."[6]

The *Examiner* report characterizes Beck's electronic-imaging equipment as updating Belson's mechanical and optical approaches. Beck's references to "sound color" art are accompanied by citations of "force," Eastern philosophy, and the proposal of a more immediate conjunction between authorial composition and audience reception: The terms he uses differ, but the themes are significant. Beck cites Fischinger as a historical source, along with Wassily Kandinsky and Pablo Picasso: This "video music television" is presented as a second, electronic modernism. The article thus attempts to clarify the broader applications now apparent: "Imagine weaving your own textile patterns on the [television] tube. Imagine the games people could play." As in Beier's and Potter's hopes for a more improvisational mode of communicating information as music during the 1940s, Beck's proposal to Zenith emphasizes technical, artistic, and educational aims, while his comments in the *Examiner* article and elsewhere make clear the motives of uplift and regeneration as well. The rhetoric of a musical negentropy tropes on informatic entropy—the larger dream of cosmos-creating musical energy informing the informatic cavern of musical sense and sensation visualized in Ib Melchior's *The Time Travelers* (1964) by virtue of Fischinger's hand-animated Lumigraph color-light instrument.

Beck's performance of electronic color music on PBS in the San Francisco Bay Area in 1974 and his reported intent to create color music in computer games revisit and project forward the dream of color music as a mode of innovating industrial-art practices, updating Beier's and Potter's articles invoking Mili's *Jammin'* or Fischinger and the Whitneys as conceptual prototypes for the new medium of broadcast television conceived as musical programming in the broad sense. Visual music in these accounts appears as ahistorical and futural; it seems somehow indiscriminately present, a familiar achievement of modernist aesthetics that is as yet technologically unfulfilled, a still-to-be concretized new medium awaiting its avatar. These repetitions confirm that visual music animation offers more than simply visualizing temporal rhetorics and metaphors deriving from musical epistemologies, studies of synesthesia or empathic gestalt, or an archaic history of color organs updated in motion graphics and computer animation. Visual music is a mode of stylizing the futural capacities of the cinema's instrumentalities—or those of television or of digital gaming.

Taken together, these examples of visual music practice and the documents of its reception begin to clarify a complex historical problem. Much more than a visualization of musical metaphor or the technical translation of psychological, phenomenal, or perceptual states, visual music animation appears as the historical font and futural horizon of a three-part problem of technique, affect, and ethics in periods of new media transition. In Beier's 1940s proposal, visual music animation requires animating not simply the framed image but to a large degree the entire production process; Beck, who did in fact produce attractive electronic pattern tapes, developed equipment that might have helped automate and rationalize such a speculative reorganization of time-based media, if it had ever come to that. But why should such a painstakingly specialized practice as visual music animation be invoked as a proposal for animating the very processes according to which the possibility of a new medium becomes a historical realization?

Potter's citations of Fischinger or Beier's citations of the jazz soundie are significant: The ontologies, epistemologies, and ethics of jazz and visual music animation had to do with modulating a continuous expression animating a block of immanent time. As the diagrammatic scores of theatrical plays that Fischinger produced in 1921 and 1922 suggest, his work was more concerned with submitting the technics of framing and the graphic capacities of cinematic space to an energetic and affective understanding of time. One early graphical score of Shakespeare's *Twelfth Night* presents organically flowing pencil gestures rolling more smoothly or more turbulently from left to right, aiming to depict the musicality of the larger succession of theatrical movements[7] rather than, as in Vsevolod Meyerhold's biomechanical diagramming,[8] the motor gestures of actors and their coordination with scenic space and props.

If that diagram depicts, as William Moritz suggests, "the changing moods, flow of emotion, intensity, style, flourish of the ideas, and the experience created by the process of the action,"[9] these are first and foremost expressed as temporalities rather than as spatial or objective elements. No localized positions are given in the graphical score, only a global overview of the moods, emotion, intensity, style, ideas, and experience of the work, sketched as graphical intensities scrolling along and above the bar lines. Energetic temporal intensities pulse and touch above the musical lines, animating the notational space.

What Fischinger sought, suggests Moritz, was a new language of dynamic visual form that, in ways similar to musical form, might transcend particular languages and cultures.[10] Although much is "new" about any one of Fischinger's films, perhaps what is "newest" today is his exploration of musical and visual form in a body of work that encompasses what constitutes the three-limit cases

FIGURE 3.1 Oskar Fischinger's *Motion Painting No. 1* (1947): Laboratory scan. (Copyright © Fischinger Trust. Courtesy of the Center for Visual Music.)

for synchronized audiovisual works. Fischinger studiously produced, using the rhetorics and motives of musical form as an analog, what might be considered a set of prototypes for synchronized motion in multiple media. His work may be divided into these three types: silent works, presenting only the image as music (such as *Liebesspiel* or *Radio Dynamics*); tightly synchronized sound works presenting the image in musical synchronization (such as *Allegretto* [1936] or *An Optical Poem* [1937]); and sound works only very loosely synchronized, or synchronized in nonlinear correspondences, between sound and image (such as the early *R-1* [1927] or the late *Motion Painting No. 1* [1947; Figure 3.1], although this last film was painted to and retains as its sound track Bach's third *Brandenburg Concerto*).[11]

Yet Fischinger's is not a cinema of language or of montage, but of pulsing, material duration. Joseph Fourier's development of what would become harmonic analyses during the early nineteenth century revealed nature as a teeming reserve of inexhaustible energy, as Anson Rabinbach[12] explains; modern time-based media are the biopolitical means of technical reproduction specific to the revelation of a unified electromagnetic spectrum. Thus, from Italian Futurism to digital media, the temporal materialities composed in visual music animation correspond to the epistemologies of electromagnetic phenomena known since Fourier, extending them to an Einsteinian worldview, where, after Werner Heisenberg, the observer is assumed to help create the phenomena he or she observes. As Fischinger states in the catalog issued by the film festival where *Motion Painting No. 1* took first prize in 1949: "The film isn't 'cut,' it is a continuity, the absolute truth, the creative truth. Any observer can verify that, and I consider myself an observer."[13] Fischinger's visual music cinema does not aim at animating semiotic elements within either the frame or according to some perfectible notational schema informed by notions of musical performance. Rather, it submits shot structure and compositional space to an energetic temporality that is brought into pulsing contact with the meter of the filmstrip. Classical visual musical animation expresses the modulating pulse of an energetic block of time.

In this chapter, I attempt to clarify what Fischinger might have meant when insisting that his statements are contained in his work. While recent curatorial practice has recognized Fischinger as part of a broader avant-garde practice than what Peter Bürger's description[14] accounts for, Fischinger's work is still routinely appropriated, if not for montage history or digital art's specificity, then for theories of synesthesia, musical meaning and technical advance in synchronized arts, or alternative modes of documentation—roughly the range of thematics proposed in two large-scale exhibitions on Visual Music (Hirshorn/MOCA Los Angeles) and Sons et Lumières (Centre Pompidou) in 2004 and 2005. These recent approaches only begin to compete, though, for the vast reception of Fischinger's work since his death, although generally on a small scale. Moritz[15] points out that screenings of his work continued immediately following Fischinger's death; my own review of more than 150 reviews, essays, commentaries, screening notices, or other documents spanning roughly the early 1970s to the present, in trade newspapers and journals from Germany, France, the United States, and the U.K., reveals that Fischinger's work has been in constant circulation and an object of comment, mostly without sustained focus or analysis. In that time, in fact, Fischinger's work has become a constant touchstone for essayistic approaches wondering how the narrative film and film music might be improved or how the expression of musical ideas in cinema might be more meaningfully executed. Visual music, as a result, has become not so much a genre of cinema but an everyday hermeneutic, as well as a mode of stylizing particular relations of affect, visuality, audition, musicality, and history. Fischinger tends to be the name that anchors a broad and popular notion of musical expression in the moving image.

If art institutions have recently and increasingly acknowledged Fischinger's work as occupying a central place within the twentieth-century arts of painting, animation, and cinema, this acknowledgment is partly because of interest in visualized musical expression prompted by the central and long historical marketing function fulfilled by cinematic narrative thematizing musical epistemologies, sound-track recordings, and musical promotion clips, and because of a more recent rise of alternative moving image formats particular to the nightclub, DJ/VJ performance, or interactive work. Fischinger's work has been "performed"—that is, remixed, usually without permission or acknowledgement—in performances for DJs of international stature at locations ranging from a recent installment of the Coachella Music Festival (2008) to small scale rave-type settings, where it has long been in rotation with computer-graphics mix tapes in chill-out rooms. Additionally, electronic and digital forms have easily appropriated the mantle of a populist avant-garde since approximately 1980. Video games, Internet-working (and, later, Web-working), or electronic music releases and events have become critical sites of aesthetico-political contestation because of their very proximity to, and capacity to represent, the investments of technocratic capital, and because of their interests in the meanings of instrumental action and intensively mediated affect. Finally, however, these digital cultural forms' explicit interests in problems of technical synchronization also emphasize the ways that expressive attempts at synchronizing digital cultural forms, digital distribution, and the affective production of sense by networked masses of receivers articulates a goal still *not* resolved in digital technologies, contrary to their claims of "real-time" eventuality: that of the fully programmable and participatory audio-visual-gestural synchronization of the expression of affect. In fact, synchronization technologies lack significantly all around, from network access—where broadband access to Web-based materials is uneven and unreliable, depending on such factors as local traffic or Web providers' configurations of consumer services—to rapid introduction of changing hardware platforms, where significant expressive resources for flexible synchronization of sound, vision, and gesture may barely be fleshed out at all. As designer Erik Loyer has remarked of his work designing "Opertoons" for the Apple iPhone, many of his efforts were frustrated because such mobile devices are often released with very limited capacities for programmable, precise, and variable synchronization of audio, visual, and gestural streams.[16] The popular *Guitar Hero* series and the automatic frequency and rhythm analyzer, which come standard with digital music players, are not the end of the line; indeed, they are more simply statements of the meanings of "visual music" as a problem of everyday hermeneutics for or stylization of uses of time as material. And although *Fantasia*'s debt to Fischinger is well known, we should also note the industrial, vernacular appeals to visual music or vernacular homage to Fischinger routinely appearing in U.S. cinema since the commercialization of computer graphics: If Steven Spielberg's color organ finale in 1977's *Close Encounters of the Third Kind* (one of the first Hollywood feature films to attempt integration of computer-graphics animation with the live-action image) is too general to be a citation, perhaps *Wall-E*'s (2008) love duet between two robots soaring through space, their exhaust trails recapitulating the glowing trails of Fischinger's *Liebesspiel,* will be allowed. In all these ways, from everyday interface to computer-graphics entertainment to challenges for further advance in interactive synchronization technologies, visual music as style and idiom is recognized as having a newly historical role to play, if for no other reason than digital technologies have much to improve when it comes to providing sophisticated synchronization techniques for expressive audiovisual and gestural streams. But if visual music is an idiom and a style, what does it say, and how does it say it? These preliminary observations, then, only beg the question: "What statements are in Fischinger's work?"

Cinema as Block of Time

Fischinger's *Wachsexperimente* (*Wax Experiments*; 1927) produced striking organic and atmospheric effects, unfurling chromium roses or turbulent clouds by slicing away and filming in stop-motion the surface of a block of wax molded to produce dynamic textures when projected.[17] *München-Berlin Wanderung* (*Walking from Munich to Berlin*; 1927) subjects a geographical region to treatment as a block of time, an early exemplar, as Moritz[18] points out, of the later flicker film. In his tightly synchronized promotional films for Electrola Records from the late 1920s and early 1930s, Fischinger used a slide rule to measure the phonographic spiral and thus calculate a common time base for the prerecorded music and the image track to be animated; the time base he calculated existed above and beyond the meter of the filmic and phonographic spirals.

More than parametrically synchronizing sound and image, Fischinger's cinema depended on working out a higher-order temporal stream. Yet it also coincided with attempts in fine-art and critical-philosophical contexts of his period to rework the ways in which contemporaneity and historicity might be measured. We are more likely to find the reflexively political avant-gardism sought by such critics as Bürger[19] in the later, more overtly political films of Hans Richter. Richter's painting and film work displays a tendency toward universalist nominalism that comprised one strain of modernist avant-garde practice; Fischinger's focus on energetic radiance emphasizes musical affect over logical information in pursuit of a not entirely dissimilar interest. In his German Constructivist paintings and films, Richter works out actual prototypes for the universal language that, he explains in a manifesto written with Eggeling, illustrates the "possibility of a language above and beyond all national language frontiers."[20]

Richter and Eggeling invoke musical strategy in their paintings and early film work to articulate an internationalist and constructivist symbolic system with revolutionary potential. Musical titles indicate the formal inspiration and the tentativeness of their achievements: Richter's 1919 painting *Präludium* shows compact and solid black and white lines and rectangles at lower left generating through increasing tension a metamorphosis that produces their opposite: lightly rendered, elongated rising rectangles at upper right, bounded by arcing curves. Music here is both inspiration and objective, but distant. Film brought it closer by concretizing the temporality that the paintings and drawings suggest. For *Rhythmus 21, Rhythmus 23,* and *Rhythmus 25* (all composed between 1921 and 1925, although Richter is believed to have backdated his works of this period in a bid for historical primacy), Richter orchestrates geometric shapes in time, attaining in film form what could be suggested only in static painting. Avant-gardists, such as Richter, recognized revolutionary Soviet aesthetic achievements. The goal of international intelligibility through abstraction was explicitly a political one: Soviet Constructivism was seen as the "expression of an optimism which swept the public along with it and promised to grant artists in the most free, abstract development a new, functional place in society. A rare moment in the history of a people, in which the efforts of government and people, artists and those who commission their works, are identical."[21]

The notion that a graphical language might learn from music ways to speak of whole, identitarian relations between self and society retains as a central concern the problematic of the constitution of the audience. I suggest in the next chapter that it is precisely the formation of the cinema audience as an emergent class of networked, mass collectivity that underlies this tendency. In any case, for Richter or Fischinger, it appears that a listening knowledge that is believed to bear universal meanings was found possible in the cinema and was prototyped on the model of music. For Richter, the move to film grants a way of gaining the temporality that this dynamic language seems to need. At the same time, the difficulty of animating graphics musically questions notions of parallelism and synchronization between visuality and musicality. This central problematic of musicality in film, as well as its perceived promise of universal intelligibility, was established almost a decade before synchronized sound tracks would become viable.

Before Fischinger, Richter made advertising films for Muratti cigarettes,[22] and, just as Richter's work does, Fischinger's visual music animation raises the intertwined questions about a universal intelligibility perceived to be possible through musicalized abstraction. But important differences have to be drawn out here: Fischinger went from engineering to film and ended by painting musical abstractions, unable to afford the cost of filmmaking. Throughout his career, he achieved innovations in the creation of special effects and the construction of apparatus for executing them for Germany's Universum Film AG (UFA) as well as for Metro Goldwyn Mayer (MGM), Paramount, and Disney Studios in Hollywood.[23] On the other hand, Richter was originally trained as a carpenter and committed to internationalist politics, successively championing constructivist idealism during the rise of the fascists, the values of surrealist subversion, and, after his move to the United States, documentary filmmaking as exemplified by the Soviets or the Italian neorealists (although his experience of Dadaist aesthetic anarchism remains part of the creative contexts of his evolving work). But more than simply their distinct talents and achievements, Richter's notes for a "Document of Universal Language" demonstrate the key difference between Fischinger's treatment of cinematic time in terms of immanence as opposed to Richter's treatment of cinematic time in terms of information.

Richter's annotated sketches on paper are essentially a study of elements for, and a key to, the more finished scrolls Richter and Eggeling were creating to be filmed. This work comprises pages of graphical transformations effected in the visual field, pencil-drawn experiments conceived quickly as elements of a language yet to be. Annotations describe the interests of the artists: permutations of proportion, intensity, color. The artists identify the formal elements of composition that could be made to affect the visual field according to rules that are considered musical. The intent here was to use those elements they identified to compose graphical scrolls that would translate directly into a universally intelligible cinema capable of communicating potentially revolutionary messages. But, once the experiment was tried at UFA (with the backing of a banker friend), Richter was disappointed to learn that no such direct translation of static forms, however musically conceived, would produce an interesting piece of film. Part of the *Präludium* scroll, did, however, appear in *Rhythmus 23*.[24]

The demonstration of universal language forms, however, contains annotations by Richter that shed further light on the problematic of synchronization, visuality, and musicality. In Richter's early conception, the notion of composing informatic *logos* for films is potentially autopoetic and generative, thus, a revolutionary liberation of aesthetic meaning. The scrolls, Richter writes, "are meant to express knowledge (knowledge) knowledge that cannot be realized in theoretical ways—only through them. Only if they exist does the theoretical knowledge of them obtain its content + form + value." And, on the same page of this key to the scrollwork, Richter notes:

> The scrolls are "machines," complicated constructions like life with organic + alive and ever-changing expression—due to the relations which they themselves really possess within these representations + those which the inventory creates within them out of its own (everyone understand—as in music). They are machines not like a hammer that bangs on your head—more like an active living power—like a radioactive element, for example, that without your knowing it transforms you.[25]

A vital and diagrammatic cinema, if it could be realized. Far beyond a robot or cyborg, such a cinema would be a living mechanism, enveloping, transforming, and moving far beyond the merely mechanical, sentient, or transforming. The graphical score—the scrolls—are machines composed according to a hermeneutic whose value is knowledge itself, the theory of which is proven in the realization of its aesthetic effect. For Richter, the guarantee of the effects of this revolutionary cinema is that it will be universally intelligible in the way that he believed music to be. The precise relationships between instance of forms, inventory of forms, and laws of transformation of forms are unclear, other than that through their own unalienated self-possession, the scrolls in projection attain a performativity through which they will transform their viewers on some supraconscious level. In an interesting comparison, Richter indicates a more basic quality of music than of formal mathematical law, which is that of vibration—here, expressed as radioactivity. Music's intelligibility effectively is equated with a living, robotic, radioactive organic cinema of metamorphosis.

The musicalization of cinema that produces revolutionary knowledge does, Richter suggests, follow a law for meaning—a logos. Musicality provides the systematization by which opposites are united: "Chaotic" intuition and "tamed" intellect are seen, in action, to follow this law:

nature + mind are
not opposites.
The one completes itself in
the other. The law lies above
them.

As I attempt to reproduce above, the text itself takes over from the penciled diagrams and begins to move itself according to its own law. Here, in the index to the scrollwork, the pages begin to be at least half full of text, as the diagrammatic transformations fulfill Richter's performance to produce their own law. The textual explanation of the penciled gestures takes over from their scribbled abstraction and brings a conclusive formula near the bottom of the page:

truth must be (1) recognized
(2) wanted
(3) created[26]

This is, in short, an aesthetic reformulation of a materialist dialectical progression between the real and desire that results in creative transformation. But this musical law—resolving in a simultaneous pathos and logos—is problematic. My contention is that the problematic revolves around the potential of synchronizing in time forms, already considered dynamic, of the visual and the sonic, in such a way that this correspondence also dynamically generates meaning. What is at stake, finally, is not formalist experimentation, but rather the instantiation in visual art of musical performativities and instrumentalities that communicate a transformative "gnosis."

Musicality as gnosis is well illustrated in Ernst Bloch's 1919 *The Spirit of Utopia*, in which he posits that the modern subject is "becoming blind to the outside."[27] Bloch's complex probing answer is to propose a historical succession of musical "carpet motifs." Through such carpet motifs, Western musical motifs are transposed in material form and in signifying capacities from Mozart's time into the time of modern music. But the implication of the complex temporality of the suprahistorical carpet motif is also that it can be applied back to modernity: The carpet motif diagrams complex historical transformations not observable to the subject, but, by the same token, such transformations are not limited to musical histories. Like Eisenstein's montage as a doubling of monadic seriation and dialectical progression, Bloch's carpet motif seems to materialize at the surface of a doubled temporality: history stalled, the subject blinded, a supratemporal dimension invoked. (Richter's scrolls follow a similar formula.)

Diagramming history in terms of Bloch's carpet motif is a speculative theory of musical-historical invention, where rhythmic repetition relates musical time to historical time (129), and orthothetic convention relates listener to collective (120). Musical process as historical process repeats historical idiom as compositional style. Mozart repeats and differentiates a "Grecian" idiom of musical historicity, Beethoven and Wagner, a "Luciferan" idiom. Although carpet motifs repeat in historical differentiations, music spatializes historical temporality and, in being heard, becomes innermost experience in the listener who colors it.

For such figures as Eisenstein, Richter, and Fischinger, the "speaking musicality" Bloch describes had arrived in the media arts. In Eisenstein's work, cinema articulates these qualities to communicate historical pathos in the virtual image and affective gesture of montage.[28] For Bloch, of course, the arrival is still to come. Bloch's listener looks forward to a fourth stage of the carpet motif, a revolutionary moment in which the listener will understand and possess the "ideogram" of the "we" through musical-historical experience.[29] Diagramming that experience in terms of carpet motifs serves to indicate a futural eventuality, Bloch thinks, where vision fails but revolution prevails.

Fischinger's musical cinema also consistently places the planning, exhibition, and reception of the cinematic apparatus within a higher-order temporal stream, synchronizing the expression of authorial sense, technical apparatus, and the sensation of the work received by the audience within its terms. The challenge of this cinema is taking an immanent but energetic block of time and articulating it according to a "musical" instrumentality conceived as technical ratio, affective relation, and historical measure of material, industrial progress that must be engineered and animated. This musical animation of energetic time requires a certain ratio of aesthetic composition, technical display, and spectatorial reception. Rather than determine the relation of author and audience in terms of techno-scientific reason, then, visual music animation treats author and audience as a problem of mensuration that is "historical" and "suprahistorical," in Bloch's terms. Musical instrumentality expresses sense in composition and impresses sensation in reception.

If Fischinger's larger aim is to express energetic temporality as musical, each attempt diverges to some degree from the last in the way that the author's sense of time is received as temporal sensation. For "sense," we might think of the way in which Gilles Deleuze describes the divergent seriation of psychic and corporeal identity; for "sensation," the way in which Deleuze describes the reception of the diagrammatic rhythm of Francis Bacon's canvases. Yet in Fischinger, sense and sensation are better understood as being not entirely distinct orders of sensual logics, but rather entangled with one another, where musical instrumentality mediates authorial style and technocultural idiom.

Painting Musical Sentences

Much of the tessellated patterning of Fischinger's *Motion Painting No. 1* was prepared in earlier canvases, such as *Plan* (1938), and later extended in *Flower* (c. 1950) and *Abstract Landscape* (1959). More familiar are the ways in which *Motion Painting No. 1* revisits graphical motifs and tropes familiar from his earliest films. In the second movement of *Motion Painting No. 1,* concentric circles are formed as a line traces its own circular curvature then closes the cycle by drawing its leading edge back to the center of the completed spiral form. These figures dynamically trace in time two figures appearing early on in Fischinger's work: the spiral and the concentric circle.

In Fischinger's *Spiralen* (*Spirals*) film experiments from 1926, among the glowing spiraling forms are also modulations of concentric circular curves as well as an array of small concentric circles that fill up the entire screen space. These spiraling and circular forms became key graphical motives across his oeuvre. They surface in his production of the first three-strip color film, *Kreise* (*Circles*; 1933), a Gaspar Color "color-play" commercial advertisement in which they feature in new radiantly colored forms; similarly, they provide one of the two graphic theses of *Radio Dynamics,* which alternates between sequences of blinking and scaling rectilinear forms and pulsing, glowing orbs. Fischinger paints continuously on sheets of Plexiglas, with the cumulative result a "motion painting." Painted to Bach's third *Brandenburg Concerto,* here Fischinger is intensely concerned with what Bloch describes as the spatial aspects of the Bachian carpet motif.

Understanding the visual music genre as the aesthetic practice of a philosophy of music instead of simply a translation of musical forms into graphical representation allows us to see the spatialization of musicality in the cinema as the drawing of carpet motifs. The primary carpet motif, the "sentence" that dynamically occurs and recurs transformed in *Motion Painting No. 1,* is the spiral. The form that conditions the very possibility of well-tempered music as it was synthesized in Bach's time, the spiral first appears reaching vertically in a calligraphic form and, on reaching its apex, dissolves the scene into an elaborate sequence of mosaic motifs. The spiral returns in varying forms but flattens out at the end, finally, in what Guggenheim Museum director Hilla Rebay, who commissioned the piece, called "Fischinger's awful little spaghettis."[30] In its recurrence, the motif of the spiral functions as the visual equivalent of the *ritornello* structure that Bach deploys in the concerto itself.[31] Just as well, it might figure the technological innovation of even temperament underlying Bach's musical invention. Finally, the spiral also emblematizes a cycling, open-ended, and improvisatory process of interpretation itself, as the audience follows sound, then image, then sound in serene and superabundant economy.

Although elaborations of circular return or other articulations of spiral form here repeatedly appear, develop, and disappear, rarely are these motifs or any of the other visual patterns synchronized to the music in the phrasal style of *Allegretto,* or the phrasal-rhythmic style of *Optical Poem.* As Fischinger conceives it:

> This music, concerto by Bach, is like a smooth river flowing on the side of open fields—
>
> And what you see—is not translated music, because music doesn't need to be translated on the screen—to the Eyes music is in itself enough—but the optical part is like we walk on the other side of the river—sometimes we go a little bit farther off (away) but we come back and go along on this river, the concerto by Bach.[32]

The film approximates, in Fischinger's words, an "optical dance" to Bach. In providing a motion painting that returns, and returns, and returns to the river of Bach's concerto, Fischinger seems to approximate in limited form what Bloch determines as the musical logic of noncontemporaneity. Moments occur when the carpet motif of the spiral and the *ritornello* form of the concerto almost resolve to one another but never really do, and when the synchronization is close, it is only so in large steps. The movement here is, as in Bloch's philosophy, toward the celestial, and where Bloch criticizes Wagner's use of pseudo-Hindu figuration, Fischinger invokes Vedic notions to clarify the design process (184–186). Here, interpretive actions in the musical dance take the soul on a journey. The gestural appearance of the time-based forms as they evolve in time is clear, but Fischinger himself emphasizes their emotional import in his private notes on the film:

> The optical thought the optical dance to the sound of the river of your soul The flowers of a mind The dance of handwriting and the song of flowers and the white of the clouds and the blue of the sky—Sometimes it is dark and you see in the darkness nothing but your own feeling your own movements your own pulse and the rapture of your heart your blood this is what you see what goes with the music—the Stars the Heaven the Darkness and the Light of your own love your own heart The Light of your mind The Dancing Light of your blood—and your feeling. (185–186)

Affect and meaning are destructured from their conventional opposition to each other in referential representation. The notes elaborating the artist's conception of the film compare to Bloch's musical immanence for a subjectivity now blind to the outside. In Fischinger's terms, "Sometimes it is dark and you

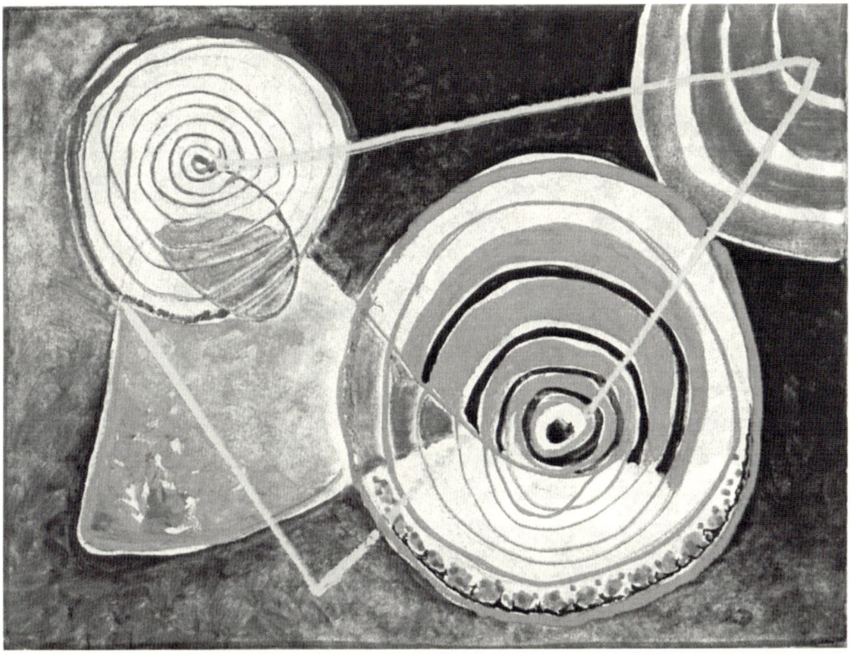

FIGURE 3.2 Kesting's *Viertalrad* (1923): *Van Ham Kunstauktionen: Moderne und Zeitgenössische Kunst,* June 9, 2005 (catalog image).

see in the darkness nothing but your own feeling" (185). But for Fischinger, illuminating musicality in synchronization results in meaning dancing between sound and image, a dance at times calligraphic and at other times broadly graphical that leads to an ecstatic state by which the body literally *becomes* feeling. The musical design of this pulsing rhythmic film makes it everything that Disney's *Fantasia* is not: unified, but heterogeneous; through composed, but progressing through distinct movements. It is as if Fischinger has drawn the film as a single, very complex line of multiple, spiraling temporalities that call, carry, distribute, culminate, and complete one another, again and again.

Motion Painting No. 1 references a modernism of pulse and phrase distinct from the musical intimations of Kandinsky, Paul Klee, or Piet Mondrian in painting or from Eisenstein's pulse in vertical montage—one that has yet to be fully accommodated in the art historical archive. The polytopic field of spiraling circles featured in the second movement of *Motion Painting No. 1,* for instance, also recalls Edmund Kesting's 1923 painting *Viertalrad* (Figure 3.2). The title of this work refers to the mechanical workings of a timepiece; the painting presents a polytopic interlinked field of spiral forms, such that the dynamic "gears" of the painting seems to pulse and to rotate, communicating with one another across the energetic canvas. Consider the second movement of *Motion Painting*

No. 1, where one spiraling composition leads to another, finally saturating the frame in darkness and disappearing into obscurity. That the variegated techniques of stroke used throughout the film were not determined in a tightly synchronized schema for the film as a whole leaves us with the suggestion that rather than an attempt at a pure cinema, *Motion Painting No. 1,* in addition to further elaborating Fischinger's intentions for a choreography of sound and moving image, also summarizes the motives and achievements of a visual culture of pulse and tact rendered for nearly a half century by 1947 on canvas and cinema screen.

In *Motion Painting No. 1,* then, a long series of interests is recapitulated and, in a sense, completed: The circle becomes the spiral, and two incompatible graphical forms are unified in terms of a larger sustained temporality in spite of historical displacement. These circles-become-spirals and the wonderful tumult of messy energy into which they finally dissipate are surely the portion of *Motion Painting No. 1* that Rebay angrily cited as "Fischinger's awful little spaghettis." Indeed, much of this sequence suggests interests other than those that Fischinger's commentators usually attribute to him: technical innovation and inner visions, a modernist pure cinema.[33]

Thus, another important possibility for interpreting this sequence of Fischinger's *Motion Painting No. 1* should be considered. Circles and spirals are not directly derivable, but they can be turned into one another by being flattened into a graphical line, gathered into what might be round bundles of threaded lines to be knitted into yet another series of spiraling derivations and then cross-stitches. It is as if the graphical pulsing thread of light were yarn that, after being collected into a ball, was knitted into a dynamically patterned surface. Perhaps this sequence of *Motion Painting No. 1* presents an analog to wife Elfriede Fischinger's design of specially knit fashion sweaters. The sweater, the result of the technical craft of knitting together color and line, is worn on body as fashion (by such customers as Bette Davis); the film, the result of the technical crafts of image and sound making, is to be mixed in the eye and ear of the cinema spectator.

Motion Painting No. 1, arguably very different from the more explicitly commercial or meditative films, demonstrates how visual music animation might survey a larger practice of the diagrammatic mode of production determining artisanal in terms of industrial cinema: (1) Recapitulate and extend the major theses, techniques, motives, and interests of the historical author; (2) express a rapport with the larger trajectory of visual cultural production from which that author's work extends or in parallel to which it continues; (3) lay out a demonstrative work that builds a self-revealing logic of variable synchronization in its own textures; (4) draw, perhaps, inspiration from other small-scale craft forms of industrial production situated in the immediate environs of everyday life; and (5) disseminate the film through whatever channels possible, including gallery or museum shows, and include statements on the intentions, techniques, and effects of the work. These five concerns characterize the broader import of *Motion Painting No. 1*; what is at stake here is not simply the goal of a meditative or affective cinema or the question of integrating or differentiating experimental art with the industrial cinemas but the larger historical logics of industrial arts, artisanal-industrial production, techno-scientific epistemologies, speculative interests, aesthetic histories, *and* conditions of everyday life. An account of the ethics and affects of visual music as style and idiom would begin with this array of concerns.

Fischinger's work should be seen in this complex series of contexts in which the avant-garde and the industrial cinemas, as David James shows,[34] worked in separation, conjunction, or divergence from one another. Carrying on the practice of artisanal cinema production in this way constitutes, beyond any single context or work, a *mode* of technocultural style and idiom that animates cinema. This modal cinema operates a divergent continuity, whether carried out during the rise of the German film industry during the 1920s, the institutionalization of fascism during the 1930s, or the conglomeration of the Hollywood studio system around the sound film or its decline during the 1950s and 1960s.

For James, as for Moritz, Fischinger's great works are those that propose the "absolute cinema" in terms of its possibilities for popular engagement, as in *Allegretto,* and then advance its motives toward a form that dispenses with the music that these critical historians dismiss as distracting or banal.[35] This reading makes sense in terms of a championing of the avant-garde in Los Angeles, but it does not fully elaborate, as I attempt to above, the greater historical catalog of aims, interests, and achievements that *Motion Painting No. 1* documents in the terms of the visual music idiom. Its variable synchronization with Bach's third *Brandenburg Concerto* is an important aspect of *Motion Painting No. 1*; as Walter Frisch clarifies, Bach's music played a particular role in the musical, critical, and cultural debates around German modernisms—debates that Bloch attempts to recast with an understanding of musical history as differential repetitions of "carpet motifs." Bach was, in brief, a musical sign for musical purity, vigor, and health—an important rediscovery for modernist German musical history and criticism during a period when modernist composers of competing tendencies were debating future directions in musical culture.

For such composers as Ferruccio Busoni, Frisch notes, music retains its absolute identity regardless of arrangements or transcriptions, since it is always "'pure': no text, context, or extra-musical additions could ever alter its basic condition."[36] Busoni, like Kandinsky, shared the idea that spirit and emotion, and nothing else, give the artwork its essential meanings. As Frisch observes, "Busoni turns the traditional definition of 'absolute' music on its head. Absolute music is not about 'form-play' without 'poetic program.' On the contrary, form is 'the opposite pole of absolute music,' which is attained only in the absence of any imposed structure" (174). Bach was the greatest example of music's unity, or "oneness." For Arnold Schoenberg, too, Bach's music provides a key historical exemplar, but here that exemplarity has to do with his project of emancipating tonal harmony. For Schoenberg's theory of harmony, Bach's music becomes a demonstration, Frisch writes, of tonality not as a natural but as an artificial phenomenon and of harmony as any group of tones sounding together rather than those tonal combinations thought universally valid on the basis of mathematical harmonics (147).

Given this context, we may also consider Eisler's recollections of Bertolt Brecht's understanding of Bach's music. Eisler recalls Brecht's sense that in Bach, musical affect does not excessively stimulate the receiver's passions but allows a measured response to the affects expressed in the work.[37] Eisler's recollections help us better understand how the reception of Bach's music as a "healthful," even-tempered relation of corporeal sense and musical sensation may have had a critical function in a modal cinema: The work expresses passion, of course, but it is measured, a commensuration of sense and sensation—that is, the scaling of an even temperament between composer, technique, instrument, and receiver.

Fischinger came of age as interpretations of Bach turned from more historicizing to more synthetic. After his early attempts to diagram musical transformations of theatrical time, Fischinger moved on to a series of technical experiments, including his well-known wax-slicing process, in which designs are shaped three-dimensionally in a wax block and then sliced as in a CAT scan to produce successive film frames that, when projected, present organic, flowing movement. Moritz notes that Fischinger was interested in the debates on expressionism and cinema, and *Wachsexperimente* produces atmospheric visions in eerie remarkable ways. Some of the wax footage turns up in *R-1* (for multiple projectors; c. 1927) as dynamic atmospheric background for the more solid repeating forms of the foreground. *R-1* approaches synchronization between multiple image tracks and musical accompaniment in terms of musicality, but only as interpreted *between* sound and image synchronized experientially, not technically (that is, by virtue of a mechanically indexed sound track). Fischinger's already sophisticated, rhythmically dynamic animated geometries in this work for multiple projectors look toward technical synchronization (which, in fact, is rapidly becoming perfected for sound cinema), though it relied on live performance when shown in 1926 and 1927.[38]

As in Bloch's work, over and over in Fischinger's films, music is taken as the range and potential for a series of expressive transformations whose ground and extent needs to be defined. Expressive ambient pieces, such as *Wachsexperimente,* led to and are combined with forms whose transformation in time is verifiable and more clearly replicable. Fischinger's craft demands the elaboration of these expressions in terms of gestures of synchronization. Although Moritz claims that such Fischinger films as *Liebesspiel* are not inspired by music and do not obtain to music, the musicality of these films is apparent, and even Moritz refers to qualities routinely associated with musical meaning and sense.[39] The difference is simply that musicality arises in the play of series rather than in synchronization to image or in some graphical representational schema that translates the idiom of rhythmic or harmonic musical form. In *Liebesspiel,* two glowing white shapes on a black background coalesce to play out a dance between them. Stripping the elements of visual music bare, the musicality of the vision here has its say in terms of the qualities that Bloch relays: rhythm attained in inflection and onset (attack). At the same time, as each shape plays off of and mirrors the other, the film becomes an emblem of the goals of visual music animation itself. The radiating ghostly images lay out a music of the self and its other, without sound. Here, synchronization in musical form is limited entirely to the visual field itself.

Still, musical synchronization across sound and image calls. *Allegretto* uses the Hollywood apparatus of multiple-layer cell animation as well as Hollywood jazz (composed by Ralph Rainger and performed by a Paramount studio orchestra) as the means to perfect visual music synchronization: glowing, radioactive, and timbrally and chromatically synchronized by phrase development. Made after Fischinger fled the Nazis and came to Los Angeles, this piece was originally to be called "Radio Dynamics."[40] The name recalls the strange immaterial materiality of the new materials of that era: electronics, but also radiation. We have seen that Richter attempts to model his universal language on music to create meanings that are radioactive; Fischinger too is taken with strange transforming power across distance common to music and radioactivity. Conceptually, then, once again, the problematic is not strictly auditory. Fischinger used the pseudonym "Raidon" in a number of early black-and-white drawings and in proposals for projects he pitched to the UFA during the late 1920s. The content of one of these proposals concerned a man from Mars who is exiled to Earth for trying to create a better world. These proposals brought him his first job in Berlin, as special-effects animator for Fritz Lang's *Woman in the Moon* (1929).[41]

In *Allegretto,* a "radioactive" musical transformation is seen literally, now in a musical form that is analogically condensed and immediately apparent: Musical supralegibility is achieved here, not through political revolution but rather through Hollywood craft and cinematic installation. Perhaps an illumination of radio broadcast is not exactly what Bloch means to prophecy, however. The Tin Pan Alley–style pop music is often denigrated, even by Fischinger's biographer Moritz. *Allegretto* has been seen as an example of what might have been, if Fischinger had been able to get funding for his own *Fantasia.* That film, which Disney had hired Fischinger to work on after his productions for Paramount and MGM, was probably inspired by his own earlier work, but he quickly resigned from the Disney Studios in profound disagreement over the direction the production had taken.

Still, the animation of *Allegretto* is masterful and successfully captures the excitement of radio-transmitted popular jazz in a form that combines Fischinger's artistry with the production values of Hollywood. And, if in the use of popular music, Fischinger reaches a Blochian goal, he further reveals the critical problematic. Are these glowing shapes a womb for revolution or the tomb of experimental cinema in a commercial industry? In fact, these films and others by artists with similar goals are crucial to multiple generations of experimental artists working under their influence: Len Lye, Harry Smith, James and John Whitney, and many others. Visual music, not music at all, in fact, may best be approached as the synchronization within and across media of musicality, with the aim of leading its audience on a journey through the very creation of affective meaning. These meanings are dynamic, composed or coordinated in motion and attaining legible effects of action experienced only virtually. While on Orson Welles's payroll during the early 1940s, Fischinger again refers to transformation achieved at a distance: He made the meditative silent exercise in "color-rhythm" *Radio Dynamics.* Here is Bloch's problematic placed in the cinema and moved through to its antithetical conclusion: The supralegibility of music is achieved, but without sound.

Fischinger wrote in 1956 about his filmmaking activities since 1919 in a catalog for the Pasadena Art Museum. As might be expected, it is an all-or-nothing proposition:

> But painting in motion, combined with music, or painting *without* motion: that is the problem. The difference is tremendous. "Motion paintings" give to the painter a new potentiality. He must develop and become something like a "visual-motionist" creating not only in space but in time. Within sixty seconds or sixty minutes he must present not only one static, framable two or three dimensional creations of a virtual nature, but he must also create sentence after sentence of moving, developing visual images changing and changing, in continuously different ways. At times, these may be composed of successive ideas, bringing new life into images. Forms are basic, but changes develop from the orchestration of forms and lines and colors. This is a tremendous new world—a tremendous new tool—a challenge to creativeness comparable only to music.[42]

A "new world": Bloch tells us that this much was likely in music. But further, a "new tool" exists: The function of the time-based means of expression is to temporalize the production of meaning, make meaning ex-static. "Sentence after sentence of moving developing visual images changing and changing, in continuously different ways" (189): This might be a description of *Motion Painting No. 1.* As for Eisenstein, Fischinger accomplishes a similar process of musical abstraction and cumulative adduction into the visual field, but to the end of animating dynamic forms on screen and, finally, to release visual music from any necessary correspondence to the sound track. The two go forward freely in parallel, returning to each other, according to the musical will of each. The important difference between the Eisenstein's musical montage and Fischinger's vision—and this is signaled early on in the fragments of graphical scores of theatrical works—is that Fischinger ultimately is not working from any objective or indexical image.

Rather, his approach is based on drafting and illustration techniques derived from his engineering background but applied to the musical imaginary. The result is musical gesture visualized, moving in time through the audience of a musical cinema world. The techniques he develops stress visual musicality being produced for either exact or noncontemporaneous synchronization with musical sound through correspondences of musical meanings. Fischinger moves the audience into a precisely timed musical cosmos, first explored with such works as *Allegretto* and *An Optical Poem.* He insists on the power of the moving image to produce musical meanings in its own right with *Radio Dynamics*: a visual music masterpiece *without* audio. This work produces musical meanings—the rhythms that suggest breaths, or cycles—that reverberate silently as a meditation on spiritual experience. And, he finally releases sound and image from their mutual grasp into an instantiation of audiovisual noncontemporaneity, or at least complex heterogeneous temporal layering, in *Motion Painting No. 1.*

Fischinger's use of what were by the mid-twentieth century considered a form of industrial pop—"light classics" overly familiar in terms of then-contemporary musical epistemologies, as David James points out[43]—should be considered in the following way: Where Brecht and Eisler, through his film scores, seek to distance the audience from the screen display, Fischinger's stylistics of the idiom of pulse and tact seek to animate an energetic block of time that ultimately may be deployed toward a conception of a situated convertibility between author and audience. *Allegretto* is, in this view, the mature culmination of the pop strain of Fischinger's modal cinema; *Radio Dynamics,* its purified poetic form; and *Motion Painting No. 1,* its critical, historical, and autobiographical exposition.

What to make, finally, of Fischinger's insertion of his own index finger, appearing as a flash at the lower center of a single frame, pointing upward at a climactic point of the final movement of *Motion Picture No. 1*? In the reading I offer here, Fischinger's inclusion of this brief flash of finger orienting the viewer's eye upward toward the suprahistorical dimension of the historically situated screen relays the stylistics of the work back to the idiom conducted via the energies of his own sustained divergent labors. This gesture reflexively points to the film's historical and autobiographical exposition of what Erwin Panofsky[44] describes as the coexpressivity of sound and image and the dynamization of space and spatialization of time. Yet visual music animation as a modal cinema deploys style and idiom transposable across the material substrates of the presentational medium—that is, beyond style and medium, the terms with which Panofsky describes cinema's dynamism. The deictic flash of Fischinger's hand is a signature effect: It rebinds the sensation of the work's reception to the sense of its authorial composition; it rebinds the historical time of the site of reception to the suprahistorical temporality where visual music animation previously performed, and would again in the years ahead, as a cipher for reframing and disseminating style and idiom in new media to come.

Musical Gesture, Star Gestures

One constant in all of Fischinger's animated films is the artist's solution to a basic problem of nonobjective animation. The animator, to effect a fluidity of motion, must use visual elements whose shapes allow them to move continuously over time as they are translated through two- or three-dimensional space. It is this choice of shapes and transformations, with the attendant movement, that comes to constitute the animator's "language," or, rather, a toolbox of dynamic visual technique. Fischinger's visual forms are designed to retain their shape while they move in a given direction (melodiously, or rhythmically, in musical terms), while moving quickly and uniquely enough to visualize a musical phrase or to simply persist in motion in the visual field throughout a given duration.

Of course, the simplest visual form that can retain its shape as it moves directionally through space is the circle. The circle, full of symbolic and metaphorical connotations, is a common motif in the work of many artists of visual music. As such, its use may provide a point of comparison between works. Comparing Fischinger's independent art productions to Busby Berkeley's lavish Hollywood production numbers by focusing on the use of circular motifs in each, for example, might help us glean an idea of how musical rhetorics complicate and subvert traditional narrative form. Such a comparison can also provide a notion of the nature of the relationship between independent artist labor and studio artist labor.

Between Fischinger and Berkeley we might identify, to begin with, a supplementary relation based on the idea of prototype. That is, Berkeley uses Fischinger's radiant dot motif as a successful experiment that, as a graphical effect, might enhance and expand his own musical adventurism. In this way, we see one relationship that helps define part of the complex dynamic between art and commodity film: The industry accommodates the avant-garde as a prototype. Berkeley, himself an avant-garde visual music artist by virtue of his transformation of singing, dancing bodies out of a strict narrative teleology and into musical form less reliant upon cause and effect and the need for closure, nonetheless functions as industry as he recovers Fischinger's graphical effects into the Hollywood musical. Berkeley takes up Fischinger's tool.[45]

Fischinger uses circular form as the figure of expansion and return, the way onward and the way home. In his earliest works, we encounter it in many instances, from ellipse to spiral. The circular motif or gesture figures prominently in all the complete works he produced while in Hollywood—namely, *Allegretto, An Optical Poem, American March* (1941), *Radio Dynamics,* and *Motion Painting No. 1.* The motif is clearest in *An Optical Poem,* whose visual forms are primarily circular dots painted a radiant golden hue that move in time to Lizst's *Hungarian Rhapsody No. 2. An Optical Poem* is closely synchronized to the musical sound track, but, unlike *Allegretto,* which retains one style of synchronization throughout,[46] it uses the two different styles of synchronization I have briefly referred to: phrasal and rhythmic. In the phrasal style, the music "draws," as Bloch would say. The animation traces precisely an instrumental line—a visualized carpet motif—heard on the sound track, moving up when the melody goes up, or vice versa. In the rhythmic style, the radiant dots simply dance around each other in a rhythmic choreography. Sometimes, in *An Optical Poem,* both styles occur at once. Routinely, the circles and circular movement imply the very poetry of celestial transport that Fischinger invokes in his notes.

This "orbit" metaphor suggests a transcendental view of the cosmos, alluding to the oldest known figures of astronomy. In this view, we see many possible "worlds" moving with and against each other in outer space. But the metaphor also suggests a microscopic view of atoms and molecules, invoking the recently gained knowledge of particle physics and atomic fission. Ever the synthesist, Fischinger switches between or combines "harmonic views," with dots following melodic contours, and "views of harmony," with dots dancing around each other. Harmonics in music, celestial mechanics, and particle physics all coexist in rhapsodic form, and the fact that you can see instrumental and choreographic synchronizations together in some views shows that in visual music, at least, duality need not imply binarism. Later, in *Radio Dynamics,* Fischinger dispenses with the music, simply putting forth a silent meditation piece that glows with pulsing rhythmic circles, among other forms. The radiating dot here is tripled in the frame, as three circles slowly give way to one that zooms out at the viewer. The effect is hypnotic.[47]

The difference between Fischinger's abstraction and Berkeley's figuration is as clear as that between dance and song. Although Fischinger's work consistently evokes the figure of return as a dance of orbiting spheres, Berkeley has a different problem: To get to the circle, the simplest geometrical form for regular repeating movement, he must allow for song but reformat the human body inside the frame[48] with the camera. Although Berkeley accomplishes this task in one way or another in all his films, for *The Gang's All Here* (1943) he adds a graphic effect never before used in his films. *Gang* is a wartime distraction starring Alice Faye as Edie Allen, a nightclub singer who learns that her returning soldier has a fiancée, leading her to perform a mournful version of the film's theme song, "Journey to a Star." Edie had serenaded her lover with this tune the night before he left for the Pacific front, and it has haunted her ever since. After she sings out her melancholy and resentment, she overhears a conversation that explains that the engagement that has broken her heart was just a family arrangement. Then Edie begins the production number that ends the show and the movie, an elaborate final sequence that radically redefines the meaning of the lyrics to "Journey to a Star," which is reprised.

The production number starts from a gag song whose lyrics intone, "The polka is gone / but the polka dot lives on." Couples of children in turn-of-the-century clothing crowd around Edie as she croons, "And gentlemen still love / the polka dotted glove." A musical fantasia breaks out: The camera fixes in close-up on a girl's glove, similar to Faye's, and this close-up dissolves to a massive facsimile of the glove, now floating in darkness. The fetishized "manu-factory" of musical stardom literally displaces the performer's gestures, its operations getting underway as the polka dot patterns begin to glow neon bright and fall away from the fabric of the glove. Becoming halos, they fall upon the heads of chorus girls in factory-worker catsuits who begin to work the neon dots into larger patterns. The work to be done, it seems, by these worker angels is to reverse-engineer musical stars out of the diegesis and place them into the cinematic heavens above the spectators. Before the stars can appear, symbols of physical desire are coded into the production, and the polka dots spill away, out of control.

Finally, Edie appears as the strange fabrication of the production number, swallowed up at the center of the frame in blue fabric, with only her head visible. While the camera hovers above her, her movements turn into a psychedelic kaleidoscope of pulsating color, and the fetishized veiling of the body that began with the glove now proceeds from her singing head as a riot of bodies moving in abstract patterns forms a circle. The production number ends as the polka dots form halos behind the heads of the stars as each star in turn sings a line from the song "Journey to a Star." And here appears Fischinger's zooming radiant dot: A complex compositing process highly unusual for Berkeley turns the dot into the halo of a musical star who is offered not only as a subject position within a narrative trajectory but also as the object of desire in an orgiastic musical display. Each star's head zooms out at the viewer, framed in circle, until finally Edie's head appears again as she sings the last line of the song. Then, all the actors' heads appear clustered around Edie's, a star field on a sky-blue background as the musical fanfare concludes.

Although Berkeley's production numbers often rehearse motifs similar to these, in this particular instance, the graphical nature of the finale is unlike anything before or since. The cosmological carpet motifs in Berkeley's and Fischinger's films are striking. In Fischinger's *An Optical Poem,* musical views of astronomical and atomic space put the viewer in a position to perceive transcendent harmony. In Berkeley's *Gang,* we are distracted from a military conflict extending around the world with the story of a singer and a war hero's romantic "Journey to a Star" at the same time as we undertake a "journey to a star" ourselves.

The allure of Hollywood replaces fears about the war, as the uncertain future of our couple is conveniently forgotten. From the dangers of war to the production of glamour, as the song suggests, "isn't very far." In both films, spectators find their relations to the world they experience completely transformed, not simply defamiliarized. By Bürger's standards, both of these films would fall into the category of practical art that "enthralls" the consumer and so performs a "false sublation of art as institution."[49] With his emphasis on Adornian negative dialectics and his somewhat naive acceptance of the avant-gardists' manifestoes as an accurate description of how their work actually performed in the social field, Bürger valorizes one style of avant-garde production at the expense of others.

Fischinger's small-scale craft production and Berkeley's large-scale industrial production can put the consumer at the center of worlds where the pleasure of musical experience allows multiple levels of meaning to become explicit in a purposefully ambiguous work. In Fischinger's case, the viewer's knowledge of the physical world might be turned into the sense and sensation of musical engagement with the real. In Berkeley's case, Hollywood conventions shamelessly expose themselves in blatant attempts to keep people's minds off the war's effects even as they are asked to cheer the war effort itself. Perhaps the sheer exhibitionism of Berkeley's pastiche is what ensured that he made very few films after this one; the musical film turned to ever-subtler integration of musical and narrative form, and Hollywood was never quite so brazen again.

I have suggested one possible relationship between Fischinger's experimentalism and Berkeley's commercialism as that of "prototyping," and others certainly exist. But at the same time, I do not want to overlook Berkeley's humiliation in Hollywood to concentrate on Fischinger's. Both are artists who were put out to pasture before their times, possibly because their prototyping was too far advanced or their productions too risky to continue being the right sort of novelty for the Hollywood cinema. What's important is how these artists mobilized musical fervency to open up the narrow flow of the traditional narrative work. The ecstatic quality of visual music has potent effects on the cinematic work. Artists use philosophical visions of music to involve spectators in a reproduction of the world that can reveal it to be deeply complex, pleasurably engaging, individually subjective, collectively mobilizing, and in sum a profound lens for reviewing the world outside the film. A major difference is in the gesture of movement each work makes.

As Martin Rubin points out, *Gang* is the Berkeley film that most radically puts narrative to the uses of music. Rubin contrasts Berkeley-esque spectacle with conventions of realism and naturalism that are generally considered "narrative." For Rubin, narrative, from this point of view, is almost an afterthought in *Gang*. Lyrics for the musical numbers reach an "extreme of nonsensicality" in the musical numbers, such as "The Polka Dot Polka." He points out the paucity of analytical editing sequences, such as those in the "shot, reverse-shot" pattern, even in comparison to musical narrative conventions of the early 1940s. The film begins with a spectacular musical number featuring Carmen Miranda as Dorita, whom Rubin describes as "a walking alienation effect." This introductory sequence is only marginally integrated into the film's excuse of storytelling—but technically, the smooth and surprising continuity from the musical world of this number to the musical world of the film's primary diegesis is pure spit 'n' polish. In general, Rubin notes, narrative space is flattened to become musical: "Space in *The Gang's All Here* is not so much penetrated or analyzed as unscrolled, spun out."[50]

It is understandable that, in arguing that *Gang* is a film that unscrolls musically without diegetic depth, Rubin opposes music to narration; this is part of the tradition of cinema studies that accommodates only with difficulty the work of Fischinger, Richter, or Bloch. Rather than say that almost no narration occurs or that the musical numbers do not resolve narrative tension, I would suggest that musical narration is taking on a greater role and taking the film someplace else all together. By flattening the diegetic world so that, effectively, it is read as performance, Berkeley simply allows music to take on almost all narrative functions in a way that is less grating than the usual story/number division. The more conventional solution during the early 1940s, and the reason why Berkeley was fired from MGM, was to more carefully craft the narrative and lyrics so that when song did burst into a scene, it was fully motivated in terms of the characters' cohesive internal worlds. Instead of the backstage musical, with its tendency to turn the external world into a stage, the Arthur Freed Unit at MGM tended to place a star at the center of a film and motivate musical numbers through his or her emotional conflicts. Splashy production numbers might come at the end to grandly resolve these conflicts constructed in terms of character interaction and character interiority.

The suspension of the usual role of cutting so that *Gang* tends to float away from analytical convention is signified above all in the "The Polka Dot Polka" scene, in which the gargantuan woman's gloved hand floats prosthetically above the chorines in darkness. This image perhaps emphasizes the lack of distinction throughout the film in what Rubin refers to as "audience/narrative" space and "stage/performance" space. But his conclusions here are based on audience interpreting narrative and performer performing musically; the implication, as usual, is that music is beyond rationale, and its magical transmission from performer to audience is the right way of producing spectacle. The audience is closed off from music, which is kept to the stage.

With Bloch's notion of synthetic cultural creation through musicality, we can better understand what Berkeley attempts in the face of the increasingly music-resistant Hollywood narrative of his day. The visual spectacle of the star, in effect, passes over into the visual spectacle of music through the cinematic space of the audience. Edie's gesturing hand becomes separated from her screen body and continues, without her, into the next number, directing the refabrication of the star into an ensemble production. Here, the visual conventions of solo-number presentation tend toward continuous musicalization, with visual elements and even body parts reforming into motifs. This fragmentation of the star's musical gesture is strained in the tension with her star body. The motif undergoes transformation beyond recognition only to reoccur in a new formation later: Edie's gloved gesture initiates the later appearance of the blooming flower of her head, which is then itself placed in orbit, in a constellation of "stars." Of course, it is more difficult to fabricate a motif out of a star's hand than a polka dot, but Berkeley shows here that it can indeed be done.

Above all, gesture in the Berkeley-esque spectacle is that of bodies become motifs for organization into a musical narrative that simply wants to carpet the audience's eyes as well as its ears. This gesture, of course, is under extreme constraints as to its transformation once it is derived from a human figure. The female figure is chosen to dissolve and to recombine, usually, simply because such anatomical nondifferentiation would be threatening if it were configured male: It would reveal a disturbing picture of male fabrication during wartime, a moment that would tend, perhaps, to display male invulnerability, not constructability. More generally, under the terms of heteronormativity, a motif in feminine construction always helps prevent the male ensemble from dissolving together, with its attendant risk of confusion of man and (musical) instrument. But finally, the very femaleness essential to the movement of the cogs in this cinematic machine becomes nominal at best once the sequence proceeds through its initial lapses of cinematic narrative convention. After the stage has been nondifferentiated from the audience space and after the performance has been nondifferentiated from the narrative, the body is simply the last thing to go. If we accept that cinema might be the staging ground for the musical interiority that Bloch projects, the destination is utopia. More than the literal representation of the gesture of a female body and beyond the fetishization of the female figure, this gesture is Hollywood's instrumentalization of the audience.

Alternatively, Fischinger's hand appears literally in his work, but only under the guarantee that it would not be seen beyond a single flicker. Robert Haller notes that Fischinger would place his hand in front of the camera to indicate a mistake in the animation process.[51] The flicker of his hand is surprising, because the visual motifs of Fischinger's films tend to aspire to fluid and nonobjective form. The hand in the frame that Haller refers to appears to be stopping the flow of time. In fact, Fischinger's gesture as painter is what guarantees the temporal transport experienced in his films. But the flash appearance of a single, clearly intentional finger gesture pointing upward suggests that gesture as music is patent in Fischinger's work and not hidden because of its obtrusiveness. Fischinger's gestural Lumigraph device would be the material instantiation of the even temperament of Fischinger's modal cinema.

In this account, then, are not simply two gestural logics of experimental cinema, as Akira Lippit[52] argues. Rather, four divergent series of gestures animate the apparatus, modulating producer and receiver, sense in composition and sensation in reception: A first series of gestures, in the preparation of the apparatus for the work, where the apparatus itself varies, is animated, over historical time; a second series of gestures in the production of the work as experiment, study, or mature work, and where the author's work develops in relation to its historical epoch; a third series of gestures, the reception of the work in any number of passive positions, whether the commercial cinema spectator, the gallery or art gallery or dome environment, or again, the camera that records the Lumigraph performance for television or cinema special effects and that lives on after the author; and fourth, the gestures of the audience member who might step "behind the screen" to animate the apparatus him- or herself, so clearly modeled by Fischinger with the Lumigraph, but also in those artists' work who acknowledge his work as influential exemplar. Here, the passive synthesis of cinematic contemplation becomes the active synthesis of calculation graphically projected through the bioenergetic or bioinformatic screen. Receiver becomes author; the historical epoch of the author is transposed to, while being displaced by, that of the receiver. Style and idiom in the modal cinema implies far more than a problem of old and new media.

Taken in this light, Fischinger's practice is not simply a decorative alternative to more critical avant-gardes, nor is it simply a neglected history finally getting its due from art-historical scholarship. I argue that Fischinger's cinema demonstrates in historical fact and consequence a subtle resistance as much as a major modality of industrial style and idiom. More than just a seminal part of the history of musical, special effects, expanded, or motion-graphic cinemas, more than an invitation to revisit a Hollywood renaissance of transnational localization of the avant-gardes, it is, in fact, an ecstatic, if difficult-to-maintain, form of resistance: to the early industrial cinemas, which marginalized the avant-gardes; to fascism, which branded it impermissible; to the Hollywood studio system, which detached its stylistics while obscuring its signatures without disseminating to any sufficient material degree an idiom through which these styles could be maintained; and also, finally, to art-historical methods that insist on a critical avant-garde antithetical to the braided seriation of the popular, the technical, and the ecstatic. It is difficult, indeed, given the great number of meditative works Fischinger inspired, to underestimate the "spiritual constructions" motivating the animated screens of many who have worked in this idiom. Yet it is more important to emphasize the material and effective nature of this mode of stylizing the idioms of transnational industrial arts and cultures.

Gesture in Fischinger's work is made explicit with his invention of the Lumigraph, a musical instrument of light he played from behind a screen. Moritz recounts an early Fischinger performance on the Lumigraph: "Soft glowing images begin to appear where the screen was. Is it a film? No, it has a luminous presence quite unlike [film]. . . . Sometimes it seems almost like a hand but then it can flicker, and swirling leave a vague trail like a comet's tail. The bright saturated colors have a ghostly three-dimensional presence. The shapes change so easily, yet are so solid."[53]

The patent diagram for the Lumigraph gives the key for the real-time performance of visual music. Describing the latex screens that are pushed out toward the audience through a band of lights to produce colored movements, the diagram notes: "RUBBER SKIN—LIGHT TOUCHES SKIN ONLY IF PUSHED FORWARD INTO THE LIGHT." These are instructions for enlightening the audience as well as for the patent office. Here, though, gesture outstrips the prosthetic.

After cinema has materialized temporality, finally, gesture emerges into temporal materiality. Visual music now happens directly through artist movements. When performing at the San Francisco Museum of Modern Art, Fischinger arranged his costume and the instrument so that only the musical gestures and his white gloves could be seen. The disembodied hand here again indicates the unseen labor of aesthetic production that underlies the movement of music into the visual field and, in this case, directly into the audience space.

Elfriede Fischinger notes that the Lumigraph was enjoyed by Lionel Hampton and his friends, was shown to Gene Kelly, and also served as the prototype for a "love machine" during the production of *The Time Travelers*. Fischinger performed with the Lumigraph in museums and galleries in Los Angeles and San Francisco. A contract was signed to use the instrument for an Andy Williams television special called *Kaleidoscope* (in the mid-1960s, apparently), but, because of low light emissions, the cameras could not adequately capture its subtle effects. Visual music on the Lumigraph was insufficiently "radioactive" for television.[54] Stephen Beck's live television performance of highly saturated electronic musical patterns, however, was only a few years away.

Radiant Historicity

This chapter's aim has been to provide a critical framework restoring Fischinger's work as well as the tendencies informing visual music cinemas to their historical positions mediating classical debates on film form (where Eisenstein stands as the central exemplar) and audience reception (where Eisler and Adorno, to whom I turn next, provide the key discussion). Doing so, too, we avoid the situation depicted in Jonathan Lethem's *The Fortress of Solitude*.[55] In this coming-of-age story set in New York City during the 1970s, Abraham, the protagonist's father, seems increasingly distant, occupied with a near-mystical painting practice. As he grows up, the protagonist begins to realize that his father is more active, too. Invited to speak on a panel at a local university, a lively discussion on painting ensues. But at least one audience member is unconvinced: He jumps up and shouts, "But what about Oscar [*sic*] Fischinger? None of you are acknowledging Oscar Fischinger!"[56]

Fischinger's stylization of cinema and the Lumigraph have been similarly constantly convoked in the developments of streaming media over the twentieth century. Thanks to shifts in accounts of avant-garde activity deriving partly from 1950s and 1960s engagements with popular culture that Fischinger helped inspire, art-historical studies have granted him a tentative place in scholarly histories, but without fully granting the importance of his work or its influences. Fischinger's practice had little to do with modeling synesthesia, visualizing sound or music, musicalizing narration, or making cinema painterly—these perspectives have merely helped condition the reception of his work.

What is remarkable, though, is that Lethem could make the joke and that the joke might be humorous in 2004. From Fischinger's steady production of musicalized cinematic space environments during the 1920s to the Lumigraph and to hundreds of diagrammatic paintings, he constantly gestured upward: beyond his branding as a degenerate in Germany, biases of language, and economic privation in Hollywood, toward, as Moritz puts it, a nonobjective world he knew "had always existed, even though European art was just rediscovering it." Moritz fittingly suggests a range of carpet motifs for Fischinger's animations and inventions: geometric color fields, organic auroras, and mathematical trajectories, Plato or the Tibetan painter of yantras, Einstein and Heisenberg and Hopi Shaman. Moritz also points to artists working with computer-generated graphics in the California school of color music—Michael Scroggins or Vibeke Sorenson—and argues that Fischinger understood that his influence would be deeply generative in spite of the difficulties of working in this style and the hardships of economic marginalization or art historical neglect that he experienced and saw others experience as well: "Perhaps [my own films] will be primitive. I think I am mostly a catalyst."[57]

Lethem's humorous scene in which the frustrated audience member calls out for acknowledgment of a properly historical exemplar of ecstatic moving painting, then, points less to Fischinger's actual reception and more to the sustained inability of advancing industrial arts in the United States to grasp the aesthetic and ethical dimensions adequate to, first, the establishment of variegated public spheres where, second, receivers might become "literate" in terms of that ecstatic affect that Bernard Stiegler[58] suggests characterizes learning to write and that is commensurate to the practices of politically vital regimes of technocultural production. For Stiegler, learning literacy means time away from and a dissynchronization with the site of writing, allowing an accommodation of literacy, with its internalization and habituation of reading and writing that shifts, in inobservable moments, the writerly systems of inscription that are habituated. In streaming media, however, the opposite tendency is vaunted as the equivalent of literacy: persistently networked habits of using streaming media appliances. A double inadequacy of the aesthetic and ethical dimensions of media reception and the time required to effect reception in ecstatic terms help explain not only the enduring appeal of Fischinger's work but also the very different meanings assigned to it as a cinematic modeling of internal synesthesia or as external technical invention of a more powerful synchronization of streaming media.

This double inadequacy of styles for expressing techno-political ontologies, epistemologies, and ethics, and of idioms adequate to their dissemination, *is* the ethical problem of modern historical time and not simply that of advanced capacities for digital composition or of remix culture posited on the model of open-software production. We know the broad outlines of this problematic, in long-standing debates around industrial design, visual anthropology, documentary practices, and mass-media publics. When a historical period, an industrial process, or a situation of reception fails to adequately condition access not simply to the tools of production but to the models, criteria, and differentiation of their uses, in mass-cultural terms, this failure points to a kind of social death, a necrosis of time, diagnosible in terms of developmental dynamics alternating between symbolic infantilization and symbolic senility. We gesture, like children, toward the opaque and carefully protected capacities of a new mass medium, only to find, as the devices and the affects we invest in them obsolesce, that we have forgotten to animate the site of technocultural reception as a place for public life. "Democracy" is the stand-in term for this repeating failure of everyday industrial or postindustrial life. For Stiegler, the reality is symbolic misery accruing in what he calls hyperindustrialism, the regime where the means for producing goods and programming "spiritual nourishment" converge.[59]

Yet since early cinema (at least, that is, from the point at which these liabilities and tendencies become clear for industrial mass cultures), faced with that failure such theorists as Bloch and such artists as Fischinger have turned to music. Fischinger's musical animation and its reception should be seen in this light: As style and idiom of a modal cinema, it constitutes a sustained example of a broader and continuing musical turn, a means not simply of radiantly illuminating the industrial screen but of reanimating the historical rhythms of industrial or hyperindustrial time. Where Eisenstein's montage diagrams hieroglyphic time as historical pathos, then, Fischinger diagrams it as futural ecstasy. Between the two, and not entirely exclusive to these, Eisler develops another classical stylistics of streaming audiovisuality that is neither anchored in historical or futural immanence, but in the site of reception itself: a dialectical stream. I turn next to the ways in which Eisler's dialectical streaming of sound and image modulates the affect of "hysteria."

4

Hanns Eisler's Dialectical Stream

Sync, Dissonance, and the Devil

> *By keeping itself at a distance, [Eisler's score] also creates a distance from its place and hour. Something of this element—the formal self-negation of music that plays with itself—should be present in every composition for motion pictures as an antidote against the danger of pseudo-individualization.*
>
> —Hanns Eisler and Theodor Adorno, *Composing for the Films*

Diagramming Cognition

In previous chapters, Sergei Eisenstein's and Oskar Fischinger's distinct resolutions to the problem of synchronizing the creative labor of production with cinema's automated technical presentation and the interpretive labor of the audience provide two crucial exemplars of stylizing the complex temporalities of time-based industrial media in what I have termed "modal cinemas." Hanns Eisler's film-scoring practice clarifies a third classical stylistic of audiovisual media synchronization. Eisler's use of post-Schoenberg musical insights; his political engagements; his wide range of scoring activities for documentary or narrative features; his seminal Rockefeller Foundation–funded experiments in cinema music composition in the Film Music Project (later elaborated, with Theodor Adorno, in *Composing for the Films* [1947]); and the historical continuity of his activities in film music between the 1920s, in his scoring for nonsynchronized cinema with Walter Ruttmann, and the 1950s, in his score for Alain Resnais's *Nuit et brouillard* (*Night and Fog*; 1955): All of these make Eisler a key figure where musicality is conceived to mediate the production and reception of a time-based work within, and yet diverging from, the dominant conditions and conventions of music production in cinema.

In this chapter, I consider Eisler's compositional methods vis-à-vis those of Bernard Herrmann. Eisler, with Adorno, provides one of the earliest critiques of Eisenstein's isomorphic correspondences, although, as I show in Chapter 2, they interpret Eisenstein's *Alexander Nevsky* chart as a parametrical informatic diagram rather than as a diagram of threatened cultural labor that might secure itself in asserting a deeply historical immanence. Nicholas Cook[1] notes that an uncritical reliance on some less than fully acknowledged notion of formal unity seems to persist in Eisenstein's *Nevsky* chart *and* in Adorno and Eisler's critiques of classical Hollywood scoring practices and of Eisenstein: "Oppositional scoring, as its designation implies, represents merely the opposite of [Eisenstein's] parallelism. It is the inversion of a principle, a parasitic concept, and its practice represents no more than the exception that proves the rule" (65).

The larger strategy of reading that Cook suggests (as discussed in Chapter 2) is that of a cognitive, "metaphoric" transfer of meaningful material from two distinct expressions. Eisenstein, Eisler, or, again, Walt Disney's elaboration of sound-image doubling in *Fantasia* illustrates three distinct models of this metaphoric transfer: conformance when similar meanings are expressed in similar terms; complementation when similar meanings are expressed in different terms; and contestation, when opposite meanings are expressed in different but somehow still comparable terms. These terms may describe the production of metaphoric meaning in multimedia musical objects, but Cook also suggests that they may characterize interpretive strategies in music criticism or scholarship. Eisler's work seems to attempt but fails to demonstrate sound and image as "contesting" one another.

Yet like Barbara Stafford's "echo object," Cook's notion of cognitive transfer of metaphoric meaning is less descriptive when it comes to the historical materialities informing Eisenstein's and Eisler's very different approaches to synchronizing the audiovisual stream or to the varying purposes to which these critiques have been put since they were elaborated. Too, the very preliminary cognitive study on which much of Cook's account depends gets little historical treatment. Cook's framework, then, serves not so much to describe cognitive metaphor as problematic but to contain unruly historical examples of music across multimedia that are fraught with multiple layers of meaning. Invoking his own terms, Cook argues that Eisler's apparent insistence on "oppositional scoring" is hard to reconcile with what Cook regards as the conventional score Eisler composed for Joris Ivens's *Rain* (1929) as part of his work on the Film Music Project: "The difficulty is not so much in understanding the principles behind Eisler's scoring [of *Rain*], but in understanding how they are meant to conform to principles set out in his text" (64).

Cook's powerful model of three tendencies of metaphoric transfer in multimedia object and criticism of the multimedia object, then, allows Eisler to be drawn into a contradiction based entirely on an anachronistic and partial understanding of *Composing for the Films*. Cook acknowledges the book as a problematic example of joint authorship but generalizes the meanings of synchronization as "fit" that Eisler presents in text and in his films as meaning close timing of significant events between sound and image rather than as a much more complex term. Rather than reading Eisler's score for *Rain* in terms of what it is—"variations" whose meaning develops over the duration of the composition and the film—Cook reads *Rain* as simply matching shifts in musical tonality with a cut from long shot to close-up.

In reading Eisler's score for *Rain* in this way, Cook risks the sort of reduction to which Eisler and Adorno subject Eisenstein—reading Eisler's notion of "fit" as an informatic "fitting" to film frame as event *and* by virtue of the rhetorical strategy of synecdochic reduction according to which Eisenstein's *Battleship Potemkin* becomes entirely a nonnnarrative cognitive object in Stafford's recent description (see Chapter 1). Viewing and listening to *Rain* make clear that the iconic links between musical figure and image sequence that Cook identifies vary throughout the film and that the score contains neither a through-composed unity nor an uncoordinated, ad hoc assembling of sequences of the sort that Eisler and Adorno critique in Hollywood practices. The score and its relations to the image track vary over time, then, and the counterpoint Cook claims Eisler fails to theorize as "concept" is an artifact not of a relation of image to music but rather a much more complex streaming effect whose meanings accrue and develop over time. Cook's reading of Eisler's film music as facilitating the emergence of icons linking sound and image continues film studies' conventional epistemology in which music must link with image to provide musical elaboration or sound effect, special effect, narrative commentary, geographical siting, temporal adjustment, or affective direction.

The problem with this analysis is that it turns a film studies cliché—that of Eisler's scoring as a political contestation of the filmic image via the musical supplement of the film score—into a conceptual error by referring Eisler's work back to the modes of production from which it diverges, and under the cover of once again reducing the film score to largely supplemental and, here, cognitive functions. *Composing for the Films* is a problematic text, complicated by joint authorship but also by misstatements that, as I discuss below, must have been intentional. But my interest lies in the way that Cook reiterates the notion of the film score as a supplement to the image by turning musical figures into conceptual objects that can be synchronized as associative icons. Cook's analysis is a valuable example of temporal diagramming, in other words, but it begs the question of how we can account for Eisler's scoring practices in terms of temporal streams rather than simply in terms of iconic conceptual objects informatically synchronized as serial events reducible to the common time base provided by the filmic or digital recording.

In the following section, I introduce the historical context in which Eisler and Herrmann moved from New York to Los Angeles. I then devote the two

FIGURE 4.1 Losey's *A Child Went Forth* (1941): Defending her water pail against a hysterical attack (frame capture). (*A Child Went Forth*, dir. Joseph Losey [National Association of Nursery Educators, 1941].)

subsequent sections to discussions of the ways in which each composer rendered hysteria in fiction and nonfiction works. I close the chapter with a discussion of the implications to be drawn from what I clarify as Eisler's "dialectical streaming." Cinema and film music studies have long attempted to ascertain how Eisler's "counterpoint" of sound and image could "emancipate" film music, as Eisler and Adorno describe their project in *Composing for the Films*. I clarify that what is at stake in Eisler's work is not simply the linkage or breakage of musical figure and framed image or image sequence but rather a larger concept of musicality in audiovisual works achieving commentary or essayistic dimensions. I show the radical ways in which Eisler's rendition of hysteria in *A Child Went Forth* (Figure 4.1) differs from Herrmann's depiction of hysteria in *Hangover Square*. Eisler's achievement here not only builds on an earlier approach in which dialectical tensions are proposed in one film and resolved in another but also provides a stylistic of synchronizing sound and image that is still relevant for cinema and digital-media studies. Eisler demonstrates in *A Child Went Forth* the qualities that would later be apparent in such films as Resnais's *Nuit et brouillard*: not a sound-image counterpoint of audiovisual icons but a larger dialectical streaming of temporalized, audiovisual materiality.

Composing Mass Listening as "Hysteria"

Eisler's approaches to film music in his U.S. period, in his rescoring of Ivens's *Rain* and in his writing with Adorno in *Composing for the Films,* respond to two distinctly U.S. approaches to mediating mass corporeality: one situated in the New York intellectual, aesthetic, commercial, and political contexts of the late 1930s and early 1940s, and the other situated in Hollywood of the mid-1940s. The first prepared the way to the second. Eisler came to Hollywood in 1942 with the practical experience, theoretical insights, and personal contacts gained from his Rockefeller Foundation–funded Film Music Project carried out at the New School for Social Research in New York, where he composed multiple variations of scores for a range of moving image types, including animation and documentary.

Threatened with deportation by the House Committee on Un-American Activities during the Red Scare, Eisler voluntarily returned to Europe in 1948 after receiving two Academy Award nominations, for Fritz Lang's *Hangmen Also Die!* (1943) and Clifford Odets's *None but the Lonely Heart* (1944), and scoring numerous other theater and cinema productions, including Joseph Losey's production of Bertolt Brecht's stage play *Galileo* (1947). Eisler's most direct critiques of cinema scoring practice may be found in his scores for documentaries, notably Resnais's *Nuit et brouillard* and the now largely neglected *A Child Went Forth* (1941; also known as *The Children's Camp*), Losey's short film about a summer day camp sold as pedagogical treatment outlining priorities in the care of child refugees during World War II. The latter film is seminal for its economy and clarity of sound-image synchronization and was central in Eisler's career development in the United States. In his work for the Rockefeller Foundation and for Resnais, working without the stringent demands and divisions of creative labor he would roundly if at times cavalierly critique with Adorno in *Composing for the Films,* Eisler makes significant historical contributions to cinema music worth considering.

Eisler's scores for these films present sound effects and commentary apart from each film's authoritative voice-over. They are not simply attempts to ameliorate film music in "musical" terms but rather aim to create, by virtue of explorations of serialist aesthetics in cinema, a mode of musical enunciation whose complex forms and effects are developed throughout the filmic text. There is also their Brechtian aspect: their attempt to achieve a degree of interpretive agency, but through musical audition. Eisler's scoring practices differ from those of functional accompaniment or even descriptive narration of framed objects or edited events in providing extended commentary on the subject matter of the work and its reception, not simply on the image. Earlier Eisler had deployed serialist strategies not to advance new harmonic combinations or the serialist method itself but to raise the aesthetic standards of composition for proletarian march songs or agitative populist *lieder* while working with Brecht or figures in Germany and France. Again, the larger goal was not simply to appeal to popular song but rather to help compose the musical function of a public that did not yet exist as such.[2]

In a similar way, Eisler's Rockefeller-funded film music experiments at the New School from 1940 to 1942 had more to do with developing a pragmatics for composing cinema music where listening might help prompt critical (and, consequently, properly historical rather than escapist) spectatorship. Still, if Eisler had earlier rejected the elitism he perceived in Arnold Schoenberg and his circle to turn to more explicitly political projects, now, he composed proletarian marches as musical cues within more subtle underscoring for narrative films, such as Lang's *Hangmen Also Die!*—a film whose antifascist politics had relatively little to do with, say, forging a public character for workers' struggles in California. If Eisler's film music in New York or Hollywood is less oppositional in intent than the actual union organizing for whose events he formerly had composed musically sophisticated agitative marches, it is nonetheless directly engaged with actual conditions of industrial cinema production. The "contestational" tone of Eisler's remarks in *Composing for the Films* or elsewhere, then, does not translate into film scores producing countercinematic icons at every juncture of musical cue and image sequence in the audiovisual stream. There is no critical need to "conform" *Composing* to Eisler's composing, inasmuch as the production process of each work necessitates different positionalities to be enjoined. Adorno's claims that Eisler overly politicizes the content of the German edition of *Composing for the Films*[3] indicate not the incoherence of Eisler's practices but rather that the book's production process proceeded through phases different from that of his film music production.[4]

Rather, Eisler's primary contribution to the U.S. cultural industries is less the production of film scores that would become canonical in cinema than the development of a pragmatics for the theoretical critique of the culture industries, deploying flexible serialist style to press against the conventions of audience listening as inattentive and parenthetical. Rather than a problem of unheard melodies, Eisler's problem in such films as *Rain* is that new recording technologies were not sufficiently advanced and still tended to neutralize much of the sound and musical resources available to the composer, even while increasingly sophisticated synchronization techniques for sound and image design rendered the exhibitionary capacities of the cinema more powerful than before. The technical "neutralization" of musical sound in the production process, then, corresponded with a neutralization of audience response in reception, as *Composing for the Films* suggests and as archival documents also make clear. New techniques might transform or worsen this condition. Eisler's concerns were as much equipmental as conceptual, but because the techniques have changed, we do not easily acknowledge the creative labor required to change them. But *Composing* presents in any case not simply a proposal of contrasting sound and image metaphors—it presents a social and technical program aimed at raising the value of musical labor in the film industry. That creative labor in the Hollywood cinema could not become expressive in material, historical terms was complicated by the conventions of the synchronized cinema: "The talking picture too is mute."[5] Eisler and Adorno's concrete, critical plan is aimed not simply at musical supplementation but the transformed, technical aspects of sound expression: "objective planning, montage [methods for sound and music], and breaking through the universal neutralization" resulting from then-inferior sound production practices and alienated mode of aesthetic production (88; and see Chapter 2).

Eisler's film scores thus raise the creative status of the film composer but also expand the expressive means and capacities for film music toward critical narration as such. Such works as the rescore of *Rain* or of the original score for *A Child Went Forth,* composed during his time as a Rockefeller researcher, demonstrate the critical, creative, and administrative pragmatics informing Eisler's revaluation of creative labor and musical expression in the production of the audiovisual work, not simply in oppositional iconic linkage between musical score and image. And despite numerous attempts within historical film studies to grasp Eisler's scores in reference to *Composing for the Films,* his commentary with Adorno does not actually describe the production process he used on the Film Music Project when scoring and evaluating such films as *Rain* or *A Child Went Forth.*

For instance, for the films he scored as part of the Film Music Project, Eisler prepared multiple variations of each score, allowing musical experts and film connoisseurs the Rockefeller staff selected to "test" the experiments in screenings at which this aesthetic, expert opinion was gathered and discussed. Eisler and his coordinators at the Rockefeller Foundation refrained from using the statistical methods and technical apparatuses that other Rockefeller researchers had developed for evaluating studies of radio reception or experiments in theatrical sound effects. His organization of multiple possible film scores with variably configurable sound-image combinations for the purposes of testing and evaluation was predicated on divisions and displacements of material, creative, and affective labor, even if he did not describe the conditions of labor in those terms. Yet the "methods" Eisler and Adorno describe leave out this last, fourth stage (*Composing,* 140); if they had described this phase as they describe the rest of the project, it would appear in the place where Eisler and Adorno resume their critique of Eisenstein, in fact. They explain their elision of the actual New York screenings of Eisler's results this way: "Sociological investigations might have been undertaken in connection with the general plan of the project. For instance, some of the feature-film sequences could have been performed for different groups of listeners, accompanied by the old music and sometimes that worked out in the project, and the reactions could have been studied under laboratory conditions, by means of questionnaires and interviews. But such investigations lay outside the scope of the project; moreover, their results would merely contribute data concerning the possible mass audience reactions to the use of modern music in motion pictures" (138).

Eisler in fact considered questionnaires and interviews of the sort developed by Paul Lazarsfeld on Princeton/Columbia Radio Research, for which Adorno was an early consultant. He also considered using the synchronized gestural feedback mechanisms Lazarsfeld's project had developed to gather audience reactions to radio programming. A budget item was included in his project for such "data" gathering. Although he finally carried out only a focus group–like gathering of experts, in *Composing,* Eisler and Adorno entirely deny any such evaluative stage of the project existed at all! In this light, not only is Eisler conceptually incoherent, as Cook claims, but he has a very short memory as well. But we need to invoke a different theoretical measure, here: Eisler and Adorno simply grant no apparent credence to the cognitive measurement of aesthetic values in terms of the popular reception of post-Schoenbergian music in terms of either discursive or rationalized gestural measurements. Eisler could hardly have believed that an audience made up of the likes of the Rockefeller Foundation's John Marshall, who coordinated Eisler's project, or Iris Berry, of the Museum of Modern Art's Film Department, represented "the masses."[6]

Despite a more radical political stance during the 1920s and 1930s, by the early 1940s, rather than drawing on the overtly agitative stylistics that characterize his earlier music aimed at building a public function for workers' rallies or Brecht's theater, Eisler composed cinema music in New York and Los Angeles that reflects a critical pessimism increasingly shared by other German émigrés during and after their exiles in the United States. As John Fuegi notes, Brecht had discarded his earlier theories of a *Verfremdungseffekt* (alienation effect) by 1948, as he turned to a new, apparently more conventionally Aristotelian and less overtly politically engaged theater upon his return to then–East Germany. Brecht's later aesthetic strategies are aimed more at resistance than agitation—as Heiner Müller observes, they are theatrical works with the "Stalinist brakes on."[7]

Eisler's compositional approaches in U.S. wartime and postwar contexts also move away from his attempts at engaged serialisms during the 1920s, designed to motivate the audience to cohere in a mass unit, toward an engineered critique of image and music relations designed to programmatically insert cognitive and affective distance between the cinema presentation and the audience. Already considered to be acting as a bloc, the audience was now regarded as a body programmed for atomization by the cultural industries at the site of reception. Eisler's U.S. film scores can be understood, then, as a pragmatics for modulating distraction with critical distance rather than as effecting a radical agitative intent. This modulation of distraction with distance indicates a diagram of music, affect, and compositional technique distinct from that associated with the avant-garde relying on a strong sense of oppositional relation.

Whereas the earlier marches or theatrical assignments are predicated on the theory that class cohesion could be an outcome prompted by performance (whether musical, theatrical, or, indeed, the cinematic montage in *Kuhle Wampe, oder: Wem gehört die Welt?* [1932], or tap dance and black song in *Niemansland* [1931]), the film music Eisler undertook in New York and Los Angeles pushes any Brechtian notion of *Gestus* beyond Brecht's conception of *Gestus* as verifiable in relation to music but stopping short of musicality as such. Very broadly, Brecht meant by *Gestus* the critically informed social reality that an actor denotes through his character's movements or attitude: "A good way of judging a piece of music with a text is to try out the different attitudes or gests with which the performer ought to deliver the individual sections: politely or angrily, modestly or contemptuously, approvingly or argumentatively, craftily or without calculation."[8] Eisler's great contribution to cinema, for his part, would be to emphasize less of a performed, performative *Gestus* on the part of a historical agent, an actor, or a musical performer or ensemble and more of a musicalized *Gestus* on the part of a cinema audience. This ostensively resistant audience reception would be achieved, unironically, by flexibly harvesting the new musical resources of avant-garde composition for the synchronized industrial cinema, whose capacities for sound reproduction continued to develop rapidly while continuing to make music and sound production secondary.[9] If Adorno comments that Schoenberg's music is "no longer aural," Eisler uses synchronized counterpoint to deploy a gestural stylistics for the intermediation of sound and image that, just so, is no longer aural. Sound cinema as a doubled site of listening and of spectatorship is, similarly and as a consequence, not unified in terms of narrative or presentation. Rather, cinema as site of musical design hosts the situational development of a divided couple, such that the site of listening and the site of viewing are mutually modulated in time. The dialectical image becomes the problem of the dialectical stream.

And what is key to recognize in *A Child Went Forth* and in *Nuit et brouillard* is Eisler's composition of not simply sound and image relations in iconic linkage but a relation between musicality as essay or commentary to audience reaction in ways that address then-contemporary concerns with affect, including hysteria. Eisler's film music thus elaborates an alternative to what Brecht or Eisler conceives as a cinematic image anchoring realist audiovisual synchronization whose passive consumption legitimates class privilege.[10] Eisler's scoring practices, like Fischinger's visual music animation or Eisenstein's cinema montage, are a modal cinema aiming at a medial ethics of reception. This project of "emancipating" film music would be analogous to Schoenberg's "emancipation" of dissonance (and, for Schoenberg, with reference to Bach),[11] but by inserting a Brechtian *Gestus*, distancing audience from exhibition while claiming access to advancing technical procedures of recording and synchronization to increase the creative autonomy of the cinema composer as creative worker.[12] In fact, Brecht and Schoenberg were paid consultants for Eisler as he prepared the final, April 1942 previews serving as the evaluative component of his research.[13]

Eisler and Adorno removed any account of the actual evaluation of Eisler's work on the Film Music Project from *Composing for the Films* not because what they heard did not conform to their theories but because neither questionnaires nor biological measurement could register the meanings Eisler felt mattered, and perhaps because they felt that reactions from roughly five years prior to the book's long and drawn-out publication were no longer relevant. Between completion of the Film Music Project and publication of *Composing*, too, Eisler's lectures on the project in Los Angeles prompted considerable interest. Eisler was invited to appear on a panel in Beverly Hills on May 17, 1945, to speak on questions that would later be presented in *Composing*, but here in anticipation of publication in the initial summer 1945 issue of *Hollywood Quarterly*, which never panned out.[14]

Rockefeller archives document the problems of mass listening that helped motivate funding for Eisler's project and mitigate Lazarsfeld's psychoanalytically inflected studies of radio reception. One of these problems, and one that Eisler refers to his method of dialectical pragmatics rather than to formal observer evaluation, is mass listening's power to produce the "mass hysteria," as observed in the radio reception of Orson Welles's October 1938 pre-Halloween prank, *War of the Worlds* broadcast.[15] *Worlds* demonstrated to Rockefeller administrators that the U.S. public was not immune to the apparent mass hysteria manipulated by Hitler's regime in Germany. Mass-media listening was not simply a problem of exhausted workers caught between unrewarding work, inadequate education, and aspiration mythified in passive reception of mass media, as Rockefeller administrator John Marshall observed, then, but also of overreactive response.

Mark Micale argues that Freud's early work marks a point at which the individual symptoms of hysteria were ceasing to be indicators of a generally recognized disorder; by 1910, without a strong etiological theory to maintain its coherence, hysteria as a unitary disorder, its "constituent symptomatological parts" were broken apart and redistributed to other medical categories (525–526).[16] Yet by the mid-twentieth century, mass hysteria had been re-created out of these parts. Hysteria was invoked to describe reactions pertaining to mass listening and helped prompt important studies of sound and music in mass media. Eisler's Film Music Project was one of these projects. It is in this context, then, that Eisler observes in *Composing for the Films* that his score for *A Child Went Forth* demonstrates affective states, such as "sadness, nervousness, even hysteria."[17] Film music should not provoke or even depict such states but rather, in a sense, diagnose them in relation to others and within a larger commentary on their conditions and development.

Yet Eisler's rising profile in Hollywood after World War II occurred amid the turbulent wave of anti-Semitism and fears around Soviet influence and the emergence of Communist China. In this context, the very mass hysteria that had helped motivate funding of Eisler's project and that Eisler had used film music to diagnose now turned against him, as he himself recognized. One pamphlet that was particularly thorough in its claims of conspiracy named Eisler's pro-Soviet journalist brother Gerhard as a secret Jewish infiltrator of the United States and went on to proclaim that although the U.S. public's hatred of "the Nazis" had become "hysterical" after cinematic dramatizations of Hitler's brutality became commonplace, because Hollywood had failed to similarly demonize Stalin, "Reds" must control all cinema writing.[18]

Eisler gave *his* response at his hearing before the House Un-American Activities Committee:

> The committee hopes to create a drive against every liberal, progressive, and socially conscious artist in this country, and to subject their works to an un-Constitutional and hysterical political censorship. It is horrible to think what will become of American art if this committee is to judge what art is American and what is un-American.
>
> This is the sort of thing Hitler and Mussolini tried. They were not successful, and neither will be the House Committee on Un-American Activities.[19]

Eisler underwent voluntary deportation in 1948.[20]

Eisler's 1942 move to Los Angeles had been facilitated by his friendships with other displaced German artists and intellectuals as well as the industry connections he had made through the Rockefeller-sponsored Film Music Project. Herrmann had arrived in 1941 as part of Welles's creative entourage. Both men's moves to Hollywood coincided with creative opportunities created by maturing sound and synchronization technologies as well as by larger political or economic urgencies. Eisler and Herrmann ultimately undertook stormy departures, although in very different times and circumstances. Herrmann enjoyed a long, if tempestuous, career as part of the Los Angeles film community but, a devoted Anglophile, finally removed himself to England after repeatedly infuriating and alienating his Hollywood employers, Alfred Hitchcock among them.[21] Despite his signature ability to move audiences' passions into realms by turns ironic (*Citizen Kane* [1941]), grand (*Beneath the 12-Mile Reef* [1951]), or diabolical (*Psycho* [1960]), the composer's tendency to openly criticize his directors made him hard to employ in the 1960s until a revival of interest in his work developed shortly before his death in 1975. During that decade, Herrmann was again often engaged in high-profile projects, but now by younger directors who began their careers in independent cinema and who aspired to create a renewed cinematic expressivity to rival that of classic Hollywood: Brian De Palma (for whom Herrmann scored the thriller *Sisters* [1973]) and Martin Scorsese (for whom Herrmann scored much of *Taxi Driver* [1976]).[22]

Herrmann rose to early fame as a conductor for NBC radio broadcasts during the 1930s, introducing the U.S. listening public to new scores from emerging (often Continental or British) composers he admired and reintroducing forgotten or neglected American ones (he was an early defender of Charles Ives, who was later recognized, partly as a result of Herrmann's efforts, as a pioneer in the incorporation of noise in the compositional techniques of modern music). Herrmann's music, distinct from Eisler's, uses dissonance and noise with respect to conventional tonal harmonics. His rousing fanfares and operatic tragi-parody in *Citizen Kane* enabled his permanent move to Hollywood by securing his reputation there in advance. Later, his scores lent metallic sheen and spectral texture to such films as *The Ghost and Mrs. Muir* (1947), in which Rex Harrison's pirate ghost appears to Lucy Muir (Gene Tierney) as something like a suddenly embodied radio signal emanating from the distant past of her mysterious home, appearing at the prompt of a musical cue. Dissonance in Herrmann's scores tends to approximate a musical sound or special effect connoting psychic unsettlement or dissolution, or corporeal dismemberment, disintegration, or disappearance, as in *Hangover Square* (1945), *Psycho*, or *Taxi Driver.* Yet like so many of the historical composers he admired (Wagner, Debussy, Ives) and like so many film-music composers before and after him, Herrmann deploys dissonance in relation to anchoring tonalities in his works, establishing complex, coloristic tensions sustained in relation to, if not always resolved into, the dominant thematics of the thus-defamiliarized setting.

Herrmann's and Eisler's work, then, provide counterexamples of the way serialist composition was deployed or resisted in midcentury U.S. cinema, radio, and theatrical music: either to provide the motivation and development of the effects of hysteria and the psycho-corporeal fragmentation such hysteria might name or to offer a dialectical stream of sound and image whereby the site of listening reception may not be reducible to spectatorship and, thus, where such affects as hysteria may be expressed for critical audition. Herrmann tends to invoke serialist dissonance as punctuation of exceptional affective states transgressing their generating conditions, so that resolution is often tentative or ambiguous. In Eisler's work, the characteristic dissonance of serialism simply recoups conventional harmonic tones as needed within compositional autonomy derived from Schoenberg's methods. Eisler thus shifts any tensions to be developed more fully into audience apperception, allowing the musical score greater formal heterogeneity even while paradoxically liberating dissonance from musical sound. Eisler's scores may often sound, or read, as "conventional," as Cook finds. But their planning and effects worked toward greater creative autonomy on the part of the composer and aimed for greater interpretive autonomy on the part of the audiovisual receiver.

Even when Herrmann's cinema music was conceived as integral to the cinematic work, the extreme of corporeal dissolution in Herrmann's cinema music exhibits the classical film's score lack of interest in making palpable the doubled complexity of sound cinema as a site of reception: cinema's doubled quasi-architectural diagram of itself as a site of image and aural exhibition. Harmonic dissonance in Herrmann's cinema music indexes the composer's struggle to maintain a sense of artistic innovation, integrity, or reputation *against* divisions of creative labor that tended to make anonymous key procedures of his work. These divisions of labor (composition, part copying and orchestration, performance, sound mixing, recording, conducting, dubbing, editing, and so on) did not innocently inherit the division of labor typical of Western art music but resulted from Hollywood's long transmedia marketing imperatives requiring greater resources for programming reception of the cinematic sensorium than the moving image itself could provide. As a Los Angeles fan wrote to the producers of *The Spanish Main* (1945) about Eisler's score of the film after its release:

> Since "The Spanish Main" first started running at the Pantages I found it impossible to forget the background music. Since then I have seen it sixteen times and I love it. The music, I mean. My request is do you know of any way that I can get a recording of it, from the very beginning to the very end. I would be very proud and happy to add it to my record collection.
>
> I would appreciate this very much, because it out does [*sic*] any background music I have ever heard, "Spellbound" and "The Song of Bernadette" included. This is, I know, a very clumsy way of putting it but I do hope you can help me.[23]

By the early 1940s, the sound-track recording was a fully commercialized object (even if not as a long-playing record).[24] Herrmann's tendencies toward grandiose musical fanfare or disintegrating corporeal affect in cinema scoring are as much narratological elements as they are indices of his resistance to the secondary status of labor granted to film-music composers. Their work, Herrmann thought, rose above difficult narrative or technical problems only to be further constrained and diverted by being packaged according to secondary marketing procedures, such as phonograph sales, that had no clear motivation in relation to the narratological problems film music had to solve and that might benefit from entirely different production practices. The paradoxical capacity of apparently passive audiences to respond so actively to marketing imperatives is the issue here.

Herrmann argues that film-music marketing detracted from what made film-music marketable:

> [Karol Rathaus] treated for the first time the music of a film as an integral emotional part of the whole, not as a decoration. Because the film [*Der Mörder Dimitri Karamasoff* (*The Brothers Karamazov*; 1931)] deals with one of the Karamazov's falling in love with a prominent harlot and visiting her in her establishment wherein a gypsy orchestra plays, the music of the picture begins with a gypsy orchestra simply playing Russian gypsy music. But as the picture progresses, the brother becomes more and more involved with the harlot, the music stops being ornamental and becomes an emotional mirror of him. It becomes more and more tragic and more and more hysterical. It reaches its greatest moment . . . when the brother hysterically drives a troika through a raging blizzard accompanied musically by a great battery of percussion instruments. Remember: this was done way back in the early 1930s! . . .
>
> I don't know why, today, a film has to cost four million dollars to push a record costing seventy cents, but it does! . . . Music for film should be no more noticed than the camera work.[25]

Film music's incorporation of dissonance, in Herrmann's work, was a strategy of disappearance that might allow hysteria to appear in the media stream, much like Lucy Muir's first disturbing, then ultimately accommodating, "ghost."

By contrast, dissonance for Eisler is a matter of synchronization understood neither simply as a mutual indexing of coexpressive narratological relationships between recorded image and sound, as in Herrmann's music, nor of immanent time circulating, via the film, between creative workers, audience, and the transposition of their mutually sensible history into the materialities of the work of (socialist) mass culture, as in Eisenstein's montage. Rather, sound-image synchronization in Eisler's music, where the site of listening reception is not entirely reducible to the site of visual exhibition, foregrounds the site of reception and the machinery of exhibition as enacting actual historical conflict between (exhibited) narrative and (unattended) audience speech. "Dissonance" in terms of listening and watching is as much an aim as the use of advanced techniques of composition. As a result, in Eisler's work, especially after his work with Losey on *A Child Went Forth,* musical narration opens to essayistic commentary as much as it engages in storytelling. The administrative rather than purely auditive *Gestus* of Eisler's film music supplies tension whereby the relationship between cinema music's audibility and the cinematic image's exhibition becomes in itself a mode of critical speech that is interpreted—but not *in itself* heard—by an active audience.

For Herrmann or Eisler, as for others, the tensions and paradoxes encountered as sound cinema entered into a new phase of transitions (and as radio broadcasting breached national boundaries with international information and the phonograph extended its aural reach into factories and homes) suggested danger: an exaggerated capacity on the part of audiences and publics for passive experience on the one hand and for unpredictable activity prompted by artificial or synthetic messages on the other. The positive version of this paradox, of course, was productivity; the negative version, hysteria. "Hysteria" in cinema as a site of mass listening, then, describes or diagnoses some too-passive state of reception alternating with, leading to, or otherwise sharing potential with a too-active state of response. It is an energetic dysfunction of networked, mass corporeality.

Despite Kurt London's influential 1936 study of contemporary film music,[26] despite the attention given to sound and music in such trade journals as *Hollywood Quarterly* (and see Chapters 1 and 3), and despite the fact that the work of such figures as Eisler and Herrmann dramatizes a thorough integration of mass-media aesthetics, critical theory, institutional policy making, and cinema-industry marketing, academic cinema studies did not significantly extend theoretical coverage of critiques of musical sound in time-based work until the 1980s and 1990s. Mass listening, which had been a first-rank problem from 1930 to 1950, was reconfigured in understandings of the film sound track as "supplement"—a much more critical treatment of Herrmann's complaint cited above. Appearing after Jane Feuer's and along with Rick Altman's analyses of the film musical,[27] works by theorists as diverse as Claudia Gorbman,[28] Kaja Silverman,[29] Mary Ann Doane,[30] Royal S. Brown,[31] or Lawrence Kramer[32] reconsider film music and film sound as supplementary to the narratological and spectatorial functions presumed to be anchored in the cinematic image. Musical sound afforded a symptomatic stratum for critical interrogation of the exhibitionary unconscious (as in Michel Chion's influential book-length analysis in *Audio-Vision*).[33]

In the most rigorously musicological of this generation of analyses, Brown also sees musical meaning as exterior to narrative and representational meaning, but not simply in terms of marketing. Rather, in this view, music represents a logic of aesthetic supplementation,[34] a conclusion that Kramer formulates explicitly in regard to music and narrative, with film scoring a primary example of music as narrative supplement.[35] A slightly later alternative to these analyses was to situate cinema music in relationship to popular music, resulting in the "pop film-score," which Smith suggests emerged in tandem with the long-playing record during the late 1940s. Here, though, the most obvious historical negotiations of music in cinema—between music industries, cinema industries, and radio industries—is drastically and retroactively shortened to the period of postwar consumer culture, against the historical evidence.[36] For example, Ivor Montagu, who accompanied Eisenstein to Hollywood in the late 1920s, later wrote of the vast libraries of commercial music held at Paramount Studios, where they visited. More recently, Katherine Spring[37] demonstrates the extent of cross-industry marketing between industrial cinema and industrial popular music at Warner Brothers.

With increasing critical attention recently given to computer games, digital downloading of music, and musical appliances, questions and doubts about how musical scores function across historical formats or media canons return.[38] Gorbman draws on Cook's analysis of musical media discussed above and, while retreating from her earlier psychoanalytic investigation into cinema music's "unheard melodies," turns to an aesthetic and rhetorical account of music in digital gaming. Gorbman suggests that music's "linearity in a nonlinear environment" emphasizes medium-specific aesthetic and rhetorical challenges prompted by the "interactivity and variability" of computational production. Artificial intelligence computationally generating dynamic musical variations now appears to threaten human intelligence, and, in doing so, prompts theoretical challenges: "What kind of blow does this replacement of human intelligence (or rather its displacement, since the musical parameters are in fact composed by humans) strike to notions of musical aesthetics and rhetoric? Is dynamic music just a giant convention/cliché machine? And if we claim it is, must we also acknowledge that the bulk of live musical performances are also convention/cliché machines? . . . The rapid evolution of technology, markets, and social functions of music make these questions all the more compelling" (24–25).[39]

In fact, whether the cultural industries' new sound technologies resulted in giant convention/cliché machines was a compelling question for Herrmann, Eisler, and many others between 1930 and 1950, although the ways in which the question was asked and answered differed from the ways in which it is raised today. But we should be careful not to overstate the case that cinema, radio, and television differ from digital works in their "linearity" (digital games are linearly encoded and proceed in generally linear patterns of development but differ in the flexibility of display and use that cybernetic programming and random-access memory afford). Nor are cinema products distinct from digital-gaming products in being limited to stand-alone one-time consumption—whether historically or in the contemporary digital markets of DVD or online downloading. Any time-based work exhibits complex temporalities and may support variable exhibition practices, regardless of the appearance of a dominant paradigm or of critical accounts affirming dominant paradigms to the detriment of our understanding of significant variability in practices of display and interpretation. What is distinct, then, in addition to the computational capacities of the medium and any stylistic variegations in its use, is the reconfigured and intensified divisions of creative labor that digital audiences actualize in terms of interactive gesture. Fans still correspond with producers asking for unavailable recordings—but handling of the request and the transaction now tends to be automated, whether in a musical download or in a computer game revealing musical pattern.

When Adorno or Eisler assail the culture industries, theirs is not simply a critique of specificities wrongly instrumented in technological mismatches of content and medium. Rather, they are concerned with a massive rationalization of the corporeal affects, social relations, and worldly knowledge, where passive consumption by audiences whose attitudes toward mass-cultural transitions seemed to border on hysteria was thought to indicate deepening social alienation. They believed that a propensity toward political delusion had its corollary in the incapacitation of critical thought. Such institutions as the Rockefeller Foundation shared their concerns, albeit without the insistence on the critical methods of dialectical materialist aesthetics. Generally, "passive synthesis," the capacity for thought to become habit, was observed as subsumed within passive consumption, such that habitual consumption replaced critical learning. This concern that passive synthesis gives way in advanced capitalism to habitual consumption without learning, of course, is the refrain of twentieth-century media studies. In the late 1930s and early 1940s, it was marked by the transposition of "hysteria" to "mass hysteria" in critical, aesthetic, and political discourses and diagnoses.

Eisler directed his Film Music Project under the auspices of Alvin Johnson at the New School for Social Research from 1940 to 1942; Adorno provided critical theoretical expertise to Lazarsfeld's Radio Project and later collaborated with Eisler on writing *Composing for the Films*. From 1938 to 1948, Harold Burris-Meyer received funding for Sound in the Theatre, a sound-design project extending Adolphe Appia's notions of "image and light" on the postromantic stage to a contemporary electronic processing of sound in the theater. Burris-Meyer applied his theatrical sound-mixing techniques to workplaces wired by Muzak and to the World War II Pacific Theater but envisioned them also as providing enhanced sound control in the cinema theater.[40] Support staffer Harry Robin moved from Burris-Meyer's to Eisler's project; all three initiatives shared access to consultants provided by the foundation's John Marshall, as well as to other institutional resources. Iris Berry of the Museum of Modern Art, New York, for example, reviewed Burris-Meyer's "Sound Show," a demonstration of his work in sound design, but also facilitated aspects of Eisler's project, researching Eisler's film work before his grant proceeded and promising to archive and to distribute the results. All three projects were coordinated for the foundation by Marshall, whose longtime interest and administrative expertise in mass-media reception, mass-cultural aesthetics, and project management helped inform the projects' methods and goals. Motivating these projects was the long-standing concern on the part of the Rockefeller Foundation that the commercial effects of mass media were undermining their social, educational, and aesthetic potential and, in the worst case, contributing to emotional exhaustion or mass hysteria.

As Caryl Flinn notes in her historically informed close readings of *Detour* (1945) and *Penny Serenade* (1941), listening and responding to music is a problematic of affect, engagement, and mobility. Flinn makes clear that affective epistemologies are visualized within narrative in terms of phonograph players, recordings, music, or performance, and as dramatic interpersonal negotiations conducted in terms of musical functions. In these films, music on and off screen reflects greater tensions at large in the *socius*—and, sometimes, their tentative resolutions. Resolutions happen in terms of affect, whether cinema music shapes a contingent, repeating utopia through feminine nostalgia in the women's melodrama (as when *Penny Serenade*'s Julie works through her doubts about marriage and motherhood to music) or through a contingent, repeating dystopia giving rise to masculine hysteria in the noir road film (as when *Detour*'s Al is tortured by a recurring pop song that brings back unwanted memories of the woman he loves and drives him to strangle the femme fatale who has led him to dissolution in a dingy Hollywood apartment). Each of these narratives presents nonlinear plots and requires nonlinear interpretation, although the exhibition format is linear. "Musical memory" affords Julie's assertion of choice in *Penny Serenade* but prompts Al's violent dissociation in *Detour*. In both films, music as passive memory or music as hysterical excess shows the ways that networked listening across radio, theater, cinema, and phonography suggests an exterior, programmed reservoir alternately drained or overflowing: a kind of impersonal inorganic affect not easily reduced to cognitive models of active or passive synthesis. Musicality in works of this period connotes this affective labor standing in reserve. Far more than simply expressing the "cinema memory" Annette Kuhn[41] has recently described, music also expresses the capacity of the audience to hold the sexed, gendered narrative of the film apart from the viewers' interpretations or to be lost to its flow of manipulations: "holes" in music's synthetic recall.[42] In what follows, I distinguish two competing modes of synchronizing musical sound in the classic sound film, whereby Herrmann attempts synchronization as overflowing affect and whereby Eisler attempts sync as a measured, temperate observation of affect, draining the audiovisual work of its potential hysteria by naming it. I show the way that Herrmann's "consonant synchronization" of music and image differs from Eisler's "dissonant" synchronization. Herrmann's work in *Hangover Square* dramatizes contemporary concerns around hysteria: the conflict of commercial media versus quality media, imagined as music, sex, murder, and sacrifice. I close the chapter with a discussion of Eisler's work with Losey on *A Child Went Forth,* which also depicts affective labor as hysteria but localizes it as an affective event in a series of affective events to deflate its power.

Musical Pandemonium in Everyday Life

Hangover Square, John Brahm's 1945 psycho-thriller for Fox Studios, presents the mid-twentieth-century threat of musical pandemonium arising in excessive listening by transposing listening cultures backward: to turn-of-the-century gaslit streets and musical salon reminiscent, in fact, of romantic auditoria. The film's title sequence opens with Herrmann's "Hangover Square Concerto," which Herrmann composed before shooting began to provide tempo and emotional pacing for the film's visual design and narrative direction. The film's finale concludes with a performance of the final concerto, but this performance is drowned out in a conflagration that destroys the musical salon and the film's disturbed protagonist, George Bone (Laird Cregar).

The final concert scene at the climax of this film specifically calls up two transformations that allow audiences to be optimally configured for the combined reception of audio and visual display. The first of these is the conforming of the seating to an arc within which perspective on the stage (and later, screen) could be established for a maximum of people to minimize visual obstruction (as opposed to the varied seating arrangements of eighteenth-century listening rooms). As we hear the elusive concerto in its "entirety" in the final moments of the film, the orchestra is seated in a half circle behind and around the pianist and conductor, while the audience is seated in a half circle facing the stage. No warranted guarantee of a centrally framed perspective on the piano performance takes place; the optimization of the musical space for the synchronization with dramatic space is not specifically pictured here. However, the camera's ability to compose the scene of musical performance makes up for its incompletely rendered historical antecedent and effects a narrative climax for the film as a whole. Herrmann's score is profoundly engaged in introducing, developing, and concluding the narratological trajectory of the film.

The second transformation is the presentation of the performance as a visual spectacle.[43] Within the film, that spectacle includes prominent use of gaslights in a brightly lit room. The feverish subjectivity of the composer, performing his overwrought composition amid flaming torches, presents a synchronized musical topos wherein his emotions burn brightly before the expectant audience. The spectators can still see each other, which is historically appropriate to the lighting of such a room and also useful for camera presentation of their responses to us, the cinematic audience. In this way, a listening situation from the classical age is reconstituted for the filmic performance of a neo-romantic concerto. The concert hall is rendered as an excessive site where musical spirit collides with musical labor, a location that recenters for the cinema audience the diabolically displaced sexual urges of a mad pianist.

Brown points out that in film, diegetic music can become nondiegetic music, and directors often play on the notion of the "invisible" music of the sound track by introducing a cue to indicate the mood of a character.[44] Brown also observes that in *Hangover Square,* the piano concerto presented in the film's fiery climax works within and outside the film's diegesis to function as source music and emotional cue. Yet this film's story is so musicalized through strategies of synchronization as to be compulsively overcontrolled by musical sound itself—just like poor, mad George Bone, the film's pianist protagonist. *Hangover Square* is an example of a film that recapitulates the position of listener as viewer, but so that a romantically scored love story becomes a musically excessive thrill-kill shocker. The modulation from romance to murder comes consistently through the overt synchronization of musical themes and cues with visual framing and characterization, so that any final division between a visual narrative diegesis and nondiegetic nonnarrative music is untenable. Instead, George's instability is presented in terms of sound passing into music through George's unstable psyche. In key moments of the film, a grating dissonant chord, heard in jostled violins or in the clang of falling pipes, sends George into a fugue state, flipping his split personality like a record and transforming him from passionate struggling artist to degenerate sex-killer.

Brahm's film sets up George as a dedicated, if poorly spoken pianist at work on a concerto he cannot quite bring to completion, partly because his murderous sexuality is "randomly" cued by those recurring, dissonant musical events. Over the film's title sequence, we hear the first tortured chords of the concerto that George is struggling to complete. George's first murder occurs during the opening moments of the narrative: Crashing chords play, the camera settles on a view through a window, and, through a shop window, we see George confronting an unknown man. As the man screams for him to stop, George sets him on fire. George then groggily wanders home to find his loving fiancée waiting anxiously. The gap inserted here, between the opening strains of "Concerto Macabre" heard over the title sequence and the initial murder following shortly afterward, is then broken out into a stream of seriated events occupying the audience's distracted attention. In due time, we learn to unfold this gap-as-development from one unreasoned motive to the next and apply it to the whole of the film: from musical overture; to illegible conflicts of desire, art, and commerce; to murder; to flames. Our gapped attention to initial title sequence, applied to the larger narrative trajectory, finally implodes in the concerto's spectacular refrain: George himself goes up in flames at the film's end, as he finally delivers the creative work he has long promised but been unable to complete.

Here, musical reasoning as an indeterminate interval of synchronized sound and image remains "irrational" but becomes increasingly concrete. This musical reasoning, irrational as it may be, nonetheless insists on narrative power, contrary to cinema studies' parceling out of primary narrative meaning to the image and supplementary modulation to the musical sound track. We never learn the precise motive for George's early morning visit to the unidentified man, but soon enough a clearer pattern emerges: George later kills vampy music hall singer Netta (Linda Darnell), who has humiliated him by making him compose pop songs for her to perform. George's problem is not musical mastery, for his talent is fully demonstrated early on (at the outset, even, if we grant that his "concerto" introduces the film). Rather, his problem is some uncertain ratio of commercial distraction to artistic production. He suffers nervous exhaustion brought about by incessant commands on his creative power to produce, whether for himself and for his art (the concerto, whose composition fulfills him when he can do it and grants him social status) or for Netta and for commerce (the cheap pop tunes, which distract him from higher pursuits). As any frustrated, romantically inclined genius might, George experiences music issuing from around him and within him—but in gas-lit London, he is surrounded by construction noise. George (and the audience) cannot know whether the music experienced is internal or external, so his fugue states begin with random musical noise emanating from his surroundings, develop with the screams of his victims, and cadence to their end in musical fire.

The threat of ambiguous sexuality is coded in terms of a musical schizophrenia whose destructive motif the narrative follows and develops. The chords that set George off can come from anywhere, inserting an element of deviant sexuality into otherwise everyday struggles; they function as musical sound both objective and subjective, transitioning from diegetic noise to musical underscore via sound effects, bringing the audience, like a moth to the flame, closer to George's dangerous musical perspective and relating to us the partial measure of a corporeality alternately slumbering in fugue states or bursting out in hysterical violence. In the body of the narrative, unlike the body of George himself (whose musical sense is stripped bare to the poverty of its commercial potential by Netta), music is doubly potential: materially ubiquitous as sound and subjectively expressive as music, exhibiting and inhibiting at the same time.

The result of these tensions on George's action is a diagram of musicalized sexuality that is intensely interior and exterior by turns. The sound track (alternating between concerto and pop song) and the settings (alternating between posh salon and cheap music hall) vampirize George's artistic potential, making a puppet of his musical will. Although the musical conflict animates pleasures, cares, and threats for all who know George, his murderous productivity nonetheless belongs intimately only to him and to his nighttime consorts. His creative labor, subjected to exhausted habitual productivity in two different directions, has its own special side effects: rising class status and excessive criminality. These tendencies cycle in a repeating pattern that finally condenses and completes itself in the climactic scene in which George immolates himself, almost singeing the fleeing audience.

Chion describes the victim's scream in such suspense thrillers as *Psycho*—whose violin stabs musically condense the sudden, upward more harmonic violin shrieks of *Hangover*'s "Concerto Macabre"—as a "screaming point."[45] Less than a sound object, Chion points out, the "screaming point" is better understood in terms of sound-image synchronization: It is a "black hole toward which there converges an entire fantastic, preposterous, extravagant mechanism—the celebration, the political crime, the sexual murder, and the whole film—all this made in order to be consumed and dissipated" (76). For Chion, this screaming point is heterosexually gendered in a straightforward way: Men shout; women scream. The woman's scream is the black hole of female orgasm, neither spoken nor thought; the woman's cry is "more like the shout of a human subject of language in the face of death" (78). While generally the screaming point is "of a properly human order," Chion asserts that in the male-directed film it poses a question of masculine "mastery"—where the male shout "delimits a territory, the woman's scream has to do with limitlessness"; it is the point at which "speech is suddenly extinct, a black hole, the exit of being" (79).

Yet such a screaming point (gendered explicitly in terms of heterosexual dynamics for Chion, within which he configures its relation to the order of language, humanity, and death) is less relevant to *Hangover Square* than a stream of screams. George's victims' screams are serial, a motif within a refrain that repeats, a crime of musical passion among men motivating the pattern. George's criminal serial identity is never made part of that pattern, and no attempt is made within the film to construct a genealogy of his crimes.

In *Hangover Square,* an entire passage of hysterical time is marked by an extended musical development in sound and image, where diegetic Foley initiates the musical fugue state and where musical score and pacing, tempo, and increasingly hurried movements in the image drive George's states of depressive alterity into manic disidentifications of creative and sexual labor. The anonymous murder glimpsed during the opening of the film is, in musical retrospect, a crime whose sexual nature becomes pointedly clear in the refrain that defers the homophobic projection of musical scream for a heterophobic one: the ambiguous and potentially explosive power of determining meaning by modulating sound and image streams. The more precisely these streams are synchronized, the more radically their meanings may proliferate through them or through the events and objects that populate them. Musicality serves to stabilize or to suspend this distributive tendency, allowing transpositions determining Bone's authorship of the concerto even as they cover up the tracks of his murderous unreason. Desire ordered as synchronized streams rather than as synchronized objects renders desire for the image as desire for the image as music. Personhood and publicity arise in terms of contact and contagion. Finally, the pianist burns out; the police clear up, and the film composer has had his say to his cinema listeners.

Hangover Square's musical score is synoptic—it models a large-scale pattern of transpositions according to which the film's meaning unfurls and that eventually determine the meaning of visual spectacle in relation to musical sacrifice. The narrative hermeneutic constantly refers to the score, the musician, and the warping of his musical expression, setting up his conflict with his environment as noise, rendering George's sanity in a push and pull between the meanings of creative labor: impulse or program? Inner drive or exterior command? Commerce or art? Still, creative labor loses the musical measure of its visually unreflected force precisely in its conflation with excessive affect and that affect's authorization in a body whose creative debts must be repaid. And because music's productive forces are properly exterior to visual quality, those debts must be assigned to the struggling musician himself. George's recalcitrant but determined creative expression patterns his inevitable downfall in the spectacular pyre: flames out of gravity.

George's crimes are not further investigated, because the sonic and musical cues reveal their logic, so he just burns up, as any romantic, criminally insane pianist should. As he collapses from strain during the final performance, the concerto hits the dissonant cue to madness that the sound track has been giving to us all along, at the last, crucial moment moving the extradiegetic key back into Bone's composition itself. His unfinished concerto is the wounded contrary side of his unbridled sexual violence. When they come together, subject, object, and any affective vectors that might distinguish them collapse in haptic spectacle. Whether the concerto on fire or the earlier clanging pipes, clattering violins, or fluttering piccolos as Netta's body burns at the top of the bonfire—all of these carefully indexed moments of synchronized cue and frame have music, even while managing to direct the story's temporal flow, punctuating or suspending what is musically excessive with that which becomes logical through visual composition (framing, editing, and pacing). Musical ratio is visually rationed while the site of listening is destroyed. Regarding the turn to extinguishing George's labor in the name of rationalizing its effects, as a psychologist tells George's fiancée while George, his piano, and the listening salon go up in flames: "It's better this way."

Herrmann thought so. For Herrmann, the film score should be as transparent as camera movement; otherwise, it might become intrusive, losing its power to measure motive and involuntation precisely by expressing them fully. The film's explicit meaning is that popular music's commercial spirit can dangerously contaminate the artistic soul, much like a prostitute can contaminate a good man—that is, after he gives up anonymous cruising. But considered more closely, the film diagrams divisions of creative labor across media industries as well as displacements of creative labor between production personnel and audiences of the time-based industrial artwork. Even when music is scored for a film before production begins; even when it is used to set the tone, pacing, and mood of the shot and sequence design; and even when it is used as narrative synopticon, musical ratio can only make secondary claims on stories industrially programmed according to, and thematically resolved within, the glassine visual reason of a world picture. That is *Hangover Square,* and that is melodrama, for the ever-frustrated Herrmann: For film music to have its say, the site of listening distinct from the site of reception of the image must be destroyed. But more than this personal stylization of the site of listening as subject to the logics of vision on the part of Herrmann, and more than evidence of the unchangeable identity of sound-track music as supplementary to the cinematic image, this stylistics of synchronization is identifiable in its particularity: This is consonant synchronization.

Consonant synchronization works to forward the complex temporal relations of the work as those that define the meaning of the exhibition of the work as the audience's reception of the work (which actually only history can define, and then only partially). Consonant synchronization deprivileges the meanings of sound or sight and their effects on the basis of the audience's laboring interpretation in favor of determining exhibition as the condition of material, technical, and affective meanings in the work. Hence, the recurring industrial concern whereby quantity and quality, commodification and art, technical display and audience corporeality are resolved as shots of burning flames. All transformative potential tends toward potential exhibited within the exhibitionary frame as object and gauge of affective measure. But this style of synchronization can go only so far—the fire that consumes George at the end of the film is the "resolution" of his masculine hysteria in a burnt offering as much as it is a statement on the limits arising in multiplex narration of affective positions, dispositions, and orientations shaped temporally in relation to the work itself. Consonant synchronization can never recoup that inevitable mutual dissonance arising between the mass corporeality of the viewing, listening audience and the complex temporal relations the work exhibits, if only because the audience and the technicized work cannot properly belong to one another's distinct ontological, epistemological, and ethical domains.

Consonant synchronization is an affective rhetoric of temporal framing and deframing: It frames temporally not simply the profilmic or animated image but the networked mass corporeality of the audience. *Hangover Square* relies on technical instrumentalities for framing and deframing and so suspends unprogrammed instrumentalities that may be active within the site of reception. This suspension is accomplished through analytic narrative and editing, realist, performative, or other formal codes but here depends on musical cuing and musical narration, mimesis, and allusion to conduct the audience into affective dispositions that the larger narrative then clarifies, continues, or explains in terms of its temporal modalities: what was, is, and will be happening. The narratological events programmed in the time-based work, then, are always themselves generated within and as serial processes whose convergence or divergence is orchestrated in processes of synchronization; the possibility of their coherence or incoherence is conditioned on the prior displacement of everyday life from the site installed to facilitate audience reception. Consonant synchronization functions by leveraging sound and image in moments of indexing these series to bind the film in packages of icono-mimetic stress.[46] The consonance of the sound track with the visual track depends on orchestrating synchronized series that deframe the audience from the temporal ontologies, epistemologies, and ethics expounded in the work. Suspense or thrill in consonant synchronization, however it is resolved in the work, also presents an open question about the audience's relation to history, actuality, and futurity beyond cinematic time. The musical flames in *Hangover Square,* precursors to Herrmann's violin shrieks in *Psycho,* exorcise the devils of creative history and creative labor, distinctly displacing the time of production and of reception. Yet to identify consonant synchronization is also to say that other modalities of synchronization challenge it, informed by different notions of parallelism between musicality and visuality and other modes of orchestrating composition, exhibition, and reception.

Consonant synchronization may deploy the effects popularly known as "Mickey Mousing," which Kathryn Kalinak[47] describes in terms of early synchronized film in Hollywood. As she points out, this form of musical illustration and repetition of visuality operates in classical scores, such as Max Steiner's for *King Kong* (1933), but is more popularly recognizable in the Disney visual musical style, as seen in animated films from *Steamboat Willie* (1928) to *Snow White and the Seven Dwarfs* (1937). It is turned to pedagogical visualizations of the sound track itself in *Fantasia* (1940) and *The Three Caballeros* (1944) but is distributed across animated and live-action films or television commercials in terms of contact and contagion: displaced material forms or resources, transitioning technology and technical systems, creative labor. Sound sources may be on screen, off screen, or in the apparatus exhibiting synchronization itself but never in the mass corporeality of the audience. Karaoke can be, thus, a mode of introducing dissonance into, of "playing" with, consonant synchronization. Consonant synchronization deploys the audiovisually correspondent gestural quality of Mickey Mousing as well as lip sync, diegetically correct sound effects, and phrasal underscoring tied to shot sequence, whether through motivic structuralization or rhythmic delineation. But it properly is concerned with confining complex temporal relations, relating the past tense and future tense of the cinematic work to the delimited time of its actual exhibition, not simply synchronizing points of coincidence between sound and image.[48]

Reading *Hangover Square* as a diagram of tensions in divisions of creative and affective labor allows us to more fully delineate the strategy of consonant synchronization in one dimension of its bedeviling of historical time: The film represents a scene conceived as a traditional music room for a cinema audience that has heard the musical motivation for that scene's, and its prime agent's, hysterical conflagration. The possibilities of the cinematic medium in terms of audiovisual synchronization and the possibilities of cinematic reception in terms of the spatially oriented and rhetorically deframed corporeality of the audience operate together to emphasize the pitches or turns of fantasy in a confined environment articulated through the exhibition of musical "symptoms." Neither these symptoms nor their logics are unconscious or unheard. Rather, as *Hangover Square* shows, they are the index of tensions between commodity and affective utterance and so between the time-based narrative work's overt temporal form and content, taken in their larger modes of historical production.

Other exemplars could be listed at length here. To give just one, in Jacques Tourneur's *I Walked with a Zombie* (1943), a Canadian nurse comes to a West Indies plantation to care for the owner's wife. The plantation's time-out-of-joint relation between the Eurocentric will to world pictorial representation and a laboring body animated beyond individual will by means of the Afro-diasporic epistemologies of voodoo is exhibited as haunting musical difference. In one sequence, after it becomes clear that an exhausted but vital life beyond death haunts the plantation, a curtain ripples mysteriously to the soft, dissonantly chromatic rise of harp strings; some distant presence from outside the plantation window communicates the movement of laboring commodities animated beyond their physical characteristics, rippling in some larger temporal stream of material corporeality that produces illness within the plantation and bodies animated beyond natural limits beyond it. These dynamics of world temporality are long rehearsed in tales of diabolic agency: vampiric contamination on the one hand and involuntary animation as golem, puppet, zombie, robot, or cyborg on the other. In consonant synchronization, cinema's world picture of energetic motion does not redeem "physical reality," as Siegfried Kracauer[49] proposes, but rather is itself redeemed in some ethics accomplished in reception via the musical streaming of world historical time.

Conversely, Eisler's active mobilization of critical faculties for audience reception can be described as dissonant synchronization. On the one hand, Eisler's was a pragmatics of musical agitation adapted for the industrial cinema. On the other hand, his concerns also aligned closely with concerns at the highest levels of U.S. cultural, corporate, and governmental policies over mass media's capacity to induce mass hysteria in audiences. Although Eisler's dissonant synchronization of music and image overdetermines musicality as modern music and the sound track as music, it rests on the larger assumption and desire that the audience be recognized not simply as actively responding, which all industrial cinema does (and which was precisely the concern of policy makers), but also *learning*, in spite of and perhaps through its material constraints, conflicts, and contradictions. Even if the lights go down while screening a film, for Eisler, the lights need not go out.

Eisler's Dissonant Modal Cinema

Contestation comes in various and complex forms, be they, as discussed in Chapters 2 and 3, the craft interventions of visual music animators or Eisenstein's montage gesture. Schoenberg's serial methods are directed toward a transformation of the aims of musical expression, from the nineteenth-century melody-oriented motif to a musical idea in the form of a tone row expressing the totality of a musical work.[50] Part of a critical movement in the arts, Schoenberg's innovations in musical composition bear comparison to Adorno's elaboration of the critical notion of a "total social process," a theoretical coherence that is necessary, finally, for rigorous critique. "Materialist determination of cultural traits is only possible if it's mediated through the *total social process*," Adorno writes to Walter Benjamin in 1938.[51] The status of music and film as cultural products occupying different strata of artistic coherence is at stake in Adorno's concern with correctly grasping totality and, ultimately, with the production of culture in a moment properly conceived as being within living and lived history. The critical engagement of cultural production within a history that is grasped through dialectical materialism requires that the great axes of Adornian method will turn on inverting the dynamics of totality: Individual experience and cultural identity are mediated only negatively through the instrumental strategies of the culture industries.

In a slightly earlier letter responding to Benjamin's only partially formalized dialectics of play and appearance in the work of art, Adorno claims that not only technicization and alienation but also appearance as such must be seen as operating dialectically. If the kitsch film is to be defended against the quality film, then so is art for art's sake, precisely because the autonomy of art is not identical with art's value:

> It would be bourgeois reaction to negate the reification of the cinema in the name of the ego, and it would border on anarchism to revoke the reification of a great work of art in the spirit of immediate use values. "*Les extremes me touchent*," just as they touch you—but only if the dialectic of the lowest has the same value as the dialectic of the highest,

> rather than the latter simply decaying. Both bear the stigmata of capitalism, both contain elements of change (but never, of course, the middle-term between Schoenberg and the American film). Both are torn halves of an integral freedom, to which however they do not add up. It would be romantic to sacrifice one to the other, either as the bourgeois romanticism of the conservation of personality, and all that stuff, or as the anarchistic romanticism of blind confidence in the spontaneous power of the proletariat in the historical process—a proletariat which is itself a product of bourgeois society.[52]

It is clear from this passage that for Adorno, even a dialectical criticism of high and low cannot be revolutionary in and of itself—an integral freedom as such will not be the result of an enterprise that seeks to bring these fields together, because not only is each alienated from the other but each also manifests its alienation in terms specific to its production and form. Effectively, no critical gesture can be made as a "middle-term between Schoenberg and the American film" (130). Benjamin, says Adorno, falls into the second kind of romanticism in suggesting that certain Hollywood films might offer a kind of value to a proletariat that would have to be liberated to actually produce such an object of its entertainment—in which case, the proletariat would neither produce the kind of kitsch that Hollywood does nor exhibit the kind of affective investments in it that Benjamin prizes. In the final analysis, the American cinema is a trap of dialectical mediation, at least in the short term. For Adorno, the critic must grasp this confinement—for the proletariat, living it more fully means it cannot be grasped. Eisler's film scoring in the United States would confront just this conundrum and crisis.

After leaving Schoenberg's tutelage, Eisler began composing for films, writing the live musical accompaniment to Ruttmann's *Opus III* (1924) before the synchronized film had been standardized in Germany. The book Eisler wrote with Adorno, *Composing for the Films,* was reprinted in English in the early 1990s and is still cited as a practical, critical, and historical source in the canon of film-music literature, especially in regard to the inadequate or manipulative nature of and motivations for Hollywood film music, as is Eisler's output for the cinema.

Brown cites Eisler's score for Resnais's *Nuit et brouillard* as a "perfect example of a nonnarrativizing, nonmythifying film score":

> Eisler's score does not even attempt to join with the visuals and the voice-over narration to create a closed-off universe of consummated effect. Instead, the composer wrote a score of chamber-like proportions—a solo flute and clarinet back the post-title sequence, for instance—that moves parallel to the filmic and verbal texts. Occasionally

> dramatic, occasionally sad, once or twice ironic . . . Eisler's often rather pastoral music communicates on a musical level what *Nuit et brouillard* often communicates in its visuals . . . the brutal irony of the indifferent ordinariness that can mask unspeakable horrors.[53]

Yet this account neglects the clear strategies of synchronization on display in *Nuit et brouillard* (or those that Cook points to in Eisler's score of Ivens's *Rain*). Still, Brown rightly distinguishes Eisler's approach from what I have called the tendency toward consonant synchronization of industrial narrative features of the same period, as we have seen at work in Herrmann's *Hangover Square*. Eisler's score for *Nuit et brouillard* does something more specific than "not even attempting to join with the visuals." Instead, it joins with them to disjoin the given sense of the affect they might otherwise recall. Meanwhile, any "brutal irony" would be only one affect that would finally have to be given over to the audience to determine. The horrors of the concentration camp may become passively "spoken" in reception instead of being mediated in terms of a mask of false remembrance or historical denial. Eisler does more than "contest" or "disjoin"—he effects a dialectical stream of dissonant synchronization, rendering a fuller spectrum of effects than either Cook or Brown describe. Brown's interpretation understands music as primarily an affective rhetoric outside of the intelligible instead of accomplishing the reverse, as I feel Eisler's score does: It renders an essayistic legibility as speech, and this speech remains to be interpreted by the audience. It *might* articulate nostalgia or denial in spite of itself while working to demythify the motives or effects that the image might assign to such affects, but it leaves the relation of affect to the audience to synthesize.

We can describe the score perhaps as actively demythifying rather than merely nonmythifying. But more importantly, this score is conducive to rendering the cinematic site of reception and exhibition as a site of contest, *not of sound and image but of exhibition and reception.* Rendering plural affects from ironic detachment from the possible (and false) familiarity of the images, from sweetness to terror to sadness, the sound-image stream is subtly synchronized for a dissonant conduction of affect that Eisler had already perfected in earlier scores.

Richard Raskin points out that one effect of Resnais's film may be to mediate an impossible experience of massive senseless horror with which all manner of complicity went unspoken and about which survivors were not fully able to speak, complicating questions around complicity. World War II was over, and the matter of responsibility, especially in Vichy France, which had under German occupation officially collaborated with the Nazi extermination of Jews, blacks, homosexuals, Slavs, and Gypsies, was ultimately complex to determine. As survivors, guilt might be felt for those who were slaughtered—how could one speak for those lost when the fact of the absence was so real? And how could one explain to loved ones or families the magnitude and degree of orchestration of violence? On the other hand, in what ways might those complicit with the horror benefit from simple denunciation as a convenient removal of their own guilt? For Raskin, Resnais's accomplishment is that the film provides a form of mediation such that those who had already been through such horror do not bear the responsibility of having to articulate it all over again. And yet, in this particular form, those with questions, those in denial, are faced with a presentation of the camps that provokes engagement rather than defers it to the unspeakable.[54]

Eisler's critical methods in this New Wave documentary raise questions that go deeper yet. How would a representation of the camps be affected by and impact the practices of postwar cinema? More precisely, this question might be broken into three dimensions: How would this Franco-German collaboration counter the Franco-German collaboration during the war? How would this documentary constitute a critical engagement with the cinematic space of confinement, where Hollywood narrative dominated international cinema? How would the narration of confinement and extermination itself be broached? The achievement of *Nuit et brouillard* is precisely in terms of essayistic narration, then, rather than content.

With the disjunctive operation of music working against the image to produce the irony Brown describes, a performative dimension in the synchronization of sound track and visual track is opened up and exposed to the audience. What is indexed more than any experience of the camps is the distantiation enacted not by theatrical performers or the work but by the audience itself—not expressly for agitation but for reorienting the address of totally mediated experience, with the massive corporeal risks of that mediation acknowledged as eminently repeatable without adequate interpretation.

As a documentary exposing the experience of the audience's mediation through sound and image and narrating the pandemonium of the death camps, the space of the cinema is called into audience knowing. But, once there, it is displaced from the totality of mediated social process. In this case, the total social process undergoes an opening. Any possible romanticizing of total war or capitalist reconstruction after winners or losers have been determined, any denial of the experiences of the war, is referred to indeterminate individual responses and, to the extent that it can be, is substituted with a questioning of mediation and collaboration toward the critical coherence of the artwork. Notably, the effects of this cinema of dissonance do not preclude a relation of affect to time that would be neither "rationalized" nor "emotional."[55]

Rather than grounding audience response either in the formal coherence of the work or the identification with celebrity performance or personality, affect is deferred to some coherence to be bestowed upon it by an audience who listens and views sound and image stream discretely and dialectically. This removes any presumption of affect on the basis of false historical relation or spectacular effect. The sense of synchronization refers to the space where the work performs as mediation and where cinema (as radio had for Lazarsfeld) has to do with learning history, not in terms of taste and everyday alienation but with the rationality of horror bequeathed by the recent historical past to the historical present. The film does not attempt to represent or even to emotionally connote in a tragic mode, because the historical trauma being mediated cannot be thought or felt in any universal way. A dissonant stylistics of synchronization forwards instead an essay on actuality (of reception) in relation to historical trauma (which informs the actuality of reception as its impossible—that is, undeniable but unknowable—historical ground). This work is facilitated by the time-based work as dialectical stream, not as dialectical image.

To clarify Eisler's role in developing the essayistic tensions of *Nuit et brouillard* and the way these tensions propose an opening of the site of reception to learning not oriented toward cultivation of taste, the development of human or social capital, or emotion as synchronized spectacular effect, I turn to the lesser-known *A Child Went Forth,* a thirty-minute documentary and the first film scored as part of Eisler's Film Music Project.[56] The score was composed using a transposed version of Schoenberg's serial methods, and Eisler attempts to prevent the pantonal serial idiom from functioning as an exclusive aesthetic ideology opposing either previous compositional methods or standardized popular music. Here, we see Eisler's style directed neither at musical agitprop nor oppositional critique but rather, as in the terms of the Rockefeller Foundation's other projects, at a potential for learning (whether in terms of "behavior"[57] or in terms of "educability").[58] As well, Eisler aligns himself with Burris-Meyer's redefinition of music as an art-technological medium transposable to radically different "theaters" of work, recreation, or war, capable of incorporating the narratological functions of sound and special effects.

At the same time, musical sound and special effects are handled in terms of the tensions between music and image and between sound track and image sequence; here, unlike in such films as *Hangover Square,* where musical listening is understood as psycho-corporeal conflict, music tends to work in tension with and against the image to emphasize musical learning as a general response to the meanings of war. These are the general characteristics of Eisler's modal cinema: He mediates the broad "social functions" identified for listening in the Rockefeller projects and their spectacularized form in such films as *Hangover Square* in the process, moving away from a strictly agitative or oppositional notion and toward an essayistic legibility for synchronized time-based media. The film makes clear that the legibility of the postwar cinema, which Gilles

Deleuze ascribes to a shift from the kinesthetic movement image to the readerly temporal signs of a cinema of the time image,[59] was always a matter of relations of synchronization broadly, first between audience and history, and secondly, mediated in terms of exhibition and reception.

In this film, Eisler shows the new theoretical strength of his film-music methods as well as their potential in practice. *A Child Went Forth,* like *Nuit et brouillard,* treats the confinement of moving bodies in restricted spaces, but under very different circumstances and conditions: Its subject is a day at a summer camp for children. Though shot at the camp Losey's children attended, it was packaged as a plea for the humane treatment of child refugees of war. The film attempts to show children's unblemished potential, but it also suggests the ways in which children replay the worlds that adults give them. We see them embracing gender equality in their play, learning to be kind to animals they care for, and constructing buildings for themselves, but we also see them in conflict with one other. The adult world is allowed a perspective on its own realities, its own desires for peace. Although the politics of the film were clearly left of center for the time, Losey sold it at a profit to the U.S. Department of State to be used as a guide for evacuating children in wartime situations.[60] Thus, a day at a progressive summer camp becomes a model for wartime evacuation of refugees.

The scores Eisler prepared for the Film Music Project, of which this film was one exercise, indicate the ways in which variable and probabilistic methods instrumentalized today as "interactivity" were already aspects of the cinema production process before modern cybernetics. Eisler's scoring of distinct versions of rain for a sequence of the eponymous Ivens documentary, for example, is a composition-intensive way of differentiating his own methods from standard film-industry procedures. Further, his development of these scores shows them to be—as distinct from Eisenstein's graphical diagram of the labor value of his and Prokofiev's collaboration—data intensive, collated as documents in a larger administration of experiment and affect. Rockefeller Foundation support personnel considered some automatic registration device of the sort sought for Burris-Meyer's measurement of audience response and Princeton Radio's recording of audience reactions to radio content.

They concluded that it was precisely the aesthetic responses of people able to articulate their opinions as to the distinct effects different score fragments provided that would in this case be necessary.[61] As the titles of the rain scores make clear, Eisler approaches the variegation of musical possibility as an expanded problem of serial stylistics: *Vierzehn Arten den Regen zu beschreiben.*[62] For Eisler, rain is a cipher, in Verlaine to Rimbaud and beyond, for *Trauer*—that is, sadness or melancholia—and these were *virtual* (*gewissenmaßigen*) stylizations of rain as sadness. "I won't say," Eisler comments in 1958, "that it is the central theme of the twentieth century; we should say that that would be an

'Anatomy of Sadness,' or an 'Anatomy of Melancholy.' But that can also appear in the *oeuvre*."[63] Eisler's work for the Rockefeller Foundation should be seen in this light: His Film Music Project scores are a highly abbreviated attempt at an affective anatomy for film music; but such a project only coheres inasmuch as it relates affect to historical time. Here, again, is the doubled potentiality of the media stream: its virtual stylization of historial relation, to be evaluated for some more concrete possible historical value in reception.

Developing a distinct order of musical ciphers for *A Child Went Forth*, Eisler plunders surprising musical territory for his material. He composes complex, delicate passages depicting children's dispositions, moods, actions, and interactions with the world around them, reworking such sources as nursery songs. Yet Eisler also achieves a mediating effect between learning and synchronization without submitting learning to the reception of spectacle; the feeling of action here is our own capacity to rethink the way we understand childhood as a time for learning. Musical listening provides the critical gesture by which our consideration of children is accomplished by calling attention to precisely our envisioning of childhood. Losey's intimate editing works together with his relatively hands-off direction and Eisler's score to make this educational film operate through more dissonant than consonant synchronization, though any final determination of effects rests finally with the audience.

The film opens with a violin narrating a theme suggesting hunting or a game of hide-and-seek, with flutes answering the stringed instrument. On screen, children arrive at the summer camp. A narrator quotes Walt Whitman and sets up the message of the film: "'There was a child went forth every day, and the first object looked upon, that object he became.' . . . How children play, how they stretch those muscles and minds of theirs is of crucial importance." Violins play a tentatively rising questioning theme with unresolved harmonics and then drop with a musical "splash" as children jump in a pool of water. By starting with a theme suggesting hunting or hiding, the music asks the audience to *wonder* what the message of the film might be. "Search like a child," the music continues to suggest, "and you will find it for yourself." The treasure found? Image and audio creating a synchronized splash. However, the prior phrasal sequences and those that follow mediate any "immersion" here; the music narrates what are in essence high-quality home movies providing the low-budget visual resources for an educational film.

In just these first few moments, musicality orders the modes of dissonant and consonant synchronizations, with an onomatopoetic splash following a question presented through unresolved yet gentle pantonal dissonance. Themes of autonomy, independence, self-confidence, and respect for nature follow. The score streams loosely along with the image, providing sound effects as well as commentary, in terms of pleasing, tentative, or contradictory emotions as we see the children play, fight, build things, or swim. The narrator suggests that children in wartime should be treated with the respect accorded to adults, referring to their similar problems and feelings and, in doing so, appealing to the audience's capacities for feeling childhood as adults. As we see one child hit another and the abused friend immediately hit back, we reflect, led on by the dry, witty, and attentive sounds we hear, that while the narration asks us to consider the children as humans, another message seems to be that adults often act just like these children, but with far more serious consequences. The first of those messages is found and emphasized through the accompanying voice-over, but the second is found primarily in the mediated gesture of synchronization, placing music in some more autonomous relation to the image to performatively narrate our capacity to learn as an audience:

> The musical problem was to save the picture from the usual saccharine sentimental and humorous romanticism of magazine stories about children. The effect of the music could be neither stirring nor funny. Its range of feeling had to include elements that usually are not associated with children: genuine seriousness, such as children often show in their play; sadness, nervousness, even hysteria; but all these conceived loosely, thinly as though inconsequentially. Above all, the music should not tap the children on the shoulder, as it were, and make them the object of adults' jokes or ingratiate itself by adopting a spurious baby talk.
>
> The form of the suite seemed most natural—in other words, not an elaborate form of leitmotifs, but a sequence of small, distinct, clearly differentiated pieces, each complete in itself with an unmistakable beginning and ending.[64]

Here again, hysteria is produced in synchronization, but according to a dialectics of media streams that submit the spectacular hysteria conducted in such films as *Hangover Square* to the audience for critical consideration. At the same time, taking the measure of hysteria in this way also undercuts the personality profiling used in radio surveys attempting to discern the motives of radio listeners who panicked and took flight during Welles's *War of the Worlds* broadcast. But, rather than through leitmotifs composed to signal interiority or emotional response, audience identification with dramatized emotion, or background environmental moods, Eisler constantly emphasizes a feeling of action taking place in the actuality of reception, of being in historical time. He moves from one distinct section of the suite to the next as the children romp from activity to activity during the course of their day. A recurrent developmental thematic never develops in the harmonic or rhythmic sense, nor does a finale sum up those developments. Musical comments are more discretely articulated around the movements and interactions of the children on screen in particular instances, yet they are more aleatory in their overall sequencing.

Synchronization here does render, then, subjective reactions as well as environmental events, but with equal weight, and the combined audiovisual effect communicates an impression of children who must play at learning in order to grow up and who live in a world that expects them to do precisely that. No foregone musical conclusion leads them, or us, along. Does *our* world place the same expectations before children? *Can* we? We watch their careful eyes and ears as we hear a woman tell them a story about other children, but she is also telling their story, just as the film tells us the story of the children we see as a story about ourselves. We learn, through the mediating effects of dissonant sync employed with consonant synchronization, that these are the two separate stories of two distinct sets of bodies, but they may become intimately related through the actions we take. Will we translate understanding into action?

The film ends with a quietly sinister march as the narrator suggests that perhaps the methods used at this camp would be appropriate for children whose parents have been killed in war or those whose mothers have been called away to work in the defense industries. But the film also implies that if we have questions about how we should care for children, the camp may present a model for times of peace and war. The music invites serious reflection without insisting on its own sonic authority, just as the images do not insist on analytical transparency; the viewer-listeners are neither persuaded nor rushed to conclusions. Still, the long summer day, the cool water, the farm animals, and the curious music all would have seemed brighter and more generous than the everyday life otherwise mediated in radio listening and cinema viewing during wartime: Perhaps a more critical, more social, even more rigorously childlike way to raise children exists. The film ends as a final citation of Whitman concludes the narration, the poet's multitudinous voicing of the American body politic punctuating the site opened out between Eisler's dissonant stream and Losey's implied antiwar message. The effect is musical thoughtfulness, questioning rather than the destructive annihilation of the symbolization of the site of listening, as in *Hangover Square.*

The use of dissonant synchronization invites mediation or negotiation between an already plural sound track and an already plural visual track, a negotiation engaged in the work's avowal of our reception of their dynamic combination. The effect of dissonant synchronization, like that of consonant synchronization, rests on the configuration of moving bodies confined in space to open out interpretive actions toward different dispositions toward the bodies and gestures screened. Eisler's musical agitation utilizes both styles of synchronization in *A Child Went Forth*; "counterpoint," in synchronization, does not necessarily translate as "opposed metaphors" in the formal sense Cook suggests but rather a tactics of conducting sound and image in a dialectical stream prompting the audience's critical and passionate investments rather than hysterical ones.

Streaming Media Pedagogies at Midcentury: The Call to Cybernetics

If the concert hall held, as *Hangover Square* postulates, a specific discovery of mass-corporeal hysteria accumulating in the tension between qualities and quantities of mass media, *A Child Went Forth* should enlighten our understanding of how musicality, deployed as a measure of opening up the site of reception as one of reflection, may mediate the spectacular pedagogies of Hollywood suspense with those of statistical analysis or art-technological orchestration of mass-corporeal effects. Thus, the theater of sound effects, distributed listening, "the children's camp," or other dynamic spaces show the ways in which total mediation (the futural specter of some triumphant historical fascism) may be amplified or mitigated through orchestrating synchronization of reception and exhibition, shedding light on our ability to see screened actuality and to hear immanent historicity or futurity at the same time. These dynamic sites of stylizing temporality contribute to our contemporary understanding of stasis and mobility, now profoundly reconfigured not so much through "new technologies" but by new divisions and mediations of material, technical, or affective labor: Interactive experiences, too, yield the orchestration of gestures of interpretation.

Perhaps we will return to understand the way music's capacities were refigured in the midcentury instrumentation of social conditions, broadly distributed through the working and recreational conditions whereby everyday life was dislocated or ameliorated. Listening, sound, and music were seen as condition and medium, not event, of social violence or war: the substance of mass-corporeal expressivity, available to investigation as an art-technological effect of synchronization and thus portable across distinct environments. These capacities for music informed a synoptics of spectacular dissolution in the consonant synchronization deployed in such films as *Hangover Square* (becoming even more graphically explicit in the spiraling titles and narrative of Hitchcock's *Vertigo* [1958]) as well as an essayistic mediation on care in a time of total war through the stylistics of dissonant synchronization in such films as *A Child Went Forth* or *Nuit et brouillard*. These were midcentury modern pragmatics for stylizing time-based materialities of musical communication to be grasped by audiences. Because of the deep histories and the continued deployment of these modes of consonant or dissonant synchronization—that is, their historical and futural values—they should not be reduced to the sound track (in cinema or in gaming) as supplement, nor should the radio listening or cinema viewing of the past be understood as at all linear. Time-based media is serial, not linear, and no instance of reception may be reduced to any one term in a series.

For these reasons, musicality and gesture are primary to the learning effects Eisler's essayistic orchestration of serial sound and image aims to produce, but these had been, since before his own Film Music Project began, primary problems encountered in attempting to understand the ways audiences create, interpret, or move locally through temporally determined modes of globalized everyday life. Modal media reception never exhausts historical time that is hieroglyphically transposed as cinematic time but rather animates the creation of more of it, engendering further divisions of labor. Recognizing the operations—synchronization, dissonance, and the devil of mass corporeality—through which Eisler configures his path through global hieroglyphic time may bring us to a pandemonium regained: the reinvention and restylization of a *musicalized* everyday life. Returning to the powerful affects attributed to musical listening in this period further allows us to observe the range of problems having to do with assigning coherent contexts and identities to network effects distributed over world space as media. As I discuss in Chapter 5, an "IBM world" had materialized for writers on jazz, such as Langston Hughes; Burris-Meyer's attempt at closely synchronized sound control, Eisler's attempt to resist it, and Herrmann's attempt to dramatize it as individual (rather than mass) hysteria give us a preliminary set of exemplars against which to measure the demand for more powerful technics for calling, carrying, distributing, culminating, and reworking the network effects of material, temporal media streams.

Eisenstein's, Fischinger's, and Eisler's stylistics of sound-image synchronization comprise the three major stylistic tendencies mediating musicality and gesture in classical cinema. As we shall see, montage, visual music, and dialectical streaming provide resources that later works will rework as they transform the historical, futural, and present tenses of the site of reception. Pathos, ecstasy, and hysteria will be reengaged in modal cinemas that pass creative labor through mass mediation. However, in Chapters 5 through 7, I show that these historical resources will not be sufficient for new, materialist cinemas or for the computational interface. In Chapter 5, I review the musical cinemas of the 1960s and 1970s, which generated a full complement of interrogations of cinema style and popular music. Of pop, rock, and jazz, jazz in particular maintained a political history whose trajectory would be commensurate to a countercinema marking the extensive development of transnational media industries in terms largely antithetical to it. At the point of its near-disappearance in the sphere of mass-market commodity recording, the free-jazz cinema achieves a critical treatment thoroughly integrating the classical stylistics of sound-image synchronization into its formal materials and narrative thematics by drawing on the epistemologies of black music. In Chapter 5, then, we observe the ways in which the problems of bioenergetic control and expression are reframed in bioinformatic terms. In the jazz cinema of the 1970s, engagements between improvisation and biopolitics become, precisely, a question of deciphering and reciphering cinema as style.

5

Black Relationship

Improvising a Black Pacific

Ultimately the phonograph records are not artworks but the black seals on the missives that are rushing towards us from all sides in the traffic with technology; missives whose formulations capture the sounds of creation, the first and the last sounds, judgment upon life and message about that which may come hereafter.
—Theodor Adorno, "The Form of the Phonograph Record"

Americans began to realize for the first time that there was a native American music as traditionally wild, happy, disenchanted, and unfettered as it had become fashionable for them to think they themselves had become. . . . Race records swiftly became big business.
—LeRoi Jones, *Blues People: Negro Music in White America*

Have you ever suffered from political despair, from despair about the organization of things?
—Fred Moten, *In the Break: The Aesthetics of the Black Radical Tradition*

Growth as inherent right.
—Cecil Taylor, liner notes for Taylor and Mary Lou Williams, *Embraced*

"Jazz Is the Teacher"
—"Magic" Juan Atkins, techno-house track title

Cinema and Jazz as Style and Idiom

In the preceding discussions of Sergei Eisenstein's "charmed" montage, Oskar Fischinger's spiraling musical animation, and Hanns Eisler's administrative synchronization of sound and image as dissonant, dialectical stream, I have identified three classical stylistics for synchronizing audiovisual exhibition as a relation of contemporary and historical time. For subjects cut off from history and from one another, and reprojecting and redefining historical meaning in exhibition, pathos characterizes the complex relation between the affective labor of composition and that of reception. Eisenstein's "charmed" montage provides the key exemplar of this stylistic of streaming synchronization. When exhibition emphasizes a continuous streaming of temporal relation above and beyond the materiality of the exhibition context, so the futural tense of the work exhibited coincides with a futural sense of the audience's ability to convene in exhibition, an ecstatic sense of affective labor emerges. Here, Fischinger's visual music provides an influential, widely recognized example. And when the affective labor of interpreters becomes excessive, whether positively or negatively, and cannot be localized either in terms of the historical or futural potentialities of the audiovisual stream, a potential for (or, in some cases, actual fact of) "mass hysteria" appears—that is, wild interpretation not on the part of an individual subject but on the part of networked mass subjects. Eisler's stylization of dissonant synchronization proposes a dialectical, streaming display of affective labor, aiming at a diagnostic capability achieved by differentiating the affective labor of interpreters from that affective and technical labor combined in exhibition. Eisenstein's, Fischinger's, or Eisler's work, then, demonstrates modalities of affective labor and attempts to stylize it in relation to historical, futural, or contemporary immanence. Each of these styles of synchronizing time-become-hieroglyphic aimed at some medial ethics by construing the materialized temporality of the media stream as music and its reception as gestural. Each of these cases, then, presents a canonical style of preparing corporeal relations to media spectacle as music and as gesture. Although each of these attempts emerged historically as responses to specific problems in specific contexts, the stylistics they demonstrate have been adopted, appropriated, and reworked far beyond their immediate concerns, conceptions, and uses.

Eisenstein's various appeals to a material kinesthetics of affect modeled on the roller coaster or circus, the biomechanical theater, drawing as choreography (or jazz or music, more generally), in addition to his concerns with the visuality of painting and drawing or the textuality of poetics of literature, make clear that he understood that cinema's historical and contemporary ontologies, epistemologies, and ethics were transmedial—that is, cinema was historical and revolutionary precisely inasmuch as its capacities to relate personhood to public being in affective terms derived from earlier media but were more expansive and more dynamic than other forms of expression. Fischinger similarly worked with cinematic composition and reception as a particular medium in relation to others—that is, as requiring transmedial resources for crafting cinematic sense and making sense of cinematic sensation. Fischinger's abstraction of parametrical data for sound-image synchronization from phonograph records, his presentation of the kinesthetics of visual music as radiophonic flight, or his elaboration of his works in terms of a medial choreography all contributed as much to the narrative Fischinger had to tell about musical expressionism, its antiauthoritarian orientation, and the contemporary relations between painting and cinema at the mid-twentieth century as to his own work. Musicality and gesture shaped affective labor to make "statements" in his works. Eisler turned from stronger to weaker claims, relying ultimately on politically incisive strategies of dissonant synchronization that nonetheless were designed only to prompt audiences to interpret what affective meanings were to be made of the compression of material and technical labor composed in and as the material, streaming work.

All these figures engaged, to some larger or smaller degree, improvisational epistemologies associated in their own times with jazz music. A range of recent scholars have observed the ways in which "noise" functions as musical and technocultural aesthetic in black musics;[1] more broadly, cultural theorist Jacques Attali influentially claims that new music foreshadows broader cultural change as a kind of annunciatory noise.[2] Typically, for Eisenstein, Fischinger, or Eisler, as for other artists of temporal media in the early twentieth century, jazz or jazz aesthetics are invoked to characterize an improvisational capacity on the part of receivers of otherwise highly programmed media streams. In this chapter, I explore in more detail how improvisation and media program are concretely characterized in transformed stylistics of synchronization after cybernetic networks had redefined relations of temporality and corporeal contact after the midcentury era. Director Larry Clark's *Passing Through* (1977), one of the films made by the Los Angeles group of independent filmmakers, which included Charles Burnett (*Killer of Sheep*, 1977) and Haile Gerima (*Bush Mama*, 1979), provides an exceptional exemplar. Jazz as relation of history and contemporaneity provides not only the structure and narrative for *Passing Through* but also the broader aesthetic resources for reworking montage, visual music, and dissonant synchronization.

Any consideration of cinema as transmedial stream suggests a consideration of cinema as the stylization of a temporal and material idiom. Cinema as style and idiom coincides not only with the long historical rise of computational technologies but also with globalizing musical forms, such as jazz (or tango, for example).[3] In this sense, jazz becomes central to considerations of transmedial stylistics in precisely the degree to which its importance for cinema tends to be neglected.[4] That cinema is a global industry while jazz is a musical genre or form is an asymmetry in terms of which industrial priorities condition the critical reception of auditory, visual, or audiovisual and gestural productions of meaning. In fact, this asymmetry and the historical abandonment it may suggest are where *Passing Through* begins. Clark's film not only is the temporal diagram of a struggle for a future cinema but also rewrites the cinematic archive in terms of jazz playing, recording, and listening. Audience reception of *Passing Through*'s sound and image track is synchronized as an improvisational seeing-hearing of jazz history as correlate of world historical struggle. If, as David James[5] argues, the film ultimately fails in its attempt to found a jazz cinema that would articulate the meanings and languages for a feature-length black cinema, the film does employ complex ciphers of jazz performance, recording, and listening to document jazz as style and idiom relating historical struggle. In *Passing Through*, styling jazz in relation to historical struggle underwrites a medial ethics where playing and hearing music opens to liberatory modes of affective labor rather than destructive and dependent ones. Here, too, musicality and gesture point to cinema as transmedial configuration and as ethical engagement as much as industry, institution, or mass cultural form.

Further, *Passing Through* provides a crucial example—at precisely that historical moment of the mid-1970s to which contemporary theorists of affective labor, such as Michael Hardt[6] or Hardt and Antonio Negri,[7] refer as characterizing the transition from "old," Fordist industrial networks to "new," post-Fordist and cybernetic models of labor—of a musical cinema whose stylistics for relating audience to personhood and to public being *historicize* affective labor as a mode of biopolitical resistance. The film reworks then-conventional sound-image relations of cinema by deploying improvisational stylistics for synchronizing sound and image. Cinema had long been contemporary and arguably capable of engaging sound and image as improvisation, as different phases or works by Eisenstein, Fischinger, or Eisler show, but for complex political, economic, and social reasons, it had not yet fully elaborated this engagement or its implications. *Passing Through,* regardless of its marginality in canons of cinema, jazz, or critical studies, not only elaborates this engagement but also dramatizes the contradictions and tensions, the doubled potential, such an engagement entails.

Free Jazz and Program Media

Passing Through functions, in some ways, as a musical cipher: It was made for the revolution but hardly surmounts capitalist contradictions on its own. Still, its achievements are numerous. First, *Passing Through*'s primary interest is not, I think, in deploying jazz to allegorize cinema production as such but rather in allegorizing, more broadly, an audiovisual medium that might project an improvisational jazz musicality in reception. Seeing the film in this light suggests larger historical currents in which jazz works as a historical resource extensible across media. Importantly, broadening our understanding of the film's rhetorical address in this way allows us to see the ways in which *Passing Through*'s transmedia jazz rhetoric corresponds to others produced in black poetry, literature, and critical social theories. Of considerable importance for interpreting the film and situating it in relation to jazz history is the way it draws on one crucial resource to present such correspondences: the jazz album cover.

Passing Through is a historical treatment, in musical narration, of the material, technical, and affective meanings of jazz in cinema, transferred to the screen by virtue of the historical meanings immanent to free jazz music's marginalized condition during the 1970s. The film begins with an affirmative dedication to "black musicians everywhere" and proceeds to a visual-music sequence that introduces the musical resources that inform its entire narrative, emphasizing the historical and contemporary sources of jazz production: black history and black performers. This sequence starts with a close-up of jazz pianist Horace Tapscott's hands, bathed in blue light, on a keyboard; he performs the music we hear as the repeating refrain slowly adds, in the image, other hands on additional instruments, their corresponding sounds joining together. This sequence presents a music whose structural density gradually expands to a chaotic sound image whose rhythmic and timbral density challenges the very auditory and visual capacities of the medium in which it is inscribed.

The film's protagonist, Eddie Warmack, is a jazz saxophonist who, having recently been released from prison, is struggling to find his sound again. He realizes that he needs to organize his former bandmates for a new recording venture to succeed; this move arouses violent anger from the record-company conglomerate that formerly held him under contract. A series of events reestablishes Warmack's friendship with a former lover as well as with his bandmates and introduces a new love interest, Maya, the single mother and photojournalist whose photographer ex-husband documented the struggle to decolonize Guinea-Bissau. The key events of the film, then, comprise Warmack's rediscovery of his signature sound, his transformation of the music that his ensemble makes together, and his working through the meanings of lost and new love. Transformations become possible, not simply potential, for Warmack because of his recognition of parallel histories, established through montage composition.

The film employs pseudohistorical recreations of recognizable yet fictionalized historical events. It includes actual newsreel footage and photographs of African revolutionaries but Clark edits them into carefully composed sequences where montage functions as forms of musical memory, speech, recounting, or storytelling. Within the narrative, for Warmack, these highly synthetic montage sequences elucidate the relationship between the struggle for African decolonization and black political recognition in the United States. Montage as pathos, then, projects personal and impersonal historical time.

Warmack's personal breakthroughs are depicted instead through the stylistics of visual music. To find his sound after being released from prison, he goes to the beach at the Santa Monica piers. Later, he loses his sense of self and sound at a point at which he again should be performing as a contributing member of his ensemble.

Here, dissonant distortion using electronic feedback synchronized with Warmack missing notes shows he is "out of sync" with the diegetic reality of his surroundings. Dissonant synchronization, then, is used to suggest a deeply personal political despair, while montage or visual music styles indicate jazz as historical resource: personal and impersonal; private and intimate.

Passing Through deploys classical stylistics but stylizes them as jazz performance of personhood and publicity. Warmack finds, as he rejoins the ensemble and relearns what it means to lead it, the means to upend political despair and to move through complex time. His musical breakthroughs, whether intimate or raucous, appear in often-hallucinatory or visionary terms: History can continue into a new phase only by virtue of a cut or interruption allowing "cut-off" memories to be recalled.

At the end of the film, Warmack retaliates against record-company gangsters who have marginalized his ensemble's economic prospects, encouraged their drug dependency, and even murdered and attacked them. Warmack kills two of the gangsters in a roadside ambush. The tenor of this sequence is doubled in terms of sense and sensation. On the one hand, armed struggle and jazz recording are depicted as parallel endeavors: They share sense. On the other, the gangsters are represented in the film according to a reversal of the logics of minstrelsy—one corporate hack pretends, in a way that is clearly embarrassingly unconvincing even to him, to be "down" with the ensemble by badly miming black gestures. The other, the head of the recording conglomerate, appears with a pencil moustache drawn above his upper lip. When Warmack dispenses with these vicious clowns at the close of the film, even as the film dispatches a sense of "realistic" catharsis, it also caricatures corporate ownership of black musical commodities as comic sensation: denuded forms of white minstrelsy and cinematic masquerade. *Passing Through* closes with a sequence of held frames presenting African independence fighters, and at the end of this historical photo album, Warmack appears in a circular matte shot: at the center of a record label, that is, which has begun to produce sound heard and recognized as historical struggle.

The significance of *Passing Through*'s narrative, like other films of the period treating music commodities, transnational media industries, and progressions of musical genre, material, form, or style, is that it elaborates the material and historical development of musical meaning in jazz as cinematic narrative. In other words, to a degree that is not achieved in other films of its period, it transposes the aesthetics and rhetorics of free jazz performance and recording to cinematic temporality. Here, jazz recording histories and musical epistemologies provide immanent historical resources transposed to cinematic spectacle, a translation of musical epistemologies that other comparable film narratives either pointedly refrain from doing or fail to do, so the differences between such films are illuminating.

In Peter Watkins's *Privilege* (1967), a highly critical film about the manufacture of pop-music stardom, rock is a carefully administrated outlet for youth aggression that functions by channeling libidinal investments—depicted as screaming teary fans and as a masochistic, self-flagellating rock star—into nihilistic consumerism that resolves tensions between the British state, public culture, transnational capital, and religious institutions. Two successive stages of pop stardom, the passage from transgressive break-out hit to iconization, are presented literally as gestural performances. First, the pop star appears on stage in a cage and, in a dramatic miming of his desire for liberation, gesturally pleads for release by police officers, who do so and then beat him. Later, to the backing of police, corporation, and state, the church adds its support, too. This second performance presents the pop star's kinesic iconography as sustained gesture of hands outstretched: canonization.

Similarly, Ken Russell's 1975 film adaptation of the Who's 1967 rock opera *Tommy* also presents the rock star's body as the center of his fans' libidinal investments, but here as directed in search of an alternative to mind-numbing postwar middle-class status. Here, rock is aligned with emergent media technologies rather than biopolitical control: In an early sequence allegorizing this alignment, pinball machines are depicted as transforming into electronic games whose iconic airplanes recall World War II bombers. In *Tommy*, media are dialectically divergent and convergent; their divergence allows fans to catch on to the exciting implications of the star's pseudotranscendent corporeality, and their convergence allows fans to catch on to the commoditization of his pseudotranscendence. Where Watkins presents the musical commodity system as a closed circuit, Russell finds historical progressions of new technology, new media, and new musical genre, in relation to which fan rebellion partially determines the passage from one rock style to the next but where any coherent social agency or actual political change that might result from fan insurrection initiating a new school of rock is illusory, when it is not regressive.

Distinct from these films in which music's capacity to relate personhood and public being is entirely contained within a critique of transnational capital's production of hysterical, corporeal affect, *Passing Through*'s central concern is rather the need to organize musical production for autonomous recording, and thus for transnational distribution and for historical archiving. Taking jazz as its form and as its narrative thematics, opening an ensemble jam and ending with an image of its protagonist as icon of recorded music, *Passing Through* presents a cinematic allegory of the musical localization and globalization of commodity and community relations. The film's ending suggests that Warmack has resolved these contradictions not simply by making sound but by recording musical sound in relation to, and as an analog of, the historical and contemporary political struggles that continue to inform its meaning. Thus, *Passing Through* presents the jazz ensemble as an improvisational staging ground for the individuation of the soloist—that is, it historicizes jazz as the aesthetic correlate of a contemporary political assembly, with the free jazz solo requiring an ethical performance guiding the ensemble to resolve tensions between commodity and community relations in some more autonomous form of laboring, affective production. Here, jazz cinema becomes a series of didactic lessons for decoding the laboring relation of black assembly and leadership as deciphered historical and musical facts. The film presents, in effect, the complex counter-narrative to Watkins's or Russell's critique of a threadbare, transnational musical postmodernism.

Where the site of jazz reception is depicted in *Passing Through* as marginalized, deprived of origins, and made threadbare in its dysfunctional dependency on the recording industry, the stylistics of Eisler's dissonant synchronization are engaged and revised. *Passing Through* uses dissonant synchronization, paradoxically, to effect a cinematic naturalism for jazz, making playing jazz a natural fact in spite of its historical neglect. In the key scene I briefly describe above, Warmack cannot synchronize his own sound to that of the players around him. His musical incapacity is correct in terms of the diegesis, although the notes he plays are wrong for the ensemble that performs in the scene. But this wrong, failed sound *is* the jazz sound track; the site of jazz production is placed in tension with the audience's reception of it. An ensuing fugue state leads Warmack to see class conflicts playing out among family members mourning the death of "Poppa" Harris, Warmack's musical mentor. Similarly, attending to the conflict between jazz as a site of production and reception, the viewer diagnoses unresolved historical tensions playing out through family, class, and history.

In another key scene, the sound of musicians rehearsing narrates a flashback in which Poppa intervenes in the overdose of a drug-addicted musician who has died in a hospital room. Again, naturalizing improvisational jazz as cinematic sound and image capable of departing from its own constraints or of interrupting its own dependencies contests what were then still-current associations of jazz with corporeal dependencies: violence and addiction. Here again, dissonant synchronization of sound and image prompts improvisational sense making whereby receivers' attention is called and then follows, notes, and interprets tensions to make conclusions about relations between production and reception. This dissonant sync leads to psychic or social insights or perhaps renewals for the film's key players. In essence, the jazz rehearsal space functions as what Vorris Nunley has termed a "hush harbor," a musical version of those quasi-public "safe spaces" Nunley sees as central to the production of community-centered knowledges since slavery.[8] Yet in projecting the cinema, too, as a musical hush harbor, *Passing Through* places the improvisational stylistic of synchronized sound and image in a powerful role, musically mediating the quasi-public hush harbor in terms of the virtual public sphere of the cinema. In the process, jazz music as deployed in *Passing Through* teaches political despair, as Fred Moten puts it, precisely because jazz's centrality in twentieth-century musical production and epistemology is routinely projected and marginalized as weak, fixed, and dependent—the opposite of what its own historical narrative knows it to be. But, in projecting despair and musically parsing the affect of despair in terms of its historical production and in terms of the affective contrariety to despair forged in love or solidarity, the film improvises toward its conclusions: Jazz is a complex streaming of heterogeneous, historical modalities of action rather than an industrial product or musical genre.

As a result, *Passing Through* finds jazz rhetoric holding immanent resources for futural movement, perhaps surprisingly depicted here in terms of visual music synchronization in the early scene I note above, wherein Warmack plays his saxophone at the beach. By projecting and playing off musical waves echoing between his instrument and the ocean, Warmack resynchronizes himself to localized temporality after the alienating temporality of prison. He also "flows" into the sound of the Pacific Ocean, which seems to connect him distantly to Poppa and to Africa. Here, again, the stylistics of visual music are turned around: Rather than transporting or abstracting, visual music instrumentalities localize a connection with global Afro-diasporic crosscurrents.

Passing Through also uses montage techniques to establish the epistemological broadening and reorientation of jazz as liberation music. In a key moment of musical narration that establishes character backstories and narratological aims, the film presents a fictional prison revolt carefully shot and edited to match newsreel footage of the 1970 Attica, New York, prison uprising, introducing photographs of African rebel fighters to position the jazz musician's historical status for comparative analysis. These parts are woven into a whole not in terms of a larger montage narrative; rather, they are patterned into the film's often-hallucinatory sequencing according to the tension established between the story of recording jazz and the story of improvising historical struggle, a tension narrated primarily in terms of or with reference to the film's improvisatory sound track.

As Todd Boyd[9] demonstrates, black musical styles, such as jazz or hip-hop, exhibit the ways in which black aesthetic expression in the United States modulates vernacular and formal. Describing a modulation of vernacular expression and techno-scientific media as a historical development, Fred Moten[10] suggests that radical black aesthetics engage recording media as a transition from the vernacular to the modern. In this regard, Moten sees Eisensteinian montage—canonical in liberal film schools and in independent and commodity film production—as crucial for understanding "the break" and "the ensemble" of black radical aesthetics. Boyd's and Moten's comments suggest black radical aesthetics as intervening practices of what Miriam Hansen[11] refers to as vernacular modernisms, whereby Hollywood globalized cinema as exportable sensorium. For Moten, in particular, Eisenstein's montage provides a theory of the dynamisms animating the transformed ensembles of techno-scientific modernity and their framing of resistant social relations: "For montage comes into its own by way of the deconstruction of the elemental status, which is to say, the staticity, of the frame. Such a deconstruction cannot but include an improvisation through the idea of the frame as pure singularity: This means not only a theorization of movement in/of the frame, but an iconization that acts as an affirmation against the very idea of the frame."[12]

As I discuss in Chapter 2, Eisenstein describes "learning to draw": his impulse toward montage as a form of "drawing" a tension between the improvisatory and the programmatic, where montage serves as a partial modal deconstruction of the frame—it does not aim entirely to negate its "idea" but to mobilize it ethically.[13] Eisenstein's "charmed" parameter passes through the frame while negotiating its political history and use. It charges cinema's historicity with framing the appearance of nonindifferent nature as dynamic historical change and as the historical indifference of cinematic institutions to some more robust exhibition of his own corporeal labor: the degree that he could "keep secrets" by simply placing them in plain view. New historical conditions do not make Eisenstein's montage directly accessible; instead, as it recedes into our own historical immanence, it awaits further improvisational informatic work. Similarly, visual music synchronization and dissonant synchronization provide additional, but immanent, gestures for framing and deframing the cinematic image and its mutually inscribed sound track.

These considerations suggest that no production of sense or sensation can simply apply the aesthetics of prior stylistics of synchronization without appropriating them for conditions other than those at which they were directed or without working through its own complex historical relationships in terms of aesthetics, politics, and ethics. *Passing Through,* reworking classical stylistics of musical audiovisuality, emphasizes free jazz as an articulation of the capacities of black musicians historically and in the 1970s[14] but without visually erasing their gestures in service of an alienated mode of abstraction, contributing to further commoditization of radical music in popular media, or visually fetishizing the bodies of jazz performers. To the degree that global media production circulates affective labor precisely in the terms *Passing Through* rejects, *Passing Through* critiques global media production while articulating the musical identity of a "Black Pacific" in relation to what Paul Gilroy calls the "Black Atlantic," a West Coast site where jazz's transatlantic epistemologies are recalled and reoriented with regard to global decolonization movements.

A Black Pacific

In articulating these historiographies and epistemologies in relation to a haptic, gestural reception of improvisational jazz poetics, *Passing Through* produces a cognate form of Paul Gilroy's version of black musical epistemologies[15] (but some two decades earlier) and instantiates what Gilroy sees as the "rhizomatic" and kinesic transversality of black historical meaning in another place: the Black Pacific. As cinema, *Passing Through* achieves the instantiation of a Black Pacific by deontologizing those extraordinarily problematic practices of synchronizing jazz as a musical function of dependency that became conventional and even praised in commercial cinemas of the 1950s and 1960s. *Passing Through* subjects montage, visual music, and dissonant synchronization to an improvisational aesthetic so their utility can be entirely contrary to conventional uses, and antithetical within the same work. Concretely, montage, visual music, and dissonant synchronization are subjected not to particularized or foundational meanings but to the poetics of antiphony. Bringing the antiphonic gesturality of improvisation to cinematic narrative and to the cinema audience, the film privileges the salient instance of antiphony, the ensemble, which Moten theorizes as the aesthetic "unit" of the black radical aesthetic.

Passing Through works through a great number of black relationships, then, testing the meanings of masculinity, sexuality, and community as lessons in biopolitical resistance and learning that loving music means loving people. Yet alienation "in the European sense," as James[16] puts it, is never shorted here, nor is the questioning of social alienation in terms of the social politics of its time. Not the least of the black relationships that the film explores brings a poetics of relationship to counter what Édouard Glissant[17] calls the "flash agents" of the transnational media industries. Since the film concludes by suggesting the recording of not only the ensemble's music but also, more pointedly, the protagonist's solo, Warmack relearns and expands his understanding of political history and jazz performance, contesting flash agencies of transnational media by drawing out the ensemble as well as drawing the soloist out of the ensemble. The future of the ensemble as community is found in the capacity for the ensemble to host the potential leadership heard in the contingent individuation of the solo.

Jazz as a musical rhetoric of social ensemble and creative individuation relates U.S. "hush harbors" to global developments—namely, the still ongoing complications of decolonization to which Langston Hughes had earlier linked jazz as historical and contemporary Afro-diasporic musical articulation, as I discuss below. Ernst Bloch's utopian notion of music as historical presentiment and utopian imagining (see Chapter 3) is reversed here. Instead of history framed through the development and recapitulation of carpet motifs that the critical imagination can entirely grasp, jazz struggles to capture, by remaking differently, a musical force field that does not subsist in supratemporal time; it struggles to recognize and construct the difference between local situation (Warmack's release from prison) and historical dissemination (Poppa's travels and death). Historical relationships are lost, fragmented, or distant to one another. Jazz as a legacy of historical temporality requires reinvention in material conditions and so takes the form of Warmack's struggle to recompose his performing ensemble as a recording unit in a privative present tense. This struggle depends on and so illuminates Warmack's ties to Poppa, his spiritual and musical mentor, albeit one who is most often displaced from the musical group and who dies before Warmack can reunite with him and his musical rootedness. The production of privation in south Los Angeles, then, means that the rhizomatic connection to global struggle is broken and must be reassembled—in musical terms, "reensembled"—not simply as event but also in commodity terms, requiring the skills of image production as well as those of musical performance.

The film's enactment of Warmack's romance with Maya, a photographer and graphic designer, notably does not deny the difficulty of creating love against the raced, sexed, and gendered histories of economic alienation and incarceration. Yet their romance plays without exploitation or stereotype, singular in American jazz film. Crucially, Maya's narrated memories provide the important point of view that connects Warmack's Los Angeles struggle, framed in terms of the legacies of the U.S. civil rights movement, to global struggle: Maya's deceased husband, the father of her child, was a photographer who documented decolonization movements in Africa. Musical production is local; distribution is global. While Poppa turns out to be the remembered link to jazz as sound, Maya's images provide the crucial contemporary production of memory as circulating vision. Together, historical sound and contemporary memory lead Warmack to the card reader Oshun, who prophecies Warmack's fortune while gifting him with a box of seemingly banal objects once belonging to Poppa. Warmack decodes these object symbols, understanding their formal hieroglyphics in a logic of temporal destiny, and maps a path toward greater autonomy.

And perhaps because so many of the visual stories of jazz, and black music in general, have been told outside filmic narrative, we find this film deriving its strategies for visualizing a jazz mode of production from graphic materials outside cinema history but belonging squarely to musical history: record album covers. These provide the visuality iconizing the key temporal junctures and disjunctures of the film whereby its lasting meanings are inscribed. If the filmmakers had few recent resources by which to mount a lasting black cinema, the film can hardly be faulted for not shouldering those historical burdens in a single work. The cryptic ending, culminating in what appears to be a jazz record label, thus invokes other historical sources from those of industrial cinema.

Although period critiques of jazz as a musical subversion of "cockroach capitalism"[18] seem obvious critical sources for the depiction of the recording conglomerate's relation to Warmack's ensemble, Hughes's literary interpretation of the child's poetry primer as jazz album with liner notes in *Ask Your Mama: 12 Moods for Jazz*[19] provides a lesser-known model of the relation of the jazz listener to the jazz commodity object, as I argue in the next section. Moten observes that jazz is an aesthetic, epistemological, and material project: "That which would be named—the sound of the structure and agency that is improvisation—is that which the crossroads only figures: the ensemble." Suggesting that improvisation in jazz amounts to a resistant gesture similar to Ludwig Wittgenstein's "ostensive gesture," an "enactment on the other side of linguistic failure," Moten asserts, "improvisation is sounding in linguistic failure": "Meanwhile, the ensemble—the complex phenomenal object—is what asserts itself at the moment when phenomenon and object each appear in the and as the eclipse of the other."[20] Moten discusses jazz performance as phenomenon and as object. *Passing Through* deploys stylistics of synchronization with regard to the ensemble to be recorded, though, as if to better handle and to archive the appearance and eclipse that Moten describes and that Warmack repeatedly enacts not only in his musical performance but, for example, in his failure to communicate with Maya or in his failure to be able to describe to his collaborators why he cannot play as he used to. In this sense, the mediation of jazz as enduring, circulating object is necessary to bridge eclipses and failures that repeat in the music and in the everyday life where music is made.

Jazz solo and jazz ensemble, as cinematic rendering of world historical meanings—that is, including radical dependency and radical liberation—pertain to the process of creating a musical recording: Warmack and his ensemble enact the crossroads where phenomenon and object appear and eclipse the other but, further, must also mine oral histories, visual production, and futural relation to circulate the ensemble and solo as media commodity. Oshun and Maya contribute these measures to the temporal relation Warmack unfolds as he gathers the affective modalities of time. In this way, Warmack's ensemble's sound proceeds to its archival, recorded temporalities, fulfilling the destiny of the improvisation as object and phenomenon that the film itself has prepared.

The questions *Passing Through* raises and answers are also taken up in other narrative allegories thematizing black public spheres and popular musical commodities. Perry Henzell's *The Harder They Come* (1972) presents a not-dissimilar narrative of a struggle to record, but set to reggae. In this Jimmy Cliff vehicle, a musician struggles to cut a reggae record amid the obstacles of drug dealing and record-industry corruption. Setting its affirmative resources in the crossroads of black production and black reception, *The Harder They Come* allegorizes the country/city binary to frame a struggle for black musical independence that is similar to that depicted in *Passing Through.*

Another, more immediate precedent for Clark's film is *Wattstax* (1973), the Mel Stuart documentary made in association with the Stax/Volt record company and for which *Passing Through* director Clark served as cinematographer.[21] *Wattstax* and *Passing Through* set out the problematic of production against the problematic of reception as a crossroads, wherein sound-image relations, stylistics of synchronization, and historical allegory develop futural calls for future responses without minimizing the difficulties of actual tensions or the violence of historical displacements.

At the time of *Wattstax*'s production, as Mark Anthony Neal points out,[22] soul music had become the dominant form of black musical speech, though it was pulled between the increasing pressures of commercialization and the notion of soul music informing a black public voice. *Wattstax* presents these two pressures and attempts to reconcile them in the concert that inspired the film, featuring artists on the Stax/Volt label and, after the concert footage itself seemed inadequate to telling the story of the music, emphasizing the community of Watts in south Los Angeles. Throughout, the film documents discussions of history, work and leisure, civil rights and American identity, and gender differences related to the experience of race that take place in casual social venues, such as hair salons or barbershops. Watts's music locales are also emphasized to show that soul music, however much an occasion for a national gathering, is also the local expression of storefront churches and neighborhood nightclubs. These last are gendered along the lines that Gilroy suggests: Masculine vocalists in the nightclub celebrate illicit love affairs and the ability to provide sexual pleasure; female gospel singers in the church stress a musical corporeality that vocalizes liberation as a spiritual deliverance. Significantly, *Wattstax* closes with Isaac Hayes, the quintessential organic intellectual as priestly musician representing the journey out of bondage that Gilroy describes and prefiguring hip-hop celebrity's preoccupation with hyperconsumerist adornment as he takes off his cape to reveal a harness of gold chains while singing "Down from the Mountain."

Much as Angela Davis describes the importance of airing grievances through song at blues gatherings or in jazz clubs in the 1920s and 1930s,[23] here again, musical antiphony is found not only to be active within specific locations but also to structure the passing back and forth of meaning between community and concert more broadly. Similarly, in *Passing Through,* the location of the nightclub where Warmack and his group practice constitutes a musical public sphere, though the film's fictional setting allows this to be presented as an overlapping of the pressures of marginalization and violence and the power of instrumental jazz music to convoke historicity and futurity in the present. When the drug dealers who cooperate with the music industry to keep their musicians dependent enter the club, the scene seems to depict "cockroach capitalism." Yet, when the music plays, framing flashbacks that provide historical context and character development, the jazz club, though without vocalists, works similarly to the ways that Gilroy and Davis describe.

Otherwise, of course, the musical styles and visual materials of *Passing Through* as a whole are very different from those of the documentation and commentary compiled in *Wattstax. Passing Through* is as interested in the rhizomatic connections of the local, national, and global as *Wattstax* is concerned with locality as a site where national discourses are anchored and reframed. Further, *Passing Through* animates meanings of musical history and collective identity in a graphical allegory, proposing that to watch the film is actually to watch the process of conceiving, rehearsing, and recording the music that sets the film's narrative in motion and propels it toward its political conclusions.

Few stories of jazz have been told in musical or narrative film with as integral a role for local music or as attuned to the ontologies, epistemologies, and ethics of jazz globality.[24] It is useful, here, to keep in mind the conflicts and tensions playing out historically between U.S. cinema and jazz performance. In such films as Leo Penn's *A Man Called Adam* (1966), a black jazzman played by Sammy Davis, Jr., proves himself too arrogant for a white agent's ego to handle. The agent retaliates by withholding bookings until Davis literally crawls to him on his hands and knees, begging for work. Accurate in its characterization of the primarily white-owned recording industry's attempt to control musical production and horrifically racist in its punitive humiliation of the character played by Davis, the movie compounds its insult by depicting Davis as being forced to sing for his supper on a tour of his hated homeland, the Deep South. Once tragic in his substance abuse, he again meets tragedy when he is killed by a white supremacist, but the music is not lost: His white protégé on the trumpet inherits his mouthpiece. Jazz here narrates national race relations but from the point of view of an appropriative white guilt that appreciates jazz music if only because the deaths of black musical stars have inspired so many talented white men to (continue to) occupy the spotlight. The gestures in question—inscribing domination, addiction, and death—are precisely those of the racial terror that Gilroy argues was unspeakable or that Moten describes in terms of linguistic failure. Here, however, they recapitulate jazz sound being delivered to dominant historical epistemologies, ontologies, or ethics.

Passing Through is also singular in its upsetting of conventional associations between musical genius and drug addiction. Consider the way that the jazz sound track of Otto Preminger's *The Man with the Golden Arm* (1955) deploys some of the angular harmonic stridencies of postbop jazz yet ties them to the exoticizing character of a bass line more appropriate to striptease. In a key sequence of *Man*, jazz drummer Frankie Machine (Frank Sinatra) can no longer resist the temptations of his neighborhood heroin dealer, Louie (Darren McGavin). Frankie, frustrated with his inability to become a professional drummer, sits at the counter of the neighborhood bar and, in the mirror hanging over the counter, sees Louie approach. Frankie visually "connects" with Louie through the reflection in the overhead glass. The sound track rises, emphasizing the exchange of gazes that leads Frankie after Louie and into the dealer's apartment. The sequence carefully choreographs the image track and the musical score to synchronize the off-kilter economy of corporeal attraction between the two men, with the dealer's seduction of Frankie taking over suspense as to his fate as a musician. The sequence musicalizes lower-class street masculinity and frustrated aesthetic aspiration as a desire for dependency and subjugation. The sequence climaxes with a melodic flourish and rhythmic thrust as Louie injects heroin into Frankie's arm. Frankie's eyes widen, then he passes out; the sound track softens and fades out. The penetration of Frankie's inept musical body by Louie's pharmacological needle shuts off Frankie's vision and, with it, the insistent rhythmic drive of need, making him deaf to the world around him.

The jazz cue here is a "record" of addiction playing again, silencing the underemployed musical worker's rhythmic "machine."

In contrast, in *Passing Through,* addiction is presented as a biopolitical equivalent of disciplinary incarceration and economic marginalization. When Maya visits the jazz club where Warmack and his musicians are rehearsing, one of the musicians tells her about his past as an addict. A flashback begins that, like many of the flashbacks in the film, is carefully photographed in black and white to match historical footage. This musical-flashback sequence follows an earlier series of flashbacks in which jazz music being played is juxtaposed with scenes of a prison uprising and a civil rights–era riot. Some of that footage is archival, but some was created to feature *Passing Through*'s players as protagonists in a history of racial conflict and demands for equality. Here, though, the jazz being played in Warmack's club takes us to a run-down room where the band member narrates, without dialog, a past heroin overdose. The narration is delivered in terms of improvised musical synchronization, recounting the struggle with addition but with a different outcome, one emphasizing jazz as an ensemble struggle for historical consciousness and working freedom rather than historical narcosis compensating for frustrated ambition. As the musical sound track becomes increasingly insistent in the flashback, we see the band member taken to a hospital, his friends and girlfriend frantic with desperation. He is pronounced dead by the attending physician. His physical stasis is diagrammed by a hospital monitoring device that traces his nonexistent pulse: He has flatlined. This diagram is a graphical scoring of techno-scientific time, of dominant time, of the biopolitical present. It is not the time of free music, which continues to play on the sound track—ragged, insistent, unstopping, hardly attached to the scene at all except for the living desperation it animates, dramatized in the desperate gestures of the musician's girlfriend in the hospital corridor. Poppa suddenly enters the hospital room, and, seeing the band member's condition, he blows a note on a folkloric horn. The note fuses with the sound track, synchronizing sound and image in musical time and taking over what had been a dead relationship between techno-scientific or biopolitical time and the still body of the comatose musician.

The note that Poppa plays to revive the musician belongs as much to the history being narrated in audiovisual terms as to the jazz being played in the present tense in Warmack's club. This complex musical narration of overlapping temporal modalities synchronizes jazz as doubled immanence, belonging to suprahistorical duration but activated in the material contradictions of the present moment. It calls the musician back into his body, but this is the musical narration of memory: Poppa's sound calls the musician back into his body, then, but from the future tense of his own musical voice. Hearing Poppa's note, we see the musician's eyes flutter and open. Here is jazz as *pharmakon*:[25] This is jazz as affective labor and as antidote to, rather than the condition of, the affective labor of addiction. Its time unfurls through doubled potentiality as traveling multiplicity, heard in the present, transversal to history and to future but remembered and related in the present. It awakens the musician, restores his body, and allows him to speak a past tense of which he was otherwise unconscious. *Passing Through*'s jazz temporality interrupts, alters, and cures by way of narrating and releasing the biopolitical confinement of the musician's body and by way of recalling the memory of jazz in the present tense of struggle.

This complex temporality informs the entire film. Between *Passing Through*'s opening shot of jazz musicians improvising and its final shot of an album cover signaling an emergent mode of record production, an exploited ensemble liberates itself by taking control of its musical destiny. The film moves from the presentation of jazz performance to presenting the film itself as a jazz recording: Performance *and* recording are storied ways of articulating jazz. With this graphical allegory of jazz as mode of production, the film also suggests a jazz model for other forms of performance and recording, such as film. *Passing Through* performs the relation between jazz and its own material, technological, and affective reproduction.[26] Whether seen as a demand for a black cinema in its own moment or as a summary of jazz as developmental music, the listening knowledge of the audience and the visual knowledge necessary for identifying African independence leaders are crucial to viewing *Passing Through.*

Jazz in the Hands of Listeners

Historically, whether in the Baroque era's "eye music" or in the long-playing album cover, the presence of auditory and visual musical materials suggests transpositions in the circulation of composed music for performance, where musical emblems diagram the affective dimensions of knowledge associated with not only seeing and hearing but also "holding" music—remembering or archiving music. Musical emblems may be otherwise representative depictions of composers or performers or may be diagrams of heard mobilities, claims on historical, social, cultural, economic, or technological relationships. In these ways, musical commodities, such as printed scores, media recordings, or album covers, may fold in an ethics apart from their notational instructions, which may be obscured by the marketing appeal such emblems may make formally. Clark's distinct aims and methods in presenting the cinematic recording of a materialist aesthetics of free jazz have numerous historical parallels or predecessors.

Consider the pun on dominant modernity and black transatlantic modernity appearing on Anthony Braxton's 1981 release (Figure 5.1). The album cover features a reproduction of Wassily Kandinsky's painting *Black Relationship* (1924); on the reverse, Braxton's diagrammatic graphical scores for improvisatory performance, presented as near hieroglyphics of shape, color, line, and text,

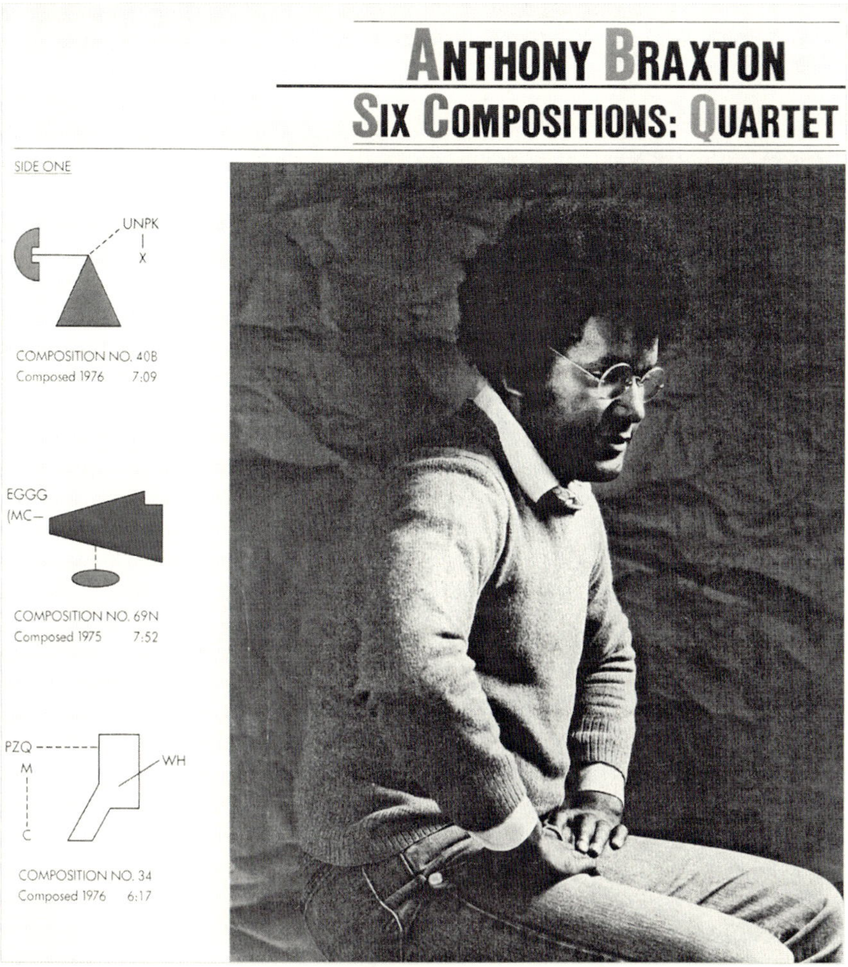

FIGURE 5.1 Anthony Braxton's *Six Compositions: Quartet* (1981): Back cover image (Antilles AN-1005-A, detail).

point to the participatory dynamics guiding the performance of each track. The thoughtful Braxton appears amid the miniature scores on the back cover, as if he were contemplating his diagrammatic work. The juxtaposition of the front and back cover imagery invites multiple comparisons: If Kandinsky's meditative paintings are part of a modernism that reacted against objective figuration through intimations of musical experience, Braxton's diagrammatic compositions describe the musical generation of open-ended works in what Braxton calls a "trans-African" idiom.[27] During a moment when jazz, as a popular music genre, had largely dissipated, and black music was renewing its energies in soul, funk, disco, and hip-hop, Braxton's cover signifies a switch in focus from the immanent energies harnessed in the musicalization of modernism's painterly image to the graphical notations indicating the compositional coherence of his highly variable musical forms. Creating music whose form depends on processes invoked in its performance, Braxton utilizes for his own notational ends spatialized geometries similar to those figured in Kandinsky's painting.

Here, the relationships between composer and score, between members of the quartet, and between performer and composition constitute black relationships. But perhaps the relationship between free jazz and mass-cultural reproduction of image and text is also a black relationship. Braxton's appropriation of Kandinsky for the front of his record humorously suggests that, rather than being considered transcendental or nonobjective, musical meanings are to be considered generative as well as concrete.

Braxton's placement of his graphical scores in the hands of his listeners can be understood by imagining the instructions for a planned yet indeterminate series of musical kinesics embedded within the instructions for another planned and indeterminate series of gestures for listening. The album sleeve sets up this contrast between two series of gestures separated into distinct regimes: one musical, the other technical; one of articulation, the other of listening—distinct regimes, of course, separated by time and space. As an invitation to listen and to reconsider the meaning of a black relationship, though, the album-cover graphics lead one to listen for productive gestures and perhaps to compensate for the absence of the performers and composers. To reclaim the visual representation of music through geometrical figures on an album-cover sleeve as reference to improvisational composition and performance at the same time provides suggestion for repeated hearings that produce variegated experiences for the listener.

If a black circle dominates Kandinsky's *Black Relationship,* a black shellac record dominates Theodor Adorno's early critique of the recording industries: "What the gramophone listener actually wants to hear is himself, and the artist merely offers him a substitute for the sounding image of his own person, which he would like to safeguard as a possession."[28] Late in life, Adorno found that opera could best be served by records' ability to be collected and listened to repeatedly. The opera auditors of Adorno's imagination are "lonely and perceptive . . . hibernating for purposes unknown" (285). He also suggests that filmic montage might inform musical production and, finally, that music must look to film for its production motifs. Adorno's emphasis tends to be on an individualized listening to composers and performers. Listening as a form of enacting or experiencing knowledge is not considered, nor is music explored as a form capable of representing cultural knowledge. Additionally, he does not consider the material gestures of listeners who have (limited) means to activate and to control their musical apparatus. In his description of girls listening to public phonographs in Nice, France (273), they are literally hooked up to the recording industry, standing below text and images advertising the songs they pay a token to hear while waiting to be picked up by strangers. It is a strangely louche yet hysterical connectivity—rather than auditory or economic mastery—that animates this image: bourgeois female bodies closing the circuits of capital precisely in offering themselves up to Adorno's troubled gaze.

If, as Thomas Levin suggests, Adorno concentrates on music's own autonomous gesture (it writes itself),[29] this emphasis discounts the immanent epistemologies within musical production where reception commands the hearing of actions exterior to recorded products. Adorno's interest in establishing the indexicality of the record groove has more to do with an interest in applying the techniques of cinematic montage to audio production. So Adorno treats culture industries as monolithic entities producing kitsch and "light music," such as jazz, when the real power of his critique might be more effectively directed at the nature of cross-holdings and conflicts of interest between various industries, forms of media, media distribution, and media properties. Also, differing economies of scale and production regimes mean products differ greatly in their relationships to reception communities. In these differences, one finds immanent contradictions not entirely registered in the material contradictions of music or cinema production to the degree that production communities and reception communities can be made coincident: immanence and information in whose synchronization a different subject of history appears.[30]

Album sleeves and recorded discs may make visual claims toward the exchange value of media products: Here are the mass visualities of advertising, promotion, and calculation or, at the material surface of the disc, indecipherability, blankness, the "picture" of the phonographic spiral, and the faint reflection of the listener. But these surfaces also may enact claims about the value of the musical experience set in motion by the gestures of listeners. The form of the commodity, its production, and its self-promotion as object of exchange necessarily are mediated by the utility of the commodity for a listener and the musical meanings to be interpreted. The phonograph album cover lacks depth but has a flipside and interiority. These are tactile diagrams of music whose visuality is turned inside out; they guide the hand toward the recording they protect, but in an open-ended invitation to hear the music they diagram. For those leaning toward Braxton's often-demanding music, the graphical scores at minimum provide an index to guide selections. Still, his scores remain largely hieroglyphic to the uninitiated; as pictures of general dynamics that produce a particular instance, they require a kind of mastery, some form of inside information. If free jazz is to be counterposed to European modernism, how exactly is free jazz to relate to audiences?

If it is a strain to hear the music within the free jazz wrapper, that is partly because here, interiority operates in relation to the exteriorities of biopolitical, bioinformatic time. The flip side, as it were, of Adorno's reflective black pane and the abyss of light music might precisely be jazz music as it records black cultural production. If Adorno—or Eisler, for that matter, as discussed in Chapter 4—wants sound recording to model itself on cinematic montage, during the 1970s, jazz composers, such as Braxton, and cinema directors, such as Clark, wanted to construct recording media as jazz history. This history and its futures have long been emblematized in and on jazz recordings, which have long provided resources for their telling. Hughes's *Ask Your Mama* literally presents his long-developed verbalization of liberation poetics from jazz musicality. The book is a musical primer of Afro-diasporic struggle that takes the form of a book-length poem designed to be read as a jazz album cover in expanded form. The poetic content of the text takes up jazz as music and as contemporary social commentary, evincing Hughes's long-standing interest in the poetics of jazz music as a historical subject and a historical form, instantiated earlier as his illustrated essay primer *The First Book of Jazz.*[31]

In *Ask Your Mama,* a score of the book's "leitmotif," the melody of the "Hesitation Blues," and a scored fragment of the melodic and rhythmic material of "shave and haircut, fifteen cents" provides additional material to the reader, who is invited to improvise, in the course of reading, an imagined musical ending for each poem. Providing a visual design based on the graphical aesthetics of the jazz album cover to support the performativities of jazz reading, the twelve "moods" included in this book as album cover constitute musical "tracks." Each mood, or poem, is printed on the left side of the page, and this is, in essence, the vocal "performance." On the right side of each page, in italics, is a poetic description of an imaginary musical accompaniment, apparently derived from scored material "gathered" for the reader from the resources of black musical history by Hughes in the preface. The book as album cover, then, is musicological archive, poetic essay, and performative reading, achieving social commentary—a historical record presented as an opportunity for improvising with the musical materials of black history. With the music heard in the process of reading generated in the engagement with the textual object, *Ask Your Mama* provides no musical sound in the auditory domain but instead uses the graphic design of jazz album covers as a musical setting and staging for the text.

Each of the twelve moods of *Ask Your Mama,* as well as the cover of the book, is introduced with a small mosaic of abstract geometric shapes—graphic emblems punctuating the title of each mood that suggest, variously, the crystalline asymmetries of postbop jazz; the integration of compositional and improvisational, directed and participatory aesthetic methods of jazz production; and the piecing together of musical meaning that is demanded of the jazz listener. The poems themselves situate the black poetic voice as emanating from "the quarter of the Negroes," an imagined locale for black articulation that is segregated, restricted, contained, and yet, at the same time, broadly historical, diasporic, with global ramifications.

At the end of the book, short texts gloss each of the twelve poems, providing a set of "liner notes" for the book as album. Significantly, while these notes are supplemental in form, given to explain and to provide context for the musical material (as in the tradition of many jazz album liner notes), they are also given in language that is less poetic only by degrees, and there is no marking off the language of "jazz exegesis" as explication from jazz as poetic language. Didactic or exegetic values of information are not delimited from musical performance. The notes, then, too, pertain to a jazz aesthetic where the poetics of idiolectal composition give reason and occasion for explanation, which is joined as a variation, or improvisation, to the musical body of the text. The textuality of the liner notes does not situate the meanings of the musical poetics given in the main text by functioning as their exterior but rather extends and folds the performativities of jazz meaning back into the body of the text held by readers.

For the reader, then, the gesture of turning pages, moving from musical track to musical context, "mood" to "liner note," is refashioned after the gestures conditioning the reception of musical commodities: the flipping or unfolding of the album cover, the drawing out of the flattened double album, the dual and reversible planes that each contain a record. The jazz poem, in book form, entreats the user to interrupt the dominant form of the book, generally separated into poetic or descriptive languages, by applying the practices of orienting oneself toward knowledge anchored in listening to recorded music. In folding these gestures into the turning of book pages, and in doing so rustling, interrupting, and resettling the conventional order of leafing through the sequential pages of printed text, Hughes's design prepares a musical grasp of the book for the reader by presenting its artifactual surface as an antiphonic progression, a sequence of calls and responses: a musical flipping or unfolding, a holding, then a folding back and a moving on. Jazz musicality passes through the book, interrupting its conventional serial form.

Just as the jazz hearer is folded into the antiphonies of black musical production, so the reader's experience of the poem comes as an antiphony, a call and response engagement with the haptic and the visual, holding and beholding. What does the listener "ask mama"? Jazz meanings are confined not to jazz musical production necessarily or to American national identity but to Afrodiasporic liberation struggles worldwide, and they are construed in the context of, on the one hand, techno-scientific production and, on the other, cold war geopolitics. The liner notes for the first mood, "Cultural Exchange," explain:

> A State Department visitor from Africa comes, wishing to meet Negroes. He is baffled by the "two sides to every question" way of looking at things in the South. Although he finds that in the American social supermarket blacks for sale range from intellectuals to entertainers, to the African all

> cellophane signs point to ideas of change—in an IBM land that pays more attention to Moscow than to Mississippi. (86)

Observing a present in which superpower politics and supermarket commodification seem not only to divide the political subject but also to endlessly particularize everyday experience in an "IBM land," Hughes presents questions and answers for musical listeners, musical readers, musical hands: black relationships.

Black liberation histories refract in mass-market packaging in differing degrees; these histories figure in distinct iconologies pointing to relationships between creative practices, musical production, and productions of identity specific to black histories and musics as well as to national and transnational ones. Gilroy develops these antiphonies as defining modernity in terms of a countermodernity. Following W.E.B. DuBois but reframing "double consciousness" in terms of transatlantic modernisms, Gilroy, too, argues that trauma is not inexpressible but rather spoken in terms of musical expression. Music emphasizes "embodied subjectivity" as kinesics communicating but going beyond abstract thought or text-based knowledge, pinpointing distinctive aesthetic components of black communication.[32]

Poppa or Warmack in *Passing Through* or even Braxton's self-presentation on his album cover recalls Gilroy's description of musical, "organic" intellectuals. Black music, for Gilroy, elaborates another articulation of a body politic in dissemination, one that clarifies the antiphonies of cultural exchange that Hughes draws as jazz poetry. Gilroy asks: "How are we to think critically about artistic products and aesthetic codes which, though they may be traceable back to one distinct location, have been changed either by the passage of time or by their displacement, relocation, or dissemination through networks of communication and cultural exchange?" (80).

Braxton's album cover folds his compositional labor against the reproduction of Kandinsky's spiritual abstraction. This fold of the album sleeve enables a flippant gesture, valuing jazz as creative labor while putting it in the place of high art: a generative substitute for high modernism. Such covers diagram relations between the recorded sound, whatever futural promises the commodity form may hold, and the auditory practices of listeners. Yet declining in influence in its commodity form, how was free jazz to extend listening knowledge after what Hughes called an "IBM land"? Clark's *Passing Through* provides one version of an answer.

A Poetics of Relating Ensemble and Solo

Given *Passing Through*'s precedents in American jazz cinema and the ways that it so thoroughly breaks with them, it is clear that the film draws on a different set of materials and intertexts than those of Hollywood for its frames, themes, motivations, and audiovisual strategies. Again, the film's opening sequence demonstrates a visuality cognate with graphic materials outside cinema history but belonging squarely to the history of the mass media: jazz and record album covers. The graphical parallels relevant to the colorized orchestration of Tapscott's performance, for example, are primarily those of the photos seen on so many jazz covers from the 1950s and 1960s.[33]

The optical overlays in the film's introductory sequence, featuring the performing hands of the jazz ensemble, are a prime example. Orchestration in jazz here means invoking traditions of improvisation and of "following," in the musical or dance sense—of aligning with a movement already established by another performer. By the time the sequence ends, the aural layers are crowded with instrumental parts responding to the musical themes laid out, and a visual cloud of colors follows the music. The image of the performers' hands on their instruments differs from narrative and documentary practices in that the musicians are not individualized as persons *before* their performance but rather attain musical identities inasmuch as they are participating in the elaboration of an audiovisual orchestration. We do not see their faces or see them standing on stage, as we might in an expressive shot of a musician during a "live" performance. This sequence lays out a diegetic trajectory established through musical line sense and not through a concert venue, club, or some other spatial constraining of musical cinematography. Above all, the musicians are not relegated to a background scene in front of which others will dance or romance; their performance is an end in and of itself, even as it prompts the narrative directly.

The visual intertexts here may be the optical overprinting typical of visual music experiment, like the optical delay effects diagramming gestural streams or visual "echoes," whether in Gjon Mili's *Jammin' the Blues* (1944; see Chapter 1) or in the cascading ballet dancers' movements in Norman McLaren's *Pas de deux* (1968). In *Passing Through,* though, relevant prior media objects would also include the two-color mood shots typical of many jazz albums—for example, those of the Blue Note record label. These album cover photographs emphasize affect and form, with jazz sound as a medium that can, as Boyd suggests black music does more generally, fuse formal aspects of musical expression with the vernaculars of specific inflections. The formal aspects of the photography stress line and tone in what is almost a two-tone chiaroscuro. Performers' articulations are communicated through expressive facial gestures and their hand movements as they play. Taken together, these values produce graphical compositions that stress instrumental mastery and emotional intensity. Often, the musicians' hands are shot according to a photographic convention that foregrounds them in relation to the rest of their bodies. In turn, this iconology of artist as expression, gesture, and instrument foregrounds an articulatory moment that, as often as not, points up the emotional meanings of the music in relation to the visual compositions.[34]

The scene in which Warmack attempts to find his sound during rehearsal also points up meanings of jazz thematized by the film and reflected in album cover art. During this jam session, another saxophonist is improvising, and Warmack appears to be trying to find a way into the music. He seems lost or confused, wondering exactly what he is hearing and thus what he is to play. The sound track here is processed with distortion and delay effects that depict the sax man's hearing as "out of sync." The film repeatedly cuts away and returns to the jam session, with each cutaway cued by sonic distortions in the sound track. Warmack, dissociated from his own musical identity by his time in the penitentiary, is able to intuit through this distortion the scene of Poppa's passing and, in so doing, begins to resolve for himself the steps he needs to take toward refinding his signature sound. The film invokes jazz as a scene of performance in which unexpected distortions can free up musical space such that a musician does not simply follow the line but may *hear* the way to a new vision of the musical legacy. The sound of jazz is a vibration, an emanation in the world—not so much unifying transcendent temporality but a form that emphasizes the place of the present in relationship to an immanent temporality that can reveal identity, and become historical, by also calling toward a futural struggle.

These themes propose jazz as an irruptive ethical epistemology—that is, where action and knowledge are mutually determining, ethical knowledge, as "pure sound," "resonance," "distortion," or "vibration," exists as sonic material to be heard penetrating through rationalized architectures that circulate exploitation. As such, jazz communicates a musical knowledge to be reshaped by the performer. Although in the film, these themes are developed vis-à-vis a performer who is struggling for personal vision to be able to rejoin his musical colleagues, similar notions of jazz (and of popular music more generally) exist as an irruptive epistemology of vibration typical of album cover iconography.[35]

Revisiting the narrative climax of *Passing Through*, in which Warmack ambushes the mobsters who have been sabotaging his efforts to organize his musicians' collective, the sound wave is similarly figured. After killing two at close range, he chases the third, their leader—whose European accent suggests the global scope of cultural exploitation—into a forest. Warmack's gunshot, aimed at the mobster's back as he flees, reverberates, and with its echo comes a freeze-frame of the man from the front, falling in midair. An optical zoom blurs the frame toward the viewer as the sound of the gunshot resonates. Here, the blurred zoom stresses the graphical composition as a visual counterpart to a sound emanating from a musician and traveling through space. Agency resides not necessarily with the man who has fired the gun but with the man whose gun's sound reaches the listener. This sort of sound event—no simple sound effect, but one with significance because it is *meant* to be heard—is also an album-cover art staple.[36] Any synthesis of musical recording and political movement is tentative and incomplete, of course—at best, a temporal diagramming rather than a completed, constitutive event. This synthesis has to be tentative, in that it indicates a tentative ground at which to articulate changed conditions and to make new demands; but, in becoming definitive, the music will have to move on.

Expanding the Archive

This stylistic of synchronization requires not simply an account of the audience's grasp of formal elements in sound track or image track but that these elements become accessible in the reception of time-based media layered as streams. In speaking of audience gestures toward screen media or media distributed through cinematic networks, instrumented through televisual networks, or articulated through digital networks, one addresses the capacity to virtually touch what Anne Friedberg[37] calls the "virtual window" of the screen. As Friedberg shows, with respect to the screen, the mobility the "virtual window" grants is conditioned within the larger historical contingencies extending haptic and kinesthetic engagements with streaming media. Mary Anne Doane suggests in her discussion of cinema's "cutting" of time as the shot that the cinematic stream of time also archives time. For Doane, two simultaneous epistemologies are archived in cinematic time: the shot as the lived time of the individual (Doane suggests that in the works of such directors as Pier Paolo Pasolini, we see a narrative epistemology) while cinema also archives an index, in the sense Charles Pierce describes, as a thermodynamic datum (operating within a probabilistic epistemology).[38] These considerations indicate that mobility conditioned by the shot and the reconfiguration of everyday life archived in cinematic time are at stake, then, in the exhibition of streaming layered media. Where the stream of cinematic time is projected via technical means to cut into the time of reception, more than liveness or the actual datedness of media streams is projected. "Virtually touching" the simultaneously informatic and narratological epistemologies of inscribed media streams as they are animated and situated in reception, as I have shown, draws on the complex technical capacities of the media installation and object as well as the complex affective capacities of receiving audiences.

Affective labor is archived in technical reproducibility, then, while necessarily being conducted in relation to it. The feeling of action we exert at the multimedia screen is modal in the sense I have described of being divergent from, yet contradictory within, the framing technics and architectures that partially determine our positions, postures, and movements during reception. No single theory of spectatorship or audition can determine this doubled immanence of affective labor, because it is always immanent to the ordering of an event within some relation of contemporaneity and historiality. Considering the affective labor of making sense and the polyform technical layering of streaming media in reference to Deleuzian understanding of affect as actualizing virtual potential, we can see, however, a clarification and a complication. Affective labor draws on the immanence of virtuality, and the affective labor of the engaged audience is never reducible to the technical operations of media exhibition. In this sense, audience conduct and contact with streaming media means that the affective experience of technical synchronization may be, in some cases or to some degree, a stylistics or means of flight through technical reproducibility that is not dependent or fully determined by it. And to the degree that events occur as technically reproduced possibilities on the basis of synchronized streams—the sound effects of visual montage or the haptic effects of audiovisual montage, for example—technical means of reproducing media streams also capture virtuality and affective labor. In thinking through the ability, apparently promised by "paperless technologies," of the virtual to be archived, Jacques Derrida questions whether transitions of inscription in media also suggest that the philosopheme of the virtual has become unmoored from the absolute opposition to the actual that it holds in Gilles Deleuze's *Bergsonism*:[39]

> What will become of this "full and effective actuality of the taking-place" when it becomes necessary to remove the concept of virtuality from the couple that opposes it to actuality, to effectivity, to reality? Will one be obliged to continue thinking that there is no imaginable archive for the virtual, for what happens in virtual space and time? It is hardly probable, this mutation is in progress, but it will be necessary to keep a rigorous account of this other virtuality, to abandon or restructure from top to bottom our inherited concept of the archive. The moment has come to accept a great stirring in our conceptual archive, and in it to cross a "logic of the unconscious" with a way of thinking of the virtual which is no longer limited by the traditional philosophical opposition between act and power.[40]

For Derrida, the opposition between virtual and actual is in a long process of shift toward "spectralization." This tendency itself is ordered within a larger historical process that is indivisible from writing, understood as the techno-politics of hominization—that is, of the advent of the human. Where, for Deleuze and Felix Guattari, the periodic table or musical scores are evidence of a signifying diagrammatic relation[41] ensuring the efficacy of affective labor that actualizes the virtual in lived corporeality, rather, Derrida argues, "information expropriation" produces a trembling, epochal shift.

But here, in jazz cinema, any such embodiment or shift is subjected to the unfolding and recalling of historical epistemologies, ontologies, or ethics suspended in traumatic experience, such as addiction, privation, or death, and, more specifically, the biopolitics of personhood and transnational public being.

Gilroy's Black Atlantic (and see my summary in Chapter 1) is reworked in *Passing Through* or *Wattstax* in terms of stylistics of synchronization deploying doubled immanence: Affective labor is work on, working out of, the relation of contemporary to historical time. Jazz articulates the meanings of citizenship, the freedom found in working in ensemble or as solo, the creativity of historical knowledge, antinomies not only raced and gendered but also sexed, as Alexander Weheliye[42] points out. In these senses, affective labor becomes the archive and the unfurling of doubled potentiality. In such a film as *Passing Through*, composition and reception along with exhibitional program are synchronized in a complex cloud of temporal modalities requiring an improvisational interpretation to decipher. The film creates a pragmatics of audience conduct and contact with the cinematic work for some nonteleological—that is, improvisational—relationship with historical transformation determined in, and interrupting, bioinformatic time. *Passing Through* expands the archives of cinema and of jazz by diagramming a historical recording of the ways in which the shifting status of the virtual between immanence and information was contested in terms of possibility.

The pathos vital for Deleuze in Eisenstein (see Chapter 2) or the pity in Francis Bacon's painting, which Deleuze sees as resolving tensions between abstract and abstract expressionist painting, is diagrammed in diastolic, systolic rhythms carrying hysteria through painting.[43] *Passing Through* draws a still broader and more conflicted outline of musical immanence, global capitalist temporal regimes, and corporeal discipline. More broadly, situating album covers as mediation between producers and audiences by way of a visuality that, when grasped, leads to listening, I have suggested two black relationships between 1970s free jazz and history that complicate Deleuze's contemporary theorization of rhythm and haptic image. First, Hughes's *Ask Your Mama* or Braxton's album cover relates jazz to the bioenergetic modernisms typified by such avant-garde figures as Kandinsky and suggests jazz as the displaced emblem of dominant modernisms that recurs within bioinformatic temporalities as mastery of historical temporalization. Second, *Passing Through* suggests the relationship of jazz to world politics and its own technological reproduction, revising recognitions of its localization in Los Angeles in terms of a larger Black Pacific. Finally, I point out a third relationship underlying both of these: the relationship of free jazz to its own history within black music—solo leadership arising in an embrace of the ensemble.

In 1977, pianists Mary Lou Williams and Cecil Taylor released the concert recording *Embraced*. The title is spaced across the cover, graphically uniting photos of the two artists beneath. On the flip side, the concept: "A concert of new music for two pianos exploring the history of jazz with love." The cover's black background is continued in the fold of the double album, which opens to reveal the artists' notes and biographies. Williams recounts her life in jazz from the 1920s on, hoping to "show the full seep and history of this music . . . together with some of the musical struggles it has been up against." Taylor claims, in writing that is equal parts poetry and criticism, "growth as inherent right."[44]

This cover acts out the project of the music: Williams composed most tracks to rehearse developments in black music from spirituals to bop, going "Back to the Blues" and ending ironically with the George Gershwin standard "Can't Get Started." Here, the ensemble becomes a duo, and the jazz avant-garde literally plays with its history as Taylor's textured variations situate Williams's more thematic material to expand its reach and demand. As jazz was languishing as a genre, Williams and Taylor attempted to invigorate it within a musical embrace—one of historiographical narration, not idealization.

For many years now, for a range of software and hardware devices, designers and technologists have attempted to revive the culture of the album cover. Album covers extended visuality and textuality in graphical, tactical objects to call listeners' responses; in these objects, musicians' gestures, image and text, or listeners' gestures corresponded asynchronously and asymmetrically within developing musical cultures. Distinct from synchronized audiovisuals, such as film or television, as well as distinct from synchronized interactive forms, such as video games, these correspondences happened out of bioinformatic time or, more properly, within a fold in it. Album covers, strangely incomplete image objects containing musical experiences, read two ways: as emblems of a particular moment in the economies and cultures of recorded music and emblems that circulate musical meanings and knowledges. In the case of free jazz, arguing for its continued relevance, three relationships usually considered as external to music and to cinema become vital to the grasp of material history: jazz as a transmedial idiom; jazz as localizing style and, in *Passing Through,* a cinematic stylization of the Black Pacific; and jazz as a complex temporal relation of ensemble to solo, of organization to leadership, of collective effort and individuation, of event to object to phenomenon. No wonder album-cover text and graphics are redesigned for digital consumer music devices, and not just for marketing reasons. They continue to suggest an opaque correspondence not between a visual world and an auditory world but rather between a visual-textual field[45] and the instrumental meanings of "handling" music as time. They effect, in the diagrammatic form of the commodity object, those legible, graspable poetics of the ethics of musical circulation and of the commoditization of historical and social meaning, and the affective labor conditioning the legibility of fixed material labor. These are the themes of *Passing Through,* a film that situates Hollywood as the antagonist within a narrative of Los Angeles' decolonization, and as a historial datum within listening distance of decolonizing Africa, and then proceeds to improvise through cinema's stylistics to screen the music of historical south Los Angeles.

6

Melos, Telos, and Me

Transpositions of Identity in the Rock Musical

> *It is as if in endlessly retracing the course of our disappointment, we might still keep open those junctures where a different outcome still seemed possible, one on which, say, Arnold won the contest, or Louise became Tulsa's partner, or Rose, at the end of the "Turn," took off a wig. Hence, too, like Boy Rose, we turn and go off, in the Star Mother's train, to seek somewhere else, at some other show, the recognition that this one has almost but not quite given us. . . . [W]ho can say it will never turn up?*
>
> —D. A. Miller, *Place for Us: Essay on the Broadway Musical*

> *I ain't never goin' back.*
>
> —Hedwig, in *Hedwig and the Angry Inch,* dir. John Cameron

Melos and Telos, or Origins of Love

On the way from a sideshow act entertaining scandal-seekers and startling diners at an unlikely home-style-buffet-cum-rock-club in Kansas City to star billing at a swank New York City rock club, where she delivers an anthemic "last waltz," Hedwig crosses territories familiar to and untrammeled by filmic melodrama, musical biopic, rock musical, and rockumentary in director and star John Cameron Mitchell's 2001 film adaptation of his long-running off-Broadway play, *Hedwig and the Angry Inch.* Hedwig's audience works through her trials and tribulations along the way: child abuse sexual (by her father) and emotional (by her mother); surgical mutilation by a crank doctor; betrayal and abandonment at the hands of a first love; lost homes and irretrievable origins; sex experienced as illicit, sad, angry, and failed relationships with gendered, raced, and classed conflicts; public infighting and intimate divisions among band members, motivated in a strange permutation of cold war geopolitics; delusions of star grandeur, tawdry tabloid fame, and celebrity stalking; stolen authorship and misbegotten millions at her own expense; emotional and physical manipulation of her closest friends, her lover, and her agent; a terrible car crash; and an apparently only imagined reconciliation with her "better half." After all this, her music stilled, the long-suffering, long-suffered Hedwig disappears, walking alone, bare but for a small tattoo, toward the dim light of an empty street.

The film is more than a series of melancholic episodes interspersed with rock-show spectacle, though. *Hedwig* proceeds not according to the narrative rules of melodrama or musical but by subverting them in substance and in form, whereby those classical film genres are filtered through postclassical formulae, such as rock opera and rockumentary, to indicate, in retrospect, that the fates of those earlier genres have long been sealed. The postclassical film genres *Hedwig* reworks come undone, too. *Hedwig* is hardly reverential of rock style as spectacular transgression, as rock opera is. And the rockumentary's "behind-the-scenes" documentation of the elusive rock performer's genius is mined to produce a fictional demythification of rock genius as highly traded public image. And as if *Hedwig*'s plundering of pop music, film style, and narrative form were not enough, the film delightfully buttresses its *combinatoire* of drag as sex-gender perplexity, its easy and constant deployment of marginal film and video musical forms, and its encyclopedic proclivity for intertextual reference with the outright bastardization of classical texts (Plato's *Symposium*) and the sacrilegious invocation of the Bible (apparently, standard and gnostic).

As we have seen for figures as disparate as Sergei Eisenstein, Oskar Fischinger, Hanns Eisler, or Larry Clark, and in the numerous critical accounts I have discussed so far, works of time-based media and critical and cultural accounts of music alike accord musicality a potentiality for and find within that potentiality a critique of utopian and dystopian imaginings. For Theodor Adorno, musicality speaks personhood and collectivity: Musicality says "we" in spite of musical labor's specific conditioning in material networks of commodity production.[1] In comparison, *Hedwig*'s take on generic and gendered expression as extended musical detour might seem more a dystopian crash of Deleuzian virtuality into the ubiquitously mediated contemporary moment. The film is a jagged palimpsest of Western philosophy, spirituality, and sexed gender expression in a mediatic scrambling of past, present, and future temporal modes, suggesting a lurching narrative engine outputting personhood as murderous telos, a failing actualization offset only in an occasional momentary kaleidoscope of selfhood exploding as musical epiphenomenon. And, when Hedwig disappears, so disappears, perhaps, our potential for identifying personhood as anything but a fragmented contingent self-awareness, the blind spot of a media supersystem engineering us in a program where retrospective melancholia defers future transformation.

In this chapter, I provide a reading of *Hedwig* as a temporal diagram of queer personhood to clarify the pleasures it takes in an apparently punishing self-expression. I am less interested in a reading of masochism or melancholia, here, than in allowing the film to present a reading of the apparent rhetoric of realism that such a bombastic, rhetorically extreme, and politically incorrect film invites. How can it be called "realistic"—the word that one midwestern U.S. educator used to justify his presentation of *Hedwig* to high-school students? And what is it about *Hedwig* that inspires YouTube remixes of image and sound track, Web fan pages, revivals of the original play in such locales as Seoul or Tokyo, and audience performances of the film in the style of *The Rocky Horror Picture Show* (1975)? The short answer is that what matters in the film is *melos,* not telos. By *melos,* I do not necessarily mean the melodic shaping of acoustic material or the properties of musical sequencing as opposed to those of unstructured noise. If the film short-circuits the telos of personhood as a production of fixed, identitarian subjectivity, the subject as fetish or fixation, then it is *melos* that provides a musical path through identity as fetish, though experience as programmed effect, such that personhood as fixation opens onto historical time. The film's *melos,* before giving a path to each scene of musical self-imagining, also provides the vehicle for moving along the narrative path in order that one may pass along toward larger ends less easily discernible (of narrative or of historical determination). In *Hedwig, melos* is something of a ruse, a mode of unfolding temporal affect as historical movement, as the film's narrative rhetorics arise out of and collapse back into its performative aesthetics. *Hedwig*'s ruse of *melos* is twofold: The film takes drag as the face of affective mobility, and it takes pop music as the instance of having been affected: a musical diagram of historical corporeality transforming its historical relation.

Hedwig's drag is not melancholic heterosexual allegory.[2] Rather, drag in *Hedwig* is the intimacy of a self becoming public in differential recapitulation and repetition: the face of nonnormative sexed gender appearing as such, once having been deferred in a reading of Stonewall as "gay liberation" but now working as transdrag in such 1990s festivals as Wigstock or *Wigstock: The Movie* (1995), the film documenting it, as well as screenings and DVD releases revisiting San Francisco's seminal Stonewall-era Cockettes performance group, such as *The Cockettes* (2002). In the mass media of the early 1970s, the exuberant and often informal performances of the Cockettes marked a dissolution of theatrical genre; media format; and gendered, sexed social norms: *Hedwig*'s largely forgotten transmedia "DNA."

In a review, gossip journalist and television personality Rex Reed[3] describes the Cockettes as mostly "hippie drag queens" but also pregnant "women, married couples, and infants" who together had produced a "landmark in the history of the new, liberated theater" with their "nocturnal happening composed of equal parts Mardi Gras on Bourbon Street, Harold Prince's *Follies,* old movie musicals, the United Fruit Company, Kabuki, and the Yale varsity show" (51). Reed cites Truman Capote's excitement over a Cockettes' performance in which Billie Holiday recordings vied with Sun-Ra posters for audience attention amid the musical chaos, partly a result of the audience's own getting in on the act: "This is the only true theater," Capote is reported to have said of a performance where he was cheered by hundreds of cross-dressers from the theater balcony, "where there is total participation from an audience that is part of the show itself" (52). In Reed's review of the Cockettes' chaotic synchronization of musical genre clichés with overturned norms of corporeal performance, the pathos, ecstasy, or hysteria of the performance demonstrates the West Coast antithesis of the "decadent," "meaningless" Warhol scene (55).

In the early 1990s, then, *Hedwig* originates after the *Wigstock* festival had been commercialized and as histories such as that of the Cockettes had begun to be reexamined. In this context, Stonewall is historically reconceived: No longer the breakthrough moment of gay liberation's visibility, it is reclaimed as a tactical street battle fought by drag queens and kings, a motley milieu of gay, lesbian, and (pre-Gender Identity Disorder) transpersons whose political affiliations would shortly coalesce out of homophile movements only to quickly fragment once again. As recent research reminds us, in New York, the Gay Liberation Front formed in 1969, but the single-issue advocacy group Gay Activists Alliance quickly splintered off that same year, followed by Radicalesbians, Gay Youth, and Street Transvestite Action Revolutionaries (S.T.A.R.) in 1970.[4] Contrary to any number of accounts of drag as allegorizing heterosexuality or some minoritizing relation to it, in *Hedwig,* queer drag allegorizes the generative and fractious relations among sexed-gender displacements, distributions, and differences. It enacts and exhibits a range of techniques and technologies for diagramming the politics of voicing a sexed and gendered self-image and so, more generally, of personifying personhood where personhood is not a given.

Rock music in *Hedwig* is also a matter of displacements, distributions, differentiations: It is rock on radio, on record albums, or in cinema or other visual media, and it is similarly reconceived. If rock in film often signals a historical moment of cultural transformation, whether accurately or nostalgically, in *Hedwig,* rock is the public face of an anterior cultural transformation (such as "the 1960s" or "the sexual revolution") whose rhetoric may be radical but that achieves that radical profile only by renegotiating its displaced premises. The story, then, is not quite that of rock recapitulated as sexual liberation but rather of 1970s rock's denial of its glam renovation being sourced from the queer cultures rock would quickly and loudly disavow. In this film, the sexed and gendered image of rock personified is not only that of David Bowie's glamorous corporeal ambivalence but also that of his commodified "bisexuality." Simon Frith[5] points out that by 1970, rock had become a dominant commercial force in a recording industry to which it had been marginal only a few short years prior. The new rock's denial of its complexly queer audiences is neither the moment of cultural transformation rock likes to recount nor the musical speech of the rock star's individual genius but a cultural tendency within rock's industrial integration (witness Elton John's detour from 1970s glam pop into tragic heteronormativity by the mid-1980s, culminating in his tastefully public "gay marriage" in December 2005, or the more complete, if less spectacular, closeting of various other rock personae).[6] Rock's expressive denial is a power not of production but of reception; it is the audience's betrayal of its own prerecorded desires, finally, its differentiation of its own displacement. This same tendentious dynamic provides the narrative thematics of Todd Haynes's *Velvet Goldmine* (1998), which attempts more romantically and less successfully than *Hedwig* to recover 1970s rock's queer ear in the same millennial moment of rock-in-film revisionism.

Thus, drag and rock as accreted historical materials are not, primarily, powers of, sources for, or signs or symptoms of expressive productivity. Synchronized in song, they speak the opposite, like the warped record functioning as a menu on *Hedwig*'s DVD release. The audience becomes its own obstacle, a jamming frequency within reception for expression of and for the audience, a blocking that the audience is neither able to incorporate nor to disavow. In this chapter, "reception" does not refer to undertaking audience-member interviews about what they remember liking or disliking in a film or a musical recording; recovering personal letters as evidence for film or recording cultures; parsing film or music criticism to reconcile critics' tastes with historical developments; or combing the Internet for evidence of conflicted, and so revealing, attachments in fan production or authorial defense. In *Hedwig*, reception is the very thematic of the film, its narrative impulse, and the form of its conclusions. *Hedwig* thus provides a signal opportunity to revise theories of media reception by undertaking more of it—that is, by reflexively exploring the performativities of reception.

As many market researchers will admit, and as *Hedwig* presupposes, reception is simultaneously willed from within and forced from without. Hedwig's relation to her own personification, withheld all the more intensely as she approaches it all the more intimately, is analogous to the audience's present-tense relationship to its own history. In this chapter, then, I read *Hedwig* as a musical diagram of deferred self-reception that displaces a representational mirroring of deluded self-reflection. Because the histories of sexed, gendered personhood continue to mediate the self-representation of sexed, gendered subjects as displaced from history, reading *Hedwig* as narrating a complex process of deferred self-reception also means receiving the film as a precise historical statement on the capacities of media reception to relay personhood as self-displacement.

So, as a child, Hansel (Hedwig's given name) listens, head in the chamber of a gas oven, to rock on the radio in the walled-off concentration camp of 1960s family life in an imaginary East Berlin;[7] eagerly receives (orally/anally) first-love Luther's "candy," which he gags on and spits out; and performs live as Hedwig (John Cameron Mitchell) only to have a bigger star, Tommy Gnosis, break into Hedwig's act by singing the songs he has stolen back to her. Hedwig's willingness to constantly receive and to repeat her own commodified alienation is not (simply) neurotic self-victimization or melancholic repetition of the traumatic. Beyond that, it is also a proprioceptive strategy learned from and reapplied to the task of traumatically navigating a displaced history of self-mediation. Musically receiving her own self-displacement aids Hedwig in ascertaining and mobilizing the next step on a journey where another stop, another obstacle, always waits on the self's reception and exhibition of personhood: "another opening, another show."

During her third-to-last stop ("Exquisite Corpse") on this trip, the musical personhood she had structured as "collage," a "montage," is entirely exhausted. She shames herself before her public, giving it not the show of her breakdown but its effects, as she berates her own worn musical self-image. Strained to breaking point, the seams of her life show up in a kaleidoscopic frame barely holding the contrary aspects of her life together. Then her self-reception and self-exhibition breaks down entirely, replaying her past traumas and abuses in flashbacks ordered entirely out of sequence. At this point, Tommy Gnosis breaks into her fragmenting personhood while singing his alternate version of "Wicked Little Town" from an entirely different venue. Hedwig's musical personhood is now more a scrambled radio broadcast than a coherently channelized film genre or rock show. Hedwig then steps into Tommy's distant arena to hear her own song sung back to her, but this time directed at her. Tommy "rebrands" Hedwig with the gnostic cross she once gave him as his trademark symbol. The final musical number, "Midnight Radio," ensues on a calmed, white stage decorated with large-scale photographic stills of a boat caught rising on a stormy sea.

Here Mitchell no longer sings as Hedwig but as himself, and, as Yitzak (Miriam Shor) is transformed into a female drag queen, he calls out the names of iconic soul, pop, and rock singers—"Tina," "Aretha," "Nona," or "Nico"—and emphasizes that the meanings of these names have as much to do with the iconic women as with the rock-and-roll "misfits and losers" who have internalized their voices as a strategy for everyday listening and everyday life. The film closes as Mitchell, out of drag, leaves the stillness of the now-transformed club and walks away into the night, accompanied by a reprise of "Origins of Love." The camera slowly cranes up as Mitchell's nude body disappears, emphasizing the synoptic importance of this particular composition by Stephen Trask for the film as a whole, along with the open-ended resistance to closure that its accompaniment of Mitchell's departure implies. This three-song sequence connotes reception forced: the culture industries' dialectic of enlightenment. But it connotes force only insofar as reception is first willed altogether differently from the way it is forced: reception as the antinomian praxis of listening as deferred, yet again immanent, speech. Reception, then, for my purposes, is the corporeal reception of biopolitics and archiving and actualization of the immanent speech therein prepared.

Neither of these dual faces of reception can be directly accessible to contemporary techniques of reception studies. As I show below, *Hedwig* offers a metacriticism of the dynamics that compel those techniques. Receptions of will and of force are the dynamics of ascesis in mass mediation.[8] These dual aspects of reception entail a problematic of narrative rhetorics coupled with performative aesthetics, animating the corporeal on both sides of a mediatic screen: specifically, queer praxes of audiovisual musicality presenting as listening and as vocalization. Modeling immanent speech in terms of reception, *Hedwig* suggests reception as an annunciatory dynamic.[9] Within commodity culture, musical reception as modulation or resonance, in coming up against the reaction formation its own expression invites, is put on ice, so to speak. At the same time, against its own partitioned history and its own false mediation, musical reception can profile a praxis of expression amid and against cultural reaction: The commodity's own frozenness points to a hardening reaction in culture and to meaning's hibernation below the popular horizon as it helps prepare the coming thaw, the future. Taking this dynamic of mediatic contemporaneity as a problem of "closet epistemologies" tends to produce hermeneutic inadequacy, suggesting the absurd need to find a "gay Socrates," as Eve Kosofsky Sedgwick[10] memorably points out. More broadly, closet epistemologies ultimately fail, because they direct a critical desire to discover the equivalent of slave narratives or female voicing but instead find historical expressions of sexed corporeality becoming emergent in divergent series and events. With the leading edge of sexed gendered personhood being the screaming baby tossed out with the bathwater of the hyperproduction of the musical self as megastar (Elton on your Walkman, Madonna on your MP3 player), culture's hardening reaction formation stands alongside refigured marginalization but is also turned aside by historical being undergoing continued transformation.

Hedwig draws on reception grounded not so much in memory or culture but rather as resounding affect of sexed expressivity placed between a cultural rock and mediatic ice. Presenting as rock revival and as drag transfigured, the film stands and gives a contradictory face to Adorno's musical "we," a "me" delivered from the morass between political marginalization newly reconfigured (after gay and lesbian identity was largely depathologized in 1974, "Gender Identity Disorder" was termed by the American Psychiatric Association in 1980, with additional revisions in 1987 and 1994) and mediatic misrepresentations freshly charged after HIV/AIDS.[11] Stemming from the moment of punk's expanded production as grunge in the early 1990s, styling genre and gender as drag rock makes so much sense. Drag and rock are not "new" idioms, and they are arresting not because of their ability to marshal productivist political or musical expression but because they work through a contrary "paragrammatics" within received systems of sexed gender and musical genre.[12] The work of affective transitioning is contrary, but sensible. Working gender expression against narrative genre gives the fabrication of selfhood as a singing dancing distortion: the autobiographical prosopopoeia Paul de Man[13] describes as "defacement," transposed by way of the "walking alienation effect" Martin Rubin[14] ascribes to Carmen Miranda. Sensible: impossible to fix in or as representation, but so long overdue.

FIGURE 6.1 *Hedwig and the Angry Inch* (2001): Audience sing-along (frame capture). (*Hedwig and the Angry Inch*, dir. John Cameron Mitchell [Killer Films, 2001].)

Surprised by the familiar sense of a scene that the audience nonetheless has not seen before, of course it *will want to* sing along (and some members do) when, during a key musical flashback, song lyrics appear on screen, timing indicated by a bouncing wig (Figure 6.1). That number is "Wig in a Box," during which Hedwig remembers, before ever singing in public, being joined in her lonely trailer-park home (in a "surprise" appearance) by the future members of her band, whom she has not yet met. The band, the Angry Inch, forms out of a nonsensical narrative event in which Hedwig's vision of their future collaboration (otherwise without exposition in the narrative) and memory of his own abandonment commingle. Drag and rock are paragrammatically woven together in a scene that can happen only somewhere between melodrama and rock opera, but not within either. As the wig "comes down from the shelf," Hedwig puts on her makeup and immerses herself in the music of the 8-track player or, later, a funky phonograph, while in come the band members, handing her the musical implements of self-poiesis. They, too, come complete with their own toy instruments, as if out of a box. Within the short space of the song, Hedwig moves from singing about the power of listening to recoup the self's nonperforming investments in the workaday world (her life as supermarket cashier) to the lyric "I ain't never goin' back," whereupon the band blows down the side wall of the trailer-home "box," forming a rock stage complete with footlights to be stomped out, Johnny Cash–style. Hedwig morphs numerous times, in sync with the lyrics, presenting as Miss Beehive 1963, where her two-foot-tall wig suggests the phallic cosmetology of the singing lipstick from 20th-Century Fox's *The Dolly*

Sisters (1945) or, alternatively, the double-flip folds of Farrah Fawcett's signature 1970s hairdo.

By the end of the number, Hedwig, backed by the band, appears as an all-white Tina Turner and, shaking in controlled musical *extasis*, triumphs on the rock stage of her imagination. "Wig in a Box" is also transfigured by this point: The first tentative piano chords suggest the intro to Carole King's "(You Make Me Feel Like) A Natural Woman," but the rousing conclusion suggests Turner's rendition of "Proud Mary," performed with all the retro-rock brio of the finale of Bowie's "Suffragette City," though with the menacing descending minor chords of that tune replaced with the jubilation typical of a T. Rex stomper or *Rocky Horror*'s "The Time Warp." The wig here, as Michel Foucault observes of sodomy, is a "confused category."[15] As a contemporary making up of the self, it is strongly feminizing; further, signaling self-presentation as artifice and as ascesis, it is phallicizing and invaginating, depending on lyrical orientation. Hedwig's hairpiece is antidote to and capstone of her body as wall and bridge, her neither/nor, both/and corporeality a transposition of sexed desire and gendered expression. Feminization itself is a transposition, keying gay-male receptivity into post-op transgender contradiction.

Always, the careening narrative speaks as a monologue of Hedwig's voice, which—totalized in her transforming aspect, searching out, occupying, and destroying melancholic, neurotic, or otherwise unsustainable subjectivities as occasions for staging impossible movements between generic and gendered identifications—returns mediated sociality as song. The set piece and performance for "Wig in a Box" fold into the time-warped narrative line to motivate Hedwig's own relentless move forward against the melancholy continually pulling her backward and to let the audience in on the joke: warped narrative sung as speech reversed. So it motivates the audience to sing along with the warping of mediatic expression, the deformed or scratched record of historical inscription, and gives occasion to actively redress its own cinematic silence (and, perhaps, its own reception of the programmed melancholia D. A. Miller[16] insists is a queer deferral written into the heteronormative Broadway musical script). This musical negotiation, capable of deflecting subjective stasis and historical incapacitation, is not dissimilar, although it is very far advanced, from Caryl Flinn's account of the utopian potentiality of nostalgic listening for Julie, the heroine struggling with contradictions of maternal affect in the classical Hollywood melodrama *Penny Serenade* (1941).[17]

Flinn describes the musical negotiation of gender constraints as melancholic immersion enduring for the length of the classical narrative. *Penny Serenade* is a long series of episodic flashbacks narrated to outdated pop; only at the film's conclusion does musical nostalgia produce agency—a change, of course, for Julie. In *Hedwig*, as with "Wig in a Box," a single musical episode collapses and explodes the impossible movement from inside (abandonment, melancholia, nostalgia) to outside (publicity, vocality, ambition), typifying the kaleidoscopic temporalities of the filmic road trip. The "making of the band" that occurs as Hedwig sings "Wig in a Box" not only recognizes its own form as cognate with contemporary media fabrication of musical commodities but also reveals its own artifice—it lays bare its plan for an exit from the dialectics of media production superpositioned over and against audience reception as it prompts its audience to affirm its capacity to sing in recognition of our deferred historical presence.[18]

So Hedwig's affectations, whether melancholic recluse or scandalous public figure, are only larger or smaller degrees of staging the twofold ruse that allows her to keep on talking. The horrors of losing the microphone, of losing her musical support, of having Yitzak sing, of letting Phyllis decide the agenda, or of allowing Tommy to ventriloquize her music—these constitute the obstacles that the trajectory of the film must surmount. What, though, does the film's musicality affect? What does it feel? Neither the violations of history experienced as melancholy nor a determined future projected as liberation on the identitarian models of the right's discourses of our historical past frame *Hedwig*'s back-assed forward movement toward indetermination. Nor are the biblical or classical references gratuitous. Rather, Hedwig explains her narrative aim early on by singing a properly etymological, anthropological, and metaphysical praxis of affective interrogation: "I want to know / the origin of love." Later comes the antiphonic refrain. Over the end credits, after the rock-operatic catharsis that reprises Zeus's lightning bolt banishes Gnosis from Hedwig's head, restores the gnostic cross to Hansel's forehead, and transforms that cross into a tattoo of a Janus-like diagram of one self receiving its other only to be again transformed, Mitchell's voice is heard: "I am / the origin of love." With the story told and Hedwig out of the picture, the audience reads the long list of contributors to the film, the transposition from vertiginous desire to affective mobility complete.

Rick Altman describes the transition between the film musical's image-centric diegetic reality, where oppositions are established in the narrative, and its music-centric fantasy episodes, where cause-and-effect relation comes undone, as an "audio dissolve."[19] It is on the basis of the transformation of reality into fantasy via the audio dissolve that the musical obtains its ability to reconcile ideological conflicts, and so, structurally, a critical hermeneutics of the audio dissolve leads to viewers' (the critics') ability to grasp the syntactic and semantic categories whose contents supply the conventions of the genre and whose transformations indicate the rise and the fall of the genre over historical time. Semantic contents become syntactic categories by virtue of becoming familiar; when the development of semantics into syntax is finally flattened, it indicates that the historical relevance of the genre has played out and that the generic conventions have finally consumed their own narrative productivity. The musical's mythological capacity to express "marriage" (of the male and female leads, of the audience and the form) is depleted. The "interpretive community" of the genre has moved on.

In *Hedwig,* though, the transition, which has to become "auditory" for Altman to clearly "see" the musical's syntactic and semantic categories and transformations, becomes distended, repeats, and carries what will turn out to be false nostalgia spectacularly entwined with futural movement. The film as a whole obtains (as a macroform) an aesthetics of sensible (if not realistic) transition. And every single transition in the film—whether moving back to East Berlin to introduce "The Origin of Love" or Junction City, Kansas, to find the "Wig in a Box," or moving forward to provide the "time is passing" modality of Hedwig and Tommy's burgeoning success as a duo—is musically motivated by chordal strains and harmonic modulations borrowed from the musical material of "The Origin of Love." The transition, here, is not a category of meaning that is collapsed as an auditory opportunity for interior character exposition or ideological reconciliation but rather is expanded to the task of complicating the systematics (in Roland Barthes's sense) of genre formation with those of gendered audience formation.

So *Hedwig*'s microform (repeating kernels of nostalgic immersion and futural movement) and its macroform (the trip from desire to affective knowledge) do not mutually resolve the syntaxes of genre or identifications of gender in a happy ending but transpose love from being a function of desire to being affective expression. The musical "me" moves from wanting to know "the origin of love" to becoming it. More, the film's metacriticism of transitioning renders the blocking-and-bridging mobility also instanced in Hedwig's filmic body. Since the film reflects that mobility within its narrative center, Hedwig's body, and its narrative course writ large, it presents a homoeroticism of the transposition: a queer reception of transgender expression. And if all these spiraling transpositions make us dizzy, well, they should: These are nothing but the sex-gendered dynamics programmed into Alfred Hitchcock's *Vertigo* (1958), applied to a reverse formatting of audience participation as a reception of mediatic historicity and visualized as rock music. *Hedwig* is neither a classical musical tripping toward Broadway triumph nor a cynical musical journey to America's overmediated heartland (as in Robert Altman's *Nashville* [1975]). It is an angry, loving bridge out of sexed and gendered Hell, and its convoluted course follows because, in crossing that bridge, one is never afforded the immediate ability to look back. As Hedwig sings, inviting Tommy and the audience to follow her voice, "Remember Mrs. Lot, when she turned around."

Finally, as Phyllis says (but not as she means), it *is* all about New York City, the Oz where the original *Hedwig* stage show moved from off-Broadway to the cinema screen. This denouement, recapitulated in the film's conclusion to be as surprising and as predictable as a reconciliation of the studied rock distortion of *Tommy* (1975) with ABBA's overproduced distraction, releases all in thrall to

FIGURE 6.2 *Hedwig and the Angry Inch* (2001): The montage-collage of the self breaks apart (frame capture). (*Hedwig and the Angry Inch*, dir. John Cameron Mitchell [Killer Films, 2001].)

move on—including Hedwig; her childish alter-ego, Hansel; her nemesis, Tommy Gnosis; director/star Mitchell; and the audience. "Gnosis" as musical affect is the expressive capacity to create and to disappear, to account for an impassible history, and to gift an indeterminate future. Reception's gift is love granted as deferred knowledge of personhood; the work of affect, a poiesis practiced as musical imagining that wrests vocality back from listening's distant, mediatic origins. Hedwig's gift of gnosis is the intimate knowledge of a public self: queer glam personhood, screened in public, at last.

But this matters only because violences of mediation underwrite the musical film and the gendered personhood sacrificed to love within its story. Hansel's failed sex-change surgery develops from a plan to alter his identity with a "simple cut-and-paste" job on his mother's passport; the lyrics and style of the shattering penultimate song emphasize identity mediated in cinema *and* the body as "collage, a montage" (Figure 6.2). Formally, techniques of collage and montage have, time and again, been subject to deadening appropriation, as David James notes. Speaking of rock theatrics in the music video promotional clip, James suggests that the music video appropriates avant-garde film and video strategies, but by way of producing a denial of the political project with which such avant-gardes have been aligned: socialist revolution. MTV clips borrow from historical avant-gardes their nonstandard angles, palettes, and textures; their representations of supposedly deviant youth subcultures and minority groups; and their strategies of parodying commercial film and television narratives. James observes that these stylistics, so claimed, tend strongly toward a sense of closure against the open-ended techniques and parodic elements they have appropriated and so deploy a lip-sync, for example, that helps assert the presence of the performers' voices: "the quasi-sexual center of pop's power." On one hand, the multiplicity of musical strategies and the heterogeneous visual accoutrements of rock culture make up one half of rock's identity, James argues; the other half is "its similarly diverse and similarly totalized functions within the economic and ideological systems of capital."[20]

Clarifying what is at stake for studies of commodity filmmaking and projects of popular music more political in their origins and intents, James suggests that tracking sound-image relations during various periods (might) generate the framework for a history of the rock-and-roll musical. Such a history would consider various subcultures' own attempts to produce themselves cinematically in the context of the assimilation of rock music, stars, and so on into the industrial cinema. The point is not to think of music film or music video merely as the illustration of the music—which is inevitably routed via the recording and so via the corporate form—but to investigate the degree to which the principles that produced the series of social and aesthetic projects mobilized as popular music were also manifested in film and in the practice of filmmaking.[21]

Hedwig's transpositionality, especially in terms of its transformation from a highly elaborated drag musical for the small stage of queer off-Broadway theater to filmic rock musical, does exactly the kind of work that James describes, but with a twist and an added difference: *Hedwig* clarifies contemporary possibilities for queer speech even as it presents a heretofore subvocalized queer history of rock, in a gesture of powerful distortion, as a music of spectacular visibility. Eisenstein's montage of pathos; Fischinger's visual-music animation of ecstasy; Eisler's administrative dialectical stream of hysteria: Just as Clark's *Passing Through* develops the instrumentalities of jazz as revolutionary transmedium by redeploying the classical stylistics of music-image relations, so does *Hedwig* redeploy montage, visual-music animation, and dialectical stream toward an origin story that culminates in a breakage and a departure. *Hedwig*'s origin of love narrates individuation and personhood according to a queer ethics of reception, where the audience's psychic investment in spectacular subjectivity is replaced with a musically mediated creative destruction.

Charting, then, along with its erotics, an ethics of reception, *Hedwig* suggests a significant difference attributable to queer aesthetic praxes, which in this view surmount the distribution of commoditized affectivity and commoditized identity. *Hedwig* shifts the conceptual orientation of lip sync as denial of audience to an affirmative accounting of the affective antagonisms of queer listening for identity in popular music. In doing so according to an ethos of reception as opposed to one of production, though, it gives a non- or antirepresentational figuration of a social, aesthetic, and corporeal project that has tended to surface as contingent, arbitrary, sporadic, or fragmented. *Hedwig* the film mediates its own theatrical rock performance as doubled potentiality to include, within the trajectory of the rock musical that never was, the practice of lip sync and playback as a primary point of access for queer transpositions of the musical image. The film plays with synchronization of image and voice across multiple forms and processes of rock mediation, since part of what rock has mediated is gender expression itself. And, finally, *Hedwig* uses rock as an audiovisual commodity form to speak a musical cinema, tracing transpositions in gender that succeed only in conflicted versions of individual history inasmuch as the corporeal mediation of gender expression produces individuals apart from their own totalized, commodified, and insufferable past identities. The film conclusively marks the ways that sexed gendered personhood, through sociopolitical shifts in gender expression and norm, is no longer necessarily defined against heteronormative sexuality. Deviance from heteronormativity opens onto transpositions between gay or lesbian politics and transgender politics.

Throughout its compulsive recycling of the mediatic bargain bin of throwaway audiovisuality, *Hedwig*'s "me" sings the audience's deferred presentation of its own history of reception. This matter of reception certainly does not surface as art film or as avant-garde or aesthetic experimentation (the "modern"), nor does it offer itself as a hypertextual resource immediately accessible for further elaboration or dissemination in commodity production (the "postmodern"). Any queer reception is powerful only to the extent that its complex sexing of identity has been historically undervalued, erased, forgotten, misdirected, or misappropriated in reception and yet continues to inform and to transform in arenas of reception that go relatively uncharted. Cultural and subcultural production relate to each other in a certain ratio of reception that divides the product of identitarian fixity and continued marginalization with an ongoing series of charmed transformations in the denominator: as if by a subject trapped behind a mediatic version of Berlin's lost wall, as if the armed forces radio service had, once upon a time, broadcast the message of rock as a call to transgender liberation.

Hedwig's origin of love, then, is not in a Deleuzian refrain deterritorializing telos in *melos* but in a receiving more nomadic and more grounded: *Hedwig* is the refrain of barred personhood transposed into spectacular corporeality by being vocalized as a demythification of sex-gender difference. Music's deferred "we" becomes the impossible, but no longer deniable, articulation of "me." *Hedwig* fabricates the origins of love and forwards the dissemination of gnosis as deferred historical knowledge (as, I explain below, rock musicals must); and yet at the same time *Hedwig* actively indetermines love as futurity. The film individuates massified song all over again; following the bouncing wig indicating the appropriate lyric to sing, audience members discover the images of their voices (even if they do not actually vocalize sound) before the screen, as if recovering from amnesia. From "we," in spite of the narrative cinema, to "me," wrought in narrative design potentially as participatory as it is spectacular, as capable of immersing its audience in the mass mediatics of the spectacular as it is of recognizing the audience and its history, *Hedwig*'s narrative entertains a transpositionality: transformations in sexed knowledges popular but inaccessible, being, as they have been, frozen out.

Transpositions: Ethics and Erotics

If *Hedwig*'s musical transposition of the corporeal and the mediatic does supply a metacriticism of reception, what would the implications of this be if, as I argue, the film is resolutely ungraspable within media studies' various productivist frameworks, whether materialist, psychoanalytic, formal, or cultural? Annette Kuhn's reception study of British cinemagoers of the 1930s and 1940s is illuminating.[22] With regard to methodology and content, Kuhn's study is synthetic—materialist, feminist, and often confirming psychoanalytic concerns; but when it is not, it draws productively on cultural studies accounts of audience or fan reception. Filmgoers are identified as heterosexual and as either male or female. Gendered sex means heterosexual identifications and courtship rituals; genres are remarkably differentiable ("horror" opposed to "musical"), even when subjects habitually attended and understood films belonging to different generic types (film genre is an industrial and demographic designation, not a hermeneutics of reception). Contradictions appear as heterosexual, national, and class differences (although a small number of Jewish filmgoers are mentioned as subjects as well—the study attends to "ethnicity").

Viewer accounts of mediatic memory are vocalized, according to Kuhn, in four enunciative modes: impersonal; past/present; repetitive; and anecdotal. Impersonal accounts stress Fred Astaire's dancing as professional, for example. This mode allows viewer knowledge a "sociological" status: The Astaire musical is an "impressive," "beautifully executed," exemplar of an American film industry "thumping out these wonderful, spectacular films that they did do, that, em, the people were living at the same time under the shadow of the cloud of war."[23] Was military activity shadow and cloud? Or is there more going on than Kuhn can draw from the subjects whom she has chosen and the methodology channelizing their speech?

Next, past/present comparisons indicate the importance of cinema memory as cultural memory; viewers remember musical films as being so much more spectacular but see that contemporary musicals no longer "put the money on the screen." Third, repetitive enunciation indicates collective as well as habitual audience response: "We all used to sit there and sigh"; or, men would watch couples make out from the "back row" of the cinema—men gathered in the back row to look at the screen and at heterosexual couples. This talk refers to narrative/spectatorial effects, cinema as cultural memory, and film spaces. Kuhn suggests that psychoanalytic readings in a limited way confirm the pleasure of spectatorial effects, such as scopophilia. The "psychical configuration of fetishism, which includes disavowal (simultaneous hanging onto and renouncing the belief that the woman has a penis) is what fuels the fetishist's perpetual fascination with what lies under the woman's skirt."[24] Scopophilia applies to "crotch shots" of Marlene Dietrich in *Der blaue Engel* (*The Blue Angel*; 1930) and to the tunnel of dancers' legs through which Busby Berkeley's musical camera enjoyed traveling, the "semantic unit par excellence" of the American film musical.[25] Finally, anecdotal accounts narrate particular events: "On a particular moviegoing occasion, this event happened." Here, the holder of the narrative places himself as a protagonist of a particular memory of going to the cinema—for example, being thrilled to have been with a particular (heterosexual) date.

Memories of the Fred Astaire/Ginger Rogers musicals emphasize the third mode of memory discourse, in which "repetitive-effects" types of stories are recalled, Kuhn notes. Kuhn suggests that the Astaire/Rogers films are remembered not simply as films but in relation to her respondents' remembered experiences of the dance hall as well. The musical cinema suggests an idealized version of the kinds of movements one might have wished to make in the dance hall; in this way, the cinema provides the "heterotopia" of which Foucault is supposed to have written:

> In [the Astaire/Rogers films'] elegant and apparently seamless combination of kinesis and heterotopia lies the ultimate dance fantasy: the everyday, the local, the rooted, and the communal—for the adolescent of the 1930s, the crowds in the dance hall—all fade from consciousness as, along with the dancers on the screen, you are carried into the space of imagination where you are utterly graceful and where the dance of courtship proceeds, with never a false step, towards its climax. The sensation imbues your body, and carries you out of your local picture house onto the familiar streets of your neighborhood, and you are moved to dance along the pavement all the way home.[26]

Cinema's heterotopic site of reception means, for Kuhn, that cinema memory mediates cultural memory such that the past is "remembered as a landscape across which cinemas are dotted like beacons in the night, and where all journeys begin and end at home."[27]

How does *Hedwig* map heterotopia (thinking that Foucault seems to have had the bathhouse in mind when he coined the term, as David Halperin suggests)?[28] *Hedwig* "remembers" temporal improbability, not a supercoherent spatial fantasy, as kinesthesia. In regards to the sociological register of memory, where viewers remember the "professionalism" of American cinema, *Hedwig* offers another point of view of the American media: At the cafeteria/rock club, as the band members hungrily help themselves to all the trimmings, Hedwig flashes a slide of a tabloid headline wherein she accuses Tommy of stealing her songs and explains that it took this "hit piece" to make audiences take notice of her authorship. "But," as she snarls at two apparently closeted gay male diners who defensively huddle into their plates, "now you're interested, ha?" Hedwig goes on, preparing a transition to the imaginary East Berlin that presents her own "past/present" discourse as "The Origin of Love"—she remembers her abusive heterochildhood as an excremental diary scrawled on toilet paper, animated in the film as visual music.

In a subsequent cafeteria appearance in Miami Beach, after a sudden jump forward from East Berlin, Hedwig stages her answer to the "repetition effect" of scopophilia. She has just recounted how, as Hansel, she fell for American soldier Luther and his gummy bears, the candy a "rainbow-colored carnage" that she gagged on and spit out. Now, in this number, "Sugar Daddy," Hedwig takes on the uniform from waist up, presenting in a shimmery gray "military" blouse and necktie, hair tightly coiffed: a wacked WAC. Earlier in the film, the "uniform" appeal of American masculinity is suggested in Luther's seductive black vocality, rhetorics of fairness and equality transposed as interracial man-boy love. Now, Hedwig's costume expresses instead the rupturing conditionality that the desiring dream of sexual equality imagined as "uniformity" covers over. Singing in up-tempo country mode and high stepping, in sneakers, from one table of (Jewish?) retirees to the next, she swings her cowgirl skirt over one elderly man's head and, rhythmically swishing its fringe, announces triumphantly as she obscures the bespectacled customer in a scopophilic excess that is obscured to us: "It's a car wash, ladies and gentleman!"

If Berkeley's crotch shot is the semantic unit par excellence of the show musical, Hedwig's body replaces that syntax with her own rhythmic mood swinging: Her tour of cafeterias is a musical series of present, transitional moments, each only a momentary cathexis of impossible past and indeterminable future. Later, after Hedwig's music teaches Tommy love as musical poiesis, she demands that he fulfill his part of the bargain and that he partake of the scopophilic pleasure that would recognize her as love's transformative potentiator, not as desire's operational object: "Love the front of me!" Telling the memory of her demand might count as an "anecdotal" instance (in Kuhn's terminology), something that happened one day while listening to a neighbor sing out of a nearby trailer window (Dolly Parton's "I Will Always Love You," loudly, for three days, "on a loop"). This anecdote about love only partially achieved and shortly denied turns out to have supreme importance: It sends Hedwig on her "American tour." Tommy flees, having felt in his hand but never faced with his eyes the surgical remainder that is less than a penis but more than a clitoris.

In Kuhn's view, scopophilia in cinema is recalled according to a de Certeauvian rationale: It marks the ways that people "make do" and so "get by" on the way to inscribing cinema memory as cultural memory. But while Hedwig's musical "angry inch," like the cinema for Kuhn's subjects, is all she has "to work with," it cannot be framed for recognition, authorship of self, or love, to say nothing of untroubled recollection accessible to cultural memory. The problematics of her angry inching toward New York, though, replacing the semantics of the musical with a transposition of genre against gender as she goes, *is* spectacular. In these moments of nonpassablity becoming impossibly bridged, *Hedwig* puts its own "money on the screen." Heterotopic kinesthesia here is neither remembered nor acted out on the walk home. Hedwig's heterotopia is that of the rock listener seeing musical cinema in disjunctive transposition and of seeing oneself sing along. Her mediatic kinesthesia is a gesture leading not homeward but from a back alley, back to the street.

Hedwig's disappearance from the musical stage at the film's close indicates that her impossible negotiation of "star status" as a thrice-complicated conflict of author status, sex-gender expression, and historical becoming remain unfixed: antitelic. The pleasures of song, of distortion, and of musical visuality suggest not so much melodramatic nostalgia investing a search for personal origins only finally to be denied but rather, as the film narrates the displacement of one frustration by another, that the pleasure of vocalizing a trajectory through these frustrations matters more than the narrative projection of melodramatic situation as fantasy. *Hedwig* replaces universalist critique with transpositional mobility, placing, as musical narrative, the melodrama of origins in relation to an appropriation of originality and playing this relation against the ultimate telos of identity fixed in cinema memory, or media memory more generally: audience reception of generic expectations.

In the film melodrama, one is not supposed to know what one knows; the viewer is the subject who is supposed to know ignorance. One cannot know that which is nonetheless suspected and so hoped against: the end of the crisis of origins. In the film musical, song and dance narrate continuity as surprise, the suspension of cause and effect; one is supposed to hear as if one has never heard before, to see as if one is doing nothing when hearing in this way. In the rock show, the viewer may sing along, but "like you have never sung before," because while the beat will undoubtedly go on (on the CD, at the next concert in the next city or town), the viewer will never be "here," at this event, again. With music television generally and the music video specifically, one may weigh in with an interpretive or gestural literacy of the music involved, but only by way of rendering musical response as lifestyle, youth cultural, or subcultural identification before, during, or after playback. So the gesture is deferred in favor of the artist's originality, as undeniable as it is commodified—until a certain obviousness of repetition in production ("lack" of a presumptive cultural relevance; warmed-over aesthetic craft; accidental exposure of lip sync, playback, or music generation technologies, on the one hand, or their overuse, on the other) works against affective engagement by destroying the illusion that the music, its history, and its performance somehow precede the momentary engagement.

In *Hedwig,* by contrast, and by virtue of its imaginative investments in presentational artificiality, failed conventionality, and pseudofolk historicization, one is *supposed* to know that the loss of historical presence is insufferable and superable. By virtue of one's presence as audience to Hedwig's wiggy impersonation of queer history as a process of mediatic reception, one is expected to sing along; again at one point, the viewer is given the words to the song, as if one needed only to be reminded of them. With the lyrics on screen, one can be surprised by one's own, possibly collective, voice. What is designed to surprise here surpasses gender conventionality, the various generic syntaxes and semantics of music in film, *and* the gestural conventions of rock's audience response, however and wherever it is mediated (in concert or as recording). *Hedwig*'s surprise is history's mediation of sexed gendered reception as musical stylization that elicits interarticulated popular knowledges within and in excess of capital's variegated production of "structures of feeling."[29]

What surprises, though, is the historicity of and for affective expression as such in the face of a commodified and propertized self: sex-gender, rock, cinema, song. This surprise is, finally, the historicity of the audience's surpassing its own unremembered song and yet having access to that song's technique. This musical stylization of history's mediation as audience knowledge is what engages, what surprises, what opens up—like an unexpected, forgotten, or unwanted gift: a "wig in a box," as it were. Singing the song, it is as though, all along, one has had access to the very histories of mediatic recognition that Miller traces as suspended expectation.

Hedwig's formal presentation in terms of the affective capacities that audience reception possesses for troubling sex-gender expectations indicates a queer aesthetics, queer style. In traversing each situation, depicted as transition from feminized gay youth to irreducible corporeal excess more than as male-to-female transgender, receptive masculinity courts and counters an aggressively improbable phallic femininity to constitute musical allure, an openly brazen invitation.[30] Mitchell-as-Hedwig's aggressively voiced masculine femininity speaks to, and of, receptive masculinity, while harmonizing with Shor's masculine backing vocals keyed to a higher, "feminine" vocal register. Throughout the narrative, forward motion comes as this antiphony dissolves the phobic trauma of reception for a gay male body. Hedwig's songs project a fictive past for a contingent present, leading to sudden unexpected futures that may recapitulate stasis or, and often at the same time, indicate the unexpected spin of the future having transformed the ground on which she stands. If queer subjectivity and queer corporeality are radically contingent, this contingency comes via variegated historical identifications in which any present movement takes shape in simultaneously retroactive (historicizing) and potential (futural) modalities.

A curious historical spiral blooms here. Generally, from the perspective of disciplining heteronormative sex and gender within an economy of the "secret," the transsexual can appear to be the new homosexual. A number of sources suggest that male femininities, evidenced in cross-dressing, the sexual behavior of the "fairy," or male homosexual subjects testifying to the desire for female body, can be located in relation to the "instincts" of sexual subjects identified, after the mid-nineteenth century, as "homosexual."[31] Cross-gender desire for either sexual or gender expression (the receptive male) once was parsed as symptom of homosexuality; analytics of "inversion" collapsed, by virtue of a double negativity embedded in that term, "inverted" sexual orientation and gender expression: "homosexual" and "transsexual." Recently, however, discursive revisions of same-sex activities have meant desires once identified as pathologically homosexual are no longer necessarily considered as such. Now, rather than the transvestite being identified under the rubric of (homosexual) inversion, the ground of feminist, gay and lesbian, and ethnic and racial interventions in the medical, legal, and religious spheres means that the transsexual or transgender individual passes out of the realm of "inverted" sexual expression to occupy the more recently clarified ground of the transperson. The transsexual now "comes out" as transgender.[32] More recently, this reconfigured dynamic figures clearly in such works as the Sundance Channel's documentary series *TransGeneration* (2005).[33]

Yet *Hedwig* suggests—against the disciplining of sex-gender expressivity as cumulative deviancy in relation to class, race and ethnicity, and biological gender—that dominant constructions of sex-gender deviance give way to negotiations between plural sex-gender identifications in terms of one another and are no longer relegated to an overdetermined negativity that would become oppositional as generic deviance. That is, the new counterarticulation of sex and gender as open resistance to the determination of sex-gender "secrecy" (constraints that the home, school, workplace, military, and media-saturated public stage of celebrity, to mention those most relevant here, have historically hosted) indicates that the discursive resources of coming out are now available to, say, persons choosing gender reassignment surgery. The out gay or lesbian, within the dynamic of dysfunctional logics of sexed and gendered closeting, is the old transgender.[34] In other words, in our histories of sexuality, the future of sex has happened again, but historically this future is the elaboration of gender identities emerging against the backdrop of gay and lesbian sexualities determined in relation to personhood and emergence, not to closeting, deviation, or transgression. Rather, these elaborations receive logics of audition and of visibility still in contest but nonetheless transposable: coming, becoming, or being out, with "outness" attaining the status of a powerful cipher demanding reading, as opposed to "closetedness" being a powerful secret deferring it.[35]

Specifically in these ways, what *Hedwig* does with the "new" film musical is radically different from various other exemplars collectively exhibiting much interest in the powers of musical reception. Lars von Trier's *Dancer in the Dark*

(2000) deconstructs the audience reception of the Hollywood "show musical" by transposing it against a dystopian version of the "fairy-tale musical." Selma Jezkova, entranced with the ideal America exhibited in the movie musical, dies because she will not obey the logics of justice lived in the realist United States that denies the value of her work and refuses to extend care in the event of her son's suffering. *Dancer* demands reception of an altogether different film from the one it seems to present, one whose resolution would have a musical finale that, as its final provocation to its audience makes clear, we cannot yet actually hear: the sound of a U.S. anti–death penalty show musical that is historically accurate. Danish director von Trier's point is clear: For Americans, his deconstruction of the show musical is to be received as the antithesis of an escapist "folk musical." Baz Luhrmann's *Moulin Rouge!* (2001) challenges its audience to recognize the songs it receives from pop-music history—though one can sing along only if one recognizes the remix and happens to know the words. Rob Marshall's *Chicago* (2002) puts the reception of the film musical through a post-feminist lens, appealing von Trier's judgment of U.S. musical-cinema ideology ("guilty!") by having singing, dancing murderesses escape the risk of state-sanctioned death to join forces on an all-female, happily scopophilic stage ("not guilty!").

Hedwig's troubling of sex and gender logics turns any genre revisionism, or any epistemology of the closet, inside out—much as male-to-female gender reassignment surgery turns the penis outside in—by articulating the unfinishedness of transgender identity as a new route "to the street" for gay-male expressivity. In *Hedwig*, interiority is less at stake than is the synthesis of personhood from processes of media reception. In the drag styles of the contingent stages improvised in queer watering holes and nightclubs like those that inspired *Hedwig*, the film mediates experience, from (fictive) intimate memories to (fictive) public appearance, as a historical problematic of sex localized in the individual body and gender located in public. Thus, the film frames the queer aesthetics of personhood as a renewed mediation of corporeal geopolitics, somewhere between diaspora and cosmopolitanism.[36] What is crucial is that Hedwig's damning of denial (in rock, in film, and in film genre and reception studies) merges high camp and low rock to claim a decidedly middlebrow acceptance of sex-gender transpositions.

More than simply a revision of the Hollywood musical or biopic, then, *Hedwig*'s elaboration of transgender-themed performance play as a new route to the queer street makes great hay of the obvious debt it happily owes to *Rocky Horror* (whose long post-release afterlife as late-night audience participation cinema might have provided the paradigmatic example of interaction between audiences as interpretive community and industrial exhibition of musical-genre cinema for Altman's study of the Hollywood musical but goes unmentioned even in his exhaustive index of works).

Hedwig, whether in the stripped-down original theatrical version or the larger-than-life, filled-out film version, mines the historical materials of filmic rock opera for its grand transpositional gestures. For my purposes, the filmic rock opera, never a coherent or conclusive category but a genre, concept, and claim of invention all rolled into a stylistic, includes such films as *Tommy, Rocky Horror, Godspell: A Musical Based on the Gospel according to St. Matthew* (1973), *Jesus Christ Superstar* (1973), *Phantom of the Paradise* (1974), *Lisztomania* (1975), and *Hair* (1979), among others. These films do not obey the generic, syntactic, or semantic conventions of the film musical Altman lays out, although they may well observe some of those tendencies. And, while they import many of the semantics of the musical image of rock as a popular commodity form into stage or film, these films also depart from the considerations of performer, voice, and image that Frith, for example, discusses.[37]

Generally, the problematic of the rock musical and the basis of its audience appeal are not, say, "coupling" and "marriage" (as Altman sees the primary ideological interest of the film musical) but rather "belonging" and "personhood." For the audience of the rock musical, the charmed musical body personified in the sacrificial figure of the rock messiah or martyr, who gathers together a musically enlightened band of insiders (the audience by proxy), sorts out the problem of belonging as musical revelation of finding identity lived as an aesthetic praxis in mass-media culture (a lifestyle). And so, as a cultural form rather than as a well-defined genre, the rock opera brings to bear a strangely direct meditation on the problematics of belief in the capitalist narrative of the self to musical subcultures outstripping their earlier places, communities, or cultural "sites" (during the late 1960s and early 1970s, rock was a "Scorpio Rising," to invoke Kenneth Anger's 1963 experimental film allegorizing this phenomenon: a paragrammatic music and youth subculture undergoing industrial integration).

In this light, *Hedwig* is all the more interesting, for it expects the audience not only to recognize generic and cultural forms but also to sing the tune of musical self-knowledge, however traumatic. These musical knowledges may be found in the discarded mediatic resources of the past, such as the rock opera, and are later refigured, in this case, by 1990s queer rock (a different example would be the 1990s return of 8-bit video-game music and its stylistic elaboration in contemporary electronic music). Hedwig's musical origins, she says and shows, are found in outdated musical technologies, such as 8-track tapes or cold war–era armed forces radio, and suggest a miscegenation between the inassimilably hip past of glam rock, banal AM radio hits, and such regional musical genres as country or urban. The film's stylistic excess directs conflicts not only between (ideological) narrative and (audience) enunciation but also between masculinity and femininity, male and female bodies, expression and orientation, property and propriety, and, most importantly for this film, between past and future identities of sexual orientation (gay, lesbian, bisexual) and identities of sexual transition (transsexual and transgender).

Hedwig's nemesis, Tommy Gnosis, is a figure of the historical misrecognition of queer enunciation contributing to narratives of rock spectacle and of the affective power of persons to affirm sex-gender expression being diverted into formulations of "sexual deviance." The glittering cross Gnosis bears on his forehead was bestowed by Hedwig's musical knowledges, a transaction leading only to his disavowal of Hedwig. Having received the sacrament of knowledge from Hedwig, Gnosis desires Hedwig as "she-male" but rejects her as transgendered; his desire lasts only as long as he can imagine her as a deviant but intact masculinity—that is, as long as she may have an "original" male phallus that can penetrate him. And he fears and rejects her to the degree that her "angry inch" signifies a remade, synthetic, and so impotent "female" phallus. As an example, then, of a generic transition of the sexed gendered knowledges invested but disavowed in the rock musical (and in the panoply of other audiovisual musical forms upon which the film draws), *Hedwig* has a lot to sing—that is, to say. Most notably, Hedwig's struggle for the authorship of her story against the father-conflicted, straight-identified, musical thief Gnosis concludes with her negotiation of a path between the respective narrative conclusions of two 1970s-era rock opera films, *Tommy* and *Rocky Horror.*

It is worth reconsidering some of the segments of the rock opera. The rock opera, within which we might include *Tommy, Rocky Horror, Godspell, Jesus Christ Superstar,* or *Hair,* varies widely in its use of popular music, narrative syntax and semantics, musical representation, and invocation of musical performance. As I have pointed out, these films by no means share what would be generic conventions in the syntactical and semantic senses that Altman lays out, and they clearly depart from the kinds of considerations of performer, voice, and image that Frith discusses—their artificiality and obvious constructedness tend to be too strong to speak simply to the embodied "grain" of the performer's voice, for example. But they do speak to what Altman calls the importance of interpretive communities for the musical, although Altman's concerns with generic definition prevent his classic study from seriously considering the rock opera. What can be seen precisely in filmic rock opera is the question of the interpretive community in relation to musical speech. All the films I have identified as belonging to the classical rock opera speak to the importance of "the interpretive community." They reflect this concern through two important qualities: They revolve around the idea of the secret and the sacred. Personhood for the audience of the rock musical, embodied in the sacrificial figure of the rock messiah, is a matter of revelation and belonging.

First, these films share a narrative telos that develops the premise of some hidden knowledge and turns this gnosis into the basis for a social identity that is to be understood within the cultural moment of the film's production. Second, popular musical cultures, especially those that can challenge dominant and established film-music conventions, become the key for decoding the sacred message: generally, of the outsider belonging, or, alternatively, of belonging to the outside or to a nondominant group. So, however fantastic the film's setting or style may be, throughout these films, the pop star appears as excluded messiah (a messiah who is also a pariah), or, more exactly, the pariah-messiah appears as pop star. The conventional narrative pattern of these films, then, across wide variations (which often exceed, and so easily come to parody, the conventions of the film musical in particular or even the scored film more generally) is that the unveiling and subsequent transmission of a hidden but life-changing knowledge takes place as musical performance and so emanates from a sacred insider or band of insiders to a wider, now musical, community (by extension, listening audience) precisely in the overt technique of musical knowledge as sound-image synchronization. A closed or esoteric subjectivity is opened up to the social, having been contained within the sound-image body of the musical outsider. Our following the revealed path to this transformation of the social that the central figure almost always personifies means that the "sacred" knowledge of the social—that is, a sense of understanding as belonging—is also reproduced for the mass of followers, by extension, for musical listeners and thus for us, the audience.

Of course, the audience's knowledge of the music animated in this way preexists and provides the basis for the cinema's depiction of it as the musical dissemination of belonging, and so the rock musical is above all a tale of the meanings of the reproduction of belonging, beyond either rock as recorded music or film musical as cinema. This is the history at stake in the rock opera, then: the story of audiences finding their own reproductions differentially, between the twin towers of film and pop music as mass-cultural productions.

The mediatic corporeality of the musical messiah, the body-to-be-consumed of the rock-and-roll outcast, is central to the way this genre mediates an audience's sense of who it is and its sense of what brings it together in the face of a disappearing, emergent, or nonexisting history over time. The narrative mode here is not historical allegory but futural retrospection; and the point of view is not one of individual nostalgia but a putatively collective point of view based in recognition and recollection of having heard the music or its meanings before, of having become able to recognize cultural values by having realized that one can never truly remember not having been able to speak. Here, musical play takes on a capacity for negation and for projection that would otherwise be denied to the musical spectator of the cinema. And so in *Tommy,* the inaccessible interior world of an unseeing, unhearing boy whose various experiences of social, substance, and sexual abuse all originate with the overlaying of a false Oedipal narrative onto a false narrative of a nationalist parental authority is once and for all shattered in a rock concert staged as a juvenile pinball tournament. In this film, mastery of a disabled masculine body (Tommy's "cultural autism") equates directly to mastering the affective potentiality of a commoditized self: the youth who has learned to "play" rock music in post–World War II youth cultures. From this point on, Tommy can now see and hear but will teach his followers to experience and to express mediatized sound and vision as a discipline of blindness and deafness. The musical body of rock here emerges in the transformation of a socialized subjectivity gravitationally compressed to the point of a black hole that has sucked up every possible pose of consumption, only to ultimately reproduce them as nullity and distraction. Tommy's rise to fame explodes in an expressive musical gesture that satisfies only by playing an appetite for mediatic musical mastery off a desire to satisfy the audience's thirst for excitement in the form of toppling the last flash in the pan. This play is depicted precisely as the audience's ability to see and to hear rock music, and Tommy brings these gifts to those who, in turn, see and hear him but whose identifications with his power must be shifted to some other rising star once he becomes "established" as a figure of worship.

The musical messiah of the rock opera accords perfectly with karaoke capitalism's congenital need for a momentary critique of the subjective and corporeal exigencies it activates in bringing sound and vision to audiences whose listening originates somewhere else and whose capacity for iconic recognition is always ultimately extradiegetic. The rock musical's messiah, then, is always written into the filmic narrative as a demand to have recognized what has already become popular knowledge, even as he or she must demonstrate the impossible emergence of that knowledge after the fact. Here, the mode of spectatorship is a paradoxical one in which the film does not defer history in allegorical displacement but rather must invent (patently false) history as a series of futural revelations phrased in the terms of grandly retrospective narratives whose meanings are largely established before spectatorship can commence. The gestures of the rock opera are always postmediatic, because for the present tense of the audience's musical knowledge to be narrated, this present tense must constitute not the audience's past but the music's future to exert a continuing hold on its audience; the music's future can unfold only after, and in spite of, the obstacles blocking its production. And so the filmic rock opera deploys that mediatic past tense common to any recorded commodity, the sense of its having been heard before, precisely because if it is any good, it will demand to be played again. This future-past tense, which is embedded but denaturalized in the playback experience belonging to listening commodities (and which would only years later become accessible to the video-store burnout), suggests not regressive listening but recognition of having transitioned, because we have repeatedly heard it all before. Distinct from either the impossible present tense of the garden variety musical, in which song and dance emerge out of the thin air of ideologically charged desire, or the nostalgic subjectivity anchored by the melodramatic underscore, the affect of the rock opera finds its power in a futural past eliciting the historical presence of the listening audience; this affect, the feeling of a remembrance of an unknowable expectation that is at the same time nonetheless already consummated as expression, rests with the audience's historically present-tense capacity to hear a music whose rupturing power can be described only by having first been depicted within the filmic narrative as coming out of nowhere or as having been hopelessly out of reach.

As Hedwig puts this retrospective futural indicative to her listener Tommy Gnosis, whom she reveals has "followed her voice" and left the "wicked little town" of Junction City: "Remember Mrs. Lot, when she turned around." The conflict of pseudohistorical narration and interpretive extemporizing here is one of biblical proportions, but this conflict always serves the interest of the rock god or goddess ("Deny me and be doomed," the film announces more than once). In just this way, the retrospective narratives of this futural mode of the audience's backward glance are grand, indeed. In *Jesus Christ Superstar,* the body of the musical rock star as transformative rupturing knowledge equates Jesus as a sensuous wrathful hippie leading his audience to salvation through a literal desert of spectacular production numbers, shot on location in Israel. In *Godspell,* conversely, the gospel is rendered as a hippie commune of Jesus freaks tripping through 1970s New York via production numbers that parody more than simply the film musical, which has more than once provided a mediatic tour of musical New York, notably in Stanley Donen and Gene Kelly's *On the Town* (1949). Too, the "canned" musical illustration and herky-jerky choreography of *Godspell* invoke the musical accompaniments and quasi-robotic movements of early cinema and generally make fun of the way in which cinema can only partially, through sound-image artifice and the limitations of the frame, capture the living (and dying) processes of the changing real. The location shoots of *Godspell,* in particular, will never be attempted again, by definition: The most spectacular number concludes with a helicopter-crane shot of the cast dancing on top of one of the World Trade Center towers. Still, the potential of the rock musical's future retrospective mode is by no means universally applicable. By the time of *Hair,* adapted for the screen some years after the filmic heyday of the rock musical and the end of the Vietnam War, the same pattern continues, but with the fading political vibrancy of the counterculture overshadowing the present-tense musicality of audience recognition. The film version of *Hair* becomes a nostalgic look at hippie antiauthoritarianism and draft dodging, knowledges increasingly impotent during the late stages of punk and the early stages of hair metal.

Like *Tommy,* which concludes with a convulsion of violence and the release of the rock-star messiah to heavenly realms of celebrity irrelevance, *Rocky Horror* confirms the way the rock musical mediates film genre, popular music form, and audience formation as the dissemination of a sexed musical body. And, like *Tommy, Rocky Horror* illustrates the sacrifice that is inevitably prescribed within this particular regime of genetic differentiation (where mediatic dissemination of the sacred gnosis implies that vital transformation takes place as mass-media reproduction and so can be transpositioned as cinema's mediation of musical gestures, gestures that outstrip the localization of subjective identifications before the screen to appear as collective knowledges driving "the music"—actually the domain of popular-music production that must be exterior to cinema for cinema to convoke it). While the reproduction of knowledge as social transformation is always a question of contact with, coming close to, or touching the outcast musical body, this body cannot live out the transformation it brings, especially if that transformation is to become definite, historical, and susceptible to narrative depiction. And so it is that the deviant bisexual Dr. Frankenfurter confesses his sins to an apparently rather more mainstream audience (songwise, his sins might be "building a man," engineering a "time warp," and otherwise enabling our view of sexual and historical identities as musical artifice) and is zapped back to his home planet of Transylvania. If an ecstatic body always appears in the rock opera—a spectacular musical image and an image of music that is "out of sight" and difficult to contain within the frame, then, to the degree that popular music provides that outcast body from outside cinema—then the death of this sexed body marks cinema's appropriation of popular listening knowledges. Of course, in these terms, this death also suggests a potential musical rebirth to come in the context of the audience itself, as the music from the film returns to other popular music reproductions: sound tracks, returns to the Broadway stage or community theater, and, of particular interest for my purposes here, the kinds of participatory postdistribution appropriation activities for which *Rocky Horror* and *Hedwig* have become notable.

Generally, then, in the rock opera, as transformative musical knowledge embodied in a charismatic figure becomes popular and threatens the authorities, a sacrifice occurs. And this pattern suggests the commodified historicity of the dynamics at stake: genre, gender, popular music. The rock opera thus makes reflexive, usually camp tragedy out of the disciplined subjectivities of youth culture in commodity capitalism; it allegorizes the limited lifespan inherent to commodifying belief in the self as an undertaking into transcendent, transparent subjective identity. During the late 1960s and early 1970s, the rock opera nicely folded together the problematic of a commodity counterculture understood as entertainment and rock music understood as having liberatory power.

The rock opera narrative complicates the older narratives of transcendent musical selves as "stars," such as that of *A Star Is Born* (1954) or *Inside Daisy*

Clover (1965), a deconstruction of that earlier film. The rock opera shifts the focus from the emergence of stardom to the emergence of an incarnate knowledge of belonging that is closely aligned with and already recognizable by a listening audience. And so in these films, the devotion of listening others is as dramatic as the central figure's transmogrification. The emergence of this form is explained with rock's new status at the end of the 1960s. No longer a dance music but a listening music, rock worked as a kind of musical avatar of countercultural populism, contributing to the idea that, since apparently revolution would not be happening, countercultural values must have some inherent and inevitable destiny of their own to fulfill in becoming mainstream commodities. The combination of this simultaneously hermeneutic and declamatory power gives the rock opera a special status: It is not simply a "rock star is born" variation on the stage or film musical but rather a musical commentary about shifts in popular systems of knowledge in which genre and gender are intertwined in the social production of belonging, of becoming a person, and whether this becoming happens in series of exclusions or inclusions.

At the conclusion of *Rocky Horror,* Dr. Frankenfurter is sent back to "transsexual Transylvania" after facing the straight audience and admitting the guilt of his pleasures. Here, drag presents a feminized male who is predatory, vampirizing both sexes—this transvestite is more bisexual than transsexual, as the diegesis makes clear, speaking to the attraction and the difficulty of same-sex identifications as well as to the overwhelming unlikelihood of transgender affiliations for the audiences of its day. *Rocky Horror* uses rock as cultural form to narrate the emergence (and untenability) of sexual desire as heterodeviance. The film presents the all-too-feared, but only to be expected, conclusion: expulsion. Deviance is always too good to last. But the film's sense of a future deferred corresponds nicely with the retro style of that period of rock and roll. The film joyously sends up as gothic sock-hop ("Let's do the time warp again!") the 1950s rock and roll of its youth, even as it consigns its newly found sexual freedoms to the formula of "transgression, contained."

On the other hand, in Ken Russell's adaptation of *Tommy,* an androgynous rock star achieves a larger-than-life persona partially in response to the heterosexual governmentality of the postwar British nuclear family but also in reaction to sexual abuse at the hands of his pedophilic uncle, who is coded as gay and perverse (this leering uncle, whose gapped teeth indicate his very facial expression as unsavory violation, reads the *Gay Times* when he is not incestuously abusing Tommy). The film suggests an overlap in the innovations of the sexual revolution ("gay liberation") with the reactionary family structures that have produced Tommy's sensual autism in the first place (depicted early in the film as a child with a cube over his head, searching for orientation as he wades aimlessly and dangerously on a seashore upon which the waves of the world are breaking). At the film's conclusion, Tommy reaches the heights of rock stardom as he is rejected by his initial fans, who finally chafe at his innovations as yet another set of constraints. He unexpectedly presides over the violence of their subsequent rebellion as they revolt and move on to devote themselves to a new musical icon on which to pin their desires. Elton John's over-the-top performance as the reigning pinball wizard, whom Tommy vanquishes during his own rise to the top, illustrates, on the level of star discourses, the simultaneously annunciatory and condemning discourses surrounding male homosexuality in rock (and in film) of that time.

Like all rock operas, *Tommy* and *Rocky Horror* each mobilize the recently recognized historical status of rock music as a rhetoric and aesthetics of cultural and historical development more generally. And as "noise" or dissonance becomes central to processes of integrating a new historical stage of popular music and capital, rock is a prime exemplar of the fact that technocultures "reproduce" not in terms of biology but in terms of historically complex diagrammatic relations of labor, technology, culture, and capital. In relation to rock music, rock in film, and our own (future) histories of sexuality, then, *Tommy* provides the opposite trope to that of *Rocky Horror. Tommy* narrates rock's historical moment of musical triumph in a vocabulary of desire displaced, of desire deviating from the subject. *Rocky Horror* camps a "future sex" transgression to the backing track of retro rock and roll that indicates from the outset that no future is in sight. *Tommy* plays rock and roll as a momentary, and therefore ultimately either contingent or false, historical triumph in the progression of musical genres, genres undermined by desire wrongly displaced from the audience to the star-as-screen erected in the institutionalization of social dysfunction as capitalist family values. For the horror-show-sex-cult-family-values of *Rocky Horror,* though, even the momentary, if illusory, future presented in *Tommy* was always already over before it started, so the transgressions underlying the appearance of a historical event as "star" are programmed to repeat upon the star's demise. Dr. Frankenfurter sings "I'm coming home" before being zapped back to Transylvania by alien storm troopers; Tommy sings "I'm free" as he finally escapes the iconic identity placed upon him by his fervent fan base and the family corporation profiting from his rock exhibitionism. *Rocky Horror* emphasizes gender-sex deviance that is a transgressive, repeating blip, easily contained (as the hybrid-cinema versions' audiences know, as they are policed into their seats and polled as to whether they are "virgins" of the show) in an interplanetary system of sexed, gendered normativity: The dark castle of outlaw rock and roll is but a fading "alternative" satellite moon in a globalizing musical economy in which rock is already dominant. *Tommy* models the historical progression of pop musical genres, with rock's transgressive power bringing it to the top of the heap, but questions masculine rock mastery as the teleological end of this progress inasmuch as rock's transgression depends on desires more expertly calculated in terms of sex and gender. If *Rocky Horror* predicates its well-oiled sensibility for tragedy by arriving at a ban on sexual transgression, *Tommy* finds gay-liberatory values not so noticeably distinct from the bourgeois family values that originally impelled the rock star toward musical transgression in the first place.

At the heart of this commutability of histories of sexuality and of rock music as either transgressive or nostalgic, both films share territory. If *Rocky Horror*'s Dr. Frankenfurter finally enters the space of audience reception to receive his banishment, whereas Tommy's fans finally ransack his music camp and flee, still, each film narrates its conclusions as a confrontation between the iconic genius (feminized to greater or lesser degrees) directing the musical spectacle and the audience who receives his mastery of feminized masculinity. And, in spite of their conclusions (*Tommy* emphasizing the fact of mediated reception, *Rocky Horror* emphasizing the fiction of liveness), each of these films gravitates around the potential for gender expressivity and sexual relational—and not gender fixity and sexual identity—to underwrite the retrospective truths popular music expresses to receptive knowing audiences.

Both films thus ultimately naturalize an identification between the cinematic work's depiction of life as musical style and rock music's claim to deliver "the live." They allow only indirect deferred self-recognition to their audiences: that audience who watches, already knowing the songs (whether because audience members have heard the songs in the theater, on phonographs, or on the radio or because they have attended numerous prior screenings of the film). Both works transpose musical recording and cinematic narrative, setting cinema to rock and rock to cinema, but use the operational artifice of synchronizing music and image as speech or song to point to the specter of the "natural," which is hermetically sealed from the song or speech of the audience.[38] *Hedwig*, clearly traveling this primrose path but with a very different destination in mind, takes a big risk in asking the audience to sing along and providing members with the words. What if no one wants to? In other words, rock and cinema, rock and visual media generally, tend to mediate gender and genre by defaulting to genius and defer their own presentational value for the mass-media audience. Rock's genius for distortion is for the rock star to sing, and cinema's genius for sex occurs against the audience's knowledge.

So, finally, it is not surprising that each film presents the rock musical as a genre where gender conclusively naturalizes sexual relation before an audience presumed to be silent and where this determination is achieved in an overtly artificial synchronization of music and image. The upshot is that *Rocky Horror* finally perversely denies the viability of any in-between or third mediation of gender and waits for the theatricalized speech of its cinematic audience; *Tommy* perversely heterosexualizes its hero at the expense of his own abuse and sends its audience on to "the next big thing." The potential for gender expressivity and sexual relationality to depart from these tragic formulations might be demonstrated, then, not with mere screen transgression or rock-and-roll social critique but with another, more important feature of exhibition: Cinema and rock would acknowledge their conventionality, speak to their own interpretation and their own mediation, *and* invite their audience's speech. Cinema might denaturalize gender and sexual relationality by upsetting synchronization conventions and asking audiences—who cannot be vocally timed or even warranted to participate—to sing along. Rock in film might more explicitly acknowledge its musical conventionality, forgoing its musical triumphalism and its annunciation of genius, by acknowledging its own circulation amid audience knowledges right alongside, say, the delivery of popular song on radio (largely lost to cinema). At least, these are the knowing truths that *Hedwig* exhibits.

Taken together, *Tommy* and *Rocky Horror* form the apotheosis of the liberatory promises of the musicalized sexual revolution. Each in its own way marks the point where the sexual revolution turns into a sexual counterrevolution. *Tommy* contributes by revealing the spectacular work of sound and image synchronization as finally counter to the aesthetics and values of rock performance, suggesting that the fans' departure from Tommy's music camp results from an excess of overmediation and results in a drive toward the next musical genre as social movement. *Rocky Horror* suggests that for the fun to go on for the audience, the tools of enforcement must be used against the transgressing doctor to contain his excess. This containment continues to be literally performed, albeit with different meanings, in the hybrid theatrical cinema of *Rocky Horror* performance today, where cast members "police" the audience into proper positions, giving them orders and largely directing the proceedings as a scripting of the potential for transgression within a "compulsory heterosexuality" that is, for the audiences I have observed, mostly a pseudonostalgic fiction. *Rocky Horror* today seems to serve, among many other uses, as a pretext for dressing up and acting out a participatory remaking of queer histories taking place as "gay-straight alliances" somewhere between the cinema screen, the audio playback device, the drama class, the community theater, the social network, and the movie audience. *Hedwig* reflexively activates these gestures in theatrical and cinema versions, and it is a testament to its success that cinema audiences have adopted *Hedwig,* like *Rocky Horror,* as a performance script for bringing live action into the movie theater. *Hedwig* has much to say about the fate of the trajectory of the film musical's reproduction of genre and gender after rock.

Hedwig challenges its audiences to deny three deviations from any naturalized orders of generic identity in relation to genre. First, *Hedwig* differentiates queer musical cinema from the film musical precisely by applying generic identifications originating in other cinematic forms than the musical: specifically, rock theatrics and album covers, but also visual music animation and the melodrama. In other words, where the film musical tends to use music to suspend cause-and-effect narration, *Hedwig* works through variegated sound-image stylistics to narrate not impossible origins but undetermined futurity. *Hedwig* transforms the ideologically suspect suspension of cause and effect in the film musical, escapist precisely in terms of the generic limitations through which it operates. Personhood is not figured in terms of a determination of biological or naturalized sex sustained through generic variations on the theme of boy-meets-girl. Instead, it is depicted in terms of the instabilities of rock and cinema mediating gender expression and audience expressivity.

Reordering telos and *melos* to construct another "me" means that the mediation of gender expression does not operate within the formal boundaries of narrative form but rather somewhat more like the way rock opera works in a proscriptive allegorical mode and, without the additional props and pointers *Hedwig* packs in, critically points to the cultural limits restricting gender expression and through which restrictions queer expression struggles. For example, the film presents a trailer-trash nonconformant gender identity sung as country music as a different mode within, but therefore analogous to, the histories in which anti-black or anti-Semitic violence are naturalized. In doing so, it suggests and problematizes affiliations between homophobic, classist, sexist, and racist violences that are at least partially renewed through the very commodities of mediatic identity inviting queer listening. In this way, the larger problematic of gender mediation is centered between and received through other analytics. These receptions are not necessarily appropriative productions of black kinesics or feminist politicizations of the personal in false or faulty identifications but rather are transpositions taken up and expressed in the processes of mass-cultural reception.

Second, *Hedwig* marks another transposition, one tangling with the ongoing project of representing gay and lesbian histories. While belonging to a historically specific moment, and while replaying historical antagonisms between less well-defined queer audiences and their identifications with media commodities, in deploying moments of identification with musical mediation and turning them against established alignments of sex, gender, and gender expression, the film refuses to render its own moment in terms of established positions for gay and lesbian identities. Rather, *Hedwig* turns productivities of media reception grounded in musical affect to a nonrepresentational negotiation of gay and queer identity or, perhaps more precisely, of the drag queen and the drag king—a negotiation that would have been impossible in this way at an earlier historical moment. The conclusion is that gay masculinity becomes mobile in terms of a divorce from its own commodified agency; a queer male body is born thanks to erotics and ethics shared with transgender politics, received in audible and visible conflicts of genre and gender expression.

Finally, a third transposition of identity accompanies these two: *Hedwig* marks the difference of mediatic music and image by applying the active reception practices associated with *Rocky Horror* to the phobic critique of rock-operatic corporeality epitomized by *Tommy.* At issue here is the way that *Hedwig* emphasizes cinematized musical mediations of gender identity as denaturalized image and sound: the lip-sync experience generally derogatorily associated with drag and music television alike. So what are we to make of the proposal Hedwig makes in the film to Tommy, and reflexively to us, about reconciling a glam *Aladdin Sane* public image with a heartfelt Dolly Parton–style composition of transgender politics capable of producing a queer male body? Hedwig's mother was wrong: It is not just a "simple cut-and-paste job."

Hedwig's transposition of listening against viewing requires, again, a praxis of queer aesthetics as an ethical stylization of the erotic idiom of personhood. It shares with contemporary queer theory an important demonstration of affect's power to resituate "historical" desires, acts, and narratives. But, by taking up a transposition between gay-male vocality and transgender politics, it manages an open-endedness, a futurity, as antiphon to a homophobic and transphobic past, where present queer theorizations may refuse past, future, or both. The difference is in receiving affective knowledge as a disjunctive musical ratio of the mediatic and the corporeal versus grasping desire as heteronormative projection. The film is hardly singular in these interests, though.

Miller rewrites the Broadway musical within his critique to refuse the seriated disappointment the musical theater inscribes; he imagines, by refusing that past, another kind of ending: perhaps one that *Hedwig* opens, with the help of its audience.[39] Lee Edelman,[40] on the other hand, works against heteronormative histories' "futurist" desire, arguing that desiring futurity fundamentally works against queer embodiment. To desire futurity as heteroreproductive "nature" indicates a pervasive violent fantasy of salvation; the future of the child is a projection exclusively screening a fictive heteronormative past while actively negating queer corporealities in the present. Edelman's synthesis of deconstructive and psychoanalytic analytics aims to reveal a "structural position" for a queer critique of heteroreproductive futurism.[41]

Against that futurist fantasy, Edelman aims "sinthomosexuality," a bastardization of linguistic orders moving through language, through symbolic orders, and through desire: The Lacanian *sinthome* is conjoined with and overlaps the textual shape of "homosexuality." The *sinthome,* he explains, is Jacques Lacan's intentional resurrection of an archaic writing of "symptom" to emphasize the inscriptive mechanisms (more generally for my purposes here, the mediatic operations of *technesis*) that enable the subject's engagement with the pleasures of the symbolic. Lacan's archaic usage exposes repetition within the symbolic order and, accordingly, the operations of the death drive, to deflate the subject's fantasy of immortality.[42] Sinthomosexuality, then, is a queer "site where the fantasy of futurism confronts the insistence of a jouissance that rends it precisely by *rendering* it in relation to [the death] drive."[43] Where the future appears in the face of the child, sinthomosexuality finds an "impasse" of language and history disavowed in the fantasy of salvaging the body politic. To succeed in that disavowal, homosexuality (and nonprocreative sexuality, generally) is called in to die in place of the inevitable symbolic death of the subjects of language and history. Disfiguring this fantasy by revealing the means of its inscription, sinthomosexuality can "pass beyond, pass through" the violent promise of salvation.[44]

The ungainly progeny of Edelman's concourse between the texts he receives and the writing device with which he prepares his reception by his reader (a pronunciation guide), his linguistic and textual bastardization is born in the negativity of the present he engages. Of course, queers must insist on equal rights, insist on "our capacity to promote the social order's coherence and integrity," and this insistence is for the present: We must not wait for a tomorrow that is "always another day away."[45] When culture fantasizes its own continuance in the figure of the child, the social order hears queer sexuality as violation, its own worst nightmare; so Edelman writes out this violation as a demand. Sinthomosexuality, a fabricated "word without a future," is a queer site created for the reception of a critical reading project—a synthetic rather than a Platonic or maternal *chora*, perhaps.[46] Edelman introduces this rhetorical device to derealize familiar narrative fantasies that frame, one way or another, futurity against the intrusive repetitive mechanism of the death drive.[47] But the deployment of sinthomosexuality as rhetorical device that can traverse and open out the narrative setting of futural fantasy comes within a larger frame, operating between two important movements in Edelman's work. Edelman first introduces his aim of revealing the violent irony at work in cultural identifications for which "the Child has come to embody the *telos* of the social order" and concludes with the disastrous effects of continued identification with puerile futurism: "endless blows. . . . Somewhere, someone else will be savagely beaten and left to die."[48] Sinthomosexuality, then, is a device for reflexive reception launched in reading queer irony through to an identitarian telos in the social: continuing homophobic violence. It travels between two powerful moments in the text: One affective gesture lays bare the scene of queer reading, and another gesture punctuates its end.

In the first gesture, Edelman engages a literally orgiastic beratement of structuring negativity. Irony is transvalued as an erotically charged textual assault against symbolic futurism:

> Fuck the social order and the Child in whose name we're collectively terrorized; fuck Annie; fuck the waif from *Les Mis*; fuck the poor, innocent kid on the Net; fuck Laws both with capital ls and with small; fuck the whole network of symbolic relations and the future that serves as its prop.[49]

Symbolic Law, and laws, before capital, or *Kapital,* then: Edelman's sinthomosexual preference is for Lacan's dialectic of desire over Adorno's negative dialectic. But the future bounces back. Because sinthomosexuality designates the conjoined overlapping indicators of the technical and the sexual woven into salvation fantasies organized around the figure of the child, sinthomosexuality paradoxically continues to be organized in relation to that futurity: "What keeps [sinthomosexuality] alive . . . is the futurism desperate to negate it."[50]

"No future" cannot be simply a statement against phobic symbolization; it is also a naming of demands for impossible recompense, for impossible justice, of impossible coherence. And Edelman does not simply dispense with futurity by diverting fantasies of symbolic control toward the death drive, which these fantasies are already practiced in refusing to face, or toward the dumb pleasure of "fucking negativity." The future always boomerangs back into frame, even as irony. Edelman shows that the ironic *can* point analytically to the inhuman real, to the unintelligible catachresis of language or history. But if the tactical power of an indeterminately oppositional queer theory rests in the ironic, the problem is that the ironic is relentlessly allegorized as a legible past for futurity's child.[51] So the rhetorical movement of any merely oppositional queer theory is arrested, held in bondage to the negating future it aims against. Negation recoups irony, while hardly thinking about it.

So, in an affective gesture emblazoning the essay's last words, irony turns to escape language and suspends history, serving not its own ends but as a pivot at which point writing sacrifices symbolic meaning and turns to musical sense: "Somewhere, someone else will be savagely beaten and left to die—sacrificed to a future whose beat goes on, like a pulse or a heart—and another corpse will be left like a mangled scarecrow to frighten the birds who are gathering now, who are beating their wings, and who, like the drive, keep on coming."[52] That scarecrow on the fence might trivially be Dorothy's symbolic prop on the child's path home through Oz but, at greater depth, is an unspoken invocation of Matthew Shepard's death. The name of this death is whispered as an anonymous index of the universalizing violence of futurist fantasy. The point seems clear—Edelman rewrites the universalist liberatory slogan "We are everywhere" in terms of a universal disidentification with the future: "Futurism makes sinthomosexuals, not humans, of us all."[53]

The power of this argument lies, for me anyway, not so much in the design of a laborious rhetorical device (the neologism "sinthomosexuality" seems designed to be difficult to say or to rewrite) but in the way it frames the device within affective gestures that work by essay's end to suspend the symbols of language within sensible gestures of its rhythmic reproduction. Edelman places the rhetorics of irony in the hands of affect, and affect is never troubled by its momentary totality; that is the only way affect can *affect.* So universal baratement

("Fuck the whole network") is answered by the "drumbeat" of continuing violence, a violence that nonetheless is suspended in ending.

Just as the catachreses of language or history disappear in irony's being allegorized away as futurity, the syntax of that last sentence finishes the semantics of opposition in Edelman's work to resolutely refuse familiar hope: "another corpse being left." Yet, in the same gesture, the writing takes another tack, marking a mediatic identification (Miller's Oz?) and a historical trauma (the violence against Shepard's body) by fluctuating between representation and rhythm. Musicality picks up this opposition and provides sense against meaning: Words turn and circle, repeating, hunting futurism's subject between music and language.

Rearranging Edelman's phrases best telegraphs the musical effect I am describing: "future's beat," "a pulse," "a heart," "a beating of wings," "the drive," "still coming," "goes on." Violence's meanings are suspended, almost visible, as sense hums mechanically. If, in this suspension, Edelman's time runs out, the affect of this writing does offer more than rhetorical devices. It answers the telos of identity, the symbolic identification achieved in projecting inaccessible history as legible future, with the *melos* of violence suspended. The beating dies out, but the resonance of having followed that beat echoes as the reader hovers now on the blank remainder of the page—along with the birds. In closing his book by aiming the affective sense of queer theory between music and language, Edelman leaves an opening for some future that cannot be written.

Who or what, after all, are these birds, beating wings, gathering "like the drive"? The circulating warrants of queer embodiment's violation? The ghosts of the inhuman, murdered Shepards haunting the negative? Or does this "drive" open dissolute history's fantasy of our disappearance to indicate another time as yet unsigned? Negativity, whatever its direction (homophobic or identitarian, exclusive or oppositional), is apparently unidirectional only as regards the sign so that it cannot offer irony as an affirming ground. Rather, moving writing into music by ending this way, something like horror—or like unfamiliar hope—is subvocalized within beratement, as beratement stops speaking. Immanence, another hope of futurity, lies here disturbed, the whispered rhythm of the unwritten.

Sinthomosexuality is a rhetorical device for opening a "structural position," but the affective charge Edelman passes through the setting of murderous fantasy suggests a larger calculus of erotics and ethics shared across queer aesthetics as praxes. So let us call sinthomosexuality an instance within a larger set of transpositional tactics or strategies, recognizable as they transpose musicality for representationalism: The rhetorical effect here is not all metaphoric, certainly not merely metonymic substitution, but the passing, the massing, of language and history into musicality as an affective disordering of phantasmatic signification. This is not a rhetoric of hyperbole. This passing passes through and beyond: It is a *diabole,* a moving expression of the powers of reception, a labor of difference.

Hedwig, too, works reception as the immanence of an agency that can be grasped as having become productive only after it becomes determined and conflicted in material and technical labors. Where studies of reception such as Kuhn's cannot recover anything other than what has been written into cinema or cultural memory, *Hedwig* suggests the praxis of an affective temporality distinct from that of historicizing force. Although this affective temporality of the diabolic frustrates productivist frameworks, it is also not bound in or to historical violence and does not mark erasure. The affective labor of *Hedwig*'s transpositional corporeality implies a larger passional dimension of the present, sensible, but not individual. Here, Gilles Deleuze's exploration of sensible time is relevant: "The future and past are rather what is left of passion in a body. But, as it happens, the passion of a body refers to the action of a more powerful body. The greatest present, the divine present, is the great mixture, the unity of corporeal causes among themselves. It measures the activity of the cosmic period in which everything is simultaneous: Zeus is also Dia, the 'Through' (*l'A-travers*) or that which is mixed, the blender."[54] For Deleuze, here, a greater and divine present *is* an affective corporeality that is the cause of its own differential expression. *Hedwig*'s achievement is to take this greater present into the moment of audience reception and so to delineate the diabolic "Origin of Love" as a mixed temporality delivering narrativity expressing speech as public knowledge: more specifically, the song of the audience. That song, as the title of the penultimate track indicates, is an "Exquisite Corpse"—Hedwig's body as the object and objective of Zeus's fury. Expressing what would normally be a marginalizing narrative as speech that is all too often barred in the very moment-to-moment progress of cinematic reception, Hedwig's transitioning body is a practical futurity. This praxis of the powers of reception confounds productivism, futurist fantasy, and historical heterodominance, suspending them in a commingling of horror and hope to diabolic effect. Transition, transversal, transposition: The *diabole* deploys reception against production and affect out of identity, transposes orders of signification and sense: image into music, *melos* over telos.

Perhaps, then, the film anticipates Edelman's critique of the child as futurist fantasy: "And what if the child is queer?" Or what if the child is the ward of queer kinship or simply grows up listening more closely to the distant wave of the radiophonic than to the familiar legacies of the patriarchal image or the mother's mirror stage? Taking her own star turn, Hedwig turns away from the sexed gendered expression of the musical as genre and turns that expression out: "Look at me Kansas City: I'm the new Berlin Wall!" *Hedwig* extends the affective work of the *diabole,* indicating the powers of reception out of which we craft our emergence, our poiesis. *Hedwig* grasps a particular moment at which transforming political struggles provide not merely identifications but affects of love and of freedom to be received in transposition by gay or lesbian struggles and to be transposed in further futural movements: transgender politics. In setting these transpositions as musical image, *Hedwig* seeks a gay-male corporeality continuing to receive its potential despite actual legacies of violence or loss (whether personhood barred to the social generally or, more specifically, continuing homophobic violence, HIV/AIDS as mismanaged crisis, new denials of rights) via leaving the stage and granting the spectacularity of the wig to female masculinities.

Hedwig is not "destiny's child" but the bastard and bastardizing of history's sexed expression as transposition from bioenergetic to bioinformatic regimes: liberation histories' "love child." If Hedwig finally exits to the street in Hansel's transformed return, with Mitchell now all grown up, that departure indicates an immanent moment paradoxically grasped in reception, not a historical erasure. History's bastard love child has gotten its legs. Its history, still struggling, will come later. For now, and for as long as our present remains violently bound to our past as its impossibility, the future is ours.

7
Stylistics of Hieroglyphic Time

Methods for Killing Time, for Reanimating Musical Time: Biolabor

In this study, I have shown the ways in which musicality and gesture have provided key terms, tropes, methods, concepts, and emblems for synchronizing streaming media throughout recent periods of technological innovation and media transitions. In each case, synchronizing streaming media for audience reception using means of greater temporal precision suggests some looming closure or totalization of media production, exhibition, or reception; in each case, musicality serves as a way of elaborating critical possibilities for synchronization in a larger sense than solely the technical means of registration and exhibition while forestalling any final totalized closed system of media synchronization. We have seen that musicality seems to function as a complex temporal diagram: It relates the time of audience reception to the time of history per se, regardless of, and all the more emphatically given, the spectacularity of the exhibition system in question. It relates contemporaneity to the historical time from which, but in terms of which, and by virtue of spectacular technical exhibition, the present seems alternately entirely exhausted or excessively new.

Musicality elaborates some serialization of praxis mediating social structure and superstructure, where structure becomes superstructure in the interest of elaborating a "historical apparatus" for critical method. Éric

Alliez points out one implication of Giorgio Agamben's observation, in defense of Walter Benjamin, that "the only materialist point of view is that which radically overcomes the separation of structure and superstructure, because praxis is posited as the only single object in its original cohesion—that is, as 'monad.' . . . [T]he monad of praxis is presented above all as a 'textual repertory,' as a hieroglyphic that the philosopher must construct in its factitious integrity, in which elements of both structure and superstructure originally converge in 'mythical rigidity.'"[1] For Alliez, pointedly overlooking the dialectics of mediation that Adorno insists Benjamin fails to adequately grasp allows us to see that it is in this disjuncture of structure and superstructure that the historical apparatus is elaborated, recognizable in the nexus established between processes of temporalization, functions of subjectivity, and systems of capitalization (the "resounding system"):

> In a praxis where one passes from one pro-position of time to another, not by reason of external social and historical determinations, nor by a dialectic of notions, but by an original motion—that is neither "originary" nor "derived"—of disjuncture by virtue of which what is held to be *aberrant* in an arrangement produces a disequilibrium, a deflection of time, or an *intemperateness* [*intempérie*], which will be invested in a new apparatus. This investment *is* the presentation itself of time as an active, "objective" temporality: as a potential-time that creates alterity and alteration—multiple processes of temporalization exceeding on all sides the metaphysical vulgarity of there being but *one* Western representation of time, which in all rigor supposes the scientific method as well as the neo-Kantian operation of subsuming being under Method.[2]

Capital begins its elaboration of the historical apparatus, Alliez argues, as the linguistic sign is made to substitute for "singular and present things it designates by lifting them to the rank of objects of an 'objective nature,'" where "to be" comes to mean "to be experienced by means of a representation" in the projection of things as objects in a world of efficient causes "for which only arbitrarily manipulable signs can hope to account" (238). Thus, on the one hand, perspectivalism, which Alliez notes in Erwin Panofsky's work, characterizes the triumph of objectification and control, the consolidation and systematization of the world as space as well as the extension of the domain of the self, but also what lies beyond perspective: the "outfitting, the transportation, the departure of being from the 'house' of language (*logos, vox*), from the cosmo-theo-psychological 'field' of time (*oikos, paupertas*)" (238–239).

A premise central to this study, however, which I discuss at length with regard to Sergei M. Eisenstein in Chapters 1 and 2, is that the expression of contemporary time as exhibition in some partial relation to historial ordering of time is that time-as-potential is doubled in the temporal exhibition of temporality. As I have shown, Eisenstein's method requires both "monadic" and "dialectic" potential: It modulates the material temporal exhibition of time in time. Historical rhythms are subjected to cinematic rhythm to communicate historical pathos: experience doubled in haptic spectacle effected in the projection of a virtual image that is received concretely as possible gesture. This exhibition, in turn, changes the cinematic-historical apparatuses of exhibition. If exhibitionary apparatuses are subject to a larger historical apparatus, they are "animated" in time, too. Thus, for Eisenstein, computation or stereoscopy would provide further means for cinema, and cinema would give way to some more powerful exhibitionary apparatus. To the degree, though, that any such animation of an exhibitionary apparatus over time would be ethical would depend on its capacity to make pathos—that is, historical experience as suffering—palpable.

Musicality and gesture in Eisenstein's pathos, in Oskar Fischinger's ecstatic musical synchronization, or in Hanns Eisler's dialectical stream: Each of these is a stylization of the double potential of streaming media as idiom. Affect conditions, as historical suffering, and recoups, as ecstatic flight or in critical distancing, the exhibitionary value of the "technological media." I have argued at length, then, that affective labor does not typify a new stage of biopolitical capital but rather conditions the transposition of one "historical apparatus" into another: the transposition of bioenergetic ontologies, epistemologies, and ethics into the bioinformatic ones that displace but rely on thermodynamic processes.

Consider, in this light, Natalie Bookchin's recent *Mass Ornament Two Point Oh!* (2009). For this digital-video installation, Bookchin animated hundreds of YouTube clips to the sound tracks of Busby Berkeley's 1930s *Gold Diggers* series of films and Leni Riefenstahl's *Triumph of the Will* (1935). Each clip is an instance of user-generated content, and each depicts its author performing calisthenics, stretching, or dance moves, often in the recognizable style of a well-known music star or in the style of contemporary fitness regimens. Bookchin's timed rhythmic presentation of the rhythmic clips varies. One clip may play alone and then fall back into a horizontal matrix of clips stretching across the width of the display. At times, clips accumulate in patterns around the screen, the progression of the patterned motif corresponding to a cadence heard in the sound track. Throughout, we are presented with familiar activity in an unfamiliar configuration, and Bookchin's video-graphic animation draws our attention to a larger regime of temporal coordination that she imposes upon them. A sense of dissonance prevails in our recognition of a larger historical regime of fitness and self-discipline and the contemporary discipline required to document the self and to upload the document as a Web-ready clip. The montage of clips, presented as cut off from the time in which they were composed; the sense of almost achieving a continuous animation of a disparate persistently networked mass of dancing or exercising figures; the critical dissonance that arises as we begin to worry about whether we are exchanging a utopian self-image for a dystopian mass present: Bookchin puts the classical stylistics of streaming media to use here in a commentary on personhood and publicity mediated in the World Wide Web.

Mass Ornament Two Point Oh! presents (although without interaction on the part of an interfacial agent) networked self-exhibition as a musical play with biopolitical power. The title of the installation suggests the two musical historical motives: self-instrumentalization as speculative gain and atrocity in the annihilation of self-difference as potential cost. As Bookchin explains, "Each YouTube dance reenacts a system that reaches further into private space in its transformation of individuals into instrumental units performing partial functions. At the same time, the dancers make small claims for embodiment and publicness in the face of their seeming disappearance in the disembodied virtuality of the Internet."[3]

Here, media celebrity and normalizing distributions of obsessive self-image determine limits of style, while the YouTube clip determines the idiom. Bookchin insists on a modicum of user style to be observed in cross-comparison from clip to clip, but she largely refuses her subjects any particular ability to originate style or idiom. *Mass Ornament* presents a largely negative view of synchronized media transactions, corresponding in some ways to the concerns Bernard Stiegler raises about the "exhaustion" of diachronic time in synchronized media networks, which I discuss at length below. The dystopian rhythm of the energetic self, appearing in terms of informatic celebrity in *Mass Ornament,* is relieved by Bookchin's choice and reanimation of clips, in which each figure appears to make "small claims" for embodiment and publicness. The immanence generating "affective labor" as biopolitical resistance in Michael Hardt's[4] account is seconded to, and reframed within, a more dialectical account of mediation, where digital self-exhibition visualizes the work of maintaining and exercising the self in the everyday "social structure" and where YouTube visualizes the "superstructure" of what Stiegler calls contemporary "hyper-industrialism."[5] Siegfried Kracauer's oft-cited critique of the "mass ornament" of synchronized dance troupes of the Weimar period is transposed to the contemporary gallery. Kracauer observes that the "bearer" of these animated linear ornaments is not "the people" but "the mass." Even if news of these large-scale coordinations of masses of people as geometric pattern traveled through newsreel networks to excite remote villages that had not yet seen them, the patterns of "girl-units" themselves are drained of organic or erotic energy. The mass ornament was an "end result . . . whose closure is brought about by emptying all the substantial contents of their contents."[6] Bookchin, paradoxically, retains a bit of "organic" energy in her ornament of persistently networked masses of digital self-exhibitors. Her reanimated clips of "girl-units" present "small claims" in her rhythmic reconfiguration of them, as she presents her *own* claims alongside those whose self-exhibition she choreographs.

Indeed, whether in Eisenstein's work, Kracauer's critique, Bookchin's *Mass Ornament,* or Stiegler's account of hyperindustrialism, rhythmic musicality contributes a common but still underrecognized trope or turn, the elaboration of a critical historical apparatus distinct from economic, linguistic, discursive, performative, or affective turns in critical thought and in historical practices of time-based media. This musical turn is pervasive, if often critically underestimated or undemonstrated. I note in Chapter 1 that for Alfred North Whitehead, writing in 1925, the Pythagorean roots of "logical harmony" renewed and redeemed an exhausted "scientific materialism." Music rivaled philosophy in articulating the limits of modern techno-science, and while Whitehead kept to philosophy,[7] less-reticent theories and practices, such as those of Eisenstein, did not hesitate to turn to music as a way of animating the streaming media apparatus in terms of affective labor. The resulting confounding musical hieroglyph is the result of problematizing the critical historical apparatus: a stylization of the hieroglyph not as text but as temporal diagram.

As I have shown in Chapter 3, Ernst Bloch's speculative account of historical progression as musical synthesis, the "transcendent counterpoint" of carpet motifs, sails over the stalled immanence of dialectic. The carpet motif travels to where a monadic historical apparatus surfaces at the outer limits of material history, bounding between ancient and modern temporalities, animating musical idiom, relaying and transforming musical styles. For Bloch, the modern crisis of representation condemns the subject to interiority, closed off to worldliness and to historical dynamism;[8] musicality reopens the closed surfaces of modern life, as if to a display of musical fireworks. Whitehead's claim for philosophy as music's rival or Bloch's turn to a musical-historical synthesis helps make the larger point emphasized in the output of creative workers whose work I have discussed. Across a wide range of media theories and practices of audiovisual media, a musical turn has been deployed where a crisis of representation becomes irremediable or irredeemable. But this musical turn has little to do with audition or musical form in the conventional senses. Rather, the musical turn makes time complex by animating it, channeling personhood and publicity in conflicts of autonomy and sovereignty. The musical turn consists in relating the time of media reception to historical temporality, the potentiality of the monad to the potentiality of the dialectic, to configure work, text, subjectivity, corporeality, conduct, national or transnational body politics, or even developmental dominants as a return of affective labor through the screen that otherwise closes off the subject from historical experience. "Closure" in this sense means not simply alienation in industrial production but, more broadly, the equation of technology with ontology.

Thus, when the streaming work (Eisenstein), the exhibitionary apparatus (Fischinger), the site of reception (Eisler), the body politic (Larry Clark), the body itself (John Cameron Mitchell), or, as I discuss in this chapter, affective labor itself is found closed, fixed, alienated, or reified in some excess of programmed synchronization where diachronic time and, accordingly, historical change are thus closed to critical intervention: In these cases, the musicalization of the temporal diagramming of ontology as technology orchestrates an opening in what is otherwise taken as a totally mediated duration of totally mediated events. The musical turn diagrams time in time, subjecting technology-as-ontology to historical observation and critical intervention in mediatic terms. Yet "superstructure" and "social structure," whether fused in monad or split in dialectic, do not directly enough address what we may call "microstructure": the mediation of temporal processes at the receding limits of the infinitesimal, where contemporary bioinformatics exhibit synchronization at deeper levels of materialized temporality.

Consider the ways in which genomic scientists may work today as musical amateurs who cut and paste DNA sequences to create Musical Instrument Digital Interface (MIDI) tracks. In "Gene2Music," for example, Rie Takahashi and Jeffrey Miller "convert genome-encoded protein sequences into musical notes in order to hear auditory protein patterns" and "make protein sequences more approachable and tangible for the general public and children."[9] Takahashi and Miller's work, in technical terms, is known as "sonification": rendering information in auditory terms to express its form and significance. But their work goes further than sonification, because they remap DNA sequences as MIDI tracks that can be played back on any personal computer equipped with a sampler. In fact, they are *not* really doing "sonification"—they are preparing "musicalization" of DNA material, and the sonification itself is done through a software protocol and personal computer hardware. The result is that tissue samples are rendered in a bioinformatic recapitulation of the industrial player piano's scrolling paper in hopes of helping children better understand the techno-biological sequencing of biotechnological life.

Alternatively, Rivane Neuenschwander's 2006 video collaboration with fellow Brazilian Cao Guimarães, *Quarta-Feira de Cinzas/Epilogue* (*Ash Wednesday*), presents a different attempt at biomusic and a different deciphering of the hieroglyphic of bioinformatic time. In this video, we see a single ant hauling a shiny object across what looks to be a frosty white surface. Then, another appears, and another, all dragging what turns out to be colored confetti across a micro-landscape enlarged for us to see. In the gallery where I viewed the piece, the ants appeared on a wall monitor that presented them at the size of small kittens—but more determined. On the sound track, a samba rhythm plays in a tonality that suggests the determined marching/dancing of the ants. Its sprightly, slightly crunching sounds were achieved by tapping matchsticks on a tabletop. Here, biomusic also appears as a kind of functional work, but the function is less "cognition" of DNA and more the work of realigning the human capacity for grasping the rhythmic correspondences associated with dance with a human

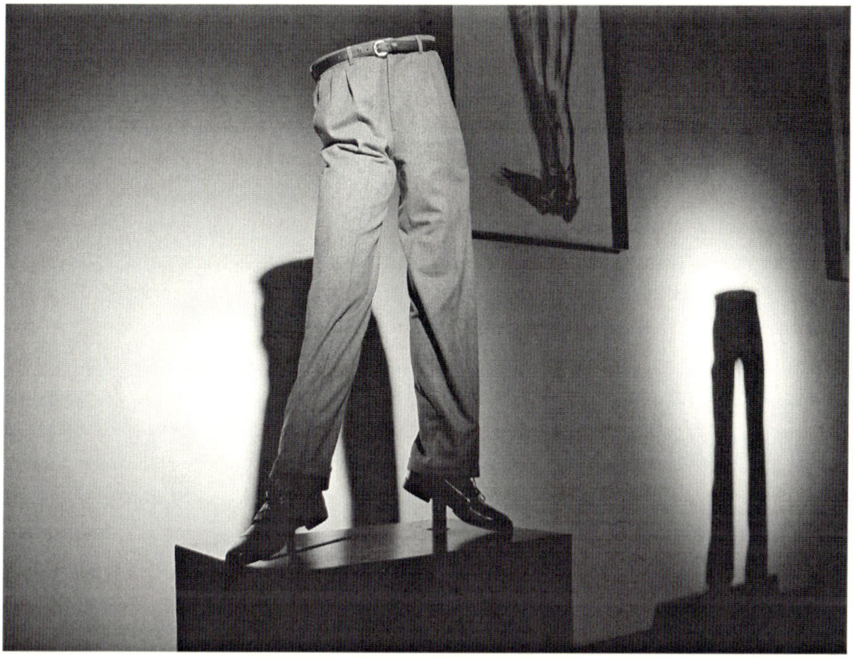

FIGURE 7.1 *Tischtänzer* (Stephan von Huene, 1988–1993). (Installation photo courtesy of ZKM, Karlsruhe, Germany.)

perspective on natural processes.[10] The musical tuning of biomusic in these cases suggests bioinformatic processes brought to face the bioenergetic processes they displace.

In this concluding chapter, I identify the musical turn at work in two recent theoretical considerations of synchronized media, those of Stiegler and of Donna Haraway, and bring these to bear on recent musical diagramming of affective labor in Stephan von Huene's *Tischtänzer* (*Table Dancers* [1988–1993]; Figure 7.1) and Steina Vasulka's *Voice Windows* (1986; Figure 7.2). In the following section, I consider the ways in which musical figuration informs Stiegler's analyses of historical diachrony and media synchronization in his multivolume series, *Technics and Time* (1994–2001). A fundamental concern of Stiegler's larger aims in the series, argued out at length in the first volume, is that the synchronized "real time" of global media networks produces a "no future," a dangerous, violent attenuation of diachronic time. Stiegler's work in *Technics and Time 2: Disorientation* (1996) provides a recent signal instance, as he discusses this attenuation of diachronic time with regard to a methodological error he attributes to Marvin Minsky, Alan Turing, and, above all, Edmund Husserl: No cognition can be construed apart from, nor can it be removed from, the technical material ensemble that in some way allows it to become coherent.

FIGURE 7.2 Steina Vasulka's *Voice Windows* (1986), with vocals by Joan La Barbara. (Courtesy of Steina Vasulka.)

Haraway's recent work, too, points out the ways in which bioinformatic regimes depend on the bioenergetic regimes they displace. Where Stiegler diagnoses a widespread condition of "symbolic misery" in contemporary hyperindustrialism, Haraway offers instances in which feminist collaborations produce resistance to biocapital.

Taken together, these accounts describe one or another form of affective labor in hyperindustrial biocapital: symbolic misery in Stiegler, or, in Haraway's account of resistance to biocapital, a revelatory "ontological choreography" of contact between humans and companion species (65), a "naturalcultural dancing" arising in multispecies "respect" (27). As temporal diagrams of contemporaneity in historical terms, that these critical accounts imply expressions of affective labor should not be surprising. Musicalizing the temporal diagramming of a historical apparatus, wherein technology effaces ontology and cuts the subject off from rhythmic historical diachrony, we find pathos without history, or "symbolic misery," in Stiegler's words. Alternatively, in Haraway's reading of broadly distributed, continuous historical resistance, we find ecstatic contact between humans and between humans and animals. These are flags, then, of those affective modalities arising in diagramming hieroglyphic temporality as broken or extended musicality.

Von Huene's *Tischtänzer* and Steina's *Voice Windows* then allow me to clarify the nonlinguistic exhibition of musical diagrams in bioinformatic regimes, revealing (as Stiegler and Haraway reveal in distinct ways) bioinformatic regimes to depend on the bioenergetic regimes they displace. These works allow me to propose a summary diagram of my own by which we can characterize the actions we take in the reception of streaming media: Music and gesture across media diagram not simply "echo objects," as Barbara Stafford suggests, nor bioenergetic or bioinformatic industries or capital but rather, more generally, *biolabor.* Beyond money as fetishized labor in Marxian accounts,[11] beyond repetitions of statements as discourse in Foucauldean accounts,[12] and certainly not a transposition of money as data: Rather, the transition from one technical ensemble to another or from one historical apparatus to another is animated in modulations, differentiations, and displacements of *biolabor.*

Hyperindustrialism and Biocapital

In volume two of *Technics and Time,* Stiegler's critique of hyperindustrialism reconsiders Husserl's phenomenology of temporal consciousness. Very briefly, Husserl proposes a "flux" of consciousness for a transcendental subject capable of temporal perception by virtue of primary (selecting) and secondary (recollecting) temporal objects.[13] By contrast, Stiegler argues that any "flux" of primary and secondary temporal objects necessarily requires an account of the material substrate and technical formatting on which time consciousness depends: "Time consciousness" is necessarily a "technical-time consciousness"; "flux" is necessarily "montage flux." Stiegler pursues this critique first through a discussion of "rhythmic" syntheses of technocultural development and second by insisting on the irreducibility of worldly melody to a transcendental consciousness of pure tone. In Stiegler's analysis, then, consideration of rhythm and melody characterizes historical temporality as the musical hieroglyph of a phenomenological subject, one that must be demystified and rendered as temporal diagram. An important part of Stiegler's aim is to critique the "symbolic misery" he believes real-time media impose to the extent that they disallow adequate time for instrumental mastery and successful individuation, whose hallmarks would be stylistic variation and idiomatic specificity. And because he is concerned with what he sees as the production of symbolic misery in global media networks rather than what others describe as the augmentation of cognitive capacity[14] or material wealth,[15] he provides in *Technics and Time* an extended critique of cognition as social capital. Yet what interests me in Stiegler's work, as well as work by such contemporary critics as Haraway or historical figures as Bloch, are the ways in which musical instrumentalities become crucial to the critique of technological instrumentalities, and not in strictly musicological or auditory terms. Musical instrumentalities in these widely disparate accounts inform and at times even substantiate critiques of techno-scientific instrumentalities' entanglements with the rationalizing logics of globalizing capital.

Haraway's *When Species Meet* (2008) invokes musical instrumentalities in distinct ways: Transpecies being is a "symphony" (2); the transpecies mesh of life is animated in "an ontological choreography" of contact zones between humans and animals (65).[16] Stiegler's and Haraway's disparate invocations of musicality are more than merely metaphoric or rhetorical. They constitute recent entries in an important trajectory of critical attempts, at least since Bloch and Eisenstein, to diagram, while intervening in, the increasing power of time-based media to synchronize everyday gestures with media time at the expense of historical time. This musical turn, which affords a critique of historical and contemporary technoculture *and* proposals for critical innovation, revolves around ostensive or explicit claims that musical relation somehow reopens an exhausted, entropic, synchronic media time to a creative, negentropic, lively diachronic historical time. Where synchronic patterning dominates diachronic differentiation, time itself appears at risk. Stiegler's and Haraway's accounts deploy musicality in critically diagramming a revitalization of everyday time.

Their musical diagrams, though, while possibly refiguring some aspects of romantic or late-romantic thought, are actually only concretely thinkable after two relatively recent developments: the standardization of planetary clock time and the transnational distribution of time-based media products during the mid- to late nineteenth century.[17] With regard to the latter, phonography and cinema are the origins of what Stiegler terms the industrialization—and now hyperindustrialization—of memory. The implications of his argument are not entirely dissimilar to Miriam Hansen's[18] observation that by 1929, Hollywood dominated the export of media sensoria. Stiegler argues that Hollywood media unified, via its mastery of the industrialization of memory, a global public image and the memory of that publicity. In effect, where Hansen describes cinema as one of a range of modern media *vernaculars*, Stiegler argues that the serial streaming of public image as the image of public memory preempts those determinations of memory and habit that would otherwise be articulated in locally differentiated *style* and *idiom*.

Stiegler's concerns begin, then, with synchronized global temporality as a historical development, where style and idiom rather than style and medium are crucial. He argues that what we call "real time" in effect kills diachronic historical time in its increasingly precise synchronization of media production and reception. This crisis reaches urgent proportions inasmuch as its intensification in "virtual reality" media technologies displaces not only the development of historically contingent and locally specific technical ensembles but further, and what is worse, historical style and idiom at large.

Still, Hollywood itself has a locale, one that has never constituted a site of production or distribution of clock registration, speed, or measure—even today's differential version of globalized time.[19] The ability to articulate style and idiom and to extend the ethical capacities of time-based media is an artifact of "Hollywood's" own multiple postcolonial locales in the world. Historical records and the history of media production, in spite of the general neglect these suffer in "Hollywood production," demonstrate that time-based audiovisual media, like Los Angeles itself, have often been the site of repeated attempts to innovate and to intervene in the media sensorium Hollywood exports in terms of musical style and idiom (see Chapters 3, 4, and 5).[20]

Two implications of the musical turn as it appears in Stiegler's work are of relevance here. The first is that even if Stiegler's characterization of "Hollywood" (in the third volume of *Technics and Time*) falls into one of Los Angeles's own favorite portraits of itself (all absorbing, impossible to turn away from), nonetheless, his account renews a long series of critical attempts at thinking of musicality, instrumentality, and historicity in ways that are extraordinarily productive. Stiegler's extension of Jacques Derrida's treatment of the signature provides a detailed proposal for understanding the ways in which media temporality is programmed within a diagrammatic mode of production whereby contemporary bioinformatic materialities displace earlier bioenergetic ones. Second, Stiegler's argument demonstrates, in the course of delineating this displacement, how musical instrumentalities help conceptualize the reopening of closed, precision-synchronized temporalities to historical diachrony and the variegation of style and idiom they might express.

Testing the streaming serial recording against the histories of technical development as well as diachronic time, instead of merely against the finite capacities of the receiving, cognizing, acting subject—perhaps we begin to open audience time to the historical diachrony that gives everyday life its meaning *as* time. Stiegler's and Haraway's musical troping indicates their execution of temporal diagrams: relating affective labor at the time of reception to the material labor displaced from the time of exhibition and to historical time (the stream of observation, the serial stream of the work, and their mutual default of memory). As historical and recent critical and cultural theory along with a great amount of historical and recent media art suggest, localizing this temporal diagram and distributing the topicality of that localization have long been thought to be a musical project.

Other Musics

Before describing the musical turn Stiegler's argument entails, I need to clarify his aims in *Technics and Time 2*. In this work, he clarifies the importance of the "temporal objects" proposed by Husserl in his work on time perception: a "primary" temporal object involved in selecting and attending to some streaming phenomenon and a "secondary" temporal object involved in retaining it.

Together, these temporal objects allow the streaming phenomenon to be grasped subjectively and, accordingly, socially and historically. As Arthur David Smith explains, Husserl's analysis of signs differentiates the Kantian notion of a unified cognitive synthesis enabling temporal perception into two: Two temporal objects are synthesized, in an "active," calculating mode of cognitive synthesis and a presubjective, "passive," and essentially receptive mode of cognitive synthesis.[21]

Stiegler's critique points out simply (though in great detail) that Husserl's temporal objects do not stand on their own and that they also imply a third temporal object: some orthothetic formatting of memory susceptible to technical intervention and to industrialization. This is the "industrial temporal object." Husserl shows that an objective correspondence of the "just-having-been" and "the remembered" is possible; it allows Husserl's transcendental consciousness to become social, to become "we." But if that is so, then that possibility of objective correspondence between given and remembered also allows the temporal objects of time consciousness to be made reactive and to be reiterated. As a result, "the possibility of ideality [is] sealed within"[22] two other possibilities: that of suspending the flux of worldly time and that of recommencing the flux of time suspended or, again, that of inscribing the object that streams forth and that of "playing back" the inscribed time. Some mode and means of technical inscription condition time consciousness, attention, and memory. The consciousness of attending to and remembering time that Husserl describes as "inward," then, depends for Stiegler on some orthographic prosthesis that always situates culture and politics as preindividual and understands subjectivity and technics as co-constitutive, at least potentially open ended in variegated techno-cultural style and idiom. Accordingly, Stiegler resituates the passive syntheses (of habit) and active syntheses (of calculation) Husserl proposes as modes of cognition in terms of a history and politics of technocultural, socioethnic, and biosocial change, because individuation *and* collectivity become possible in the techno-politics of that evolution. Stiegler repeatedly returns to this techno-politics of democracy, literacy, or industrialization in light of the productivity of global programming industries in this series of works and elsewhere. He is developing a Derridean insight: Attention and retention are subject to technical intervention and to techno-politics. If industrial culture developed a third temporal object as phonogram or cinematogram, it also transformed the politics of memory.

Stiegler's procedures in *Technics and Time* volumes one and two can fairly be described as diagrammatic. His critique clarifies that if we accept Husserl's description of temporal objects, the subject's time consciousness is never simply "in the present": Past and present time consciousness are synthetic, a "flux." The relevant comparison is Henri Bergson's famous diagram of memory, a "cone" of time suggesting that virtual duration is compressed as it passes into the momentary "disc" of actual memory.[23] Stiegler points out that Husserl illustrates the flux of time consciousness with a diagram of his own: a triangular vector diagram depicting temporal perception and recollection as a singular dynamic flux wherein past and present are not definitively divided. Stiegler resolves the two diagrams: He suggests that the Bergsonian duration of virtual time is inscribed in terms of and gives shape to an orthothetic framing of the flux of consciousness Husserl describes in terms of temporal objects. As Stiegler puts it, "The temporal object is a *vortex* within a flux—that is, a spiral."[24] Transposing Bergsonian duration in terms of Husserl's flux of temporal objects, in Stiegler's description, the spiral of an industrial memory disc—phonograph, film reel, videotape cassette, or digital disc—appears to be wrapped in a spiral *around* the subject's apprehension of time, memory, perception, *and* technological instrumentality. Stiegler thus follows Paul Ricoeur's reading of Husserl's "cosmic connectors" as needing to be recast as "technological connectors" (242). And, as a technological connector, the industrial object of memory is also subject to further technological development: It will be networked.

Stiegler's subsequent work in the *Technics and Times* series and elsewhere develops the implications. Hyperindustrial production of synchronized temporal objects unifies the production of material goods and spiritual "nourishment."[25] Hyperindustrialism intensifies active syntheses projecting the calculation of regimes of memory in a synchrony that can never be localized and so can never be adequately differentiated in diachronic situations allowing style and idiomaticity to emerge. This synchronized unification incurs a symbolic misery that typifies not contemporary capital's power but rather its loss of spirit, its loss of the transductive relationship between psychic individuation and collective individuation. Or rather, the transduction of individual and collective is "disarticulated" in today's "cognitive capitalism."[26] This disarticulation has a history and a capital: "Hollywood."[27] In these ways, *Technics and Time* provides a distinct treatment of a global Hollywood that emphasizes Americanization rather than economic policy or aesthetic considerations specific to cinema production in Los Angeles: "A process of global unification takes place through the cinema, which [Upton] Sinclair tells us could only have happened under the leadership of North America."[28] Hollywood, not the networks of finance capital or political capital, became the globe's technocultural metropolis, the capital of the industrialization of memory.

Whether we accept Stiegler's description of the hyperindustrial exploitation of memory, there is no denying that he prepares his critique of Husserl's active and passive syntheses by drawing heavily from André Leroi-Gourhan's account of corporeal rhythm as the source of social, cultural, and symbolic value in *Gesture and Speech.*[29] Active and passive syntheses are no longer modes of cognition in Stiegler's work. Instead, individual or collective being becomes historical in an "epochal redoubling" expressing "rhythmic stabilities" at "specific socio-ethnic and individual levels."[30] Rhythm in this larger (and unheard) sense enables sustainable technological adoptions or appropriations as well as that process of appropriation called "modernization":

> The operation of epochal redoubling (the addition of a new programmatic level partially suspending previous levels' effectiveness) is a passive synthesis; it is also the genesis of the "what" in general. The second epochal redoubling, an "appropriation" by the "who" of the first redoubling, is an "active" synthesis. We must use these quotation marks when referring to appropriation and activity insofar as this redoubling of redoubling is always already in the process of clearing a new path to the technical tendency and to a new stage of passive synthetization.[31]

We can see here that Stiegler's understanding of technocultural differentiation relies on a very broad proposal of rhythmic-historical synthesis. With active and passive syntheses established as technocultural processes rather than cognitive ones, Stiegler proceeds to a critique of Husserl's account of the apperception of tone. He charges that Husserl reduces melodic heterogeneity *and* the orthothetic (or technical) formatting necessary to make sense of heterogeneous temporal phenomena to the false purity of tone perceived by a transcendental "I." Husserl, Stiegler argues, introduces a "unity where it is not yet established, when on the contrary it is released, *après coup*, from the flux of a multiplicity" (207). Husserl posits intersubjectivity "*in advance* as individual," where for Stiegler, individuation emerges "trans-individually" from "a pre-individual base" (207). In a way, then, Stiegler's critique implies that what Hollywood does to local industrial productions of memory, Husserl's transcendental phenomenology does to thought. Husserl eradicates idiomaticity as he "erases the musicality of everything heard," when in reality "all tone is individuated on the pre-individual ground of musicality, all language 'sings'; the smallest noise rises up from the world's symphony. The ear is originarily musical, and this is precisely its temporality. All temporal objects detach from this grounding, incessant musicality from which they are projected and to which they are linked as a 'fade-in'" (210).

In *Technics and Time 2,* rhythmic musicality accounts for the sustained metastability of historical technocultures *through* time; melodic musicality accounts for the temporality of lived experience *in* time. Throughout, the deconstruction of textuality, authorship, and archivization Derrida carries out at length becomes for Stiegler a more pointed questioning of a crisis in historical consciousness, corporeal habit, technological change, and technocultural memory. Herein lies the importance for Stiegler of Leroi-Gourhan's analysis of the supervention of traditional socioethnic programs by modern programming technologies. Leroi-Gourhan is indeed concerned with the ways in which media networks have a normalizing power greater than the power of receivers to respond to them, resulting in a schematically oriented superhuman time and space corresponding to "the ideally functioning synchrony of all specialized individuals, each in his function and his space."[32]

If Stiegler's extensive reliance on Leroi-Gourhan appears conservative in some ways, his proposal of "epochal rhythms" of active and passive syntheses enabling technocultural differentiation and individuation extends Derrida's critique of Husserl's phenomenology beyond textual criticism to media criticism proper. The result is a critique of the subject *along with* a critique of the equipment of that productive diagramming of relations between instrumentality and historicity we know as technological modernity. Stiegler's claim that programming industries underwrite the activity of "the transcendental imagination" means that the relation of temporal flux and subjectivity is prosthetic rather than "transversal." Still, this treatment relates instrumentality and historicity in terms of rhythm and melody—that is, in terms of musicality. It invokes musicality *as* nonsubjective (or preindividual) temporality. Or, at least, musicality expresses the subjective and collective limits of historicity and instrumentality.

Technics and Time's style and idiom consistently engage the characteristics of the diagrammatic mode of the hyperindustrial production it critiques. Stiegler's great concern is that the contemporary crisis of hyperindustrialism is enabled in its denial of any necessary substrate for "information"; if the cybernetic formulation of information denies the energetic materiality it depends on, then our critique of it may aim at locating the historical error whose forgetting enables this denial to proceed. Thus, Stiegler tests his conclusions diagrammatically, bringing Bergson's diagram of memory to bear on that of Husserl. His formulation is also diagrammatic in that he describes a historical transformation that shifts from industrialism to hyperindustrialism through a reorganization and intensification of orthothetic capacities: One historical structuration shifts to another. Relating the musicality of its engagements—technocultural rhythm, worldly melody, the deferral of prosthetic relation in phenomenological thought, industrialization of memory—*Technics and Time 2* enacts a long-form rendition of the image of streaming media as musical hieroglyph requiring elaboration as a temporal diagram of historical diachronic time.

Two striking concerns arise with regard to this diagramming of instrumentality, musicality, and historicity in Stiegler's work. First, Stiegler does not theorize musicality according to musicological, auditory-cultural, or cinema-sound studies. Instead, he draws on rhythm or melody as questions of the dynamisms of historical epochality and durability and of expressive style and idiom. Each of these dynamisms is dampened in the hyperindustrial programming of memory, he argues. Second, if musicality in Stiegler is temporal, material, technical, preindividual, and expressive, but also industrial and hyperindustrial, then, like so many others before him, Stiegler engages a musical turn not only to describe the larger diagrammatic mode of media production reaching a point of planetary crisis but also to defer the inevitable question that arises as to the historical subject by asserting the primary diagnostic symptom of the problematic in terms of affect. Primordially, that symptom indicates discordant melancholia, as Stiegler adduces in *Technics and Time 1: The Fault of Epimetheus* (1994). But in subsequent works, and with regard to contemporary network media, that symptom indicates "symbolic misery." This contemporary condition of misery in knowledge, labor, or recreation results from shared orientations toward space and time undergoing upheaval with the intensification of global archiving systems enabled by digital networks after World War II. This intensification and the symbolic misery characterizing it provoke "enormous resistances; fundamentalisms, nationalisms, neo-Fascisms, and other regressive phenomena are the manifestations."[33]

The concern with technocultural style and U.S. dominance, of course, is a long-standing postwar concern.[34] But Stiegler's is a different account of affect and biopower. In Stiegler's analysis, hyperindustrialism proceeds according to the imperatives and the affordances of techno-scientific capital; however, any autonomous resistance in the form of affective labor, as Michael Hardt and Antonio Negri propose, is not a given: "But we can thus ask whether there is not in this new commerce an explosive contradiction, source of a loss of reasons—we understand by that a loss of motifs, of capacities for projection."[35] Again, this concern with loss and melancholia as symbolic misery is hardly new to technocultural analysis.[36] Yet few go as far as to retailor the technological-adoption-as-modernity thesis to address the historical rise of U.S. media influence, on the one hand, and "convergence theory" after Turing, on the other, in terms of musical instrumentalities.

Stiegler's questions are centrally relevant in extending the critique of technological modernity to a critique of biopolitical personhood: Who commands and controls the criteria according to which the models of synchronized simulacra are orchestrated and disseminated? What capacities do such orchestrations allow for differential adoption of techno-scientific equipment? Who owns the past or determines how we synthesize the future out of it? His preoccupation with grounding these critical questions in a thorough deconstruction of subject and instrumentality along with the musical turn he deploys, while distinct in method and in spirit, may be compared fruitfully to Haraway's recent work on transpecies encounters and biotech ethics.

Perhaps surprisingly, both Stiegler and Haraway invoke musical engagements in a critique of biopolitical technics. Haraway's concerns in *When Species Meet*[37] begin with what she metaphorically refers to as the "symphony" of human, animal, and machine co-constitution. If 10 percent of human cell matter is occupied by genomic material, she reasons, the other 90 percent is "filled with the genomes of bacteria, fungi, protists, and such, some of which play in a symphony necessary to my being alive at all." . . . [C]ompanion-species approaches *must* actually engage in [what Isabelle Stengers described as] cosmopolitics, articulating bodies to some bodies and not others, nourishing some worlds and not others, and bearing the mortal consequences. . . . All of this [*respecere,* looking back, holding in regard] is what I am calling 'sharing suffering.' It is not a game but more like what Charis Thompson calls ontological choreography. I act; I do not hide my calculations that motivate the action" (3–4, 88). Haraway and Stiegler, then, are concerned with biotechnological ethics between theory and practice—what Stiegler calls a "passage to the act"[38] or, as Haraway puts it, "practices and imaginative politics."[39] Each diagnoses the affect of suffering in contemporary cognitive capitalism: Stiegler relates the techno-political ethics of its historical derivation, while Haraway relates that it is the transcorporeal "sharing of suffering" demanded by mutual respect. Methodologically speaking, each wrestles with some version of what Quentin Meillassoux[40] calls "correlationism," which is "any current of thought which maintains the unsurpassable character of the correlation [between thinking and being, such that 'we only ever have access to the correlation between thinking and being, and never to either term considered apart from one another']."

Correlationisms inevitably hypostatize "some mental, sentient, or vital term": representation, nature, mind, will, will to power, memory, life (37). While Haraway and Stiegler clearly attempt to avoid the tendency to hypostatize any particular relation as general or universal, both nonetheless strain toward a politics of biotechnology in the present without positing either a "nonmetaphysical absolute," as Meillassoux does, or submitting engagement with techno-scientific production to what Meillassoux sees as "the fundamental property or trait of *Galileism,* which is to say, of the mathematization of nature" (113).[41]

For Stiegler, the key term in thinking the co-relation between human and technology is "transduction," a term adopted from Gilbert Simondon that in Stiegler means "a relationship whose elements are constituted such that one cannot exist without the other—where the elements are co-constituents."[42] For Haraway, more broadly, relation as such is reflexively co-constitutive, such that "companion species is a permanently undecidable category, a category-in-question that insists on the relation as the smallest unit of being and of analysis."[43] As well, "respect" for significant otherness means that Haraway understands autonomy not in terms of autopoiesis but in terms of "trans-acting," where autonomy "is the fruit of and inside relation" (164); here, meaning arises in a "web" of cross-species kinship transacting material-semiotic practices. Haraway's "ontological choreography" describes a tactics of respect wherein diachronic, historically situated actions inform the value of any digital cultural production. Haraway is moving toward, while attempting to critique, some theory of value in biocapital. Her examples include citizen activists who educate themselves in genomic sciences, gathering DNA datasets and coauthoring academic papers with open-minded academic researchers, and challenging the proprietary, commodified breeding practices that have led to an increase in genetic diseases even in only recently classified dog breeds (95–132). This choreography of contact anchors and distributes the activist epistemologies in and throughout the "symphonic" web of relations she describes. Her choreography of contact fairly demands attention to stylistic and idiomatic variegation over historical time. But to be clear in describing Haraway's citizen biotech activism as a tactics, we should specify that where the activist networks her production at the digital interface, this tactics becomes teletactics and, to that degree, the extended rhythmic transduction of technoculture in Stiegler may correspond to some sustained choreographic transaction in Haraway, although for her, respect makes suffering transindividual *and* transpecies.

Stiegler and Haraway, in spite of the vast differences in their approaches and understandings, risk a correlationist engagement with contemporary biotech understood in terms of global programming industries capable of determining the texture and quality of affect in postgenomic everyday life: subject and tool in Stiegler, human and animal (or human and machine) in Haraway. To avoid hypostatizing the co-relation of one term to another, Haraway and Stiegler invoke musicality and musical instrumentalities. For Stiegler, the redoubled rhythmics of active and passive syntheses of historical technocultural production provide the anchor for his account of synchronization producing nonknowledges. But Haraway thinks that questions of technique or calculation "will never take us into that kind of open where multispecies responsibility is at stake" (81). Her question is how not to separate those who may kill and those who can be made killable (89), and she finds her method in a "choreography of contact" between bodies entangled in "braided, ontic, and antic relatings" (165). This involves texturing the diachronic situation of any digital network within a larger and much more complex cross-species web of kinship. Haraway asks, "How is 'becoming with' a practice of becoming worldly?" (95, 3). Her answer is a co-relation of philosophy and play within a diffuse "dance of relating" (25) historicity and musicality.

Stiegler's rhythmic redoubling and Haraway's choreographic web: One re-animates historically and the other futurally a techno-species-being now out of time. For both, the deadening temporality of corporeal motricity industrially coordinated and programmatically synchronized in serialized sequences of events distributed on a global scale precludes the improbable while reaping the endless violences on which this factic, fictive empire feeds. Globalized media temporality implies in both cases the entropy of historical time, where the human animal is subjected to the removal of the human to accomplish the technical abstraction of the animal, in a spectacular synchronized world picture animated as biotechnological puppetry. Each critic presses his or her case differently: a mortification of rhythm in Stiegler; the enlivened choreography of contact in Haraway; Stiegler's rigorous refusal of U.S. technologists' belief that the body can be removed from its movements; Haraway's ontological, epistemological, ethical dance.

But the time for a historical movement toward the present (Stiegler) and the present movement toward a different future (Haraway) is musical temporality for both. If Gilles Deleuze characterizes philosophy as an admixture of the detective novel and science fiction,[44] these treatments might be described as resisting falling into an unreflective admixture of the science-fiction novel and the musical. Cinema memory itself is beholden to corporeal memory, reinscribed on the basis of not only "new technologies" harvesting its effects but also intervening modalities of temporal change: a choreography of contact enacted across disciplines and instrumentalities, media memory and media reception.

Whether in works of interaction art, such as those of Bookchin or of Gene2Music, or in Stiegler's or Haraway's theories of time and action in hyperindustrialism and biocapital, a certain ratio of affect and instrumentality rendered as musical play mitigates the instrumentalizing effects of techno-scientific reason.[45] The human-animal-machine whose memory of lived time is exhausted in being synchronized to bioinformatic process is musically reanimated and placed back in diachronic time, however ordinary, unfamiliar, or fractured. Synchronized time closed to diachrony is opened up to a critique of models and criteria, while the improbable destabilizes what Stiegler describes as the non-knowledges of marketing or media programming. Musical play allows commodity subjectivity and corporeality to be resituated in terms of the historical and the expressive. History returns, bearing a future.

Perhaps, though, media art diagramming contemporaneity and historiality best emphasize the tensions between Stiegler's and Haraway's critical methods. At stake in any analytics of a possible "alter-globalization" is the degree to which only *techno-scientific* possibility preempts the virtual such that representational schematisms enter into a general economy of equivalence to produce reason as proprietary knowledge and, as a result, overdetermine the meanings and potentials of media receivers' actions, habits and memories, and everyday lives. If the industrialization of memory instrumentalizes the virtual of duration as techno-scientific reason's retroactive possibility, then musical play matters beyond "play" considered as rule-bound contact, exploratory agency, or the transfer of agency learned in games to broader orders of everyday life organized as information systems.[46]

Musical play in these accounts matters more for its temporal capacities and affordances. Musical play affords the temporalities for a variegated adoption of technocultural style and idiom, constituting a kind of teletactics, perhaps, for the networked regime of conduct Stiegler refers to as "tele-action." Any account of musical diagramming, though, reaches its greatest value when revealing—or positing—that techno-scientific mediation recoups *all* divisions of labor in time, where the techno-ontological is programmatically hitched to the material ontic, so that, conversely, musicality handles the ethical risk entailed in that totalization of historical temporality. Musicality handles the risk, then, of *conducting* historical memory and ethical futurity, and because writing is also a teletactics, this risk is writ large in the accounts I have presented here. If, for Haraway, an "other worlding" is possible by engaging in a choreography of contact, for Stiegler, the cosmos is at risk in reducing the musicality of world historicity to a single global imaginary: "It is the heart of cultures and societies that is in play, their most intimate relations with the cosmos, with their memory and with themselves. To ignore or neglect this could have the most tragic consequences. Because calendarity and cardinality are the elementary warp and weft of vital rhythms, of beliefs, of relation to the past and to the future, the mastery of apparatus of orientation will come to be that of the global imaginary."[47]

To Play, to Play Back, to Play With

Here we can reconsider Bookchin's claim, cited above, that the Internet consists of a "disembodied virtuality" in light of Stiegler's exposition of the performativities of the signature. Stiegler follows Bergson in equating virtuality with temporality,[48] but he argues that if the contemporary programming industries have breached an epochal divide in which the possible is technicized, as in Minsky's problematic of "virtual space," then this contemporary risk emanates from techno-scientific reason's belief in a removable body. Stiegler's consideration of performativity suggests that identifying possibility with its realization results in a conflation of the virtuality of time as duration and some technologically accomplished spatialization, with the result that the techno-scientific possibility becomes an unquestioned virtue. As Stiegler argues in his reading of Minsky, "the structure of the biological synthesis of the living being's memory is perfectly homogeneous with . . . the absolute disruption of the biological event's status."[49]

This homogeneity of the epistemology of the structure with the disruption of its temporal ontology consists in the disruption's retroactivity: "Must possibility precede its real-ization? Must it be stated retrospectively that a possibility was suspended there, before?" Yes: "Such a modern science crosses science, philosophy, ethics, and politics even as it spans media. It is the question of fiction out of which we must now think the possibility of truth."[50]

What reality posits its own retroactive possibility where no possibility existed before? This is the problem presented in the synchronization of techno-scientific possibilities across geopolitical milieus, this catastrophe whereby the retroactive performativities of techno-scientific possibility "materialize time"—that is, capture or take over the temporal virtual as the technical possible. "Digital interactivity" is a statement of this capture in and as play, but its substance is not the cybernetic interface—it is biolabor. And the simultaneously thermodynamic and informatic nature of biolabor is entangled in musical diagrams engaging "technology" as "ontology" or as "natural history" in recent media art.

Von Huene's (b. 1932–d. 2000) sculptural installations often critically deploy musicality as thematic and aesthetic means for animating intermedial process as a problem of bioinformatic reception. For von Huene, too, musicality is never given in any conventionally musical way, as his *Der Kaleidophonische hund* (*Kaleidophonic Dog*) and *Tischtänzer* sculptures make clear. Von Huene applies tropes of musicality working across displacements, distributions, and differentials of aesthetic labor to ask, as he does in a 1997 installation project, "What's Wrong with Art?"[51] What is wrong with art in von Huene's works is that it conflates creative and affective labor; they are indissoluble, but disjunctive. In mobilizing this conflation as disjunction, von Huene demonstrates musicality as mediatic gesture, turning art into a demonstration of informaticized everyday life. In von Huene, the reception of art as experience manifests in a disjunctive systems theoretic where music provides the necessary expressive and demonstrative transpositions between two modes of aesthetic labor: creative production and creative reception.

Von Huene's *Der Kaleidophonische hund* (*Kaleidophonic Dog*; 1964–1967) is an automaton of dissonance: It overlays wood carving and musical instrumentation in an upside-down "hell hound" whose legs and head move stiffly as if running nowhere. For von Huene, Gregory Bateson's system theories of cultural expression as broadly "cybernetic" provide his point of departure from earlier attempts at differentiating the process of making from the process of apperception.[52] Drawing on information theory, for von Huene, art had become a matter of differential symbolic expression.

The *Tischtänzer* sculpture dates from two decades later and encapsulates a more specific techno-political history in its operations. The torsoless and headless dancing legs that compose the work are styled in masculine businesswear trousers and hang above the viewer in a series of four pairs. While the attention to sartorial effect suggests Joseph Beuys's suits made out of felt, the ways that political message, department-store technologies, and bureaucratic administration are deployed in this sculpture might remind a gallery visitor of the robotic doubles used as concert substitute, album-cover graphic, and Web site icon by the electronic music group Kraftwerk.

The four musical automata that perform in Kraftwerk's stead in one portion (generally a closing sequence) of the group's live concerts comprise identical torsos and mechanical arms whose rods and pistons are visible, with individual heads replicating the faces of each member of the group. As robotic proxies of Kraftwerk's players, their sweeping hand gestures seem to orchestrate, in the musicians' absence, the technicized production of Kraftwerk's highly sophisticated machine music. If Kraftwerk's musical automata seem vaguely bureaucratic, they are also vaguely futuristic, although in a slyly "old future" way. Von Huene's table dancers are the antithesis of Kraftwerk's robotic administrators of dance music synchronized with image projection and commodity circuit. Von Huene's "table dancers" lack torsos entirely, and their costuming suggests not a return to fantasies of the technological future but to an authoritarian past now distributed as wireless communication similar to that used in supermarkets.

Tischtänzer demonstrates the ways in which postconceptual aesthetic automata, immersed in systems theory and the circulation of electronic data, have become coupled with the homeostatic feedback loops typified by late-twentieth-century systems of consumption, political theater, and interactive installations. The table dancers are activated by a wireless feedback loop between gallery visitor and work. They are fully "interactive," according to one paradigm of interactive art installation. Visitor movement in the gallery is subject to sensors that activate the artwork as an interactive system, but the artwork itself moves according to a different set of affordances than the viewer's own ambulatory movements. You walk; they dance.

Passing by the four pairs of legs trips wireless sensors that set off a mysterious "tap dance" by each. Spotlights throw the shadows of this dancing on the white gallery walls. The viewer's leg movements also trigger an accompanying sound track, a loudspeaker symphony made up of sampled fragments of political speeches by Joseph McCarthy. The 1950s department-store style of the legs' trousers, then, is matched by the backing track of 1950s political pronouncements. Herbert Marcuse's *One Dimensional Man* (1964) is multiplied into a quartet, and yet this "series" is fuzzy: The viewer's gestures are not at all the same movements as those of the tapping table dancers. The isomorphism suggested between human-leg movement and the tap-dancing automata is nominal and conceptual, but it is immediately differentiated in form, style, and meaning. The material movements, the durations, and the meanings of the viewer's gestures and of those of the automata make sense in their difference. The process artwork is, as in the work of Gerhard Rühm and others, displaced into a tension of systematization and disruption.

The dancers' movements displace one's own material labors; their technical display distributes one's input and propagates it across a time-based stream of display; and the viewer is left to interpret the difference between those mediatic gestures and his or her own embodied gestures. The invisible wireless communication between the viewer's legs and those of the automata is, then, an integrally expressive part of the display of this affective tableau presenting the variegated labors of visitor movement, mechanical dance, and political theater. Bureaucratic administration is projected as a historical shadow theater of the art-technological work.

Von Huene's automata take technologies routinely used in department stores and political theaters and lend them to the task of critiquing interactive art not as a "new medium" but rather as a systematic means of questioning historical displacements, distributions, and differentials of laboring expression. His point is not that interactive art is embedded within and indebted to capitalist and nationalist circuits, although that is partly a concern. More importantly, *Tischtänzer* makes the point that critical practices in the aesthetic institution can activate an expressive force by means of which the difference between embodied and mediatic gesture is displayed. The museum gallery is not simply a reweaving of political or economic systems that are claimed to determine aesthetic practice, because the viewer's own movements are necessarily differentiated among the material displacements and network distributions that can allow theaters of consumption and politics to operate and to interoperate as art. The viewer's steps do not claim, "I dance the same old song and dance, too, the gallery is a militarized version of the department store." Instead, the viewer's legs *ask,* as von Huene does in his own writing, "What's wrong with art?" Rather than producing systematized information, then, the installation visitor produces a disruptive difference in the system of art exhibition. This inquiry, then, enacted in the difference between one's own steps in the gallery and the soft-shoe routine of the automata, is an ethical one about technicized expression. Navigation of the installation means diagramming its programmed potentiality, as one produces a dynamic display out of a static one by triggering a series of information events captured by the sensors as one passes through a gallery space that, by virtue of cheap commercial wireless technologies, becomes a hyperindustrial site of creative, observer-generated aesthetic value.

Consider, in this light, Sven König's more recent *sCrAmBlEd? HaCkZ!* (2005). For this project, König uses algorithms to divide audio recordings or music video by acoustic data, segmenting them into chunks like "notes" of different duration and timbre. These chunks are compiled and mapped in a database storing the resulting "cloud" of sound signatures. Inputting a sound signal into the database results in the resequencing of original sound samples matched to the input sound signal. Essentially, you are navigating a music-video database by speaking or singing into it, and the database outputs a stream of sound, recreating the sounds you have produced. It does not understand sound or song; it simply matches like sound signatures. This database "cloud" is made up of discrete bit-based sequences of logical value. It is addressable by logical instruction derived from any auditory input, such as your voice.

The samples remain, in his demonstration, attached to the bits of video with which they were originally synchronized, so that speaking or singing into the microphone will output a jerky montage of, say, Michael Jackson "saying" what you have said instead of what he was recorded saying. As König points out, vocal input becomes concrete sound poetry: *sCrAmBlEd? HaCkZ!* recapitulates the commonly made claim that cut-and-paste piracy is a distant offspring of the historical avant-gardes. In König's demonstration of the software, this poetry is mapped through the "star bodies" of transnational music production to make its point. Your vocalization is output as a cut-up of appearances or videos by Jackson, Adamski & Seal, M. C. Hammer, and Kurt Cobain or Nirvana, in which they seem to parrot back to you what you have said. The project can also be used as a performance instrument.

Copyright violation expresses personal memory retained in relation to global processes of media publicity. The "symbolic misery" Stiegler associates with transnational media programming closed to reuse or redefinition is transformed into the expression of concrete poetry for installation or DJ-based performance in nightclub settings. König's music machine can hardly compete with the more powerful programming of lip sync prototyped in the mid-1990s in *Video Rewrite: Photorealistic Synthetic Lip Sync* (see Chapter 1). But technical automation of media production processes is not the point. As König describes the project, the point is rather to put copyright infringement to work: to enunciate transnational popular musical memory synchronized in propertized musical data. *sCrAmBlEd? HaCkZ!* is "conceptual software" treating audio samples as concrete musical memory. For König, growing up as an MTV viewer, "the music and the video are inextricably linked" in personal memory. The choice of video material compiled in the database of samples is instructive of the concrete material making up König's musical memory matter: A recent Michael Jackson interview is demonstrated, probably from around 2005; otherwise, it is a 1990s revival: Hammer's 1990 "U Can't Touch This," Adamski & Seal's 1991 "Killer," and Nirvana's 1991 "Smells Like Teen Spirit." *sCrAmBlEd? HaCkZ!* is organized, then, as a conceptual mash-up not of sound and image but of copyright violation and interface design in a "mind music machine." Artistic strategy here aims at clarifying intellectual property laws and frameworks as discursive performativities: "*sCrAmBlEd? HaCkZ!* is the result of an effort to develop an artistic strategy that could shed some light on evident but very confusing problems of intellectual property. Intellectual property is a misconception deeply conflicting with the basic principles of any cultural production because it is completely negating its collaborative nature."[53]

In fact, though, there *is* a slight delay, giving the musical *gestus* a stuttering quality that König does not fully acknowledge in his explanation of the project. Localized, "good-enough" "real-time" utility upsets the dream of globalized music distribution as all-determining media event. But noticing this dissonant gesture, the stutter between vocal input as animating energy and audiovisual output as informatic montage, is crucial. *sCrAmBlEd? HaCkZ!* displays the propertized mediality of musical data in a disjunctive relation to the performer's voice. It contests the process of consumption of streaming media objects in transnational contexts by indexing those objects as archived cultural or personal memory, not simply in terms of logical technical memory. The stutter of the vocal input and the output of the musical sequence, a kind of anti-*karaoke gestus,* localizes "concrete" musical memories in a collaborative demonstration of biolabor. *sCrAmBlEd? HaCkZ!* argues against subjecting cultural or individual memory, cognition, or performance to digital-rights management. It presents an ethics of media by instrumentalizing the synchronized sound and image of musical commodities for "personal" vocal recall as database navigation. Its use from site to site—installation setting or club setting—means that its mediation of personhood and publicity is modulated: This, too, is a modal practice of digital media, where "symbolic misery" is turned into a musical exhibition of shared, if unfamiliar, memory.

Steina's (b. 1937) work also demonstrates an ethical, modal practice of audiovisual interaction, particularly in collaborative modes of production. Steina's work provides an exemplar for an ethical, often collaborative, questioning of that technocratic present tense that affords "participation" as a form of informal, unrecognized labor—and that often passes for aesthetic achievement, technical merit, or economic viability in digital media, installation art, or contemporary social media. Further, the ways in which Steina relates contemporary, bioinformatic nature to the bioenergetic processes that produce it teaches us to grasp bioinformatic temporality in relation not only to its histories but also to futures otherwise closed off by the determination of possibility as technological realization. Very often, Steina deploys musical instrumentalities to diagram contemporary conceptions of information in terms of more broadly historical processes whose exhibition suggests futures not yet made possible in terms of technology. Like von Huene, König, and the subjects of previous chapters, then, Steina masters the stylization of musical diagrams as media prototypes. And often, this diagrammatic musicality is given over not to relating the personhood of the user, observer, or audience to the digital production of publicity but to engaging a call and response with the complex streaming materialities of the complex world around us. Any notion of data simulation as self-generating or of "bodies in code"[54] is less important than a streaming ethics of interaction, where "interaction" means some complex, deeply entangled contact between action and transaction. What makes her work crucial to my purpose, then, is its engagement with the questions Haraway has developed at length since her 1985 "A Cyborg Manifesto: Science, Technology, and Socialist-Feminism in the Late Twentieth Century."[55] "Modeling" the world as a bioinformatic simulation relies on creating precomposed "tables" of database information that can be parametrically modulated. Von Huene critiques this "tabling" of aesthetic experience in *Tischtänzer* as the commoditization of aesthetic experience in cold war ideologies; König turns it into a "tabletop" hacking of musical media commodities in the interest of exhibiting and remixing shards of shared commoditized memory. Steina deploys musical instrumentalities to modulate interaction with such tables in its own right as a problem of action and transaction. Key instances of her work undertake musical diagramming of tabular media in terms close to what Haraway calls "a choreography of contact." These works take the form of trenchant interrogations of technology-as-ontology's hardened temporal framing.

In July 1998, veteran media artist Woody Vasulka exhibited a series of six cybernetic "tables" he titled *The Brotherhood.* As documented on the artist's Web site, the Daniel Langlois Foundation Web site, and in Nippon Telegraph and Telephone (NTT) videotapes of the event, Internet protocols as well as MIDI protocols provide the network architecture for the cybernetic machines; custom code was created to operate these machines using Internet access over Ethernet (local network). The operating system used is Linux, an open-source operating system.[56] Each of these hybrid object/image "tables" is outfitted with a combination of sensors, network technology, articulated sculptural elements, image projectors, and sound-producing capabilities.

The six robotic installations making up *The Brotherhood* have an intimate relationship with military and consumer genealogies of the digital technologies they repurpose. Each networked sculpture is conceived as a table, suggesting database tables, the tables of mathematics or chemistry, or allegorical *tableaux vivants.* They describe a range of responses to what is for Woody Vasulka an apparently essential relationship between heteromasculine identity, technological armament, and technologically determined estrangement or self-destruction. The tables incorporate numerous rejected or neglected technological hardware produced for war by U.S. firms, suggesting the interdependence between American technological progress and military prowess as well as the reuse of these technologies for critical artistic intervention. *The Brotherhood* thematizes the construction of heteromasculinity, then, as fraternal order by repurposing the technologies built in quest of the domination of nature:

> This [reorganization of nature] leads to conditions of polarization and antagonism in various social and philosophical stratifications. Foremost, it supports the male justification of warfare as an accepted and integral part of human evolution. Repeatedly it banishes all concepts of human utopia from its practices and in exchange, it offers male sexuality and its perilous values, most explicitly in form of threats, posturing and eventually in conduct of war. *The Brotherhood* does not argue for a reformist agenda or in a defense of male strategy. It stands sympathetically on his side, but it cannot resist an ironic glance at his clearly self-destructive identity.[57]

Woody Vasulka's tables deploy found hardware, including a plotting table, calibration devices, projection systems, portions of bombing devices, automatic data-writing machines, and other devices whose functions have been lost. Each table is an interactive image object hovering between energetic materiality and informatic computation (in regard to an earlier phase of *The Brotherhood,* Woody Vasulka describes the spatial construction itself as a dialectical struggle between "the real" and "the virtual").[58]

Table six, "The Maiden," is the only component featuring anything resembling a human form, and the form is specifically gendered female. This masculine construction of the female turns out to be a repurposed medical examination table outfitted with a skeletal articulation that appears to recline atop it. It can flop its feet, has arm-like limbs, and can lift and drop its head. A programmed sequence of movements has been prepared, with interactive systems driving the Maiden's movements, triggered, like *sCrAmBlEd? HaCkZ!* by audio signals that visitors to the installation speak into a microphone. The Maiden in particular, then, diagrams techno-scientific knowledges "enunciating" feminization as "hysterical" incorporation.

Viewer interactivity is via microphone but without specific rhetorical function on the level of object hierarchy, and so probably without producing immediately coherent "response" for the interactor. Rather than a programmatic mapping of sound-to-action-to-object, interaction is on a more general level of bodily gestural expression in vocal terms to animated networked action. One speaks musically—any change in pitch will do, apparently[59]—and the body of the cyborg Other moves. Here, the labor of synchronization is parametrical, but it is also denaturalized and generalized from being a question of instrumental control or production of lip sync. Further, the historical hardware and historicizing feminist critique built into *The Brotherhood* tend to work against that repetition identified by Rita Raley of "the same solitary, and sedentary, aesthetic" characterized in the "hollowness and emptiness of *Space Invaders*"[60] that is often risked in the tactical media projects she describes, despite their ethical and poetic achievements.

Raley's observation that tactical media attains "virtuosic" performance in the sense of Paulo Virno's description of activity finding its fulfillment without objectifying itself (29) may be productively reframed here. *The Brotherhood* radically objectifies heteromasculinity. Woody Vasulka stages virtuosity in his fulfillment of diagramming the divergence of the installation's historical composition and uses from the historical progression and resources on which it draws. In this sustained divergence, *The Brotherhood,* too, indicates a modal media practice, where the object experienced belongs as much to performance as to animated sculpture. Its critical dimensions arise in the virtuosity of the way it diverges from processes of material objectification. Collaborator David Dunn, in his text on Woody Vasulka's "electronic theaters," emphasizes the constraints of this staging of virtuosity in *The Brotherhood.* He notes that the installation prioritizes the material labor of the artist in relation to the art technological work and its functioning for the interactor, but, as Dunn puts it: "The role of the viewer is conceived to be altogether different, the audience is not readily invited to control the action like a video game and therefore enact a preconceived ritual of pseudo-interactivity. [Woody Vasulka's] environments remain autonomous with only a potential for perturbation by an intruder into their drama and therefore assert a specific kind of interaction: these are autonomous worlds that define their closure through their emergent language, forcing the spectator to swim in the intrinsic cultural code of the machine."[61]

From e-mail-coordinated processes undertaken between artist and curator, to computing protocols used in the machines themselves to project documentation, and to the composition of the *The Brotherhood* project using off-the-shelf, custom-built, open-source systems, "code" is as much memorial and cultural as it is contemporary and "protocological," in the sense developed by Alexander Galloway.[62] Drawing on a vast historical archive of culture and memory as code, *The Brotherhood* extends this "archive" to a national-industrial archaeology of hardware and to historical biosocial conditions typified by gendered, sexed identity. And although parts for *The Brotherhood* were gathered from surplus yards from Buffalo to Los Alamos to Los Angeles over decades, their deployment may have a critical, autobiographical, and memorial function as well: Woody Vasulka recalls playing with detritus dropped from warplanes during World War II as a child in what is now the Czech Republic.

The animated image objects of *The Brotherhood,* then, track the histories of bioinformatic construction back to the bioenergetic demands that prompted their contemporary derivation in bioinformatic terms. Too, the installation develops concerns earlier and extensively explored in now-canonical works of video art, such as Woody Vasulka's *Art of Memory* (1988): The aesthetic and cultural code programmed into these machines indexes the progression of both Vasulkas' interrogation of the video frame vis-à-vis the cinema frame since the 1970s. Intensively invested in "interaction" as a contemporary mediation of a larger historical array of programmed temporalities, *The Brotherhood* stages animated, networked, interactive sculpture in a virtuosic performance of "tactical media" diagramming complex relations of contemporary to historical time. The "syntaxes" of action explored here are those of extreme instrumentalization, bringing Woody Vasulka full circle, in Marita Sturken's view, in terms of autobiographical memory, heteromasculine identity, and the destructive expression of time.[63]

The staging of aesthetic research into material and computational incorporation in the tables of *The Brotherhood* suggests aesthetic fabrication and action in ways resonant with Haraway's discussion of "situated knowledges." Haraway's concern with the cyborg ultimately suggests more open-ended possibilities for intervention into the technological domination of "natureculture" or "material-semiotic" processes: As Haraway famously puts it, "only a cyborg has a chance": "This world-as-code is, just for starters, a high-tech military field, a kind of automated academic battlefield, where blips of light called players disintegrate (what a metaphor!) each other to stay in the knowledge and power game. Techno-science and science fiction collapse into the sun of their radiant (ir)reality—war."[64]

For Haraway, in spite of the great mobilities and fluxes enabled in informatic epistemologies, their standardization reflects their debts to patriarchy (168). Because such mobilities are possible only once a higher standard is in place and so already implies the prior work of marginalization, violence, or trauma, Haraway suggests "situated knowledges"—partial visions whose self-avowed limits ensure that objectivity ensues only through the avowed interconnectedness of those knowledges being situated (instead of self-generating systems). This notion of interconnectedness is, again, more recently elaborated in terms of "choreographies of contact" in which citizen activists collaborate with scholars to intervene in the biocapitalist propertization of genomic data, as we have seen in *When Species Meet.* Where Haraway has worked out a mesh of situated knowledges as "choreographies of contact," *The Brotherhood* suggests the staging of a sited hermeneutic that is subject to modulation.

Steina's July 1998 performance of *The Brotherhood* pushes Woody Vasulka's staging of material-informatic object networks into a "choreography of contact." They configure her MIDI violin to control the tables' movements in response to her musical gestures, thus animating and modulating *The Brotherhood*'s complex historicity. As if resisting her commands, a harsh concrete music of machine noise results as the tables begin to move. A shell-like contraption spreads and contracts, as if a fan or an accordion—a physical, animated, musical icon for Aphrodite, perhaps. Even more dramatic are the movements of the Maiden's skeletal armature, jerking in fits and starts to the gestures communicated from the violin. Meanwhile, on a video projection screen, a man, clearly suffering the psychic pain of something like hysterical amnesia, addresses the audience, muttering or shouting words that make sense only to him. The video frame places him within an institution cell of some sort, as if he is modularly isolated and confined, his movements and speech subject to manipulation as if through object-oriented programming. "I know who I am," he cries. "Tell me who I am!" Steina stands off to the side of the stage, to the audience's left, dressed in black, as if invoking a feminist Paganini puppeting the tableau of cyborg sculptures as live performance instead of expressing the ecstatic or tortured interior of the romantic listener.

After Manfred Clynes's[65] formulation of the cyborg as a prosthetic evolution necessary for travel to distant stars, Haraway's influential treatment[66] was a determinedly ironic reworking of Clynes's original suggestion: the cyborg as "ironic allegory" of feminist socialist engagements with "the informatics of domination." Margaret Morse[67] and N. Katherine Hayles[68] each extend the treatment of the cyborg. Hayles suggests that the instant that you notice your subjectivity bound up in the interactive feedback loop of the digital instrument, your subjectivity becomes "cyborg." Morse, on the other hand, takes a more suspicious stance: "What does a cyborg eat?" she asks, surveying the "smartfood" culture of the mid-1990s (144–145). For Morse, the cyborg is more ironic symptom than ironic allegory of resistance. At issue is rather the way the interface, imagined to produce bodies not requiring actual sustenance, produces immersive experiences that drown the body out.

In her response to Char Davies's influential virtual reality installation *Osmose* (1995), Morse describes the installation's use of a harness tracking the user's breaths for upward or downward navigation as generating the corporeal threat of suffocation. *Osmose*'s successful exhibition of corporeal "immersion" in simulated data space causes Morse to experience the memory of her own asthma. Rather than a sense of immersion in computationally plastic, navigable, naturalized "virtual space," she experiences the fear of drowning—panic resulted from the symbolic power of the breath-tracking display.[69] Perhaps *Osmose* insufficiently historicizes its technical innovations; the notion of "navigating" by breath gesture suggests the bioenergetic nineteenth-century pneumograph but outfitted for virtual reality. The promise of a rhythmic "breath gesture" also recalls the "breath gesture" Eisenstein claims to have composed with Sergei Prokofiev in *Alexander Nevsky* (1938; see Chapter 2).

Yet such a breath gesture, whether bioenergetic or bioinformatic, is biolabor: Whether Eisenstein's or Davies's breath gesture, each has as its larger motivation what Haraway calls the "apparatus of bodily production"—the construction of corporealities in material-semiotic terms in biocapital.[70] As Steina composes the Maiden to the video image of institutionalized "Man" in a "love duet," she reveals the deeply productive, if often profoundly depersonalizing, generativity of bioenergetic and bioinformatic logics as biolabor. Musical gesture originating in the affordances of the musical instrument is applied to the staging of hysterical man's creation of hysterical maiden. The gestures by which Steina animates this "love duet" become a complex and dynamic emblem of the conjunction and disjunction producing personhood and publicity in the transition of bioenergetic to bioinformatic capital.

Steina's noisy performance is virtuosic, then, in a way that is different from Woody's virtuosic installation staging. Her performance of the Maiden is configured for remote control by live violin rather than by voice. And her performance recalls and modulates her own long practice of using the gestural form factors or musical sound of the violin-as-interface, dating back to the age of laserdisc in such works as *Violin Power* (numerous versions). Steina's performance, then, deploys the musical instrumentalities of the MIDI violin within a long-sustained modal media practice to effect historiographical, critical, autobiographical narration as musical play. As we have seen, such films as *Passing Through* (1977; see Chapter 5) and *Hedwig and the Angry Inch* (2001; see Chapter 6) similarly accomplish layered modes of narration and musical play by deploying pragmatics of synchronization in which historical invisibility is diagrammed as powerfully informing affect. Seen in the same light, Steina's performance of *The Brotherhood* becomes legible as a neglected chapter of feminist cyborg theory, but rather than in critical text in the virtuosic tactical performance of biolabor: material, technical, and affective labor placed into complete historical relation and made palpable.

The use of the violin as interpretive device here, too, mediates not simply the memory of a romantic performing artist but also the memory of the nineteenth-century inventor. As David Hounshell observes, nineteenth-century telegraph pioneer Elisha Gray discovered the possibility of musical telegraphy, multiplex telegraphy, and voice telegraphy by attaching an electric current to, first, the body of a bathtub (noticed during his nephew's play "taking shocks" with his electrical conducting materials) and then to the body of a violin.[71] This latter configuration of the violin body as resounding receiver of electric current was publicly demonstrated, Hounshell notes. Gray's inventions inspired a contest for patents on telephonic voice conduction with Alexander Graham Bell and his backers, resulting in a settlement separating the telephony and telegraphy industries. Steina composes her love duet using the software-authoring package Image/ine, whose graphical interface allows for the mapping and filtering of one stream of data to another. Navigating data using MIDI instruments modulates informatic simulation in and as media performance rather than deploying an energetic model of harmonic series for telecommunications. In Steina's hands, then, the MIDI violin reverses the historical relationship of heteromasculine identifications with technological control of time and space that Woody Vasulka indicates as the thematic content of *The Brotherhood.*

Steina's performance of Woody's staging of *The Brotherhood* presents a "sound figure" for her audience. History adds up, but differently: The hystericization of heterofeminine bodies modeled as violins is revealed to be a projection of the unreason of heteromasculine logics seeking to contain the world as model. If irony tends to return the critical gesture toward its own sublimation within dominant subjectivities, in this case, an ironic instrumentation of musical gesture circulating through the cyborg tableau and placing it within a historical stream it denies nonetheless holds surprising power to provide that for which artist Stelarc claims there is no more time: "the meditative moment."[72]

Steina's work routinely deploys musicality to diagram ways around the epistemological endgames of subject or object, monad or dialectic, observer or observed that often trouble descriptions of informatic objects as autonomous ends in their own right, whether the supposedly self-generating systems of finance, military automata, or tactical media simulations. Generally, musicality provides means for introducing a dimension of temporality into the sited hermeneutic that itself is dynamized in historical relation as a result. The result is a modal, autobiographical aesthetic faction—fabrication and action—of the real.

A final example of her work may provide a historical diagram for contemporary studies of the interactive, audiovisual, computational, networked interface. Steina's *Voice Windows* was made in collaboration with performance artist Joan La Barbara, and it anticipates the choreography of contact toward which Haraway has moved. It presents an orchestration of the audiovisual display as traveling sound and image, animated in a call-and-response between vocal performance (La Barbara) and video production (Steina). Steina captures the perspective from a moving car as it travels out of a southwestern U.S. city toward the desert, and La Barbara records a facsimile of birdsong. La Barbara's warbles and melodies, her chatter and calls, are transformed, using frequency analysis, into a dynamic video-matte, jumping and scattering across the screen. The dynamic vocal-matte, synchronized to the sound of La Barbara's voice, begins as bar lines keyed over a pure black screen, then over the city through which the viewer moves. The energetic image of the moving panorama, suggesting movement in immersive space, is filtered with the voice of birdsong provided by La Barbara (who remains invisible). Where the dynamic shapes of the frequency analysis are matted into the frame of the city, we see through to the background scene "behind" it: a desert landscape. Animality as vox establishes the location toward which we are traveling, but as the background of where we already are: We are displaced from, but head toward, the "natural habitat" of the "bird" whose voice we "see through." Dynamic locale is personified in an animal vox cutting through the panoramic image, even as our location is displaced from belonging either to the human or the technical. Animal vox touches human movement, but in a dynamic mutual displacement of moving sound and moving image from one another and visualized through the complex apparatus.

The process at work in the matting of landscapes belongs to the practice of listening: The ear picks up many sounds at once, and only if their frequencies coincide does a nearer or louder sound mask a more distant or softer sound. The process at work in the visualization of the audio and the framing of the two layers of moving imagery, though, belongs to practices of seeing. And as the practice of listening is applied to those of seeing, we are moved through not only two different landscapes but also two different senses. The source of the sound is never certain—so the disembodied omnipresent birdsong is more powerful as an evocation or a message that can join one world with another. *Voice Windows* is a rendition of sight interrupted by the sound for which sight strains. What is exhibited, then, are two overlapping but distinct sensoria at once, at least when the birdsong is audible and visible. Musicality gives a historical temporality to the heterogeneity of overlapping sensory worlds made legible in song's tension with moving image as speech. To return to the concerns with which I begin this chapter, then, *Voice Windows* is a temporal diagram tracking vox in flight from the house of technology-as-language, from the historical apparatus where technology becomes ontology. *Voice Windows* suggests that "interaction" begins when the displacing tendencies of apparatuses of technological production become graspable, developmental, and subject to use rather than when they become "natural" as technicized ontology.

Musical diagramming, then, provides critical modes of making action possible. The production of temporality as fiction, whereby a symbolic epistemology is programmed to the ontic materiality to accumulate risk while averting the improbable or the indeterminable, this unhitching of rhythmic diachrony in favor of technicized reason is a form of play: the capture and modulation of the doubled immanence of monadological univocity and dialectical progression. This means that if the instrumentalization of reason proceeds through the automation of judgment and the production of symbolic misery, it is also accompanied by an instrumentalization of temporality whose ethical figure is play as complex time—and very often, musical play. Play in this musical sense is the differential instrumentality, the "certain ratio" not reducible to the instrumentality of techno-scientific reason.

Musical instrumentalities of rhythm or melody—that is, discrete or continuous change in time—allows the subject of play time to learn, and so, rather than simply imposing a miserable experience of being out of diachronic time, allows a critical and affecting, rather than miserable, experience of being out of media time. The musical diagrams I have presented here combine the heterogeneous historical capacities of automaton with the visualization practices associated with the nineteenth-century Chladni figure, whereby a small pile of sand forms a harmonious visual pattern when activated with musical vibrations: the instrumentation and revelation of unseen patterns of living energy in a working, moving model. Since Bloch's time, such temporal diagrams have become deeply instrumental rather than "merely" rhetorical; routinely produced as tertiary temporal objects, they now crystallize a third mode of synthesis: the active reception of the dynamic audio-visual-gestural diagram that is the media as interface. Musical diagramming of "monadic" and "dialectic" potential animating exteriorization and interiorization underlies the ways we grasp the hieroglyphic time of a techno-political world. The worlds we live in, to some degree, change in accordance with the temporal models we diagram in time, but temporal nature also returns to destroy the instrumentalities we form.

From Eisenstein, Fischinger, and Eisler, or Clark, Mitchell, and Steina, the "play" of doubled potential has allowed historical, futural, and present temporalities to be exhibited in terms of the pathos of trauma, ecstatic continuity, or critical contemporary distance. Steina's virtuosic tactical musical diagramming continues and compounds such attempts to now function as a historical exemplar critical for the contemporary stylization of the interface as idiom.

The efficacy of this displacement makes it possible for "the technical tendency" to operate as the generalized mediality of a political and social dominant *and* as the remediation of the effects of that dominant: digital epochality and its new medium. If bioenergetic materialism exhausts the bodies of workers and bioinformatic materialisms exhaust their minds, musical instrumentalities allow an opening for play in terms of material labor, technical operation, and affective labor. Instrumentalizing the instrumentalities of techno-scientific reason in a musical ratio of affect and ensemble reopens media time to that diachronicity that gives it its ipseity while relating to its audience a play of style and idiom allowing us to diagram lived, but illegible, hieroglyphic time.

In diagramming hieroglyphic time as musical play revealing energetic and informatic biolabor, we find the resources marshaled in hyperindustrialism and distributed in biocapital. The works I have discussed, as well as those of many more critics or artists, provide critical exemplars for medial ethics. By situating the hermeneutics of data modeling in a complex relation to the historical time that has called it, perhaps we can avoid being destroyed ourselves, even as we inevitably allow less useful models of information as immanence to be swept away as a memory of so much cognitive rubble. To be sustained, to sustain in the face of the disappearing world and the appearance of unknown bodies: The musical diagrams of interactions with hieroglyphic time I present in *Sync* suggest that interfacial composition and reception may be acts of love in a time of destruction. In this time, we are concerned not with the interface as a site where bodies are encoded in binary digits but with the interface as a site of historical, contemporary, and futural synthesis. Sustaining this instrument is beyond the capacity of the networked computer or the persistently networked mass; the diagram is less than and more than, before and after, the program. Yet perhaps with instruments invented through the faction of the aesthetic, we shall realize the computer is a part of our loving destruction. Grasping this temporalizing instrumentality, we may deprivilege the apparatus separating bioinformatic nature from its bioenergetic history and determining lived time as a hieroglyph where the technological realization of possibility displaces futural duration. This other instrumentality will foreground, instead, those processes of biolabor in which temporal nature arises—and will continue to naturalize itself.

Notes

CHAPTER 1

1. Michael Cowan, "The Heart Machine: 'Rhythm' and Body in Weimar Film and Fritz Lang's *Metropolis,*" *Modernism/Modernity* 14, no. 2 (2007): 225–248.

2. For discussion of *Metropolis* and aesthetic modernisms, see Andreas Huyssen, *After the Great Divide: Modernism, Mass Culture, Postmodernism* (Bloomington: Indiana University Press, 1986), 65–81; for *Metropolis* in terms of modernity, spectacle, and technological distance, see J. P. Telotte, *A Distant Technology: Science Fiction Film and the Machine Age* (Hanover, NH: University Press of New England for Wesleyan University Press, 1999), 47–71; for *Metropolis*'s gendered, anatomical gaze, see Allison Defren, "The Anatomical Gaze in *Tomorrow's Eve,*" *Science Fiction Studies* 36, no. 108 (2009): 235–265.

3. Christian Hite, "Eating Machine: Discipline, Digestion, and Depression-Era Gesticulation in Chaplin's *Modern Times,*" *Spectator* 21, no. 2 (2001): 40–55.

4. Rick Altman, McGraw Jones, and Sonia Tatroe, "Inventing the Cinema Soundtrack: Hollywood's Multiplane Sound System," in *Music and Cinema,* ed. James Buhler, Caryl Flinn, and David Neumeyer (Hanover, NH: University Press of New England for Wesleyan University Press, 2000), 341.

5. Rick Altman, "Moving Image, Moving Target," *Music, Sound, and the Moving Image* 1, no. 1 (2007): 5–8.

6. Emily Thompson, *The Soundscape of Modernity: Architectural Acoustics and the Culture of Listening in America, 1900–1933* (Cambridge, MA: MIT Press, 2002), 295–316.

7. See Altman, Jones, and Tatroe, "Inventing the Cinema Soundtrack"; and Helen Hanson, "Sound Affects: Post-Production Sound, Soundscapes and Sound Design in Hollywood's Studio Era," *Music, Sound, and the Moving Image* 1, no. 1 (2007): 27–49.

8. Michel Chion, *Audio-Vision: Sound on Screen* (New York: Columbia University Press, [1990] 1994), 113.

9. Jean-Louis Comolli, "Machines of the Visible," in *Electronic Culture: Technology and Visual Representation,* ed. Timothy Druckery (New York: Aperture, 1980), 108–117.

10. Martin Jay, *Downcast Eyes: The Denigration of Vision in Twentieth-Century French Thought* (Berkeley: University of California Press, 1994), 484.

11. Friedrich Kittler, *Gramophone, Film, Typewriter,* trans. Geoffrey Winthrop Young and Michael Wutz (Palo Alto, CA: Stanford University Press, [1986] 1999); and Friedrich Kittler, *Discourse Networks, 1800/1900,* trans. Michael Meteer (Palo Alto, CA: Stanford University Press, [1985] 1990).

12. Charles Altieri, *The Particulars of Rapture: An Aesthetics of the Affects* (Ithaca: Cornell University Press, 2003).

13. See Felix Guattari, *The Anti-Oedipus Papers* (Cambridge, MA: MIT Press, 2006), 415; and see note 41, Chapter 5, herein.

14. See especially Gilles Deleuze and Felix Guattari, *Capitalism and Schizophrenia, Vol. 1: Anti-Oedipus,* trans. Robert Hurley, Mark Seem, and Helen R. Lane (Minneapolis: University of Minnesota Press, [1972] [1977] 1983); and Gilles Deleuze and Felix Guattari, *Capitalism and Schizophrenia, Vol. 2: A Thousand Plateaus,* trans. Brian Massumi (Minneapolis: University of Minnesota Press, [1980] 1987). See also Guattari's notes collected in *The Anti-Oedipus Papers.*

15. Here I am referencing the manuscript version of Sobchack's September 2005 talk at New York University and gratefully acknowledge her for providing an electronic draft of it. See also Vivian Sobchack, "Final Fantasies: Computer Graphic Animation and the [Dis]Illusion of Life," in *Animated "Worlds,"* ed. Susan Buchan (Eastleigh, U.K.: John Libbey, 2006), 171–182.

16. Vivian Sobchack, "Final Fantasies: Computer Graphic Animation and the [Dis] Illusion of Life" (presentation at New York University, 2005), 10–15, manuscript version.

17. See Stephen Prince, "True Lies: Perceptual Realism, Digital Images, and Film Theory," *Film Quarterly* 49, no. 3 (Spring 1996): 27–37.

18. Barbara Stafford, *Echo Objects: The Cognitive Work of Images* (Chicago: University of Chicago Press, 2007).

19. And see my discussion in Chapter 2.

20. Sergei Eisenstein, "Dickens, Griffith, and the Film Today," in *Film Form [and] the Film Sense,* ed. and trans. Jay Leyda (New York: Meridian, [1944] 1957), 235. See also the more recent translation in Sergei Eisenstein, "Dickens, Griffith, and Ourselves," trans. Michael Glenny, in *Selected Works Vol. 3: Writings, 1934–1947,* ed. Richard Taylor (London: BFI, 1996), 193–238.

21. Collected as "Vertical Montage" in Sergei Eisenstein, *Selected Works Vol. 2: Towards a Theory of Montage,* ed. Richard Taylor and Michael Glenny (London: BFI, 1994), 327–399.

22. Sergei Eisenstein, "Synchronization of Senses," in *Film Form [and] the Film Sense,* 88. Additional citations here are also from the Leyda edition.

23. Eisenstein, "Dickens, Griffith, and the Film Today," 235.

24. Eisenstein's citations of Whitman imply that what he is after in streaming montage beg a treatment of Whitman rather than Griffith; Eisenstein, "Dickens, Griffith, and the Film Today," 231.

25. See Gilles Deleuze, *Bergsonism* (New York: Zone Books, [1966] 1991), for a useful, widely consulted introductory summary.

26. See Michael Hardt, "Affective Labor," *Boundary 2* 26, no. 2 (1999): 89–100, for a treatment of affective labor in post-Fordist production networks.

27. James Tobias, "Cinema, Scored: Towards a Comparative Methodology for Music in Media," *Film Quarterly* 57, no. 2 (Winter 2003–2004): 26–36.

28. Vuillermoz, quoted in Richard Abel, ed., *French Film Theory and Criticism: Volume 1, 1907–1939* (Princeton, NJ: Princeton University Press, 1988), 131 (emphasis added).

29. See Lev Manovich, *The Language of New Media* (Cambridge, MA: MIT Press, 2001), 47; and see D. N. Rodowick's critique of Manovich in *The Virtual Life of Film* (Cambridge, MA: Harvard University Press, 2007), 175–177.

30. Carl Beier, Jr., "A New Way of Looking at Things," *Hollywood Quarterly* 2, no. 1 (October 1946): 1–10.

31. Leyda's 1957 bibliography of Eisenstein's writings in English indicates the broad dissemination of the director's writings and interviews in English by 1946, so some adaptation of the Soviet director's ideas may be in evidence in Beier's proposal.

32. Beier, "A New Way of Looking at Things," 2.

33. Eisenstein, "Dickens, Griffith, and the Film Today," 244.

34. See the discussion of Yutkevich and Eisenstein in Chapter 2.

35. The U.S. television industry followed the model that Lynn Spiegel outlines in her 1992 study of televisual flow and suburban sprawl, in part influenced by official or de facto segregationist housing policies. In addition, creative responsibility in U.S. television has tended to lie with producing roles rather than directing roles, which frequently change in episodic television.

36. See my discussion in Chapter 3.

37. A digitized version of *Jammin' the Blues* may be viewed at www.dailymotion.com/video/xngw7_jammin-the-blues-by-gjon-mili-1944_music (accessed December 31, 2008).

38. Arthur Knight, "*Jammin' the Blues*, or the Sight of Jazz, 1944," in *Representing Jazz*, ed. Krin Gabbard (Durham, NC: Duke University Press, 1995), 11–53.

39. The approximately ten-minute length of the film comes close to approximating the quarter-hour programming slots that radio broadcasting had programmed using large-format transcription discs since the late 1920s and that had grown by the mid-1930s to a large programming and library business, with important facilities and distributors located in Los Angeles (who tended to regard network broadcasters as monopolistic). Since the 1920s, those same quarter-hour discs had also been used on Hollywood soundstages for synchronizing performers' movements to musical playback.

40. Clora Bryant, "Clora Bryant," in *Central Avenue Sounds Jazz in Los Angeles*, ed. Steven Isoardi (Berkeley: University of California Press, 1998), 357.

41. Horace Tapscott, "The East Side at High Tide," in Isoardi, *Central Avenue Sounds Jazz in Los Angeles*, 299.

42. Paul Gilroy, *The Black Atlantic: Modernity and Double Consciousness* (London: Verso, 1993).

43. For the ways in which the politics of information during the blacklist era were allegorized on screen in terms of confessions of information, see Jeff Smith, "*The Robe* as Anti-Fascist Allegory," in *Un-American Hollywood: Politics and Film in the Blacklist Era*, ed. Frank Krutnik, Steve Neale, Brian Neve, and Peter Stanfield (Piscataway, NJ: Rutgers University Press, 2007), 24.

44. Oskar Fischinger, "True Creation," available at the Web site of the Fischinger Trust and Archive, www.oskarfischinger.org/True%20Creation.html (accessed February 2009).

45. David James, *The Most Typical Avant-Garde: History and Geography of Minor Cinemas in Los Angeles* (Berkeley: University of California Press, 2005).

46. Archival documents of the production budget of his Rockefeller grant show that he hired a conductor when recording the scores he composed; the films and film fragments, of course, had been directed by sympathetic colleagues, such as Joseph Losey, whose *A Child Went Forth* [*The Children's Camp*] Eisler rescored as part of his Film Music Project.

47. Alfred North Whitehead, *Science and the Modern World* (New York: Mentor Books, [1927] 1948), 20–39.

48. William Moritz, *Optical Poetry: The Life and Work of Oskar Fischinger* (Bloomington: Indiana University Press, 2004), 137–147; and see Chapter 3 herein.

49. Examples of a range of prototypes designed by Mountford's team, which included Geoff Smith, Andrew Herniak, Amy Evans, Leo Villareal, and others, were demonstrated in Palo Alto, California, and London in late 1994 and in 1995.

50. Christopher Bregler, Malcolm Slaney, and Michele Covell, "Video Rewrite: Driving Visual Speech with Audio," in *Proceedings of SiGGRAPH 97* (New York: ACM Press, 1997), 353–360.

51. See Antonio Negri, *Marx beyond Marx: Lessons on the Grundrisse* (New York: Autonomedia, 1991), 21–40.

52. See Deleuze, *Foucault*, trans. Seán Hand (Minneapolis: University of Minnesota Press, [1986] 1988), 1–22.

53. James Elkins, *Six Stories from the End of Representation: Images in Painting, Photography, Astronomy, Microscopy, Particle Physics, and Quantum Mechanics 1980–2000* (Palo Alto, CA: Stanford University Press, 2008).

CHAPTER 2

1. Sergei M. Eisenstein, *Nonindifferent Nature: Film and the Structure of Things*, trans. Herbert Marshall (Cambridge: Cambridge University Press, 1987).

2. Gilles Deleuze, *Cinema 1: The Movement-Image*, trans. Hugh Tomlinson and Barbara Habberjam (Minneapolis: Minnesota University Press, [1983] 1986), 32–40; and, Gilles Deleuze, *Cinema 2: The Time-Image*, trans. Hugh Tomlinson and Robert Galeta (Minneapolis: University of Minnesota Press, [1985] 1989), 157–163.

3. The statement on contrapuntal sound, for example, indicates the ways in which Eisenstein and his fellow *montageurs* understood the "coming of sound" not in terms of a straightforward introduction of new cinema technology but as a broadening of expressive potential for montage expression. See Sergei Eisenstein, Vsevolod Pudovkin, and Grigori Alexandrov, "Statement on Sound" [1928], trans. Richard Taylor, in *Film Theory and Criticism*, 6th ed., ed. Leo Braudy and Marshall Cohen (Oxford: Oxford University Press, 2004), 370–372.

4. Cf. in this regard Mary Anne Doane's understanding of "cinematic time" as both probabilistic and narratological; and see Chapter 5.

5. Walter Benjamin, "Moscow," in *Selected Works*, vol. 2, trans. Rodney Livingstone et al. (Cambridge, MA: Harvard University Press, 1999), 41. The trial in question was that of a peasant woman charged with medical misconduct resulting in a mother's death. She received a two-year sentence, followed by dramatic and pedagogical pronouncements of the need to build hygiene centers in rural areas.

6. Benjamin, "Introductory Remarks on a Series for L'Humanité," in *Selected Works*, 2:21.

7. Benjamin, "Reply to Oscar A. H. Schmitz," in *Selected Works*, 2:17.

8. Benjamin, "Moscow," 30.

9. Benjamin, "Reply to Oscar A. H. Schmitz," 18.

10. Benjamin notes in "Moscow" that with the proletariat class "protected" by the caste dictatorship of the party, "message and subject matter are of primary importance" (38). Everyday buildings, factories—the built, modern *milieu*—were "hopelessly sad" for Benjamin ("Reply to Oscar A. H. Schmitz," 17). See also Max Pensky, *Melancholy Dialectics: Walter Benjamin and the Play of Mourning* (Amherst: University of Massachusetts Press, 1993), for a discussion of Benjamin's aesthetic dialectics as melancholia. Graham Greene addresses the matter of national-imperial melancholia with regards to Eisenstein's exuberantly violent affect in *October* (1928) in a March 27, 1936, review in the *Spectator*, comparing *October* to Berthold Viertel's *Rhodes of Africa* (1936): "After ten days I can remember very little of [*Rhodes of Africa*] but a sense of gentle titillation, of being scratched agreeably in the right spot. But the talkies have come, and stereoscopy and colour no doubt will come, without destroying the vivid memories of *October*" (which screened at the London Film Society in 1934). Its mass movements recalling *Potemkin*'s massacre on the steps, the vivid impressions that "only a participant would have thought of presenting," its playing revolution for comedy—Rhodes's "Cape to Cairo" ambitions are presented on film with no such "air of happiness": "Now as an Empire we are too old, the pride isn't there, the heart seems to have failed once too often." Collected in Graham Greene, *The Graham Greene Film Reader: Reviews, Essays, Interviews, and Film Stories*, ed. David Parkinson (New York: Applause Theater Book Publishers, 1994), 86–88. Greene sees the Soviet revolution as openly imperial but ecstatic in its vigorous transvaluation of icons of power. Technological progress—stereoscopy, color—bores him in their inevitability.

11. Bernard Stiegler, *La technique et le temps: 3. Le temps du cinéma et la question du mal-être* (Paris: Galilée, 2001), 30; a citation from Eisenstein provides an epigraph orienting this volume of Stiegler's work.

12. In part, the need to configure a critical logic of medial succession is a legacy of Karl Marx's determination of technology as an expression of objectified material labor and creative or interpretive labor—that is, affective labor—as symptoms of the ideological superstructures within which labor power is objectified (and in Benjamin, whether by capitalist or socialist authoritarianisms).

13. See, for example, the studies by Annette Michelson or David Bordwell cited below.

14. Portions were published in the Leyda editions as "Synchronization of Senses."

15. Sergei Eisenstein, "Vertical Montage," in *Selected Works Volume 2: Towards a Theory of Montage*, ed. Richard Taylor and Michael Glenny, trans. Michael Glenny (London: BFI, [1939] 1994), 327–399, esp. 398.

16. Eisenstein also perhaps helps Eisler distance himself from charges of being a Soviet agent that were leveled against him at the time *Composing for the Films* (New York: Oxford University Press, 1947) was published; Graham McCann's introduction to *Composing* notes that Adorno removed his name from the book partly for this reason.

17. Christian Metz, *Film Language: A Semiotics of the Cinema* (Oxford: Oxford University Press, [1968] 1974), 36–37.

18. Peter Wollen, *Signs and Meaning in the Cinema* (Bloomington: Indiana University Press, 1972).

19. Tom Gunning, "The Cinema of Attractions: Early Cinema, Its Spectator, and the Avant-Garde," in *Early Cinema: Frame, Space, Narrative*, ed. Thomas Elsaesser (London: BFI, 1990), 56–60; and see the summary in David Bordwell, *On the History of Film Style* (Cambridge, MA: Harvard University Press, 1997), 125–128.

20. Marc Davis, "Media Streams: Representing Video for Retrieval and Repurposing" (Ph.D. diss., MIT, 1995).

21. Nicholas Cook, *Analyzing Musical Multimedia* (Oxford: Oxford University Press, 1998).

22. Marsha Kinder, "Screen Wars: Transmedia Appropriations from Eisenstein to *A TV Dante* and Carmen Sandiego," in *Language Machines: Technologies of Literary and Cultural Production,* ed. Jeffrey Masten, Peter Stallybrass, and Nancy Vickers (New York: Routledge, 1997), 160–182.

23. Henry Jenkins, *Textual Poachers: Television Fans and Participatory Culture* (New York: Routledge, 1992).

24. As Davis explains in a later article, "current cultural practices of re-purposing popular media give us a glimpse of how people might use computational media in their daily lives if video sequences could be quickly and easily assembled, retrieved, processed, and transmitted like dolphins sending and receiving their sonar 'movies' or like the conversations of people raised to use computational video as a mother tongue." Davis, "Garage Cinema and the Future of Media Technology," *Communications of the ACM* 40, no. 2 (1997): 42–48, esp. 46. Video computing software might transform media audiences into a "landscape of ubiquitous participatory video" (46–47), whose early signal instances he thinks include *America's Funniest Home Videos,* the Rodney King videotape, and video karaoke bars.

25. Kinder, "Screen Wars," 160–161.

26. She writes, "By now it should be clear . . . that this essay reflexively traces the trajectory of my own career, which began . . . with an essay on [Henry] Fielding's experimentation in the theater in relation to his novels, and then turned in succession through an ongoing process of 'promiscuous' analogic thinking to movies, television, video games, CD-ROMs, and other forms of popular culture" (180).

27. Sergei Eisenstein, "P-R-K-F-V," in *Sergei Eisenstein: Notes of a Film Director,* trans. X Danko (Moscow: Foreign Language Publishing House, 1959), 149–167. If each piece of "representation" has its own internal "canons," so does Prokofiev. Eisenstein says that the composer "listens and hears" something "within himself" (158), which turns out to be a "profoundly national" and "international" character (165), "Byzantine," that has his proper "place amid microphones, klieg lights, celluloid spirals of film, the faultless accuracy of the meshing sprockets of synchronization, and mathematical calculations of length in film montage" (166). Eisenstein routinely made similar claims, mingling contemporary cultural labor with distant art-historical references for his own work. His general point is that the two artists share historical orientations and occupy the same laboring order, but further are bound in some suprahistorical temporality to one another, toward mutual being in time mediated and registered as temporal diagrams—of which one is the rhythmic audiovisual montage of *Alexander Nevsky* (155).

28. For a discussion of Eisenstein's concept of the "spherical book," see Oksana Bulgakowa, "Eisenstein, the Glass House and the Spherical Book: From the Comedy of the Eye to a Drama of Enlightenment," *Rouge* 7 (2005), available at www.rouge.com.au/7/eisenstein .html (accessed October 31, 2006).

29. Kinder in conversation (July 21, 2008) cites additional CD-ROMs from the period aiming at a similar effect, such as *Scrutiny in the Great Round,* which uses QuickTime VR less for perspectival navigation of a panoramic, quasi-immersive landscape than for the presentation of navigable hypertext data.

30. Barbara Stafford, *Echo Objects: The Cognitive Work of Images* (Chicago: University of Chicago Press, 2007).

31. Stafford, *Echo Objects*, 84. Stafford's strong cognitivist-realist reading of Eisenstein's montage as a diagrammatic emblem event unifying audiences does not account for the historical range of interpretations I have surveyed here; see also the suggestion, in regards to *¡Que Viva Mexico!*, that Eisenstein's corpus generally may be taken as a "multitextual" production open to historical reeditioning. Barbara Evans Bixby, "The Weave of the Serape: Sergei Eisenstein's '¡Que Viva Mexico!' as a Multitext" (Ph.D. diss., University of Florida, 1979).

32. See Russell Merritt, "Recharging Alexander Nevsky," *Film Quarterly* 48, no. 2 (Winter 1994–1995): 34–47. On correspondences, see also Eisenstein, "Vertical Montage," 378.

33. See, for example, Karl Marx, *Grundrisse: A Contribution to the Critique of Political Economy*, trans. Maurice Dobb (Moscow: Progress, [1859] 1970).

34. Sergei Eisenstein, *Beyond the Stars: The Memoirs of Sergei Eisenstein; Selected Writings*, vol. 4, ed. Richard Taylor, trans. Michael Powell (London: BFI, 1995), 589.

35. Prokofiev was also said by his wife to have had "homosexual tendencies"; and see note 27, indicating the ways in which Eisenstein in effect made Prokofiev's sensibilities into a profoundly patriotic aesthetic trait.

36. On the energetics of human bodies and industrial machines around the problem of fatigue, see Anson Rabinbach, *The Human Motor* (Berkeley: University of California Press, 1990).

37. On postgenomic bioinformatic corporeal ethics, see Nikolas Rose, *The Politics of Life Itself: Biomedicine, Power, and Subjectivity in the Twenty-first Century* (Princeton, NJ: Princeton University Press, 2006).

38. N. Katherine Hayles, *How We Became Posthuman: Virtual Bodies in Cybernetics, Literature, and Informatics* (Chicago: University of Chicago Press, 1998).

39. See Deleuze, *Cinema 2*, for his account of the "spiritual automaton" in cinema; and Gilles Deleuze, *Spinoza: Expressionism in Philosophy*, trans. Martin Joughin (New York: Zone Books, [1968] 1990), for his treatment of the automatonic and the ethical in Spinoza. Among numerous more recent accounts of popular cinema's spectral past offered in glimpses of mummies, androids, golems, somnambulists, and automata, see Eric G. Wilson, *The Melancholy Android: On the Psychology of Sacred Machines* (Albany: State University of New York Press, 2006).

40. Alan M. Turing's foundational work on universal computation, for example, was undertaken at the same historical moment Eisenstein turned back to the symbolic and conditional aspects of Meyerhold's theater. See Turing, "On Computable Numbers, with an Application to the Entscheidungs Problem," *Proceedings of the London Mathematical Society, Series 2* 42 (1936–1937): 230–265, with corrections later published in *Proceedings of the London Mathematical Society, Series 2* 43 (1937): 544–546. On nineteenth-century "cybernetics" as a model of social governance in France, see David Mindell, Jérôme Segal, and Slava Gerovitch, "Cybernetics and Information Theory in the United States, France and the Soviet Union," in *Science and Ideology: A Comparative History*, ed. Mark Walker (London: Routledge, 2003), 66–95.

41. Ronald Levaco, "The Eisenstein-Prokofiev Correspondence," *Cinema Journal* 13, no. 1 (Autumn 1973): 1–16, esp. 1, 9; these events are also discussed by numerous other studies of the period cited here.

42. Deleuze, *Cinema 1*, 178.

43. D. N. Rodowick, *Gilles Deleuze's Time Machine* (Durham, NC: Duke University Press, 1997).

44. Deleuze, *Cinema 2,* 40.

45. "What relationship is there between human struggle and a work of art? The closest and for me the most mysterious relationship of all. Exactly what Paul Klee meant when he said: 'You know, the people are missing.' The people are missing and at the same time, they are not missing. The people are missing means that the fundamental affinity between a work of art and a people that does not yet exist is not, will never be clear. There is no work of art that does not call on a people who does not yet exist." Gilles Deleuze, "What Is the Creative Act?" in *Two Regimes of Madness* (Cambridge, MA: MIT Press, 2006), 324.

46. Important in regard to this play of possibility and virtuality in Eisenstein's work are the accounts by Annette Michelson of Eisenstein's "epistemophilia" and, more recently, by Anne Nesbet of the director's "figural philosophy," both of which have shown the great capacities for epistemological excess resident within Eisenstein's cinematic diagram. These accounts of "epistemophilia" and "figural philosophy" show that Eisenstein's various developments of montage practice develop alongside emergent scientific, economic, and artistic epistemologies in the Soviet context. Michelson shows the ways in which Eisenstein's stylistics in *Old and New,* a film made at the juncture of the NEP period and the succeeding period of centrally planned economy, corresponds to the material ontologies of Soviet reality. More recently, Nesbet's discussion of epistemology in Eisenstein indicates the ways in which a "figural" image of social knowledge in Eisenstein's montage opens onto the corporeal and the affective, giving rise to interminable chains of possible critical interpretation. For Michelson, see below; see Anne Nesbet, *Savage Junctures: Sergei Eisenstein and the Shape of Thinking* (New York: I. B. Taurus, 2003).

47. Oksana Bulgakowa, "Spatial Figures in Soviet Cinema of the 1930s," trans. Jeffrey Karlson, in *The Landscape of Stalinism: The Art and Ideology of Soviet Space,* ed. Evgeny Debrenko and Erik Naiman (Seattle: University of Washington Press, 2003), 53.

48. Joan Neuberger, "Eisenstein's Angel," *Russian Review* 63, no. 3 (July 2004): 374–406.

49. Stalin's complaints in his meeting with Eisenstein included: "Ivan the Terrible was very cruel. You can depict him as a cruel man, but you have to show why he *had* to be cruel." Richard Taylor, ed., "Stalin, Molotov, and Zhdanov on *Ivan the Terrible Part Two,*" in *The Eisenstein Reader* (London: BFI, 1998), 161.

50. Oksana Bulgakowa, *Sergei Eisenstein: A Biography* (San Francisco: Potemkin Press, 2001), 210.

51. Bulgakowa, *Sergei Eisenstein,* 210–224. Bulgakowa argues that Eisenstein draws on Otto Rank's alternative to Freud's Oedipal theory with a theory of the body's emergence from the maternal womb as trauma.

52. Sergei Eisenstein, "Montage in 1938," in *Sergei Eisenstein: Notes of a Film Director,* 62–98. The BFI translation of this passage replaces the Bergsonist overtones of the discussion suggested in the Russian translation of 1959 with "has to arise or be born from something else." See Sergei Eisenstein, "Montage 1938," in *Selected Works,* 2:309.

53. Eisenstein's comments on Henri Bergson elsewhere make it clear that the Soviet director believed, or could only say, that the significance of Bergson's work had to be limited to the conditions of production of its own, prerevolutionary context: that is, for Soviet academicism, a presocialist, and therefore, possibly interesting but not entirely admissible, source ("Charlie the Kid," in *Sergei Eisenstein,* 171). Bergson was an early encounter for Eisenstein, Bulgakowa shows (*Sergei Eisenstein,* 15).

54. Dziga Vertov, "I Wish to Share My Experience" (1934), in *Kino-Eye: The Writings of Dziga Vertov,* ed. Annette Michelson, trans. Kevin O'Brien (Berkeley: University of California Press, 1984), 120; see also Annette Michelson, "The Kinetic Icon in the Work of Mourning: Prolegomena to the Analysis of a Textual System," *October* 52 (Spring 1990): 16–39, esp. 18. See also Michelson's treatments of Eisenstein in "Camera Lucida/Camera Obscura," *Artforum* 11, no. 5 (January 1973): 30–31; "Reading Eisenstein Reading Capital, Part 1" *October* 2 (Summer 1976): 27–38; and "Reading Eisenstein Reading Capital, Part 2" *October* 3 (Spring 1977): 82–89; and "Eisenstein at 100: Recent Reception and Coming Attractions," *October* 88 (Spring 1999): 69–85.

55. David Bordwell, *The Cinema of Eisenstein* (Cambridge, MA: Harvard University Press, 1993), emphasizes Eisenstein as stylist, and suggests that "musical analogies" were deployed for organizational purposes of film style; see also Cook's more detailed study of musical analogy as cognitive metaphor in time-based media, discussed above.

56. Robert Weinberg, *The Revolution of 1905 in Odessa: Blood on the Steps* (Bloomington: Indiana University Press, 1993), 132–133.

57. Here, as Stathis Kouvelakis explains, a rereading of Hegel's *Logic of Science* led Lenin to theorize that "Law is relation ... relation of essences or between essences." Stathis Kouvelakis, "Lenin as a Reader of Hegel: Hypotheses for a Reading of Lenin's Notebooks on Hegel's *The Science of Logic,*" in *Lenin Reloaded: Toward a Politics of Truth,* ed. Sebastian Budgen, Stathis Kouvelakis, and Slavoj Žižek (Durham, NC: Duke University Press, 2007), 164–204, esp. 187. The treatment of dialectical material transformation here, for my purposes, should be compared to the "diagrammatic" understanding of temporality, materiality, and change in Deleuze and Felix Guattari's notion of "diagram." Deleuze and Guattari rework Charles Sanders Pierce's notion of diagram as relation so that it becomes, more specifically, an asubjective icon of relation operative across a range of forms of material production: "Diagrammatic interactions ... in our present terminology, are opposed to semiological redundancies. The former make sign systems work directly with the realities they refer to; they work at the existential production of referents, whereas the latter represent, by giving 'equivalents' that have no operational function. Examples: mathematical algorithms, technological charts, computer programming, all participate directly in the process of engendering objects, whereas an advertisement gives only an extrinsic representation of its object (though it is also producing subjectivity)." See Felix Guattari, *The Anti-Oedipus Papers,* trans. Stéphane Nadaud (New York: Semiotexte, 2006), 419. Guattari mentions musical writing, computer syntax, and robotics (415) as examples of diagrammatic production, indicating the broad applicability the authors intended with this asubjective dynamics of relation.

58. Historicism requires an event, and "revolution," a historical determination of the transformative event whereby the party becomes the state, provides it. A triangulation of party, state, and revolution come to determine and delimit the historical dynamism of the political such that a larger political sequence becomes unthinkable in the historicization of revolution as founding event. See Sylvain Lazarus, "Lenin and the Party," in Budgen, Kouvelakis, and Žižek, *Lenin Reloaded,* 260–261.

59. In practice, in the 1920s, the Soviet socialist economy proceeded to a state of ruin compared to even pre-1914 levels. Christopher Read, ed., "Social Modernization," in *The Stalin Years: A Reader* (New York: Palgrave Macmillan, 2003), 23–25, esp. 24.

60. Elizabeth Waters, "The Modernization of Russian Motherhood, 1917–1937," in Read, *The Stalin Years,* 25–38, esp. 32.

61. Dan Healey, "Sexuality and Gender Dissent: Homosexuality as Resistance in Stalin's Russia," in *Contending with Stalinism: Soviet Power and Popular Resistance in the 1930s,* ed. Lynne Viola (Ithaca, NY: Cornell University Press, 2002), 139–169.

62. At different points, a mixture of foreign lending or transfer and domestic innovation, but by World War II, largely domestic.

63. Orlando Figes, *The Whisperers: Private Life in Stalin's Russia* (New York: Metropolitan, 2007), 192–226.

64. See Read, "The Great Fatherland War," 145–148; and John Erickson, "Soviet Women at War," 148–168, both in Read, *The Stalin Years.*

65. Figes, *The Whisperers,* 157. The larger historical outcome, then, was that after external debate and dissent had been destroyed by Lenin to achieve Bolshevik supremacy, the Communist party itself would become the locus for the internal extermination of debate and dissent after the revolution had become historicized. The project of building a contemporary socialism for the future was elaborated with all its contradictions in the relative prosperity for an elite middle class in the early to mid-1930s (149–226).

66. Historical studies of industrial and cultural policy in this period show that a "genetic" tendency (an evolutionary or adaptive socialism, based on education and cultural production) competed with a "teleological" one (where social change was instrumentally implemented in interventionist programs); see Daniel Peris, "The 1929 Congress of the Godless," in Read, *The Stalin Years,* 41–65; Read, "The Drive to Industrialize," in *The Stalin Years,* 66; and Alexander Erlich, *The Soviet Industrialization Debate: 1924–1928* (Cambridge, MA: Harvard University Press, 1960). These tensions are already evident, however, in Marx's observation that in capitalism, "the commodity form of the product of labor—or the value-form of the commodity—is the economic cell-form." See Marx, *Capital* (Oxford: Oxford University Press, 1999), 3. Eisenstein, of course, famously conceives the "shot" as a montage "cell" in "Beyond the Shot," in *The Eisenstein Reader,* ed. Richard Taylor, trans. Richard Taylor and William Powell (London: BFI, 1998), 82–92. Meanwhile, Soviet artist theorists had also argued that by collapsing "economy" and "creativity" and embedding "genetic" and "teleological" tensions in the analytical problematic of immanence and materiality, aesthetic production would provide the means for collectivizing individuation. See Kasimir Malevich, "The Question of Imitative Art" (1920), in *Art in Theory, 1900–1990,* ed. Charles Harrison and Paul Wood (Oxford: Blackwell, 1992), 294. The tragic reality, of course, was that artists who advocated such yet-to-be-defined collectivism through creative individuation became threats to the party as state.

67. For accessible histories of the period, see Figes, *The Whisperers,* 148–315; or Simon Sebag Montefiore, *Stalin: The Court of the Red Tsar* (London: Weidenfeld and Nicholson, 2003).

68. Even colleague Sergei Tretyakov criticized Eisenstein's *The Strike* (1924) as "formal experimentation" (Bulgakowa, *Sergei Eisenstein,* 50), a charge that was continually leveled at the director throughout his life and continued after his death.

69. In *Sergei Eisenstein,* Bulgakowa catalogues a cascade of politicians and artists' arrests, executions, or murders in 1939, including those of early Eisenstein collaborator Sergei Tretyakov, mentor and theater director Vsevolod Meyerhold, and shortly afterward his wife Zinaida Raikh, who had taught Eisenstein biomechanical theory and practice in Meyerhold's studio in the early 1920s. Bulgakowa's account shows that the "script" of the supposed "artist plot" against Stalin included the names of Eisenstein and Shostakovich as conspirators, Trotskyites, and terrorists directed by André Malraux (*Sergei Eisenstein,* 200), confirming the assertions Marshall makes in his 1983 introduction to the first English

translation of Eisenstein's autobiography, *Immoral Memories: An Autobiography,* trans. Herbert Marshall (Boston: Houghton Mifflin, 1983), and in Marshall, *Masters of the Soviet Cinema: Crippled Creative Biographies* (London: Routledge and Kegan Paul, 1983).

70. Sergei Eisenstein, "How I Learned to Draw (A Chapter on Dancing Lessons)," trans. Richard Taylor, in *Eisenstein at Ninety,* ed. Ian Christie and David Elliot (Oxford: Museum of Modern Art Oxford, 1988), 62.

71. Eisenstein, "How I Learned to Draw (A Chapter on Dancing Lessons)," in *Beyond the Stars,* 588.

72. Seton's account gives Eisenstein his chance to reframe the question of homosexual identity; she also helpfully includes an appendix of documents in which Soviet officials disavow any homosexual identity as Soviet. Marie Seton, *Sergei M. Eisenstein: A Biography* (New York: A. A. Wyn, 1952), 437; and see the appendix. Jacques Aumont reads the director's autobiography to find Eisensteinian ecstasy as *jouissance* at play, recycling desire constantly in a production of mastery that is complicated by the recurrent figure of the repressed: by far the more common reading of Eisenstein and sexuality in the West. See Jacques Aumont, *Montage Eisenstein,* trans. Lee Hildreth, Constance Penley, and Andrew Ross (London: BFI, 1987). Hakan Lövgren reads a sublimated violence in Eisenstein's drawings as a symptom of traumatizing homophobia, similarly to Bulgakowa's biographical claims of "creative sublimation." Hakan Lövgren, "Trauma and Ecstasy: Aesthetic Compounds in Dr. Eisenstein's Laboratory," in *Eisenstein Revisited: A Collection of Essays,* ed. Lars Kleberg and Hakan Lövgren (Stockholm: Almqvist and Wiksell International, 1987), 93–111. Taylor more recently argues that homosexuality must have made Eisenstein and his cultural labor more vulnerable to the Stalinist politics of terror; Richard Taylor, "Sergei Eisenstein: The Life and Times of a Boy from Riga," in *The Montage Principle: Eisenstein in New Cultural and Critical Contexts* (Amsterdam: Rodopi, 2004), 25–43, esp. 37. The question such claims raise, however, is: more vulnerable than whom? For the claim that rather than a novel theorization of materialist, sexed affect, Eisenstein's films are informed by concerns around gender, see Chris Robé, "Revolting Women: The Role of Gender Sergei Eisenstein's *Que Viva México!* and U.S. Depression-Era Left Film Criticism," *Jump Cut: A Review of Contemporary Media* 48 (Winter 2006), available at http://www.ejumpcut.org/archive/jc48.2006/ (accessed February 24, 2010).

73. Susan Buck-Morss, *Dreamworld and Catastrophe: The Passing of Mass Utopia in East and West* (Cambridge, MA: MIT Press, 2000), 184.

74. Buck-Morss, *Dreamworld and Catastrophe,* 184. For a useful discussion complicating identifying sexual identity as "sexual" or as "identity," see Douglas Crimp, "Don't Tell" (1993), in *Melancholia and Moralism: Essays on AIDS and Queer Politics* (Cambridge, MA: MIT Press, 2004), 239.

75. Eisenstein jokingly suggests that he is restraining the narration of his memories in order not to offend U.S. readers, probably reflecting Eisenstein's experience in Hollywood and with Sinclair Lewis, who joked about his wife, who managed Eisenstein's Mexico project, as having no idea about "homos"; Lewis blackmailed Eisenstein in correspondence with Stalin, stating in a letter that Eisenstein was homosexual; Eisenstein's "joke," then, is not too difficult to understand; Nesbet's account in *Savage Junctures* reviews some of these details.

76. Victor Shklovsky and Richard Sheldon, trans., *Zoo, or Letters Not about Love* (Ithaca, NY: Cornell University Press, 1971), 136.

77. Healey, "Sexuality and Gender Dissent," 189.

78. Meanwhile, Eisenstein received Meyerhold's personal archive on request from the daughter of Zinaida Raikh, Meyerhold's teaching assistant and later wife, murdered in her

apartment after Meyerhold's arrest in July 1939, hiding it in his dacha after Meyerhold had been killed at Stalin's orders. Bulgakowa, *Sergei Eisenstein,* 214.

79. Bordwell, *The Cinema of Eisenstein,* 22.

80. Eisenstein, more so; others, less so: "When Eisenstein was still in Mexico he gave his friend Strauch written advice on how a film director should behave [toward those commanding the film industry]: 'pressure them, be diplomatic, grovel, be sly, and then pressure them again.'" Bulgakowa, *Sergei Eisenstein,* 150, citing Eisenstein.

81. Montefiore, *Stalin,* 530. The closing image of Pier Paolo Pasolini's *Salò: 120 Days of Sodom* comes to mind: The politico-narratological sadism of Italian Fascism, and of that film, is summed up by the ambivalent image of a slow dance between two young soldiers in uniform.

82. Bulgakowa, *Sergei Eisenstein,* 220.

83. See Deleuze's theory of the cinema as simulacrum and its "power of the false." Gilles Deleuze, "The Simulacrum and Ancient Philosophy," in *The Logic of Sense* (New York: Columbia University Press, [1969] 1990), 263. Of more than passing interest here with regards to simulacral "machinery" and "the power of the false" is that Eisenstein and Deleuze had a keen appreciation for Carrollian nonsense. See Sergei Eisenstein, "Charlie the Kid," in *Sergei Eisenstein: Notes of a Film Director,* 167–197, esp. 178.

84. Eisenstein's memoirs or his early theater spectacles would not be the only "circus" of "homosexual desire" in postrevolutionary Russia. For cosmopolitan youth coming of age in St. Petersburg (as Eisenstein did), Healey explains, St. Petersburg's Cinizelli circus was a well-known center of the "little homosexual world," whose architecture, route map, and surveillance Healey documents for the period from the 1880s into the 1920s. Dan Healey, *Homosexual Desire in Revolutionary Russia: The Regulation of Sexual and Gender Dissent* (Chicago: University of Chicago Press, 2001), 31–32, esp. 36.

85. Alma Law and Mel Gordon, *Meyerhold, Eisenstein, and Biomechanics: Actor Training in Revolutionary Russia* (Jefferson, NC: McFarland, 1996), 75.

86. In biomechanics, Meyerhold understood body movement as an object in and of itself. Gravity, speed, orientation, movement, mass, and the relation between one body and another become key factors in the actor's dramatic projection. These qualities of biomechanical diagramming comprise not only a means to communicate the ontologies and epistemologies of sound and acoustics in the time stream assembled as montage; their modulation, since they no longer presume an autonomous, individual coherence of a single body-anchored perspective, also tends to preempt subjective emotional reflection. Law and Gordon, *Meyerhold, Eisenstein, and Biomechanics,* 75. On Eisenstein and Meyerhold, see also Kristin Thompson, *Eisenstein's Ivan the Terrible: A Neoformalist Analysis* (Princeton, NJ: Princeton University Press, 1981). Nesbet's analysis provides a philosophical treatment for the excess of interpretation associated with Eisenstein's work, in different ways, by Michelson or Thompson.

87. Sergei Yutkevich, *Kontrapunkt der Regie* (Berlin: Henschelverlag, 1965), 342–343.

88. Alma Law, "Meyerhold Speaks . . . ," *Performing Arts Journal* 3, no. 3 (Winter 1979): 68–84.

89. Yutkevich, *Kontrapunkt der Regie,* 355–356.

90. Wollen, *Signs and Meaning in the Cinema.*

91. Yutkevich, *Kontrapunkt der Regie,* 356–357.

92. For example, those of Appia, documented more generally in the late-nineteenth- and early-twentieth-century period by Jo Leslie Collier, *The Transposition of Romanticism from Stage to Screen* (Ann Arbor, MI: UMI Research Press, 1988).

93. Yutkevich, *Kontrapunkt der Regie,* 384.

94. Bordwell's *Cinema of Eisenstein* suggests that Meyerhold exaggerated his influence on Eisenstein (3) and that prevalent theories of reflexology or eurhythmics were a more relevant influence. An earlier U.S. version of this view had been advanced in Malcolm Eugene Bowes, "Eurhythmics and the Analysis of Visual-Musical Synthesis in Film: An Examination of Eisenstein's 'Alexander Nevsky'" (Ph.D. diss., Ohio University, 1976), 73. Eisenstein had studied eurhythmics prior to apprenticing with Meyerhold, but he claims to have mastered it under Meyerhold. See Eisenstein, *Beyond the Stars,* 589. See also, with regards to Kuleshov and Eisenstein, *Kuleshov on Film,* ed. and trans. Ronald Levaco (Berkeley: University of California Press, 1974). Buck-Morss also points out the influence of Taylorism, another influential form of industrial physical culture in the early Soviet era, in *Dreamworld and Catastrophe.*

95. Yutkevich, *Kontrapunkt der Regie,* 376, 380.

96. When making *Old and New,* Yutkevich recalls, Eisenstein became frustrated when editing the famed milk-separator sequence and screened *Potemkin* by himself for nights on end to isolate the effective principle of the Odessa Steps sequence, "but the mechanical re-application of montage construction from one film to the other didn't achieve the desired effect. The exquisitely assembled scene remained expressionless" (*Kontrapunkt der Regie,* 382–383). Most critics seem to agree that the latter scene fails to reach the pathos of the former but neglect to point out that the milk-separator sequence is designed to express the other side of pathos: ecstasy. In any case, in Yutkevich's view, montage as information fails montage as immanence.

97. Healey examines the methodological obstacle of denial of access to archival materials on such figures as Eisenstein and other cultural figures in Russian and Soviet empires. Healey, *Homosexual Desire in Revolutionary Russia,* 267n12; Dan Healey, "Homosexual Existence and Existing Socialism: New Light on the Repression of Male Homosexuality in Stalin's Russia" *GLQ* 8, no. 3 (2002): 349–378. His historical method thus draws on canonical queer studies, including Michel Foucault, *The History of Sexuality Volume 1: Introduction* (New York: Pantheon, 1978); and Eve Kosofsky Sedgwick, *Epistemology of the Closet* (Berkeley: University of California Press, 1990).

98. Eisenstein's position as creative laborer, with an international reputation as well as useful skills as a director, would have put him in a slightly different position than that of others. In the postrevolutionary Soviet context, the Bolshevik party completely decriminalized same-sexuality between 1918 and 1922 in the postrevolutionary overhaul of the civil code; by the mid-1930s, recriminalization and uneven enforcement based on status, gender, ethnic identity, or other informal factors produced largely incoherent effects at enforcement, impacting the Soviet film industry as well as practices of everyday life. For example, in 1937, when the second version of Eisenstein's *Bezhin Meadow* was canceled two years after the first version had been stopped, Ivan Siniakov, a Mosfilm executive, was arrested and charged with having sexual relations with twenty military and seven civilian men between 1927 and 1937 (whom Siniakov met in locales ranging from the stables of the Moscow Circus to Sverdlov Square in front of the Bolshoi Theater); he was sentenced to eight years of prison labor. Siniakov's confession, however, allowed his partners, many of whom were sailors or soldiers, to go unpunished, demonstrating the ways in which a suspicious, unhealthy masculinity tended to be found guilty of corrupting otherwise "healthy" masculine subjects after the 1933–1934 acts recriminalizing sodomy. See the various articles mentioning the Siniakov case in Healey, "Homosexual Existence and Existing Socialism," 365; Dan Healey, "Masculine Purity and 'Gentleman's Mischief': Sexual Exchange and

Prostitution between Russian Men, 1861–1941," *Slavic Review* 60, no. 2 (Summer 2001): 233–265, esp. 261–263; and Healey, "Sexuality and Gender Dissent," 139–169, esp. 160. For comparison, too, consider that in the U.S. context, same-sex dissidence would not be fully decriminalized until 2003, while sexual nonconformance currently remains a marker of second-class status.

99. Nesbet, *Savage Junctures,* 79.

100. Bulgakowa, *Sergei Eisenstein*; Nesbet, *Savage Junctures.*

101. Versions range from the earliest ones produced by Upton Sinclair in attempts to recoup his investment in the film, in, for example, *Thunder Over Mexico* (Lesser, 1933); to Seton's critically reviled version; to more recent restoration attempts, such as Alexandrov's *¡Que Viva Mexico!* (1979) or Oleg Kovalov's *A Mexican Fantasy* (1998).

102. And see the analysis of Clark's *Passing Through* in Chapter 5 herein.

103. As Healey's work reveals at length, female same-sex desire was much less likely to be named as prohibited and to produce punishments for transgression than male same-sex desire in this period; on the other hand, homosexual desire in the non-European Soviet republics was more likely to be disciplined than in the European Soviets.

104. Eisenstein, *Beyond the Stars,* 453.

CHAPTER 3

1. Michelle Snow, "User since Forever: Yoshi Sodeoka," available at https://wiki.brown.edu/confluence/display/mcm1700n/Yoshi+Sodeoka (accessed February 12, 2010).

2. Fischinger's extensive museum and gallery exhibition record are a stark counterpoint to his relative marginalization in film theoretical or art historical studies of twentieth-century cinema.

3. Carl Beier, "A New Way of Looking at Things," *Hollywood Quarterly* 2, no. 1 (October 1946): 1–10.

4. Ralph Potter, "Audivisual Music," *Hollywood Quarterly* 3, no. 1 (Autumn 1947): 66–78. This article, or the Beier article cited above, are only two of several articles that appeared in the early volumes of *Hollywood Quarterly* on the subject of visual music as a privileged site for exploring problems of audiovisual synchronization; see also, on the Whitney Bros., Leon Becker, "Synthetic Sound and Abstract Image," *Hollywood Quarterly* 1, no. 1 (October 1945): 95–96.

5. Stephen C. Beck, "Proposal for Investigating New Uses of Color Television" (unpublished manuscript, 1969).

6. Judy Stone, "Bringing Video Art to the TV Screens," *San Francisco Examiner,* March 20, 1976.

7. William Moritz, "The Films of Oskar Fischinger," *Film Culture* nos. 58–60 (1974): 37–175, esp. 41; and William Moritz, *Optical Poetry: The Life and Work of Oskar Fischinger* (Bloomington: Indiana University Press, 2004), 5–7.

8. Sergei Yutkevich, *Kontrapunkt der Regie* (Berlin: Henschelverlag, 1965).

9. Moritz, "The Films of Oskar Fischinger," 41.

10. Moritz, "The Films of Oskar Fischinger," 53.

11. This last film especially would have satisfied Paul Klee, who also lived in Munich during the time Fischinger lived there and who makes numerous references and analogies to music in his private diary. Writes Paul Klee, an accomplished violinist, in March 1910: "I must some day be able to improvise freely on the chromatic keyboard of the rows of water-

color cups." Paul Klee, *The Diaries of Paul Klee* (Berkeley: University of California Press, 1964), 244.

12. Anson Rabinbach, *The Human Motor: Energy, Fatigue, and the Origins of Modernity* (Berkeley: University of California Press, 1992).

13. Oskar Fischinger, "True Creation," The Fischinger Trust and Archive, available at www.oskarfischinger.org/True%20Creation.html.

14. Peter Bürger, *Theory of the Avant-Garde,* trans. Michael Shaw (Minneapolis: University of Minnesota Press, 1984).

15. Moritz, *Optical Poetry.*

16. Erik Loyer, "Stories as Instruments" (public talk and demonstration at the University of California, Riverside, April 7, 2009).

17. Some of this footage was later included in *R-1* (1927) and *Spiritual Constructions* (1927) and, like the expanding or contracting senses of screen space in the *Spirals* fragments, demonstrates the larger aims and trajectory of his work: animating a block of immanent time by musically modulating its energies.

18. Moritz, "The Films of Oskar Fischinger."

19. Bürger, *Theory of the Avant-Garde.*

20. Hans Richter, cited in Justin Hoffman, "Hans Richter: Constructivist Filmmaker," in *Hans Richter: Activism, Modernism, and the Avant-Garde,* ed. Stephen C. Foster (Cambridge, MA: MIT Press, 1998), 76.

21. Richter, cited in Bernd Finkeldey, "Hans Richter and the Constructivist International," in Foster, *Hans Richter,* 111.

22. Marion von Hofacker, "Richter's Films and the Role of the Radical Artist," in Foster, *Hans Richter,* 127.

23. Moritz, "The Films of Oskar Fischinger."

24. Hoffman, "Hans Richter," 78.

25. The "Demonstration of Universal Language" would seem to be from 1920, the year that Richter and Viking Eggeling first attempted to film the scrolls. However, while the manifesto explaining their intentions is dated from that year, the "Demonstration" is not dated, nor attributed a date, in the Foster edition. Richter, compiled in Foster, *Hans Richter,* 191.

26. Ibid., 208.

27. Ernst Bloch, *The Spirit of Utopia* (Palo Alto, CA: Stanford University Press, [1919] 2000), 34.

28. See Sergei M. Eisenstein, "Montage in 1938," in *Sergei Eisenstein: Notes of a Film Director* (Moscow: Foreign Language Publishing House, [1939] 1958), 77; and my discussion in Chapter 1.

29. Bloch, *The Spirit of Utopia,* 141.

30. Moritz, "The Films of Oskar Fischinger," 73.

31. The *ritornello* form is fundamental to *The Brandenburg Concertos,* and the Third, used by Fischinger, epitomizes the classical type of *ritornello,* despite a historical resistance to describing the concertos in these terms; see Malcolm Boyd, *Bach: The Brandenburg Concertos* (Cambridge: Cambridge University Press, 1993), esp. 48–49. Boyd also notes that the Third Concerto is notable for calling for an improvisation in its "Adagio" movement (81).

32. Oskar Fischinger, "A Document Related to *Motion Painting #1,*" in Moritz, *Optical Poetry,* 185.

33. For a selection of discussions in English, see the range of entries relevant to Fischinger in *The Film Index, Vol. 1: The Film as Art* (New York: Museum of Modern Art Film

Library and H. W. Wilson, 1941); Roger Manvell and John Huntley, *The Technique of Film Music* (London: Focal Press, 1957), especially with reference to synthetic sound; Richard Whitehall, "Introduction," in *Bildmusik: Art of Oskar Fischinger* (Long Beach, CA: Long Beach Museum of Art, 1970), 4–16; Cecile Starr and Robert Russett, "Notes on the Origins of New Art," in *Experimental Animation: Origins of New Art*, 2nd ed. (New York: Litton, [1976] 1988), 13–31; William Charles Wees, *Light Moving in Time: Studies in the Visual Aesthetics of Avant-Garde Film* (Berkeley: University of California Press, 1992); Moritz, "The Films of Oskar Fischinger" and *Optical Poetry*; Robert Haller, *Galaxy: Avant-Garde Film-Makers across Space and Time* (New York: Anthology Film Archives, 2001); David James, *The Most Typical Avant-Garde: History and Geography of Minor Cinemas in Los Angeles* (Berkeley: University of California Press, 2005); and Web sites maintained by the Center for Visual Music: www.centerforvisualmusic.org/Fischinger/OFFilmnotes.htm; and www.oskarfischinger.org (accessed February 14, 2010).

34. James, *The Most Typical Avant-Garde.*

35. See Moritz, "The Films of Oskar Fischinger" and *Optical Poetry*; James, *The Most Typical Avant-Garde*, 254–261.

36. Walter Frisch, *German Modernism: Music and the Arts* (Berkeley: University of California Press, 2005), 174.

37. Hanns Eisler and Hans Bunge, *Gespräche mit Hans Bunge: Fragen Sie mehr über Brecht* (Munich: Rogner and Bernhard, [1963] 1976).

38. Moritz, *Optical Poetry*, 202–204; and "The Films of Oskar Fischinger," 44; and see also Cindy Keefer, "'Raumlightmusik': Early 20th Century Abstract Cinema Immersive Environments," *Leonardo Electronic Almanac* 16, nos. 6–7, available at www.leonardo.info/LEA/CreativeData/CreativeData.html (accessed February 14, 2010).

39. See, for example, Moritz, "The Films of Oskar Fischinger," 139.

40. This title was later given to the meditative, silent work of 1942.

41. Moritz, *Optical Poetry*, 24.

42. Fischinger, "A Document Concerning *PAINTING*" (1956), reprinted in Moritz, *Optical Poetry*, 188–189; and see also the earlier reprint in Moritz, "The Films of Oskar Fischinger," 188.

43. James, *The Most Typical Avant-Garde*, 257.

44. Erwin Panofsky, "Style and Medium in the Motion Picture" (1934), in *Film Theory and Criticism*, 6th ed., ed. Leo Braudy and Marshall Cohen (Oxford: Oxford University Press, 2004), 289–302.

45. Whether Berkeley intentionally borrowed from Fischinger's "original" would be hard to prove; at any rate, such a line of argument might still overlook the fact that in the cultural field, Fischinger solved a series of problems in musicalizing the cinematic stream before Berkeley did, and with a quite different emphasis on graphical and painterly sophistication. Berkeley tended to resolve these concerns through mechanized sets, clever camera set-ups, montage, choreography, and a range of techniques considered "special effects."

46. *Allegretto* uses what I term a "phrasal" style of synchronization; visual elements have movements that correspond to instrumental phrases of the music, notably the melody line carried by violins, reeds, or brasses. The film can be seen as an expressive "visualization" of the sound track, because the phrase-by-phrase animation works to depict the flow, hence "meaning," of the musical composition.

47. According to Moritz, "The Films of Oskar Fischinger," this film prepares the way for the meditative films of James Whitney or Jordan Belson. Other effects in this film seem to anticipate the structural and flicker films of the 1960s and 1970s.

48. Eisenstein, on the other hand, explains that his theory of "Vertical Montage" builds on his earlier theorizations of interframe juxtapositions. Rhythmic or compositional line can be traced across and through the frame as entire sequence.

49. Bürger, *Theory of the Avant-Garde,* 54.

50. Martin Rubin, *Showstoppers: Busby Berkeley and the Tradition of Spectacle* (New York: Columbia University Press, 1993), 163.

51. Robert Haller, "Oskar's Hand," in program notes for *Kinetica-2: Abstraction, Animation, Music; A Centennial Tribute to Oskar Fischinger* (Los Angeles: IotaCenter, 2000).

52. Akira Mizuta Lippit, "Digesture: Gesture and Inscription in Experimental Cinema," in *Migrations of Gesture,* ed. Carrie Noland and Sally Ann Ness (Minneapolis: University of Minnesota Press, 2008), 113–132.

53. Moritz, "The Films of Oskar Fischinger," 76.

54. Elfriede Fischinger, undated museum catalog; presumably compiled by William Moritz.

55. Jonathan Lethem, *The Fortress of Solitude* (New York: Random House, 2004).

56. Lethem, *The Fortress of Solitude,* 141.

57. Moritz, *Optical Poetry,* 148.

58. Bernard Stiegler, *Technics and Time Vol. 2: Disorientation* (Palo Alto, CA: Stanford University Press, 2008); Bernard Stiegler, *Acting Out* (Palo Alto, CA: Stanford University Press, 2008); and see my concluding discussion in Chapter 7.

59. Stiegler, *Acting Out,* 55.

CHAPTER 4

1. Nicholas Cook, *Analyzing Musical Multimedia* (Oxford: Oxford University Press, 1998).

2. Albrecht Betz, *Hanns Eisler: Political Musician* (Cambridge: Cambridge University Press, [1976, 1982] 2006), 45.

3. Cook, *Analyzing Musical Multimedia,* 64.

4. On the tensions in the authorship of *Composing for the Films* and its different versions, see Philip Rosen, "Adorno and Film Music: Theoretical Notes on *Composing for the Films,*" *Yale French Studies* no. 60 (1980): 157–182, esp. 157n2.

5. Hanns Eisler and Theodor Adorno, *Composing for the Films* (London: Athlone Press, [1947] 1994), 76.

6. Theodor Adorno describes Paul Lazarsfeld's gestural feedback device indicating listener like or dislike in "Scientific Experiences of a European Scholar in America," in *The Intellectual Migration,* ed. Bailyn Fleming (Cambridge, MA: Harvard University Press, 1969), 344; and see Graham McCann, "New Introduction," in Eisler and Adorno, *Composing for the Films,* xxii; McCann's introduction nonetheless misrepresents the actual production of Eisler's scores, which *did* include an evaluation component, Adorno's later recollection of Lazarsfeld notwithstanding. Reference to the screenings at which expert feedback was generated appears in documents archived along with the rest of the Rockefeller Foundation project documents. But see McCann, "New Introduction," xxi–xxii. Eisler and Adorno began the manuscript in 1942 and finished it in 1944. The translation of their German manuscript appeared from Oxford University Press in 1947, but Adorno withdrew his name in the midst of the political turmoil that resulted in Eisler's testimony before the House Un-American Activities Committee and his voluntary deportation in 1948. For Eisler's version, see Hanns Eisler, *Gespräche mit Hans Bunge: Fragen Sie mehr über Brecht* (Munich: Rogner and Bernhard, 1976), 283.

7. Cited in John Fuegi, *Brecht & Co.: Sex, Politics, and the Making of the Modern Drama,* 2nd ed. (New York: Grover Press, [1994] 2002), 535.

8. Bertolt Brecht, "On Gestic Music," ed. and trans. John Willett (New York: Hill and Wang, [1964] 1992), 104–106. See also Kurt Weill, "*Gestus* in Music," trans. Erich Albrecht, in *Brecht Sourcebook,* ed. Carol Martin and Henry Bial (New York: Routledge, 2000), 61–65.

9. Eisler and Adorno, *Composing for the Films.*

10. See Eugene Lunn, *Marxism and Modernism: An Historical Study of Lukács, Brecht, Benjamin, and Adorno* (Berkeley: University of California Press, 1982); Annette Davison, *Hollywood Theory, Non-Hollywood Practice: Cinema Soundtracks in the 1980s and 1990s* (Surrey, U.K.: Ashgate, 2006).

11. See Walter Frisch, *German Modernism: Music and the Arts* (Berkeley: University of California Press, 2005), 145–148; and Arnold Schoenberg, *Theory of Harmony* (Berkeley: University of California Press, [1911] 1983).

12. On Adorno's rejection of Brecht's politicized art and Eisler's sense that Brechtian approach could be integrated with a critical theoretical approach, see McCann, "New Introduction," xxix.

13. Archival documents indicate that Schoenberg received $300, and Brecht received $250. "Statement of Expenses: Hanns Eisler—Rockefeller Music Fund" 4, in 200R New School 62-42 1.1 200 260.3096.

14. Letter to Eisler from Samuel T. Farquhar et al., early 1945. In Folder, "Hollywood Quarterly," in the Eisler documents held in the Hanns Eisler archive of the Feuchtwanger Library at the University of Southern California. The panel was to address the following questions: "1. Is contemporary film music really contemporary? 2. Does it express today's attitude toward musical forms and aesthetics? 3. To what extent is the modern musical idiom exploited on the screen? Does it work to the advantage of the film? Could its greater use enhance the significance and enjoyment of pictures? 4. Has the use of music in American films kept pace with that of Europe, especially France and Russia? 5. How can film musicians cooperate more closely with film writers? 6. How soon can we expect recognition of the place of music as an integral part of film drama, and not merely as background or a technical bridge?"

15. Hadley Cantril, "The Impact of Terror on the Radio Listener," Rockefeller Archive documents: PRR 1938 200R 1.1 Box 271 Folder 3236, which provides Cantril's explanation of listener panic. Shortly, theatrical sound designer Harold Burris-Meyer received funding for further elaboration of sound-processing equipment, explaining in a proposal document that "one use of sound effects in the Stevens Theatre produced what was really mass hysteria"; Eisler's Film Music Project was the third project funded at this time to investigate audience reception of sound and music, after the Radio Research Project (which Lazarsfeld took over from Cantril, employing Adorno for a brief period), and Burris-Meyer's Sound in the Theater, which shared staffer Harry Robin with Eisler for a brief period. A memo from John Marshall to David Stevens makes it clear that Eisler's Film Music Project was coordinated as a parallel project for film music to Burris-Meyer's sound design and the much larger Radio Research projects. See Program and Policy—Public Opinion 1942: RG 3, Series 911, Box 5, Folder 49, memo, March 26, 1940, "DHS from JM." Further, Rockefeller funded an expansion of the Radio Research project dedicated to monitoring German state radio broadcasting in collaboration with the BBC and analyzing their contents. Rockefeller Foundation Resolution Grant 42030 4/2/42. The former coeditor with Freud of *Imago* and editor of the German edition of Freud's collected works, Walter Ernst Kris, was tasked with

Hans Speier to head this effort, since despite his background in art history and psychology, "the common problem being that of man's reaction to the appeal of symbolic stimuli."

16. Mark S. Micale, "On the 'Disappearance' of Hysteria: A Study in the Clinical Deconstruction of a Diagnosis," *Isis* 84, no. 3 (September 1993): 496–526.

17. Eisler and Adorno, *Composing for the Films*, 141.

18. Rockefeller Archives, 200 R New School for Social Research Music Filming 1939–1941 RG 1.1, Series 200, Box 259, Folder 3097.

19. Hanns Eisler, "Fantasia in G-Men," *New Masses*, October 14, 1947, p. 8.

20. And see David Blake, ed., "Chronology of Eisler's Life," in *Hanns Eisler: A Miscellany* (Luxembourg: Harward, 1995), 467–470. Letters written by Louise Eisler, held in the Feuchtwanger Archive of the University of Southern California, indicate that voluntary deportation allowed Eisler to avoid being sent by U.S. authorities to the U.S.-administered zone of divided Germany, where she feared that Eisler would be incarcerated with former Nazis who might kill him.

21. An authoritative biography is available in Steven Smith, *A Heart at Fire's Center: The Life and Music of Bernard Herrmann* (Berkeley: University of California Press, 2002).

22. For a summary account of Bernard Herrmann's significance as auteur along with Martin Scorsese, Robert De Niro, and Paul Schrader on *Taxi Driver*, see Jonathan Rosenbaum, *Essential Cinema: On the Necessity of Film Canons* (Baltimore: Johns Hopkins University Press, 2004), 295–300. Herrmann was hired by the "New Hollywood," though precisely because of his recognized status as auteur.

23. Edith Newcomb, letter to Constantin Bokoleinkoff, Feuchtwanger Library, Hanns Eisler Archive.

24. See Jeff Smith's contrary claim in *The Sounds of Commerce: Marketing Popular Film Music* (New York: Columbia University Press, 1998) of film-music marketing as essentially a result of a convergence between Hollywood film marketing and that of the long-playing record beginning in the late 1940s.

25. Evan William Cameron, *Sound and the Cinema: The Coming of Sound to American Film* (Pleasantville, NY: Redgrave, 1980), 119.

26. Kurt London, *Film Music: A Summary of the Characteristics of Its History, Aesthetics, Technique; and Possible Developments*, trans. Eric S. Bensinger (London: Faber and Faber, 1936).

27. Jane Feuer, *The Hollywood Musical* (Bloomington: Indiana University Press, 1982); Rick Altman, *The American Film Musical* (Bloomington: Indiana University Press, 1987).

28. Claudia Gorbman, *Unheard Melodies: Narrative Film Music* (Bloomington: Indiana University Press, 1987).

29. Kaja Silverman, *The Acoustic Mirror: The Female Voice in Psychoanalysis and Cinema* (Bloomington: Indiana University Press, 1988). Mary Ann Doane and Silverman argue for attention to a psychoanalytically observed "voice" in cinema, and both locate this voice primarily as the ideological construction of lip sync. In these formulations, the auditory is read in a critical positioning of sound as necessary extra. Listening is not located as a practice of knowledge on the part of audiences but rather as a guilty pleasure bound up within the operations of synchronization that might possibly signify a site for political reformations of cinematic practice.

30. Mary Anne Doane, "The Voice in the Cinema: The Articulation of Body and Space," *Yale French Studies* no. 60 (1980): 33–50. As Doane puts it, little "space in the cinema" is left over for anything else: "The supreme achievement of patriarchal ideology is that it has no outside" (50).

31. Royal S. Brown, *Overtones and Undertones* (Berkeley: University of California Press, 1994).

32. These analyses also interrogate spectatorship in terms of cognition, as in Cook, *Analyzing Musical Multimedia,* ch. 1.

33. Michel Chion, *Audio-Vision: Sound on Screen,* trans. Claudia Gorbman (New York: Columbia University Press, [1990] 1994); for an alternative point of view demonstrating the avowed importance—for audiences and production workers alike—of music in "silent" period cinemas, see Martin Marks, *Music and the Silent Film: Contexts and Case Studies* (New York: Oxford University Press, 1997).

34. Brown, *Overtones and Undertones,* 19: "The degree to which there is a tendency to deny aesthetic status to the styles of the 'everyday' is the degree to which the cinema also needed something to de-iconify its temporal and spatial images in order to justify its existence as an art form. Music is one, but not the only, way in which this was accomplished."

35. Lawrence Kramer, *Classical Music and Postmodern Knowledge* (Berkeley: University of California Press, 1995), 111–112: "Emotionally suggestive and technically arcane, music adds itself to the closed circle . . . of an acknowledged story. . . . The narrative circle breaks; the music becomes the primary term and the story its mere accompaniment. Why bother to follow all that stuff Wotan is saying to Erda when we can just listen to the doom-laden procession of the leitmotifs?"

36. See Smith, *The Sounds of Commerce.*

37. Katherine Spring, "Pop Go the Warner Bros., et al.: Marketing Film Songs during the Coming of Sound," *Cinema Journal* 48, no. 1 (Fall 2008): 68–89.

38. For a range of useful essays, see Daniel Goldmark, Lawrence Kramer, and Richard D. Leppert, eds., *Beyond the Soundtrack: Representing Music in Cinema* (Berkeley: University of California Press, 2007).

39. Claudia Gorbman, "Aesthetics and Rhetoric," *American Music* 22, no. 1 (Spring 2004): 14–26. For Gorbman, Cook's account of "metaphor" is crucial.

40. The Rockefeller Foundation declined to fund work proposed by Burris-Meyer for "Music in Industry"; his "Sound in the Theater" project was suspended when Burris-Meyer's expertise and equipment were requisitioned by the U.S. military. After the war, Burris-Meyer submitted a report to the foundation outlining his contributions to "Project Polly," which produced two distinct configurations of an airplane mounted with massive speaker systems designed to broadcast messages to the battlefield while in flight. Burris-Meyer claimed that "Polly" encouraged significant numbers of Japanese troops to surrender and thus saved a significant number of U.S. soldiers' lives in the process.

41. Annette Kuhn, *Dreaming of Fred and Ginger: Cinema and Cultural Memory* (New York: New York University Press, 2002).

42. Digital games routinely assign significant value to programmed digital play in terms of linearity: You are generally a "better player" the "faster" you get through a level or the more levels you can complete; "levels" may be considered as "chapters"; and so on. Espen Aarseth's notion of "ergodic text" requiring nontrivial efforts of interpretation similarly neglects the massive differences of use, interpretation, or repetition that accrue in any use of technically inscribed memory. See Espen Aarseth, *Cybertext: Perspectives on Ergodic Literature* (Baltimore: John Hopkins University Press, 1999). Digital games do not necessarily require nontrivial effort; however, they do routinely reward any measure of effort, awarding status or points once that effort has become conventionalized in user gesture—that is, "mastered."

43. In these ways, the film deploys as narrative design that larger historical transposition of late-romantic epistemologies to cinema design that Jo Leslie Collier documents in

From Wagner to Murnau: The Transposition of Romanticism from Stage to Screen (Ann Arbor, MI: UMI Research Press, 1988).

44. Brown, *Overtones and Undertones,* 67. A joke can be played here, he points out: For example, in Woody Allen's *Bananas* (1971), Allen opens a closet door to find the harp that is playing the cue.

45. Michel Chion, *The Voice in Cinema,* trans. Claudia Gorbman (New York: Columbia University Press, [1982] 1999).

46. I'm referring to Brown's usage of musical iconicity here.

47. Kathryn Kalinak, *Settling the Score: Music and the Classical Hollywood Film* (Madison: University of Wisconsin Press, 1992).

48. Thus, the rhetorics of affect enabled through practices of consonant sync may inform both the underscore and the completely musicalized film. On the other hand, consonant sync also affords a renewed dream of an imaginary production device: cinema as a graphical scoring machine allowing sonic material to be mapped to visual, and thus, manipulable, signs; see the discussion of visual music in Chapter 3, herein, and Norman McLaren, "Notes on Animated Sound," *Hollywood Quarterly* 7, no. 3 (1953): 223–229; Roger Manvell and John Huntley, *The Technique of Film Music* (London: Focal Press, 1957); Roy Prendergast, *Film Music: A Neglected Art* (New York: Norton, [1977] 1992); Stanislav Kreichi, "The ANS Synthesizer: Composing on a Photoelectronic Instrument," *Leonardo* 28, no. 1 (1995): 59–62; and Douglas Kahn's review of efforts around visual synthesis of sound in the commercial and aesthetic modernisms of the 1920s in "Art and Sound," in *Hearing History: A Reader,* ed. Mark Michael Smith (Athens: University of Georgia Press, 2004), 36–50. Any device capable of completely translating sound and image, contrary to new media rhetorics, is necessarily imaginary, because ultimately this proposal presumes that the complex temporalities of the time-based work in reception can be entirely subsumed to those of its production. Such a device, then, could never be perfected in the instrumentalization of a merely parametrical or informatic process but rather suggests the ability to abstract the affective labor of the audience itself as production labor: a dream of total synchronization.

49. Siegfried Kracauer, *Theory of Film: The Redemption of Physical Reality* (Princeton, NJ: Princeton University Press, [1960] 1997).

50. Julian Brand and Christopher Hailey, eds., *Constructive Dissonance* (Berkeley: University of California Press, 1997), 149.

51. Theodor Adorno, "Letters to Walter Benjamin," in *Aesthetics and Politics: The Key Texts of the Classic Debate within German Marxism,* ed. Ronald Taylor (London: Verso, 1977), 129.

52. Theodor Adorno and Walter Benjamin, *The Complete Correspondence, 1928–1940* (Cambridge, MA: Harvard University Press, 2001), 130.

53. Brown, *Overtones and Undertones,* 30–31.

54. Richard Raskin, *Night and Fog* (Amsterdam: Aarhus University Press, 1987), 160–167.

55. Lazarsfeld had once briefed his senior staff on the "role of 'deep' psychology" in the Princeton Radio project. The project's heavy use of subjective interview material was useful, though systematic analysis of such material was difficult at best, because "descriptions of psychological processes" could be deduced from these interviews. In what appears to be either a pragmatic framing or perhaps a reduction of Adorno's contributions, Lazarsfeld notes that the goals are indeed to arrive at generalizations, but to be useful these statements have to be supported by interview material: "Dr. Wisengrund [*sic*, meaning Adorno] thinks

that the less 'emotional' a person's attitude toward music is, the more he knows about it. It is evident that even a few cases should prove or disprove such assumptions. It would be worthwhile to conduct a systematic investigation as to where this kind of statement could be found in the different sections of the project." Paul Felix Lazarsfeld, "Princeton Radio Research Project," Princeton Radio Research Project 1938 RG 1.1, Series 200, Box 271, Folder 3236.

56. Records at the archive of the Rockefeller Foundation show that the score for this film, the film itself, and the other materials produced as part of the Film Music Project carried out by Eisler at the New School for Social Research were all to be archived by the Museum of Modern Art in New York City, but no record shows that the materials were deposited there. Recent archival research in Germany has turned up scored materials that appear to be those for Eisler's experiments with *The Grapes of Wrath,* and it is probable that whatever Eisler was able to take with him back to Europe, he did.

57. See Hadley Cantril's letter to John Marshall of the Rockefeller Foundation explaining the goals of what would become the Princeton Radio Project; Princeton Radio 1936 200R Box 271 Folder 3233, Letter to John Marshall, December 31 1936, 3.

58. See, for example, Lazarsfeld, "Princeton Radio Research Project," a summary presentation on Lazarsfeld's orientation of Princeton Radio and his achievements with the project, filed May 12, 1938; Princeton Radio 1938 200R Box 271 Folder 3236, 7.

59. Gilles Deleuze, *Cinema 2: The Time-Image,* trans. Hugh Tomlinson and Robert Galeta (Minneapolis: University of Minnesota Press, [1985] 1989).

60. Edith de Rham, *Joseph Losey* (London: Andre Deutsch, 1991), 47.

61. Eisler and Rockefeller administrator John Marshall discussed audience evaluation and measurement techniques, but Marshall states in a memo his beliefs that no psychological test exists that could measure results in this case and suggests instead gathering qualitative feedback not from a lay audience but from the collection of statements characterizing and describing the effects in question by articulate receivers aware of their emotional reactions. He also mentions Lazarsfeld's device developed at Princeton, which consisted of a small box with two buttons: one pressed for favorable response, one pressed for a negative response. These responses were recorded on a moving tape that could be synchronized with movements of a musical score. Eisler was interested, and Lazarsfeld had already indicated willingness to cooperate, so the $500 budget item for evaluation was projected for tests using both qualitative feedback and Lazarsfeld's device. However, compared with budget items in both Lazarsfeld and Burris-Meyer, this was a very small amount of the total grant funding.

62. That is, "14 Ways [the German *Arten* can also mean 'styles'] for Describing Rain."

63. Eisler, *Gespräche mit Hans Bunge,* 16.

64. Eisler and Adorno, *Composing for the Films,* 141.

CHAPTER 5

1. See, among many notable exemplars, Tricia Rose, *Black Noise: Rap Music and Black Culture in Contemporary America* (Hanover, NH: University Press of New England/Wesleyan University Press, 1994); Lindon Barrett, *Blackness and Value: Seeing Double* (Cambridge: Cambridge University Press, 1998), 55–93, esp. 63; Jed Rasula, "The Jazz Audience," in *The Cambridge Companion to Jazz,* ed. Mervyn Cooke and David Horn (Cambridge: Cambridge University Press, 2002), 55–68, esp. 60; or David Brown, *Noise Orders: Jazz, Improvisation, and Architecture* (Minneapolis: University of Minnesota Press, 2006).

2. Jacques Attali, *Noise: The Political Economy of Music,* trans. Brian Massumi (Minneapolis: University of Minnesota Press, 1985).

3. In a related context, see Marta E. Savigliano, *Tango and the Political Economy of Passion* (Boulder, CO: Westview Press, 1995).

4. The designation of "transmedia" is generally attributed to the to digital production processes informing contemporary knowledge production; see Marsha Kinder, *Playing with Power in Movies, Television, and Video Games: From Muppet Babies to Teenage Mutant Ninja Turtles* (Berkeley: University of California Press, 1991); Henry Jenkins, *Convergence Culture: Where Old and New Media Collide* (New York: New York University Press, 2006).

5. David James, *The Most Typical Avant-Garde: History and Geography of Minor Cinemas in Los Angeles* (Berkeley: University of California Press, 2005).

6. Michael Hardt, "Affective Labor," *Boundary 2* 26, no. 2 (Summer 1999): 89–100.

7. Michael Hardt and Antonio Negri, *Empire* (Cambridge, MA: Harvard University Press, 2000); Michael Hardt and Antonio Negri, *Multitudes: War and Democracy in the Age of Empire* (New York: Penguin, 2004).

8. Vorris Nunley, "From the Harbor to Da Academic Hood," in *African American Rhetoric(s): Interdisciplinary Perspectives,* ed. Elaine B. Richardson and Ronald L. Jackson (Carbondale: Southern Illinois University Press, 2004), 221–241, esp. 223; and see Dara N. Byrne, "The Future of (the) Race: Identity, Discourse, and the Rise of Computer-Mediated Public Spheres," in *Learning Race and Ethnicity: Youth and Digital Media,* ed. Anna Everett (Cambridge, MA: MIT Press, 2008), 15–38, esp. 17.

9. Todd Boyd, *Am I Black Enough for You? Popular Culture from the 'Hood and Beyond* (Bloomington: Indiana University Press, 1997).

10. Fred Moten, *In the Break: The Aesthetics of the Black Radical Tradition* (Minneapolis: University of Minnesota Press, 2003).

11. Miriam Hansen, "The Mass Production of the Senses: Classical Cinema as Vernacular Modernism," *Modernism/Modernity* 6, no. 2 (1999): 59–77.

12. Moten, *In the Break,* 121.

13. Sergei Eisenstein, "How I Learned to Draw (A Chapter on Dancing Lessons)," in *Beyond the Stars: The Memoirs of Sergei Eisenstein; Selected Writings,* vol. 4, ed. Richard Taylor, trans. Michael Powell (London: BFI, 1995), 567–591.

14. As James observes, *Passing Through* allegorizes its contradictions as it attempts an autonomous mode of black film production. He writes that the material and historical premise of that attempt rests in the history of black feature filmmaking. Because the free-form jazz musical style and often abstract aesthetic strategies of *Passing Through* do not correspond with the popular black musical cultures of its time, James concludes that the film envisions a jazz cinema that it could not itself achieve. See James, *The Most Typical Avant-Garde,* 323.

15. Paul Gilroy, *Black Atlantic: Modernity and Double Consciousness* (Cambridge, MA: Harvard University Press, 1993).

16. James, *The Most Typical Avant-Garde.*

17. Édouard Glissant, *A Poetics of Relation,* trans. Betsy Wing (Ann Arbor: University of Michigan Press, [1990] 1997).

18. See Frank Kofsky, *Black Nationalism and the Revolution in Music* (New York: Pathfinder Press, 1970), 145; or the somewhat earlier Immamu Amiri Baraka [LeRoi Jones], *Blues People: Negro Music in White America* (New York: Morrow, 1963).

19. Langston Hughes, *Ask Your Mama: 12 Moods for Jazz* (New York: Knopf, 1961).

20. Moten, *In the Break,* 121, 139, 142.

21. The scenes in *Passing Through* in which a group of black musicians argue about how to proceed with the project of producing their own music seem to be based on the dialogical styles of discussion presented in portions of *Wattstax*.

22. Mark Anthony Neal, *What the Music Said: Black Popular Music and Black Public Culture* (New York: Routledge, 1999), 86–88.

23. Angela Davis, *Blues Legacies and Black Feminism: Gertrude "Ma" Rainey, Bessie Smith, and Billie Holiday* (New York: Vintage Books, 1998).

24. As James explains, the histories of black film production have for the most part been at loggerheads with mainstream Hollywood's goals of international control of film markets, to the detriment of articulating the voices of black communities. When independent or experimental films borrow jazz as a model of direct expression or spontaneity, they avoid an integral presentation of jazz performance. David James, *Allegories of Cinema: American Film in the Sixties* (Princeton, NJ: Princeton University Press, 1993); see also Krin Gabbard, *Jammin' at the Margins: Jazz and the American Cinema* (Chicago: University of Chicago Press, 1996), for extensive discussion of the entangled histories of cinema and jazz.

25. For Jacques Derrida's discussion of the *pharmakon* as medicine and poison, see his *Dissemination*, trans. Barbara Johnson (Chicago: University of Chicago Press, 1981).

26. The composer of *Passing Through*'s sound track, Horace Tapscott, who also appears in the film as one of the ensemble members, is one such musician, but many others built collective performance ensembles and recording ventures around a notion of music as an integral part of community, including Sun Ra and his Solar Arkestra; Muhal Richard Abrams and the Association for the Advancement of Creative Musicians (from which came the Art Ensemble of Chicago); Steve Reid and his Mustevic label; Detroit's Tribe, with Marcus Belgrave, Byron Morris, and Unity; and Black Artists' Group (BAG) with Oliver Lake and Julius Hemphill (later of the World Saxophone Quartet).

27. For a discussion, see Braxton's comments in Graham Lock, *Forces in Motion: The Music and Thoughts of Anthony Braxton* (New York: Da Capo, 1988), 26, 65–70; for Braxton's explanation of composed improvisation as creative method, see *Tri-Axium Writings*, vols. 1–3 (Lebanon, NH: Frog Peak Music/Synthesis Music, 1985).

28. Theodor Adorno, "The Curve of the Phonograph Needle," in *Essays on Music*, ed. Richard D. Leppert, trans. Susan H. Gillespie (Berkeley: University of California Press, 2002), 271–287, esp. 274.

29. Thomas Levin, "For the Record: Adorno on Music in the Age of Its Technological Reproducibility," *October* 55 (Winter 1990): 39–41.

30. Uneven technological and media development, the gaps and fallows between the industrial dominance and differing economies of scale, allow the industrial production of oppositional or, at the very least, noncompliant cultural forms within one sphere (music and recording, for example) as opposed to another (the film industry).

31. Langston Hughes, *The First Book of Jazz* (Hopewell, NJ: Ecco Press, [1955] 1997).

32. Gilroy, *Black Atlantic*, 74–76.

33. Specific to *Passing Through* is its emphasis on the musical form of jazz, its performance and production of musical sound, and the orchestration of the image in terms of instrumental parts. Unlike many of the experiments in visual music abstraction, here the jazz performers' bodies are integral to the production of the music heard in the film but not restricted to literal views of musical performance.

34. Or see Grant Green's *Feelin' the Spirit* (Blue Note BST 84132, 1963), whose cover portrays the artist toned in blue-gray against black, his hands on the guitar foreground, his

head thrown back in soulful, almost worshipful expression. Blue Note musicians photographed in such styles often appear alone in their cover shots, mythologized as sensitive, exalted, or defiant jazz giants. The style of the photographs emphasizes them as artists who have "found their sound" and seems to present this genius directly to the record buyer. The scenes that open *Passing Through* borrow the conventions of the Blue Note iconography but, significantly, deemphasize the individual performers to bring focus instead to the sequential orchestration of the musicians' coming together in ensemble performance.

35. Lee Morgan's album *Sixth Sense* (Blue Note BST 84335, 1967) pictures overlapping cascading square photographs of a forest, with Morgan standing in the center of the sound event suggested by the "zoom" effectively created by the successive enlargements of those photos. Morgan retains clarity in the overall design, suggesting that he is the source of the sonic disruption. Here, the artist as hearer of the crystalline sound vibration produces the surfeit of knowledge of time and space that is music. In a more or less contemporaneous example from rock that is instructive for its difference, Creedence Clearwater Revival's *Bayou Country* (Fantasy 8387, 1969) also places the musicians in a forest scene, playing their instruments. An optical zoom blurs the photo from the center out, suggesting an amplified mind-altering music of distortion, with the band in this case blurred along with the "sound." Here, the listener identifies as a blurry distortion the identity of the band, not any larger irruptive potential that would open a musical path to the future.

36. See, for example, Creedence Clearwater Revival, *Bayou Country.*

37. Anne Friedberg, *The Virtual Window: From Alberti to Microsoft* (Cambridge, MA: MIT Press, 2006).

38. Mary Anne Doane, *The Emergence of Cinematic Time: Modernity, Contingency, the Archive* (Cambridge, MA: Harvard University Press, 2002), 107.

39. Gilles Deleuze, *Bergsonism* (New York: Zone Books, [1966] 1988).

40. Jacques Derrida, *Archive Fever: A Freudian Impression,* trans. Eric Prenowitz (Chicago: University of Chicago Press, 1996).

41. See also Deleuze's and Felix Guattari's derivation of Charles Pierce's "icon" as "a-signifying diagram of relation" producing sense without necessarily producing signification, meaning, or representation: "'A-signifying semiotics' work from syntagmatic chains without signification, and so are susceptible of entering into direct contact with their referents in the context of diagrammatic interaction. An example of an a-signifying semiotics: musical writing, a mathematical corpus, computer syntax, robotics, etc." Felix Guattari, *The Anti-Oedipus Papers* (Cambridge, MA: MIT Press, 2006), 415.

42. Alexander Weheliye, *Phonographies: Grooves in Afro-Sonic Modernity* (Durham, NC: Duke University Press, 2005).

43. Gilles Deleuze, *Francis Bacon: The Logic of Sensation* (Minneapolis: University of Minnesota Press, [1981] 2003).

44. Mary Lou Taylor and Cecil Williams, *Embraced* (Pablo 2620108, 1978). A fragment of Taylor's poetic critique of style as fashion: "Style in itself ringeth a most narrow paradigm genuflecting to the cultural mores of a given time having as implied fact a temporal sense easily dated and quick to age."

45. Martin Jay points out the useful distinction psychologist James Gibson makes between the visual field and the visual world: space as projected ocularly and space seen as a world with depth. With the advent of perspectival painting, Jay writes, "the visual field now replaced the visual world." Further, Jay suggests that "the differentiation of the visual from the textual was . . . intensified by the differentiation of the idealized gaze from the corporeal gaze and the monocular spectator from the scene he observed on the other side

of the window" (55–57). Perhaps, then, in album-cover art, these differences may be recompressed as the visual field is put to work in communicating musical meaning to a listener. The space of the record album cover provides for text and reproduction of painterly space, but it almost always falls flat when it comes to providing visual depth. See Martin Jay, *Downcast Eyes: The Denigration of Vision in Twentieth-Century French Thought* (Berkeley: University of California Press, 1993).

CHAPTER 6

1. Theodor Adorno, *Aesthetic Theory*, trans. Robert Hullot-Kentor (Minneapolis: University of Minnesota Press, 1997), 167.

2. Judith Butler, *Bodies That Matter: On the Discursive Limits of Sex* (New York: Routledge, 1992).

3. "The Cockettes," collected in Rex Reed, *People Are Crazy Here* (New York: Dell, [1974] 1975), 51–56.

4. See Stephen Cohen, *The Gay Liberation Youth Movement in New York* (New York: Routledge, 2007).

5. Simon Frith, *Sound Effects: Youth, Leisure, and the Politics of Rock 'n' Roll* (New York: Pantheon, 1981).

6. For example, among many others, Chuck Panozzo of Styx and Rob Halford of Judas Priest, who have in recent years come out.

7. "East Berlin" here is shorthand for all manner of historical ideations misrecognized or misremembered: (1) perhaps, an homage to Nina Hagen, the former child singing star of DDR television exiled along with her dissident stepfather; (2) Hedwig's origins as a site producing corporeal excess, "bridge and wall," a counterpoint to the constrained and channelized circulation between binarized East and West at "Checkpoint Charlie"; (3) the undeterminable receivers of rock music's meanings within military-industrial complexes—that is, the creative listeners of "armed forces radio"; (4) the crumbling of the ideality of a televisual present: The Berlin Wall, which *is* crossed in the film, as Hedwig watches it on television news, comes down in a present tense that is for Hedwig, stuck in Junction City, very far away. Generally, *Hedwig* the film mispronounces, misremembers, and misuses history. For example, Yitzak describes Hedwig as the new Berlin Wall in the first number performed by the Angry Inch in the film: "reviled, graffitied, spit upon." Of course this description would be inappropriate for any purveyors of Eastern Bloc rock. In East Berlin, the wall was closely guarded, could not be approached by ordinary residents of East Berlin, and offered no sustained access that would afford graffiti art or even spitting. Further, in West Berlin, and in the Western geopolitical imagination, only one Berlin Wall existed. But the wall in the East was doubled a few years after the initial construction: a smaller wall roughly a city block away from the larger wall at the border with West Berlin was built, delimiting not the perimeter of a line to be crossed but a vacant "no man's land"—a zone of exception between East and West. This smaller eastern wall visible to East Berliners was, in fact, a monochromatic gray-white.

8. I am thinking, here, of David Halperin's reading of Foucauldian ascesis as a self-discipline of transformation, though I depart from Halperin as I see such self-transformation as a problematic of expression in a more Deleuzian sense: ascesis as poiesis. See Michel Foucault, *The History of Sexuality Volume 3: The Care of the Self* (New York: Random House, 1986); or David Halperin on Foucault's ascesis in *Saint Foucault: Towards a Gay Hagiography*

(Oxford: Oxford University Press, 1995); and on Deleuze and expression, see Gilles Deleuze, *Expressionism in Philosophy: Spinoza* (New York: Zone Books, 1990).

9. This suggestion is comparable in some ways with Jacques Attali, *Noise: The Political Economy of Music* (Minneapolis: University of Minnesota Press, [1977] 1985): the notion of music as noise, though that account privileges not reception but "composition" in its broad sense.

10. Eve Kosofsky Sedgwick, *The Epistemology of the Closet* (Berkeley: University of California Press, 1990).

11. See Kenneth J. Zucker, "Gender Identity Disorder in Children and Adolescents: Introduction," in *Treatment of Psychiatric Disorders,* 3rd ed., ed. Glen O. Gabbard, 2001, available at http://online.statref.com/ (accessed February 5, 2006).

12. The term "programmatics" is from Roland Barthes, *Sade/Fourier/Loyola,* trans. Richard Miller (Berkeley: University of California Press, [1971] 1976), who observes in Fourier's textual "systematics" a paragrammatic: "Namely, the superimpression (in dual hearing) of two languages that are ordinarily foreclosed to each other, the braid formed by two classes of words whose traditional hierarchy is not annulled, balanced, but—what is more subversive—disoriented: Council and System lend their nobility to tiny pastries; tiny pastries lend their futility to Anathema, a sudden contagion *deranges* the institution of language" (93). For my purposes here, the paragrammatic materials in question are not classes of language but of mediatic and corporeal orders: rock, film; sex, gender.

13. Paul de Man, "Autobiography as De-Facement," in *The Rhetoric of Romanticism* (New York: Columbia University Press, 1984), 67–82.

14. Martin Rubin, *Showstoppers: Busby Berkeley and the Tradition of Spectacle* (New York: Columbia University Press, 1992).

15. Michel Foucault, *The History of Sexuality: Introduction,* trans. Robert Hurley (New York: Pantheon, [1976] 1978).

16. D. A. Miller, *Place for Us: Essay on the Broadway Musical* (Cambridge, MA: Harvard University Press, 1998).

17. Caryl Flinn, *Strains of Utopia: Gender, Nostalgia, and Hollywood Film Music* (Princeton, NJ: Princeton University Press, 1992).

18. In doing so, the film also presents a continuation of early cinema sing-along practices documented by Rick Altman in *Silent Film Sound* (New York: Columbia University Press, 2004). Altman describes a range of uses of early cinema as a sing-along presentation device facilitating live audience participation, although such sing-along directives turn up later in "soundies," in 1930s Chinese cinema, or 1950s and 1960s American television, for example.

19. Rick Altman, *The American Film Musical* (Bloomington: Indiana University Press, 1987).

20. David James, *Power Misses: Essays Across (Un)Popular Culture* (New York: Verso, 1996), 235, 242.

21. Ibid., 245.

22. Annette Kuhn, *Dreaming of Fred and Ginger: Cinema and Cultural Memory* (New York: New York University Press, 2002).

23. Ibid., 178.

24. Ibid., 178, 179, 162.

25. Ibid., 162; Altman, *The American Film Musical,* cited in Kuhn, *Dreaming of Fred and Ginger,* 156.

26. Kuhn, *Dreaming of Fred and Ginger,* 192.

27. Ibid., 12.

28. Halperin, *Saint Foucault.*

29. Raymond Williams, *Marxism and Literature* (Oxford: Oxford University Press, 1977).

30. Following Deleuze and Felix Guattari, Guy Hocquenghem sees the homosexual as "sliding towards the transsexual" in a process of desublimating phallic signification; "anal desublimation" is one point on this slide. Here I am suggesting that receptivity in gay identity presented as excessive transgender identity (the phallus is lost, but an angry inch is gained) indicates phallic *and* vaginal desublimation. Arguably, then, Hedwig is neither man nor woman, but male-to-female and female-to-male, a problematic of orienting sexed desire and expressing sexed gender. Guy Hocquenghem, *Homosexual Desire,* trans. Daniella Dangoor (Durham, NC: Duke University Press, [1972] 1993), 103.

31. For a range of useful academic discussions from different perspectives, see Henry Minton, *Departing from Deviance: A History of Homosexual Rights and Emancipatory Science in America* (Chicago: University of Chicago Press, 2002); George Chauncey, *Gay New York: Gender, Urban Culture, and the Making of the Gay Male World, 1890–1940* (New York: Basic Books, 1994); and the seminal analysis by Hocquenghem cited above.

32. For activist discussions in the period of *Hedwig*'s theatrical duration, see Pat Califia, *Sex Changes: The Politics of Transgenderism* (San Francisco: Cleis Press, 1997); Leslie Feinberg, *Transgender Warriors: Making History from Joan of Arc to Dennis Rodman* (Boston: Beacon Press, 1996); and Kate Bornstein, *Gender Outlaw: On Men, Women, and the Rest of Us* (New York: Routledge, 1994), among others.

33. In avoiding the "closet" narrative or any other "before and after" narrative trajectory, *Hedwig* has perhaps more in common with aspects of that series that are shared with other recent transgender documents and features: namely, the thematic of the family, after transgender politics, as a transposition for belonging. These new "transgender family values" works, such as *Southern Comfort* (2001), *Transamerica* (2005), or even MTV's *Real World: Brooklyn* (2009), wherein the family unit is replaced with an extended family of friends selected by the network, look and sound nothing like *Hedwig,* but their emphasis on family and questions of personhood and belonging rather than on "closet epistemologies," visibility, and some supposed naturalness for a "heterosexual matrix" suggest the terrain that *Hedwig*'s queer rock spectacle plows through.

34. See Foucault, *History of Sexuality Volume 1*; Michel Foucault, *Abnormal: Lectures at the Collège de France, 1974–1975,* ed. Valerio Marchetti and Antonella Salomini, trans. Graham Burchell (New York: St. Martin's Press, 2003); and Sedgwick, *The Epistemology of the Closet.* For star discourse and sexuality, see, among others, Richard Dyer, *Stars* (London: BFI, 1982); and Richard Meyer, "Rock Hudson's Body," in *Inside/Out: Gay Theories, Lesbian Theories,* ed. Diana Fuss (New York: Routledge, 1991), 259–288.

35. Or, to put it in terms of the reception of *American Idol* finalists, for example, the preference for 2009's Adam Lambert versus 2003's Clay Aiken.

36. Such clubs as Squeezebox, where *Hedwig* originated, or other contemporary gatherings, such as *Hippie Chix*; in these locations, unlike in Butler's 1992 formulation in *Bodies That Matter,* drag was not performed as "heterosexual melancholy" but rather as aggressive counternorm.

37. Simon Frith, *Performing Rites: On the Value of Popular Music* (Cambridge, MA: Harvard University Press, 1996).

38. See Kaja Silverman, *The Acoustic Mirror: The Female Voice in Psychoanalysis and Cinema* (Bloomington: Indiana University Press, 1988); and Amy Lawrence, *Echo and Narcissus: Women's Voices in Classical Hollywood Cinema* (Berkeley: University of California Press, 1991).

39. Miller, *Place for Us.*

40. Lee Edelman, *No Future: Queer Theory and the Death Drive* (Durham, NC: Duke University Press, 2004).

41. Ibid.

42. Edelman explains, "As the template of a given subject's distinctive access to jouissance, defining the condition of which the subject is always a symptom of sorts itself, the *sinthome,* in its refusal of meaning, procures the determining relation to enjoyment by which the subject finds itself driven beyond the logic of fantasy or desire. It operates, for Lacan, as the knot that holds the subject together, that ties or binds the subject to its constitutive libidinal career, and assures that no subject, try as it may, can ever 'get over' itself—'get over,' that is, the fixation of the drive that determines its jouissance" (ibid., 35–36).

43. Ibid., 35–38.

44. Ibid., 34.

45. Ibid., 29–30.

46. Here I am thinking partly of the vocal production by which Wayne Koestenbaum rewrites what Catherine Clément describes as the operatic "undoing of woman"; see Catherine Clément, *Opera, or, the Undoing of Woman* (Minneapolis: University of Minnesota Press, [1979] 1988); Wayne Koestenbaum, *The Queen's Throat: Opera, Homosexuality, and the Mystery of Desire* (New York: Poseidon Press, 1993).

47. The narrative settings range from Charles Dickens's opposition of Scrooge to Tiny Tim through Jean Baudrillard's treatment of reproductive technologies and end with Alfred Hitchcock's parable of a malevolent nature's attack on children, *The Birds.*

48. Edelman, *No Future,* 11, 154.

49. Ibid., 29.

50. Ibid., 5, 66.

51. Ibid., 151–153.

52. Ibid., 154.

53. Ibid., 153.

54. Gilles Deleuze, *The Logic of Sense* (New York: Columbia University Press, [1969] 1990), 163.

CHAPTER 7

Acknowledgment: I gratefully acknowledge NTT Japan for providing me with the videotape documentation of the performance and the additional three-hour workshop given by the Vasulkas at NTT in July 1998.

1. Giorgio Agamben, "The Prince and the Frog: The Question of Method in Benjamin and Adorno," in *Infancy and History: Essays on the Destruction of Experience,* trans. Liz Heron (London: Verso, [1978] 1993), 107–124, esp. 121–123; and see Eric Alliez, *Capital Times: Tales from the Conquest of Time* (Minneapolis: University of Minnesota Press, [1991] 1996).

2. Alliez, *Capital Times,* 241–242.

3. C.O.L.A. exhibition catalog (2009), 20.

4. Michael Hardt, "Affective Labor," *Boundary 2* 26, no. 2 (Summer 1999): 89–100.

5. Bernard Stiegler, *Mécréance et Discrédit, 3: L'esprit perdu du capitalisme* (Paris: Galilée, 2006), 18.

6. Siegfried Kracauer, "The Mass Ornament," in *The Mass Ornament: Weimar Essays* (Cambridge, MA: Harvard University Press, 1995), 76–77.

7. Alfred North Whitehead, *Science and the Modern World* (New York: Mentor, [1925] 1948), 20–39.

8. Ernst Bloch, *Spirit of Utopia* (Palo Alto, CA: Stanford University Press, [1919] 2000), 130.

9. Samples of the resulting scores and documentation of the project are available at www.mimg.ucla.edu/faculty/miller_jh/gene2music/home.html (accessed May 3, 2007).

10. See also the review of *Ash Wednesday* in Kristin M. Jones, *Frieze*, January 1, 2007, available at www.frieze.com/issue/review/rivane_neuenschwander/ (accessed February 14, 2010).

11. See Antonio Negri's analysis of Karl Marx's critique of money and value in the *Grundrisse* in Negri, *Marx beyond Marx: Lessons on the Grundrisse*, trans. Harry Cleaver, Michael Ryan, and Maurizio Viano (New York: Pluto Press, 1991), 21–40.

12. See Deleuze's discussion of the statement in Michel Foucault's development of discourse analysis in Gilles Deleuze, *Foucault*, trans. Seán Hand (Minneapolis: Minnesota University Press, [1986] 1988), 1–22.

13. The primary work Bernard Stiegler discusses in this regard is Edmund Husserl's *On the Phenomenology of the Internal Consciousness of Time*, trans. John B. Brough (Boston: Kluwer, [1966] 1991), but he is careful to place this work in the context of Husserl's phenomenology as a whole.

14. See Pierre Lévy, *Collective Intelligence: Mankind's Emerging World in Cyberspace* (Cambridge, MA: Perseus, 1997).

15. See Yochai Benkler, *The Wealth of Networks: How Social Production Transforms Markets and Freedom* (New Haven, CT: Yale University Press, 2006).

16. Donna Haraway, *When Species Meet* (Minneapolis: University of Minnesota Press, 2008). Haraway's notion of "contact zones" is informed by Clifford's elaboration of the phrase in James Clifford, *Routes: Travel and Translation in the Late Twentieth Century* (Cambridge, MA: Harvard University Press, 1997), esp. 204.

17. Clock time was globally standardized on the "Universal Time" of the Greenwich meridian in 1884. Today's common standard, Coordinated Universal Time (UTC) is a transnational undertaking by such agencies as the U.S. National Institute of Standards and Technology in Boulder, Colorado, which calculate it by periodically subtracting leap seconds from International Atomic Time (TAI), measured since 1958 in Cesium electrons' quantum leaps to higher or lower levels of energy. Universal Time (UT1, the prior UT or Greenwich standard) continues to be calculated on the basis of planetary rotation in mean solar days. Relating "universal time" to "coordinated universal time" means composing a discontinuous difference between distinct ensembles of time-keeping instruments, one of which operates subatomic quanta, and the other, Earth's rotational frequency. This differential universal time is abbreviated as "DUT," is calculated as "DUT1 = UT1 − UTC," and is monitored by the International Earth Rotation Service, available at www.iers.org/ (accessed May 31, 2009).

18. Miriam Hansen, "The Mass Production of the Senses: Classical Cinema as Vernacular Modernism," *Modernism/Modernity* 6, no. 2 (1999): 59–77.

19. See note 17.

20. See Chapter 5; and on history and place in Los Angeles, see Dolores Hayden, *The Power of Place* (Cambridge, MA: MIT Press, 1997); on the specificities of geography and policing in Los Angeles, see Steven Kelly Herbert, *Policing Space: Territoriality and the Los Angeles Police Department* (Minneapolis: University of Minnesota Press, 1997); on community production of music and jazz as local memory, see Steven L. Isoardi, *The Dark Tree: Jazz and the Community Arts in Los Angeles* (Berkeley: University of California Press, 2006); on independent cinemas in Los Angeles since the early twentieth century, see David James, *The Most Typical Avant-Garde: History and Geography of Minor Cinemas in Los Angeles* (Berkeley: University of California Press, 2005).

21. Arthur David Smith, *Husserl and the Cartesian Mediations* (London: Routledge, 2003), 125–132.

22. Bernard Stiegler, *Technics and Time 2: Disorientation,* trans. Stephen Barker (Palo Alto, CA: Stanford University Press, [1996] 2009), 241.

23. Henri Bergson, *Matter and Memory,* trans. Nancy Margaret Paul and W. Scott Palmer (New York: Dover, [1911] 2004), 211.

24. Stiegler, *Technics and Time 2,* 210–211.

25. Bernard Stiegler, *Acting Out,* trans. David Barison, Daniel Ross, and Patrick Crogan (Palo Alto, CA: Stanford University Press, [2003] 2009), 52–55.

26. Stiegler, *Mécréance et Discrédit, 3,* 26.

27. Bernard Stiegler, *La technique et le temps, 3: Le temps du cinéma* (Paris: Galilée, 2001), 67.

28. Ibid., 138.

29. André Leroi-Gourhan, *Gesture and Speech,* trans. Anna Bostock Berger (Cambridge MA: MIT Press, [1964] 1993), 282–297.

30. Stiegler, *Technics and Time 2,* 107–108.

31. Ibid., 96.

32. Ibid., 91. Leroi-Gourhan's concerns may be seen as the paleoanthropological articulation of the modernity thesis as a problematic of technological development and adoption, an earlier form of the contemporary "new media thesis," articulated by Victor Hugo in *Notre Dame de Paris*: "This will kill that"—that is, the printing presses assumes the cultural functions once associated with the cathedral. On the latter, see Elizabeth Emery, *Romancing the Cathedral: Gothic Architecture in Fin-de-Siécle France* (Albany: State University of New York Press, 2001), 15–22. Leroi-Gourhan's concern with innovation and mediation, then, is no longer simply national history and cultural legacy but cultural and ethnic diversity in its deepest paleoanthropological sense and in relation to modernization grasped as possibly appropriate technocultural development but, alternatively, as technological imperialism.

33. Stiegler, *La technique et le temps,* 203.

34. As the mid-twentieth-century philosopher and poet Octavio Paz puts it in "The Other Mexico," drawing on Georges Dumézil in a critique of U.S. cultural "monolingualism": "[Intrahistorical] structures are the origin of the distinctive traits that are civilizations. Civilizations: styles of living and dying." In Octavio Paz, *The Labyrinth of Solitude and Other Writings* (New York: Grove Press, 1985), 253.

35. Stiegler, *La technique et le temps,* 204.

36. Richard Coyne's *Technoromanticism: Digital Narrative, Holism, and the Romance of the Real* (Cambridge, MA: MIT Press, 2001) expansively documents a tendency for romanticist metaphors and analytics in critiques of cyberspace generally. The claim that musicality

equates to preindividual temporality may well be an artifact of a larger reconfiguration of nineteenth-century epistemologies in light of twenty-first-century prospects.

37. Haraway, *When Species Meet,* 3–4.

38. Stiegler, *Acting Out,* 8–9.

39. Haraway, *When Species Meet,* 89.

40. Quentin Meillassoux, *After Finitude: An Essay on the Necessity of Contingency,* trans. Ray Brassier (London: Continuum, 2008), 5.

41. See also Peter Hallward, "Reviews: Quentin Meillassoux, *After Finitude: An Essay on the Necessity of Contingency,*" *Radical Philosophy* 152 (November–December 2008): 51–57.

42. Stiegler, *Technics and Time 2,* 2.

43. Haraway, *When Species Meet,* 165.

44. Gilles Deleuze, *Difference and Repetition,* trans. Paul Patton (New York: Columbia University Press, [1968] 2004), xix.

45. Cf. the discussion of democracy, politics, and play in Jacques Derrida, *Rogues: Two Essays on Reason* (Palo Alto, CA: Stanford University Press, 2005), 25; 46.

46. In the sense discussed, for example, by Ian Bogost, *Unit Operations: An Approach to Video Game Criticism* (Cambridge, MA: MIT Press, 2006).

47. Stiegler, *Technics and Time 2,* 204.

48. Stiegler, *La technique et le temps,* 207.

49. Stiegler, *Technics and Time 2,* 152–154.

50. Ibid., 155.

51. For documentation, see the catalog raisonné: *Stephan von Huene 1962–2000: Klangkörper/Resounding Sculptures: Klangsculpturen, Objekte, Assemblagen* (Ostfildern-Ruit: Hatje Cantz, 2002); and www.stephanvonhuene.de/echo/wrong.html (accessed February 14, 2010).

52. See the documentation in *Stephan von Huene.*

53. See www.popmodernism.org/scrambledhackz/ (as of February 2010 no longer available).

54. See Mark Hansen, *Bodies in Code: Interfaces with Digital Media* (New York: Routledge, 2006).

55. Donna Haraway, "A Cyborg Manifesto: Science, Technology, and Socialist-Feminism in the Late Twentieth Century," in *Situated Knowledges: The Science Question in Feminism and the Privilege of Partial Perspective* (New York: Routledge, 1991).

56. Project correspondence from Woody Vasulka to curator Hisanori Gogota at ICC, Japan.

57. Woody Vasulka, "The Brotherhood: A Series of Interactive Constructions," c. 1988; available at www.vasulka.org/Woody/Brotherhood/Brotherhood.html (accessed February 14, 2010).

58. David Dunn and Woody Vasulka, "Digital Space: A Summary," available at www.vasulka.org/Woody/Brotherhood/Text.html#03 (accessed February 2010). I take this comment to be a rough translation of the problem I describe in Chapter 5: shifts in the status of the virtual. For Deleuze, of course, virtuality was the dyadic couple of "actuality." "Real" was coupled with "possible," after Bergson. And yet, for Derrida, the status of the "virtual" seems to be shifting in a long historical transition.

59. According to the curator's description, pitch activates the installation.

60. Rita Raley, *Tactical Media* (Minneapolis: University of Minnesota Press, 2009), 30.

61. David Dunn, "The Electronic Theaters of Woody Vasulka," available at www.vasulka.org/Woody/Brotherhood/Text.html (accessed February 2010).

62. Alexander Galloway, *Protocol: How Control Exists after Decentralization* (Cambridge, MA: MIT Press, 2002); and see Raley, *Tactical Media,* 11–12.

63. Marita Sturken, "Steina and Woody Vasulka: In Dialogue with the Machine," in the exhibition catalog *Machine Media: Steina and Woody Vasulka,* ed. Marita Sturken (San Francisco: SF Moma, 1996), 42.

64. Donna Haraway, "Situated Knowledges: The Science Question in Feminism and the Privilege of Partial Perspective," in *Simians, Cyborgs, and Women: The Reinvention of Nature* (London: Routledge, 1991), 185.

65. Manfred Clynes and Nathan Kline, "Cyborgs and Space," in *The Cyborg Handbook,* ed. Chris Hables Gray (New York: Routledge, 1995), 29–34

66. Haraway, "A Cyborg Manifesto."

67. Margaret Morse, *Virtualities: Television, Media Art, and Cyberculture* (Bloomington: Indiana University Press, 1998).

68. N. Katherine Hayles, *How We Became Post-human: Virtual Bodies in Cybernetics, Literature, and Informatics* (Chicago: University of Chicago Press, 1999).

69. Morse, *Virtualities,* 209.

70. Haraway, "Situated Knowledges," 200. For biocapital, see Haraway, *When Species Meet*; and Kauchik Sunder Rajan, *Biocapital: The Constitution of Post-genomic Life* (Durham, NC: Duke University Press, 2006).

71. David A. Hounshell, "Elisha Gray and the Telephone: On the Disadvantages of Being an Expert," *Technology and Culture* 16, no. 2 (1975): 133–161.

72. Stelarc and Marquard Smith, "Animating Bodies, Mobilizing Technologies: Stelarc in Conversation," in *Stelarc: The Monograph,* ed. Marquard Smith (Cambridge, MA: MIT Press, 2005), 223.

Index

Page numbers followed by the letter f *refer to figures.*